Liability for Products in a Global Economy

Liability for Products in a Global Economy

The Comparative Law Yearbook of International Business

Special Issue, 2004

PUBLISHED UNDER THE AUSPICES
OF THE CENTER FOR INTERNATIONAL LEGAL STUDIES

General Editor

Dennis Campbell
Director, Center for International Legal Studies
Salzburg, Austria

Volume Editor

Susan Woodley

A C.I.P. Catalogue record for this book is available from the Library of Congress

ISBN 90-411-2385-7

Published by Kluwer Law International,
P.O. Box 85889, 2508 CN The Hague, The Netherlands.
sales@kluwerlaw.com
http://www.kluwerlaw.com

Sold and distributed in North, Central and South America
by Aspen Publishers, Inc.
7201 McKinney Circle, Frederick, MD 21704, USA

Sold and distributed in all other countries
by Extenza-Turpin Distribution Services
Stratton Business Park, Pegasus Drive,
Biggleswade, Bedfordshire SG18 8TQ
United Kingdom

Printed on acid-free paper

Printed in the Netherlands

The Center for International Legal Studies

The Center for International Legal Studies is a non-profit research and publications institute established and operating under Austrian law and with its international headquarters in Salzburg, Austria.

The Center has operated since 1976 in Salzburg, and it has had a close cooperation with the Faculty of Law of the University of Salzburg, the Austro-American Institute in Vienna, and numerous other universities and educational institutions in Europe and the United States.

The Comparative Law Yearbook of International Business prints matter it deems worthy of publication. Views expressed in material appearing herein are those of the authors and do not necessarily reflect the policies or opinions of the Comparative Law Yearbook of International Business, its editors, or the Center for International Legal Studies.

Manuscripts proposed for publication may be sent to:

The Editor
Comparative Law Yearbook of International Business
Postfach 19
A-5033 Salzburg, Austria

Table of Contents

Editor's Note

This year's volume of the *Comparative Law Yearbook of International Business* deals with the subject of product liability law. This is a growing area in which manufacturers and suppliers are finding themselves more and more responsible for the quality of their products and for the consequences flowing from any defects therein. This book discusses a wide variety of topics which come under the umbrella of product liability, ranging from liability for injuries caused by the use of asbestos and other toxic substances to the responsibility of air carriers in hijack situations. There is a growing amount of litigation throughout the world tackling the problems arising from the safety of products. These laws take into account the manufacturing process, the transportation, storage and delivery of goods, the intended use of products, their fitness for such purpose, and any warnings or instructions as to use given to consumers and end users.

This publication also covers the question of jurisdiction in product-related litigation, particularly in crossborder transactions. In many instances, a plaintiff will attempt to bring his action in the United States due to the large amount of damages, especially punitive damages, awarded there by juries in civil actions. Defendants, on the other hand, seek to counter this by raising issues such as *forum non conveniens*. There also is the question of state versus federal jurisdiction within the United States, as well as a discussion focusing on the possible growth of federalism within the European Union and its impact upon product liability nationally and at a European level.

A comparison of the divergent cultural attitudes towards property in China and the United States, including the different emphases placed upon the ownership and role of property in society, demonstrates the different views of product liability. Another aspect of defective goods dealt with here is liability for the recall of a dangerous product. There is a chain of responsibility stretching from the manufacturer, through various levels of suppliers, to the final retailer of goods, which is obviously important when attempting to remove dangerous products from the market as quickly as possible before they can cause widespread injury to consumers. This has been shown to be particularly relevant in cases involving automobiles and food products.

Overall, therefore, product liability law is a vital part of the general law protecting consumers, both on a national and an international basis, which makes this book a very interesting and useful read for anyone involved in this area.

Susan Woodley, Editor
Center for International Legal Studies
Salzburg, Austria

Product Liability in Argentina: Ten Years of the Consumer Protection Law

Lisandro A. Allende and Enrique Schinelli Casares
Brons & Salas
Buenos Aires, Argentina

Introduction

Year 2003 will be remembered in Argentina for many different reasons, such as for being the first year of office of recently elected President Kirchner or being the year that marked the end of the downward spiral of economic crisis and the beginning of a slow cautious recovery. In this regard, the Government, led by President Kirchner, implemented a series of measures aimed at attaining economic recovery on the basis — among other principles — of the devaluation of the Argentine peso *vis-à-vis* the United States dollar, which should enhance Argentine exports and encourage labor-intensive private ventures that should, in turn, help to reduce high unemployment rates. Generally speaking, and although the long-term strategy of the new government is still not clear to many analysts, the new authorities appear to tend towards an economic model based on local production and increase of exports, rather than the "services and finance" orientated model that ruled during the past decade, which was primarily based on convertibility.

The Government intends to show a much more active State, which should closely control the private sector and protect the general public more actively than in the past decade. An example of this approach is the direct involvement of the Executive Branch in the negotiation of the tariffs to be charged by public utilities. Therefore, a much more present and active public sector can be expected, as well as closer and tighter control of private companies.

Year 2003 also marks the tenth anniversary of the enactment of Consumer Protection Law Number 24,240 (CPL), a benchmark in consumer protection legislation in Argentina. Therefore, this is a good opportunity to look back and review the progress made, and also to try to imagine the future developments that can be expected.

Product Liability and Consumer Protection in Argentina

Argentine product liability legislation evolved from a fault-based system to a strict liability system. This evolution took nearly thirty years, but it reached its peak between October 1993, when the CPL was passed, and 1998, upon the enactment of Law Number 24,999. It should be borne in mind that the Civil Code chapter on civil liability was based on the principles of the French Napoleonic Code. Therefore, product liability, as well as any other liability, was centered on the concept of fault (*faute*). Thereafter, a series of legal principles applied to pursue and obtain redress for damage caused provided, however, that fault was a *sine qua non* requirement, or, as stated by doctrine, "there is no liability without fault". Section 1109 of the Argentine Civil Code states that "Any person who, acting negligently, damages another is obliged to cure said damage. This obligation is governed by the same provisions to which torts are subject".

In 1968, the Civil Code was amended, and Section 1113 introduced the concept of "strict liability", establishing that whenever damage is caused by the risks or defects of a thing, the owner or custodian will only be released from liability, in full or in part, upon proof that the damage was caused due to fault attributable to the victim or to a third party for whom the owner or custodian of the thing is not responsible. In this case, the liability of the owner or custodian terminates in the event that the thing has been used against his express or implied consent. The introduction of this cause and effect presumption set aside the general principle of fault-based liability referred to above. Since damage caused by risky and defective things entails strict liability, an injured person only needs to prove:

(1) The existence of the damage;
(2) That the thing or product is risky or defective; and
(3) The bearing of the thing upon the damage caused.

Although this reform was a benchmark in civil liability, further laws were required to ensure full protection for consumers. In October 1993, the CPL was enacted. Thereafter, the CPL was amended many times, including by Law Number 24,999 in 1998. In addition, the National Constitution, as amended in 1994, states that:

> "Consumers and users of goods and services are entitled, in the consumption relationship, to the protection of their health, safety and economic interests; to adequate and truthful information; to freedom of choice and equitable and reliable treatment. The authorities will provide for the protection of said rights, the education for consumption, the protection of competition against any kind of market distortions, the control of natural and legal monopolies, the control of the quality and efficiency of public utilities and the organization of consumer and user associations. Laws must establish efficient procedures for conflict prevention and settlement and the regulatory frameworks applicable to national public utilities. Such laws will take into account the necessary participation of consumer and user associations and of the interested provinces in supervisory agencies."

In turn, the abovementioned CPL introduced the concept of consumer protection to the Argentine legal system that was later recognized by the Constitution. The CPL establishes that all parties involved in the chain of production and distribution of goods are jointly and severally liable *vis-à-vis* the consumer, and such liability is strict. In this respect, Section 40 of the CPL, as amended by Law Number 24,999, provides that:

> "If damage to a consumer results from a defect in or risk connected with the thing or the rendering of the service, liability will fall on the producer, manufacturer, importer, distributor, supplier, seller and whoever has affixed his trademark on the thing or service. The carrier is only accountable for damage caused to the thing by reason of or during transportation. The parties are jointly and severally liable without detriment to any right of contribution that may exist. Total or partial discharge from liability only applies to anyone who may prove that the cause of the damage had nothing to do with him."

The concept of consumer protection, together with the application of a strict liability system as regards product liability, produced major changes in the way private companies conduct business in practically every industry. This chapter will briefly comment on the duty of prevention and safety, and then we will analyze the two spheres of product liability: contractual and non-contractual liability, and their effective application by the courts.

Prevention of Damages to Consumer

As a consequence of the above-described evolution, a legal system that was centered on the redress for damage started to focus on a more effective approach: preventing such damage from happening. This concern is clearly evidenced by Section 5 of the CPL, which states:

> "Things and services must be delivered or rendered in such a way that, if used under predictable or normal conditions, they do not pose a risk to the health and physical integrity of consumers and users".

This provision notwithstanding, it is necessary to point out that this obligation, commonly known as the duty of safety, already existed, although not as clearly stated. In this regard, since 1968, Section 1198 of the Civil Code states the obligation of the parties to perform, interpret and comply with the contracts in good faith. The duty of safety, interpreted as a duty to maintain the other party free from any risks to its health and integrity, is considered a derivation of the principle of good faith, which must govern the performance of contracts.

In any event, taking into account that Argentina's continental legal system is based primarily on the letter of the law, the enactment of Section 5 of the CPL cleared up any doubts regarding the enforceability of the duty of safety. The prevention of damage is now a relevant concern for manufacturers of mass consumption goods in Argentina, and this concern will become even more significant in the near future.

Contractual Product Liability

As mentioned before, product liability is governed not only by the CPL, but also by the general provisions of the Civil Code, since not all damage caused by defective products falls within the rules of the CPL, for instance, the purchase of goods for the purpose of including such goods in production, transformation or marketing processes or services to third parties does not fall within the scope of the CPL.

According to the Civil Code, liability may be contractual or non-contractual. Contractual liability arises from breach of a contract for any reason whatsoever. Non-contractual liability arises from the violation of the general obligation "not to damage" imposed by law. With respect to product liability, legal doctrine has concluded that liability of the manufacturer-seller, or seller non-manufacturer, is contractual. In turn, liability of the manufacturer non-seller, or of any of the participants in the distribution chain, is non-contractual.

Cases Not Included within Consumer Protection Law

In cases of damage caused by defective or faulty products that may not be included in the provisions of the CPL, the following situations arise.

Liability of the Manufacturer-Seller to the Buyer This is a typical case of contractual liability based on the violation of the duty of safety mentioned above. The manufacturer-seller's liability is strict. He is liable for ordinary and normal damages caused by breach of the contract, and only in cases of malicious failure to fulfill obligations is he liable for extraordinary damages. Ordinary damages are considered to be the value of the loss suffered plus loss of profits due to the damage caused. Depending on the circumstances, the court may also include moral damages as part of the compensation. Since this is a case of contractual liability, the statute of limitations for this action is ten years, depending on the type of transaction.

Liability of the Manufacturer-Seller to a Third Party Where the injured person is not the direct buyer but a third party, and the manufacturer's products are distributed through different intermediaries, there is no contractual liability in this case between the manufacturer and the injured person, and liability will be governed by the rules of tort liability. Even though there is no uniform opinion, the majority of the authors consider that liability is strict.

Cases Included within Consumer Protection Law

In those cases where the CPL is applicable, if damage to the consumer results from a defect in or risk connected with the thing or the rendering of a service, liability falls on the manufacturer, importer, distributor, "retail supplier", supplier, seller and whoever has affixed his trademark on the thing or service.[1] The abovementioned parties will be jointly and severally liable without detriment to any right of contribution that may exist, and total or partial discharge from liability will only apply to anyone who may prove that the cause of the damage had nothing to do with him.

Contractual liability is legal, binding and admitted among the parties to a contract, but it cannot be invoked *vis-à-vis* third parties or consumers in order to seek a release from the obligations imposed by law. In this regard, note that, pursuant to Section 37 of the CPL:

> ". . . a) the sections that alter the obligations or restrict the liability for damages; b) the sections that imply the waiver or restriction of the consumer's rights or that increase the rights of the other party will be regarded as non-stipulated sections".

Actions for Hidden Defects

In addition, the purchaser may also resort to a "hidden defect" (*vicios redhibitorios*) action. According to the last paragraph of Section 1414 of the Civil Code, the seller "is also liable for the hidden defects of the thing sold". This is not public policy and, therefore, this obligation may be waived or extended by the parties. However, in those transactions covered by the CPL, this provision restricts the possibility of waiving liability for hidden defects by stating, in Section 18, that "the enforcement of the aforementioned provisions does not prevent the survival of the legal warranty for hidden defects. In case of hidden defects: a) Section 2176 of the Civil Code applies by operation of law at the request of the consumer. b) Section 2170 of the Civil Code cannot be enforced against the consumer". Hidden defects are the:

> ". . . hidden defects of the thing the title, use or enjoyment of which was conveyed for consideration, existing on purchase, which render the thing unsuitable for use, if they detrimentally affect the use thereof so that, if known by the buyer, he would not have purchased the thing or he would have paid less for it".[2]

---

1 Consumer Protection Law, Section 40.

2 Civil Code, Section 2164.

In order for this action to be enforceable, the defect must be hidden, important (that is, not insignificant) and existing at the time of the acquisition. This action is not enforceable where the buyer knew or should have known of the defect due to his art or profession. In the case of hidden defects, the buyer may claim termination of the contract, returning the thing and recovering the price paid, reimbursement of part of the money paid (*acción quanti minoris*) or specific performance of the contract.

According to Section 4041 of the Civil Code, the statute of limitations for filing such a claim is three months from the time the defect becomes apparent or is discovered by the purchaser. There is no specific time limit for the buyer to notify the existence of the defect. The only requirement is that once the hidden defect becomes apparent, the claim must be filed within three months and the defect should have existed at the time of the acquisition. However, if the seller maliciously failed to fulfill its obligations, the statute of limitations is extended to two years.

The National Court of Appeals held in a leading case that the Civil Code does not provide for a limited term within which to discover the hidden defect, which may be detected at any time, always provided that the purchaser can ascertain that it existed at the time the thing was delivered, and, therefore, after detecting the defect, within such unlimited time period, the purchaser has just three months within which to sue.

If the sale of the thing having a hidden defect is deemed a commercial sale, the buyer has six months to notify the seller of the existence of the defect. The statute of limitations for filing such a claim is four years. In the case of defects that are apparent at the time of acquisition, the buyer has only three days to notify the seller of the existence of the defects.

Non-Contractual Product Liability

As mentioned above, non-contractual ("tort") liability arises from the violation of the general obligation "not to damage" imposed by the law (the Roman law principle of *neminen laedere*). Liability of the manufacturer non-seller, or of any of the participants in the distribution chain, is non-contractual. For those cases that fall within the scope of the CPL, Section 40 provides a strict liability system that can only be discharged in cases where the party can prove that the cause of the damage had nothing to do with him. For those cases falling outside the scope of the CPL, Section 1113 of the Civil Code applies.

As opposed to contractual liability, the manufacturer will be liable for ordinary and extraordinary damages, plus any unforeseeable damage that occurs as a result of considerations that the doer of the act should have borne in mind when performing the act. However, in this case, the statute of limitations is only two years from the date upon which the injured party becomes aware of the existence of the damage.

Damage

In this regard, a distinction must be made between damage or deterioration suffered by the product because of its intrinsic defects and damage suffered by the customer based on the contractual or non-contractual liability of the manufacturers and/or sellers. In the first case, liability would be based on hidden defects or express warranties. Any damage caused could be indemnified through:

(1) Reimbursement of the price paid;
(2) Repair or substitution of the damaged item; and
(3) Compensation in cash for the lesser value of the damaged item.

In the second case, in addition to the indemnification mentioned above, Section 1083 of the Civil Code applies, which states that:

> "Compensation for damage shall consist of the reinstatement of things to their prior state, except where this is impossible, in which case, indemnification shall consist of a monetary amount. The injured party may also opt for indemnification in money."

Therefore, no limitations apply in this regard, and Section 37 of the CPL also applies.

Application of the New Legislation

Two judgments specifically referring to product liability shall be taken as examples of decisions rendered after the enactment of Law Number 24,999, which introduced the concept of strict liability. The case of *De Blasi de Musmeci, Claudia* v. *Sevel Argentina S.A.* was decided by the National Commercial Court of Appeals on 10 October 2001. On 6 October 1994, Claudia De Blasi was driving her car with her son and daughter, her mother (that is, the children's grandmother) and the grandmother's sister along a very modern highway: Route Number 2. Suddenly, the car went completely out of control and overturned in a serious accident that resulted in the death of Mrs. De Blasi's son. Mrs. De Blasi and her husband filed a claim against the manufacturer, Sevel Argentina S.A., the owner of the vehicle's brand (Fiat Argentina S.A.) and against the direct seller, which was a different company (Luva S.A.). In the end, the action was pursued only against the manufacturer.

The court at first instance ordered a number of analyses, as a result of which an expert witness concluded that one of the parts of the vehicle — the steering system — was defective. As all such models had the same parts, this determined the clear existence of the manufacturer's liability. The first instance judgment concluded that the manufacturer was liable on the basis of the CPL and, therefore, ordered a full indemnification in favor of Mr. and Mrs. De Blasi. The compensation for the death of the child was fixed at US $600,000. The defendant was ordered to make payment jointly and severally with its insurance company. The defendant appealed against the judgment on the basis of the excessive amount of the compensation, since the boy was not wearing his safety belt at the time of the accident.

This is the first concept that the Court of Appeals analyzed in detail: the duty of safety that the manufacturer must observe as part of its implicit contractual obligations *vis-à-vis* the obligation of care that can be expected by consumers. In this regard, the insurance company asked for a significant reduction in the amount of the compensation, since it was proved that the boy was not wearing a safety belt. The boy was seated in the middle of the back seat of the vehicle, between his grandmother and his grandmother's sister.

The rationale followed by the Court of Appeals was:

(1) The boy was seated in the back seat, as safety regulations dictate for children;

(2) He was seated between two adults, which was the safest location for a little boy; and

(3) Notwithstanding the fact that the back seat of the car allows for three persons to be seated, the car does not have a safety belt for the person who is seated in the middle of the back seat.

Therefore, the manufacturer could not argue that the consumer acted negligently in this case, since such an obligation could not possibly be complied with. In addition, the absence of a safety belt for the third passenger implies a failure to comply with the duty of safety expressly provided for in Section 5 of the CPL.

In addition to this significant conclusion, the final judgment ordered that the car defect that caused the fatal accident should be informed to the Secretary of Trade for the competent authority to analyze the facts and, if necessary, take pertinent measures. Certainly, this was a remarkable decision of the Court of Appeals that evidences the growing concern for the effective protection of consumers and the active role that the courts and government agencies should play.

The case of *L.M.A.* v. *O.A. S.A.* was decided on 31 August 2001 by the same Panel of the Court of Appeals that handled the previous case. The claimant filed a lawsuit against a company called O.A. S.A. alleging that, in 1991, he had purchased from O.A. a prosthesis that his doctor had prescribed to cure a malformation of his backbone. Although the initial surgical procedure was successful, a routine check carried out in 1993 discovered that the prosthesis was broken.

The first instance judge ruled against the claimant on the basis that the alleged damage had been caused by hidden defects. Consequently, the plaintiff should first claim for termination of the contract and, only then, for the ensuing damage. The judge understood that this was a simple sale and purchase contract and that any claim related thereto should be resolved pursuant to the rules applicable to such contracts. Since the claim based on hidden defects had become statute-barred, the plaintiff did not have a cause in support of his claim.

The claimant filed an appeal on the grounds that the judgment was arbitrary, that is, it was not a reasonable derivation of the law in force. The Court of Appeals analyzed this argument and concluded that the judgment was not arbitrary. This notwithstanding, the legal framework under which the first instance judge had reached his conclusions was incorrect. The rationale employed was that, although the purchase of a prosthesis for final use by the customer is effectively a sale and purchase contract, it also implies the purchase of a product by a final customer. Thus, the provisions related to the duty of safety that, in principle, mean that the seller should guarantee that the purchased good will not cause damage to the purchaser provided that the purchased item is used normally, become applicable.

Therefore, the manufacturer is obliged to furnish goods that are free of defects and, where the purchaser suffers damage attributable to hidden defects, strict liability shall apply, by virtue of which the purchaser will simply have to prove the existence of the damage and that it was caused by the purchased item. The sellers' negligence is presumed and does not need to be proved. This obligation of safety forms part of the business risk assumed by the seller.

On this basis, the Court of Appeals firstly rejected the defense based on the running of the period of limitations, since this particular action has a statute of limitations of ten years. The court then analyzed whether it had been proved that the prosthesis was defective, that is, if the fact that the prosthesis finally broke was due to a manufacturing defect. In this regard, the expert witnesses informed the court in their reports that such a prosthesis is subjected to multiple forces that may actually break the item, which, in addition, is not intended to sustain the backbone by itself, but rather to provide a support while the bone regenerates. This conclusion, added to the proven fact that the claimant's malformation had continued increasing over the years, led the court to conclude that, in this case, the breakage of the prosthesis was not caused by a manufacturing defect, but by the multiple forces that had acted on it over the years.

This judgment shows that the courts are well aware of the legal framework applicable to product liability claims and are concerned about considering these claims in the light of the pertinent regulations, irrespective of the arguments put forward by the parties.

Conclusion

References made to current legislation lead to the conclusion that Argentina has modern and comprehensive legislation regulating product liability and consumer protection. Therefore, legislative bodies have done their part and future developments should be expected from the interpretation of such laws by the courts, which, in turn, will depend upon how strongly the general public will claim protection of its rights as consumers.

Although the average consumer in Argentina is still not as sophisticated as in other countries, people are becoming aware of their rights and that they, through their joint action, can make changes happen. For instance, consumers will participate in the negotiations regarding the possible increase in public utilities tariffs. Therefore, one should be optimistic as regards consumer protection awareness in general, and this is due, to a great extent, to modern product liability legislation and an effective application of such laws.

The Italian Product Liability Experience

Sara Biglieri, Andrea Pupeschi and Christian Di Mauro
Rucellai & Raffaelli
Milan, Italy

Introduction

European Union (EU) Directive 85/374/EEC of 25 July 1985 concerning liability for defective products (hereinafter the Directive) was implemented in Italy by Presidential Decree Number 224/1988 (hereinafter the Decree), which came into force on 29 June 1988. The Decree, in accordance with the Directive, is aimed at ensuring a high level of consumer protection against any damage caused by a defective product to consumers' health or property.

Although the implementation of the Directive was welcomed in Italy as a great step forward for consumer protection, after fifteen years, the application of the product liability legislation is not as satisfactory as expected. Indeed, the Decree has been applied by Italian courts in few and minor cases and, to date, no more than fifteen court decisions based on the product liability legislation have been published.

In order to examine and understand the reasons for such little Italian litigation as regards product liability, it is useful to first outline the main provisions of the Decree and to review some of the more significant Italian product liability cases, with specific reference to the burden of proof being on the consumer, as well as to the amounts awarded by Italian courts as recovery of damages.

Main Provisions of Decree 224/1988

Principle of Objective Liability

The Italian product liability legislation is based on the principle of objective liability (or liability without fault) on the part of the producer for any damage caused to consumers' health or property by a defective product. In other words, the producer of a defective product shall compensate any damage caused to the physical well-being or property of the consumer, whether or not there has been negligence on the part of the producer. Therefore, the injured consumer is not required to prove the negligence or fault of the producer in order to be compensated for any damage suffered. The Decree also provides for joint and several liability of all operators in the production chain in favor of the injured consumer, so as to provide a financial guarantee of compensation for damage.

Liability of Producer

Pursuant to Section 1 of the Decree, the producer shall be deemed liable for any damage caused by a defective product. According to Section 3, Paragraphs 1 to 3 of the Decree, "Producer" shall mean:

(1) The manufacturer of a finished product;
(2) The producer of any raw material;
(3) The manufacturer of a component part (this provision implies that all producers involved in the manufacturing process shall be liable, insofar as the finished product, component part or any raw material supplied by them is defective); and
(4) Any person who, by putting his name, trademark or other distinguishing feature on the product, presents himself as its producer.

Moreover, without prejudice to the liability of the producer, pursuant to Section 3, Paragraph 4 of the Decree, any person who imports into the EU market a product for sale, hire, leasing or any form of distribution in the course of his business shall be deemed to be a producer and shall, therefore, be liable as a producer.

The consumer who is injured by a defective product is entitled to claim full compensation for any damage suffered from all operators involved in the production chain. In fact, Section 9 of the Decree provides that all the aforesaid operators shall be deemed jointly and severally liable. This implies that the injured consumer is entitled to claim full compensation for the damage from any of these operators.

Liability of Supplier

According to Section 4, Paragraph 1 of the Decree, where the manufacturer of the product cannot be identified, each supplier of the product shall be treated as its producer unless he informs the injured consumer, within a reasonable time, of the identity and address of the producer or of the person who supplied him with the product. Pursuant to Paragraph 6 of Section 4, the same principle shall apply in the event of an imported product, if this product does not indicate the identity of the importer, even if the name of the producer is indicated. The supplier is, therefore, liable only in the following three cases:

(1) When he is the importer of the product into the EU;
(2) When the producer of the product cannot be identified by the injured consumer; and
(3) When the identity of the importer is not indicated on the product.

Pursuant to Paragraphs 1 to 3 of Section 4, the injured consumer is obliged, in order to claim the supplier's liability, to formally notify the supplier in order to enable the latter to provide, within a reasonable time, details of the producer or of a previous supplier.

Section 4, Paragraph 1 of the Decree specifies that the supplier shall notify the injured person within three months, while Section 3, Paragraph 3 of the Directive does not specify the time limit, but provides that the injured person must be notified by the supplier within a reasonable time. Section 3, Paragraph 3 states:

> "Where the producer cannot be identified, each supplier of the product shall be treated as its producer unless he informs the injured consumer, within a reasonable time, of the identity of the producer or of the person who supplied him with the product. The same shall apply, in the case of an imported product, if this product does not indicate the identity of the importer referred to in Paragraph 2, even if the name of the producer is indicated."

Moreover, Section 4 of the Decree (unlike the Directive) provides that the request of the injured consumer shall be in writing, shall indicate the defective product, the place and (with reasonable approximation) the time at which the product was purchased, and shall contain the proposal to examine the product, if still existing. The Decree also provides that, in the event that a lawsuit is brought by the injured consumer against the producer, without a previous request for information, the supplier is entitled to give such information within the following three months.

It must be noted that, excluding the aforesaid three cases, the liability of the supplier of defective products is not governed by the Decree, nor by the Directive. In order to invoke the possible liability of the supplier, the injured consumer must, therefore, refer to the contractual and/or non-contractual liability system provided by Italian legislation.

Defectiveness of Product

Section 5 of the Decree defines the defectiveness of the product in terms of the safety that a consumer is entitled to expect in relation thereto. The existence of a defect in the product must, therefore, be assessed having regard not to the product's fitness for use, but to the lack of safety that the public at large would be entitled to expect. In determining this test of safety, all circumstances must be taken into account, including (but not limited to):

(1) The manner in which the product was put into circulation, the presentation of the product and any instructions or warnings given by the producer in relation thereto;

(2) The evident features of the product (the safety of the product must be assessed, having regard to any notorious information that the consumer may be expected to know and that may be relevant for proving possible contributory negligence of the consumer);

(3) Whether the product is being put to reasonable use and the behavior which, in relation thereto, may be reasonably predictable — the level of safety that a consumer is entitled to expect in relation to a product is assessed by excluding any misuse of the product that would be deemed unreasonable under the circumstances. The reference to "predictability" is a sort of corrective to the principle of reasonable use, as an unreasonable use of the product may be predictable in certain cases (and shall, therefore, imply the producer's liability) having regard to all circumstances (as, for example, the age of the consumer; indeed, it may be deemed predictable that a child puts a toy in his mouth, although such behavior may be considered unreasonable);

(4) The time at which the product was put into circulation — the defect is, in other words, only the "primary defect", that is to say, the defect that may be assessed at the time the product was put into circulation on the basis of the scientific and technical knowledge available at that time. This circumstance shall, therefore, be evaluated having regard to the "development risk" provided by Section 6(e) of the Decree, which will be examined later;
(5) The age of the product — the fact that a new product is safer than an older product will not necessarily mean that the older product was not, at the time it was put into circulation, as safe as consumers are generally entitled to expect (reference should be made to manufacturing and design defects); and
(6) A product is defective if it does not offer the same degree of safety offered by other products in the same range (this circumstance refers to manufacturing defects).

This list of circumstances is more comprehensive than the corresponding list provided by Section 6 of the Directive, which provides:

> "A product is defective when it does not provide the safety which a person is entitled to expect, taking all circumstances into account, including: the presentation of the product; the use to which it could reasonably be expected that the product would be put; the time when the product was put into circulation. A product shall not be considered defective for the sole reason that a better product is subsequently put into circulation."

Nevertheless, such difference does not seem to be substantial, since the list of circumstances set out in the Directive is not exhaustive, and further circumstances, although not expressly mentioned, may well be added to this list, for example, the price of the product, mandatory technical standards that the producer must comply with in manufacturing the product, the state of the art and the possible testing to which the product had or may have been submitted.

Exclusion of Producer's Liability

Section 6 of the Decree, similarly to Section 7 of the Directive,[1] provides that the producer of a defective product shall not be liable in the event that he proves the existence of certain exonerating circumstances. In particular, the producer shall not be liable if he proves:

(1) That he did not put the product into circulation;
(2) That, having regard to all the circumstances, it is predictable that the defect that caused the damage did not exist at the time when the product was put into circulation by him or that the defect came into being afterwards (this means that the producer, to be sure to avoid liability, shall prove the existence of a fortuitous event, of circumstances beyond his control or fault of a third party or the injured consumer);
(3) That the product was neither manufactured by him for sale or any form of distribution for economic purpose, nor manufactured or distributed by him in the course of his business;
(4) That the defect is due to compliance of the product with mandatory regulations issued by the public authorities;
(5) That the state of scientific and technical knowledge at the time when the producer put the product into circulation was not such as to enable the product to be considered defective; or
(6) In the case of a manufacturer of a component, that the defect is attributable to the design of the product in which the component has been fitted or to the instructions given by the manufacturer of the product.

1 Section 7 of the Directive provides: "The producer shall not be liable as a result of this Directive if he proves: that he did not put the product into circulation; or that, having regard to the circumstances, it is probable that the defect which caused the damage did not exist at the time when the product was put into circulation by him or that this defect came into being afterwards; or that the product was neither manufactured by him for sale or any form of distribution for economic purpose nor manufactured or distributed by him in the course of his business, or that the defect is due to compliance of the product with mandatory regulations issued by the public authorities; or that the state of scientific and technical knowledge at the time when he put the product into circulation was not such as to enable the existence of the defect to be discovered; or in the case of a manufacturer of a component that the defect is attributable to the design of the product in which the component has been fitted or to the instructions given by the manufacturer of the product".

Development Risk

Section 6(e) of the Decree and Section 7 of the Directive set out the "development risk" or "state of the art" objection. As a matter of fact, the producer may exclude his liability by proving that the state of scientific and technical knowledge at the time when the producer put the product into circulation was not such as to enable the product to be considered defective. Such defense in favor of the producer has been provided by the Directive[2] in view of the fact that technological innovation gives rise to increasingly complicated product design and manufacturing processes, and that, over the course of time, higher standards are developed and the state of science and technology progresses.

Section 15, Paragraph 1(b) of the Directive provides:

> "Each Member State may, by way of derogation from Article 7(e), maintain or, subject to the procedure set out in Paragraph 2 of this Article, provide in this legislation that the producer shall be liable even if he proves that the state of scientific and technical knowledge at the time when he put the product into circulation was not such as to enable the existence of a defect to be discovered".

The provision allowed the legislation of each Member State to exclude this exonerating circumstance, since it may be deemed to unduly restrict the protection of the consumer. Nevertheless, unlike other Member States, such as Luxembourg, Finland, Spain (with respect to food and medicinal products), Germany (with respect to pharmaceutical products) and France (with respect to products derived from the human body or marketed before May 1998), the Decree did not derogate from the Directive provisions.

The producer who intends to raise the development risk objection in order to avoid liability shall prove that he adopted every scientific and technically known method in manufacturing the product so as to enable the existence of a defect to be discovered. In order to use this defense successfully, not only must a producer comply with mandatory standards, but he must also prove to have complied with developing and non-mandatory standards. Moreover, it is not sufficient for him to prove to have complied with typical procedures adopted by the

2 Directive 85/374/EEC, Section 7(e).

average manufacturer; he is also required to prove that he adopted all measures to avoid the defect that a manufacturer was able to take. The producer should, therefore, meet far more onerous standards than those required by mandatory regulations.

As a matter of fact, it is extremely difficult for the producer to prove that the defect could not be detected on the basis of the technical and scientific knowledge that was available when the product was put on the market.

Contributory Fault of the Injured Consumer

Section 8, Paragraph 2 of the Directive provides:

> "The liability of the producer may be reduced or disallowed when, having regard to all the circumstances, the damage is caused both by a defect in the product and by the fault of the injured person or any person for whom the injured person is responsible."

In accordance with this Section, Section 10 of the Decree states that the producer's liability shall be reduced, according to Section 1227 of the Civil Code, when the damage is caused both by a defect in the product and by the fault of the injured person. Section 1227 provides:

> "Contributory fault of the creditor — If the creditor's fault has contributed to causing the damage, the compensation is reduced according to the seriousness of the negligence and the extent of the consequences arising from it. Compensation is not due for damage that the creditor could have avoided by using ordinary diligence."

This means that the contributory negligence of the injured consumer may reduce or disallow the producer's liability. Such evaluation shall be made on the basis of the degree of the consumer's contributory fault and of the consequences derived therefrom. The Decree, unlike the Directive, also provides that compensation is not due to the injured consumer when the consumer, although being aware of the existence of the defect and of the risk of damage arising therefrom, nevertheless voluntarily exposed himself to such risk.

Recovery of Damages and Financial Ceilings

Section 16, Paragraph 1 of the Directive allows each Member State to set a limit upon the producer's financial liability for damage resulting from death or personal injury caused by a defective product, specifying that such limit may not be lower than €70-million. In Italy,[3] unlike in other Member States (Germany, Spain and Portugal), a maximum limit upon compensation for personal injury is not provided; the liability of the producer is, therefore, unlimited. However, compensation for property damage is subject to a threshold, amounting to ITL750,000 (nearly €380), as opposed to €500 provided by the Directive.

Burden of Proof in Product Liability Cases

Paucity of Italian Product Liability Litigation

The lack of product liability litigation, which characterizes the Italian experience, may probably be imputed to the following reasons:

(1) The burden of proof on the consumer provided by the Directive is, to some extent, stricter than the burden of proof provided by the Civil Code rules, which continue to be applied where possible;

(2) The amount of damages awarded to consumers is still low compared, for example, to United States standards — the low amount of damages awarded by Italian courts is probably due to the impossibility of assessing punitive damages and to the absence of juries, as the assessment of damages is left to the decision of judges; and

(3) The prohibition against applying the principle of "no win no fee" and the low involvement of consumers' associations in the product liability battle.

Rules of Burden of Proof under Decree

As already explained, product liability is construed as an objective and no fault based liability. A consumer injured by a defective product is not, therefore, required to prove that the defect was caused by

---

3 Decree Number 224/1988, Section 11.

fraud or negligence on the part of the producer. However, the consumer must prove the defect in the product, the damage and the causal link between the defect and the damage. The examination of some product liability cases will show that the task of proving that a product is defective and that the damage was actually caused by the defect may be difficult in some cases, depending on the circumstances of the use of the product, for example, when the product is destroyed during use, or on the nature of the product, for example, as regards disposable products, and depending on when the damage occurs, for example, the damage is suffered some time after the use of the product.

Italian Product Liability Cases

Mountain Bike and Bed Cases

After the implementation of the Directive in 1988, the first product liability case regarding a defective mountain bike was decided by the Court of Monza (Milan) in 1993.[4] The case involved a cyclist who was cycling on his mountain bike on a mountain track when the mountain bike frame gave way and he fell off and was injured. Due to the simple nature of the defective product concerned (a mountain bike) and the circumstances in which the damage occurred (simultaneously with the use of the mountain bike), it was easy for the cyclist to prove the defect in the product and the causal link between the defect and the damage.

The defect of the product was proved by means of an expert opinion, which deemed that the mountain bike frame was made of low carbon steel with an insufficient thickness to guarantee an adequate level of safety. For the first time, the court applied the principle of evaluation of the safety of the product in relation to the "normal and proper use" of the product itself. In other words, the court stated that, as the normal and proper use of a mountain bike is its use on a mountain track, the features of the mountain bike frame must guarantee safe use on a mountain. The causal link between the defect of the mountain bike and the damage was proved by the plaintiff by means of individuals who witnessed the accident.

Likewise, a product liability case regarding a bunk bed, which was designed in a way that did not guarantee the safety of the product, was

4 Tribunal of Monza, Decision of 20 July 1993, *Giurisprudenza Italiana* (1999) at p. 323.

decided by the Court of Milan in 1995 on the basis of the outcome of an expert opinion.[5] When the product is simple in nature, the proof of the defective nature may be supplied by the consumer by means of a simple expert opinion.

Bottle Case

In a case decided by the Court of Rome in 1998, a consumer bought a small bottle of water from a self-service counter in a motorway restaurant.[6] The bottle exploded in the right hand of the consumer, while the consumer was opening the bottle, and the consumer was injured. During the lawsuit, it was easy for the consumer to prove the purchase of the bottle by means of witnesses, and the damage suffered by means of witnesses and medical doctors. However, after the explosion, the bottle was no longer available as evidence. Therefore, during the lawsuit, the consumer was unable to supply evidence of the defective nature of the product and of the causal link between the defect and the damage.

Notwithstanding the above, the court deemed that the explosion of the bottle of water was per se sufficient to prove the abnormal features of the bottle. According to the court, a bottle that explodes does not guarantee the level of safety that consumers may reasonably expect. In other words, the court did not request that the plaintiff actually prove the defective nature of the bottle, but deducted *prima facie* the existence of a defect from the occurrence of the damage itself.

Disposable Products

Another two cases that may be of some interest concern two product liability claims involving disposable products: disposable fifteen-day contact lenses and a disposable medical device. Both cases are still pending before the Court of Milan. In the contact lenses case, a consumer suffered a serious infection to her right eye after applying a couple of disposable contact lenses. Following a preliminary examination, the consumer was diagnosed with a corneal abscess originating from the bacterium pseudomonas aeruginosa, which, according to the plaintiff, was present in the contact lenses and in their original

---

5 Tribunal of Milan, Decision of 13 April 1995, *Danno e Responsabilità* (1996) at p. 389.

6 Tribunal of Rome, Decision of 17 March 1998, *Foro Italiano* (1998) at p. 3060.

preservation liquid. The contact lenses were thrown away by the consumer and, therefore, are not available as evidence in the lawsuit. However, the consumer has kept the case where the contact lenses had been preserved during the fifteen-day period of use when taken out by the consumer. The contact lense case was examined after the accident and revealed the presence of the bacterium pseudomona aeruginosa.

The defendant objects that the plaintiff did not prove that the presence of the bacterium in the contact lense case is imputable to a defect in the contact lenses, as it could have been determined by a number of other causes. As a matter of fact, the contact lenses might have been infected due to their incorrect use by the consumer, who might not have followed the correct hygiene procedure, for example, by washing the contact lenses with tap water. Moreover, the infection might have been caused by the presence of the bacterium in the sea water where the consumer probably went swimming the day of the accident or by other factors totally independent of the use of contact lenses, but deriving, for example, from contact with infected water.

In another case, a surgeon maintains that after the use of an ultrasound energy medical device during surgery, he suffered paraesthesia in his right hand due to the ultrasonic vibrations transmitted from the generator to the handle of the device. However, the paralysis was diagnosed only one month after the use of the medical device. Therefore, in this case, not only is the disposable medical device not available as evidence, but it should be more difficult for the surgeon to prove the causal relationship between the use of the medical device and the paraesthesia, as there is no direct contemporary coincidence between the two events. In this case, it should be more difficult for the court to assume the liability of the manufacturer only on the basis of *prima facie* evidence.

Civil Code and Dangerous Activities

An examination of the product liability case law reveals that the burden of proof imposed by the Decree on the consumer may be difficult due to:

(1) The nature of the product, for example, a disposable product;
(2) The circumstances of the accident, for example, the destruction of the product during the accident; and

(3) The fact that the damage occurred some time after the accident.

As mentioned above, although the burden of proof of the defective nature of the product is imposed on the consumer, Italian courts have, in some cases, overcome the consumers' difficulty in proving the defective nature of the product by considering *prima facie* defective a product that has caused damage and, therefore, does not guarantee an adequate level of safety.

An alternative route for consumers to overcome the burden of proving the defective nature of the product is the possibility of starting a legal action on the basis of the rules provided in Section 2050 of the Civil Code when the sale of such a product may be deemed a dangerous activity. Important product liability claims have actually been started in Italy not (or at least not only) on the basis of product liability legislation, but on the basis of Section 2050 of the Civil Code, which states:

> "Liability deriving from carrying out dangerous activities — Whoever, in carrying out a dangerous activity, with respect to the nature or to the means used for such activity, causes damage shall be deemed liable, unless he proves that he adopted all measures suitable to avoid such damage."

Section 2050 provides for the liability of whoever has caused damage as a consequence of carrying out a dangerous activity, liability which is excluded only if the producer/supplier proves that he adopted all measures suitable to avoid such damage. Pursuant to Section 2050, the injured person must prove that:

(1) The activity carried out by the producer/supplier is a dangerous activity — the evaluation of the danger must be made on the basis either of the nature of the activity or of the nature of the means used for such activity; and
(2) The damage is a consequence of carrying out the dangerous activity (causal link).

If the above two elements are proved, in order to avoid liability, the producer/supplier must prove that he adopted all measures suitable to avoid the damage. In other words, it is not sufficient for the producer to prove that the dangerous activity was carried out with due care in compliance with the relevant laws and rules, but that all precautions for avoiding the damage have actually been taken. In practical terms, courts usually exclude liability for dangerous activity only when the producer/supplier has proved that the damage has been caused by a third party, by act of God or by *force majeure*.

Three well-known product liability cases were decided in Italy on the basis of Section 2050 of the Civil Code and not on the basis of the product liability legislation: the first relating to a pharmaceutical product and the other two relating to tobacco.

Sale of Pharmaceutical Products

In a recent case, the Court of Rome ordered the Italian distributor of a pharmaceutical slimming product manufactured by a French company to pay compensation for damage caused to a consumer by the use of the product.[7] As a consequence of the consumption of the slimming product, the cardiac valve of the consumer suffered detrimental effects.

The court stated that the sale of pharmaceutical products is a dangerous activity, as it is subject to a number of EU and Italian Government authorizations and controls. According to the court, whenever an activity is subject to a number of legal controls and precautions, this activity must be considered as a dangerous activity. During the lawsuit, the plaintiff proved that the damage suffered was due to the consumption of the pharmaceutical slimming product and that the pharmaceutical ingredient contained in the product might, according to clinical experience, cause detrimental effects on cardiac valves. According to the rule in Section 2050, the plaintiff had no need to prove that the pharmaceutical product was actually defective. The burden of proof was, in fact, shifted to the defendant, who was unable to prove the adoption of all possible measures to avoid the damage.

In this case, proof of the defective nature of the product would have been, in any case, quite easy on the basis of the product liability legislation. The court would probably have assumed the defective nature of the product from the clinical experience that pointed out the risks of danger deriving from the use of the pharmaceutical ingredient contained in the slimming product on patients who are cardiac valve wearers. However, the application of Section 2050, instead of the product liability legislation, enabled the plaintiff to sue the Italian

7 Tribunal of Rome, Decision of 20 April 2002, *Diritto e Giustizia* (2002) at p. 58.

distributor rather than the French manufacturer and rendered it more difficult for the distributor to prove that the liability should have been excluded.

Sale of Cigarettes

Section 2050 was also applied in two Italian tobacco cases decided by the Court of Rome in 1997[8] and 2000.[9] On the waive of the United States tobacco litigation, the relatives of a man killed by lung cancer sued Philip Morris and the state producer of cigarettes for damages. In both cases, the Court of Rome rejected the claim of the plaintiff, one of the main arguments being that the sale of tobacco cannot be considered as a dangerous activity. The court held that smoking tobacco is not per se dangerous. What is dangerous is the reiterated use, that is to say, the abuse, of tobacco. Smoking tobacco is compared by the Court of Rome to eating fatty foods: in both cases, the abuse (and not the use) of tobacco, as well as of fatty foods, may damage the health of individuals.

According to the Court of Rome, as selling tobacco cannot be deemed a dangerous activity, the shift of the burden of proof onto the producer does not apply, and it remains for the plaintiff to prove that the damage was caused by the producer's negligence. It is also common knowledge that the abuse of tobacco may be dangerous for health. Therefore, tobacco producers cannot be deemed liable for not having warned tobacco smokers about the risks deriving from such activity before 1990, when the warning on cigarette packages became mandatory.

Needless to say, the decisions of the Court of Rome have been strongly criticized for a number of reasons. First of all, it is not true from a scientific prospective that the use of tobacco is not per se dangerous and that only its abuse may cause health damage. Secondly, it appears difficult to share the opinion that all consumers (regardless of their education and scientific background) are fully aware of the risks deriving from tobacco, as well as its addictive nature.

---

8 Tribunal of Rome, Decision of 4 April 1997, *Danno e Responsabilità* (1997) at p. 750.

9 Tribunal of Rome, Decision of 11 February 2000, *Giurisprudenza Italiana* (2000) at p. 1643.

Compensation for Damage

What damage may be compensated according to Italian product liability legislation? According to Italian product liability legislation, consumers may claim compensation for:

(1) Damage caused by death or personal injury; and
(2) Damage to, or destruction of, any item of property other than the defective product itself, which was used by the injured consumer for his own private use or consumption.

In the latter case, no compensation is available for damage in an amount lower than €390.

Death or Personal Injury

According to the general principles of Italian tort law, which also apply to product liability cases, and according to the leading case law, it is possible to identify different categories of damage. In fact, an injured person may claim compensation for:

(1) Non-material damage, that is, damage to health, which includes damage caused to a person's physical or psychological well-being; and
(2) Moral damage, that is, the consequent pain suffered by the injured person.

The injured person may also claim compensation for material damage, including expenses incurred and loss of profits suffered as a consequence of the damaging event. In product liability cases, this is the use or consumption of a defective product.

Italian case law has recently referred to a different type of damage called "existential damage", which cannot be categorized as either non-material or material damage.

Damage to Health

Damage to health is defined by the leading case law as any permanent or temporary, total or partial, injury to the physical or psychological well-being of an individual, apart from the capacity of such individual to earn income. Therefore, damage in relation to health may also be compensated, for example, in the case of the unemployed or children. Needless to say, such damage must be ascertained by a medical expert on the basis of a medical or scientific evaluation of the injuries suffered.

Therefore, the assessment of the amount of damage to health involves a medical expert and a judge. The medical expert determines the percentage of invalidity, namely, the seriousness of the injury suffered, and the judge assesses the amount of damages on the basis of a schedule drawn up by each court in the light of the court's precedents. Such a schedule assigns specific coefficients to each percentage of invalidity and to each range of victims' ages. The judge shall multiply the coefficient corresponding to the percentage of invalidity by that corresponding to the age of the injured person and then express this value in Euros. The judge may then adjust such amount in the light of the circumstances of the specific case, for example, the possible outcomes of the injury suffered and activities carried out by the injured person.

Moral Damage

The leading case law defines moral damage as any pain suffered by the injured person as a consequence of damage to health caused by the use or consumption of a defective product, for example, the pain suffered by the victim as a result of hospitalization, surgery or medical examination. Pursuant to Section 2059 of the Civil Code, compensation for moral damage may be awarded provided that the producer is deemed criminally liable for the damage suffered by the injured consumer. In other words, where the conduct of the producer may be theoretically construed as a crime, without the need for a decision of the criminal court, judges may decide to award compensation for moral damage in relation to the pain suffered by the victim.

Only in a few product liability cases has compensation for moral damage been awarded on the basis of a *prima facie* evaluation of the possible criminal liability of the producer. Judges do not usually compensate moral damage, as the injured consumer does not need, in order to claim compensation, to allege and prove the fault of the producer, which is one of the elements necessary to establish the criminal liability of the producer.

As regards the assessment of moral damage, pursuant to leading case law, the amount usually awarded is between approximately twenty-five and fifty per cent of the amount awarded for damage to health.

Material Damages

Material damages include:

(1) Expenses incurred by the injured person as a consequence of personal injury suffered, for example, medical examinations not covered by the national health care system and surgery undergone in private hospitals; and

(2) Loss of profits suffered as a consequence of personal injury, the amount awarded usually being assessed by the judge on the basis of:
   (a) the income of the injured person at the time of the accident;
   (b) the reasonable expectation of prospective income; and
   (c) the capacity of the injured person to earn income.

For persons with no income, for example, a housewife or unemployed person, the amount of damages is usually calculated on the basis of triple the social pension.

Existential Damages

As mentioned before, existential damages are a new category of damages which has been expounded by recent Italian case law. Existential damages are awarded to compensate the person who, as a consequence of the injury suffered, can no longer carry out his normal day-to-day activities, for example, normal sexual relations, a normal working life or enjoyment of holidays.

This new category of damages might be qualified as a *tertium genus*, which differs from non-material damages. In fact, unlike damages for health, existential damages do not take into consideration the physical or psychological injury suffered by the individual, nor do they compensate the pain suffered by the individual as moral damages do. Existential damages differ also from material damages, as they do not take into consideration either expenses incurred or loss of profits suffered by the individual as a consequence of the injury.

The amount of existential damages is usually assessed on an equitable basis, taking into account the personality of the injured person, their working activities and any changes made to their family, social and working life caused by the injury.

Quantification of Damages

As regards the criteria for the quantification of damages, there are no general regulations thereon and, therefore, Italian courts play a very important role in determining the amounts to be awarded as damages. To provide examples of the amounts actually awarded by Italian courts in product liability cases, three Italian cases will be examined that are of some interest regarding compensation for damage, namely:

(1) The already mentioned bunk bed case, which was decided by the Tribunal of Milan in 1995, and where the injured plaintiff was awarded an amount as damages for health, loss of profits and moral damages — in fact, in this case, the judge, on the basis of a *prima facie* evaluation, established the criminal liability of the producer;
(2) The textile machinery case, decided by the Tribunal of Monza in 1995,[10] which ordered the defendant to pay moral damages without evaluating whether the producer might be deemed criminally liable or not; and
(3) The already described bottle case decided by the Tribunal of Rome in 1998, where the judge did not order moral damages.

Bunk Bed Case

An assembled modular bunk bed broke and seriously injured the boy who was sleeping in it, causing a laceration to his throat. The parents of the injured boy sued the producer, as well as the seller who had assembled the furniture, and claimed compensation for the permanent and temporary injuries caused to their son. The Tribunal of Milan stated that the modular furniture was defective as it did not comply with the necessary standards of safety in relation to either the manufacturing process or the information and warnings offered by the producer. Therefore, the Tribunal jointly and severally ordered the producer and the seller to pay:

(1) Approximately €148,000 plus interest as damages for health;

10 Tribunal of Monza, Decision of 11 September 1995, *Responsabilità Civile* (1996) at p. 371.

(2) Approximately €88,000 plus interest as loss of profits due to the inability of the person injured to work for two years from the date of the accident; and
(3) Approximately €78,000 plus interest as moral damages, as the conduct of both the manufacturer and seller, who respectively produced, marketed and assembled an unsafe product, might be construed as a criminal act.

Textile Machinery Case

In this case, a worker sued the shareholders of a company claiming compensation for damage suffered from the use of textile machinery produced by the company. The Tribunal of Monza stated that the product was defective due to the lack of normal standards of safety and, therefore, condemned the defendants to pay:
(1) Approximately €114,000 plus interest as damages for health;
(2) Approximately €14,500 plus interest as loss of profits due to the partial inability of the person injured to work for a year from the date of the accident; and
(3) Approximately €25,000 plus interest as moral damages.

The abovementioned case seems to be debatable. In fact, the judge, notwithstanding the provisions of Section 2059 of the Civil Code, omitted to evaluate whether the producer might be deemed criminally responsible or not for the injuries suffered by the plaintiff. The judge awarded an amount of €25,000 only on an equitable basis.

This decision is exemplary as it shows that, since there is no general regulation as regards the criteria for the assessment of damages, the wide discretion of judges in this field may lead to uncertainty, which does not help in avoiding a lack of litigation as regards the product liability legislation.

Bottle Case

As regards this case, the relevant facts have already been described above, and so attention will be focused on the amounts and categories of damages awarded by the judge. In this case, the Tribunal ordered the producer to pay:
(1) Approximately €35,000 plus interest as damages for health; and

(2) Approximately €4,500 plus interest as expenses incurred due to the injury suffered.

No moral damages were awarded by the judge, who stated that, in this case, no fault on the part of the producer was alleged and proved by the plaintiff and that, therefore, no crime could be construed.

Conclusion

The tobacco cases described above are a paradigmatic example of how Italian courts are still far away from a consumer-oriented approach. The Decree is hardly being applied by Italian courts, and the amounts of damages being awarded under such legislation are definitely low. A step forward for consumer protection could probably be made over the next few years if:

(1) New rules to facilitate the burden of proof on consumers are passed as regards disposable products, such as foodstuffs and pharmaceutical products;
(2) Consumers' associations become stronger and more proactive; and
(3) The interest of consumers in claiming compensation for damage increases as a result of an increase in the amount of damages awarded by Italian courts.

In this regard, the new category of existential damages expounded by recent case law, with reference to other torts cases, might be used by judges to increase the amounts awarded as non-material damages in product liability cases.

Consumer Protection in Turkey

S. Murat Celikten
Murat & Murat Law Office
Ankara, Turkey

Introduction

This chapter provides an overview of the way the different Turkish laws address the problems raised by the liability for goods and services and draws attention to both similarities and differences. The countries in the continental law system, by virtue of their legal culture, have either supplemented or amended the provisions of the Civil Law or, where they do not have a Civil Code, have laid down specific legislation to meet the problems related to contracts concluded by consumers. Although Turkey has a Civil Code, it has laid down specific legislation, the Consumer Protection Law (CPL).[1] The provisions of the Civil Code (CC) and the Code of Obligations (TCO) are designed to protect the purchasers of goods. While these laws apply to sales in general, the provisions of the CPL are designed to protect only consumers. Furthermore, the Turkish Commercial Code (TCC) contains provisions concerning commercial sales.

Product Liability

The complex history of liability for loss or injury caused by defective products illustrates well the gradual development and changing perceptions of the role of the law of torts and its inter-relationship with the law of contract. Although there exists no explicit legislation concerning product liability in the Turkish legal system, one can evaluate the subject with two main distinctions. Product liability may either arise from a previous relationship between the person responsible

1 Law Number 4077 dated 23 February 1995, *Official Gazette*, Number 8, March 1995, as amended by Law Number 4822 dated 6 March 2003, *Official Gazette*, Number 14, March 2003.

and another, that is, a contractual relationship, or there may exist no relationship, that is, a tort. However, in some instances, the claimant may base his action on both provisions, as the contractual relationship and the tort may appear at the same time.

Product Liability Based on Contractual Relationship

In product liability, the main problem seems to be whether a consumer's claim for losses should be made against the producer or the seller (retailer). If the economic superiority of the producer is ignored, this distinction makes no difference to the consumer, as his only goal is to recover damages. A claim for a defective product, as a rule, is directed towards the retailer by the consumer, unless the sale contract is entered into between the producer and the customer directly. However, where the sale is made by the retailer and damages are obtained from him, the retailer still has the opportunity for recourse from the producer, who is primarily liable to pay compensation. In any case, the basis of these analyses will deal with the liability of the producer since, in the chain of liability, he is the ultimate person who will compensate for damage.

Distinguishing the type of damage arising from a defective product is of crucial importance. This is because of Article 205 of the TCO, which states that the buyer may claim from the seller for damage directly caused to him by the delivery of defective goods. In addition to that, according to the last paragraph of the same Article, "The seller is obligated to compensate for further damage unless he proves that no fault at all is attributable to him".

The existence of a contractual relationship between the injured person and the producer is sufficient for the application of Article 205 of the TCO. This relationship exists between the parties to the contract, that is, the producer, the wholesaler, the retailer and the customer. When the damage resulting from the sale contract is direct, the producer is considered liable without the need for the customer to prove the producer's fault according to the second paragraph of Article 205. Instead, the burden of proof is put on the producer if the claimant demands compensation for other damage according to the third paragraph of Article 205.

The purchaser is under an obligation to examine the subject matter of the contract and to notify the seller of any defects for which the seller is liable under warranty according to Article 198 of the TCO.

However, Article 207 of the TCO states that the time limit for actions based on warranty is one year from the date of delivery to the buyer, unless the seller has undertaken a more extensive warranty, the time limit applying notwithstanding later discovery of the defect.

Article 25 of the TCC sets forth different provisions for commercial transactions. According to the third paragraph of the Article:

> "If it is clearly evident, at the time of delivery, that the commodity is defective, the purchaser shall inform the vendor thereof within two days. If it is not clearly evident, the purchaser shall examine the goods or have them examined within eight days after their receipt and if the examination shows that the goods are defective, he shall inform the seller within the same term, in order to preserve his rights."

The second and third paragraphs of Section 198 of the TCO shall apply in other cases. The fourth paragraph of the same Article mentions that the statute of limitations period, which is one year in Article 207 of the TCO, will be six months for commercial sales between merchants. Furthermore, the law enables merchants to reduce this six-month period.

It should be noted that contractual liability may arise only among the parties to a contract. The parties are the sole claimants for damage arising from the contract. For example, a person who acquires a good as a gift may not claim damages even though he is the last consumer. The other point is that third parties who suffer damage cannot claim for such damage directly from the producer. For example, a pedestrian injured by a car that has a defective brake system cannot claim damages from the producer; he must act against the party who signed the sale contract who, in his turn, will have the right to seek reimbursement from the producer.

In the light of these explanations it should be underlined that a contractual relationship may exist between the producer-wholesaler, producer-retailer, producer-customer, wholesaler-retailer, wholesaler-customer and retailer-customer. As there will exist a group of sale contracts among these parties, they will seek recourse against the other party to their sale contracts after compensating the injured party. However, the reimbursement procedure between different levels of the sale relationship might take time and the period under the statute of limitations is relatively short. If certain procedures, such as notification of the existence of a lawsuit, are not followed, a party might lose his right of recourse.

Product Liability Based on Provisions Other Than Contract

As product liability that centers around the provisions of a contractual relationship is not satisfactory, there is an aim to solve the problem according to tortious liability contained in the TCO. This requires the harmonization of the terms of tortious liability with product liability of the producer. The general provisions relating to tortious liability are set out in Articles 41 to 44 of the TCO. Article 41 of this Law states that:

> "Every person who causes damage to another in an unlawful manner, be it willfully or be it negligently or imprudently, is liable for compensation. Every person who, *contra boni mores*, willfully causes damage to another is also liable for compensation."

On the other hand, the first paragraph of Article 44 of the TCO affirms that:

> "The court may reduce or refuse compensation where the injured party has assented to the injury, or where circumstances for which he is responsible have contributed to the origin or the aggravation of the damage or otherwise prejudiced the position of the liable party."

According to Article 41 of the TCO, if the conditions of a tort exist, then the injured party may claim compensation. The judge shall decide the amount of compensation in two stages. First, the judge determines the amount of damage that the injured person has actually suffered. The person claiming compensation must prove the damage.[2] The judge subsequently determines the amount of compensation after taking into account the circumstances and the degree of fault.[3] The judge may reduce or completely deny any compensation if the injured person has consented to the tortious act, or if circumstances for which he is responsible have caused or aggravated the damage or have otherwise adversely affected the position of the liable party.[4]

---

2 Code of Obligations, Article 42.
3 Code of Obligations, Article 43.
4 Code of Obligations, Article 44.

On the other hand, Article 98 of the TCO, under the title "the effect of non-performance", states that "The debtor is in general liable for any wrong. The degree of the liability depends on the particular nature of the transaction. In particular, in the absence of intention to benefit, the debtor is considered in mitigation". It then determines that "Subject as aforesaid, the provisions regarding the measure of liability for torts shall, as far as applicable, likewise govern contractual wrongs". Due to the provisions of this Article, the provisions of tortious liability are also implemented with regard to contractual liability whenever applicable.

Consumer Protection Law

Scope of the Law

In recent years, the problem of consumer protection has received a good deal of publicity and many legislative changes have come into force in Turkey. The leading one was the Law on the Protection of Consumers,[5] which was followed by a number of Regulations and Communiqués. The purpose of the Law was stated as taking protective measures, illuminating matters related to the health and security of consumers, educating them on their economic benefits, compensating them for damage, enabling the protection of consumers from environmental hazards, encouraging their initiatives to protect themselves and encouraging volunteer organizations to make policies in this arca.

The Law on the Protection of Consumers has been amended by Law Number 4822 (the new Law) as a result of the efforts to harmonize Turkish legislation with that of the European Union (EU). The amended Law has expanded the definition of "goods". Distance selling contracts made and/or concluded by electronic methods are also included within the scope of the Consumer Law. Briefly, the concept of goods in the new Law includes any intangible assets that are used in an electronic environment, such as audiovisual products, and the TCO provides that all rights provided by Law Number 4077 also apply to online transactions besides those with consumers from 14 June 2003.

5 Law Number 4077.

Defective Goods and Services

The liability of the seller arising from defective goods or services is stated generally in Articles 194 to 207 of the TCO. However, the former CPL contained special provisions under the heading "defective goods or services", Article 4 thereof giving the following definition:

> "Goods or services which are not of the quality and/or quantity indicated on their packaging, label or information and user manual, or promised by the seller, or prescribed in the standards relating to them, or which contain material, legal or economic deficiencies that reduce or remove their value in terms of their application or utilization or the benefits expected by the consumer from them shall be treated as defective goods or defective services."

The new Law extended the definition of defective goods and services. If the goods have an explicit defect, then it is enough for the consumer to notify the seller by any means within thirty days. If the defect arises while using the goods, then the period of liability for the defect is two years from the date of delivery of such goods to the consumer. In the case of immovable property used as a domicile or for holiday purposes, then this period extends to five years. For defective goods, the new Law gives the consumer the option to either:

(1) Withdraw from the contract;
(2) Request that the goods be exchanged for goods which are not defective;
(3) Request a price reduction equal to the diminution in value caused by the defect; or
(4) Request free repair.

The consumer may also request compensation in addition to the alternative rights stated above. The consumer's right to demand compensation is regulated in parallel with EU Directive Number 85/374.

According to the CPL, goods or services may contain three basic types of defects. These defects may be material, legal or economic. The dealer, agent, manufacturer/producer and importer shall be jointly and severally liable to the consumer for the defective goods. Furthermore, lack of knowledge about the defect in the goods shall not relieve them of liability.

If the seller has not given a guarantee for a longer period, actions arising from defective goods must be brought within two years of the date of delivery of the goods to the consumer. If the good is a residence or real estate used for holidays, the limitation period is five years. Claims for any loss and damage caused by defective goods must be brought within three years of the date of delivery. However, if the seller has fraudulently hidden the defect in the good sold from the consumer, he may not benefit from the two-year limitation period.

Harmful and Dangerous Goods and Services

The heading of Article 18 of the amended CPL is "Harmful and Dangerous Goods and Services". According to this Article, if the goods and services offered to consumers may be harmful or dangerous to human and environmental health, the producer is under a duty to place explanatory information and warnings in a clearly visible and legible manner on the goods and services or in the user manuals. The explanatory information and warnings should be given as to the safe usage of the goods. The Ministry of Industry and Commerce, in cooperation with other organizations, is under a duty to determine and announce those goods and services that must contain explanatory information and warnings and the form and location of such information and warnings.

Quality Inspection

According to Article 19 of the amended CPL, the relevant Ministries have the duty of determining and announcing principles and procedurcs for the certification of goods, services and facilities, as well as quality inspection in relation to consumer safety, protection of property and environmental health and the duty to provide information on these subjects. These duties shall be subject to the relevant standards or, if there are no relevant standards, the characteristics thereof should be specified in order to constitute a basis for standards.

Labeling

Article 12 of the CPL concerns labels. According to this Article, goods that are subject of trade and offered for retail sale, or their packaging or containers, must bear labels that contain information on the origin, type and price of the good in a readily visible and legible manner. Where such labels cannot be placed on the goods themselves, lists that contain the same information must be posted in suitable places in a visible manner. If there is a difference between the labels, the price lists and the price mentioned by the cashier, the price in the consumer's favor is deemed to be the valid one.

If the price of goods and services is determined by the Council of Ministers, public associations and institutes or professional institutes, it is forbidden to sell these goods or services with a higher price than determined. The duty of issuing regulations specifying the form, content, procedures and principles for labels and price lists is given to the Ministry of Industry and Commerce. The Ministry and the municipalities have the duty to enforce this Article and to control its effectiveness.

Organizations for the Protection of Consumers in Turkey

General and Civil Organizations

Article 3 of the amended CPL defined consumer organizations as "associations, foundations and consumption cooperatives established with the purpose of protecting consumers". Consumer organizations in Turkey are not sophisticated, as in Europe and America. The main reasons for this are allegedly the provisions of the Turkish Constitution, which limit the organizing efforts of the public. Although the new Law supports the establishment of consumer organizations and their activities, consumers cannot be defined as highly organized. There are, however, still organizations of consumers in Turkey despite all of these disadvantages, the leading organizations being the Consumer Rights Association (*Tüketici Haklari Dernegi*), the Consumer Protection Association (*Tüketiciyi Koruma Dernegi*), the Protection for All Consumers Association (*Tüm Tüketicileri Koruma Dernegi*), the Consumer Protection Unity Foundation (*Tüketiciyi Koruma Birligi Vakfi*) and the Türk-Is Consumer Office, which is an office of the Türk-Is Syndicate.

Government Organizations

As mentioned above, there are few civil organizations that protect consumer rights. Consequently, the Government decided to establish governmental organizations to educate and protect the rights of the consumers more effectively. The leading organizations are the General Directorate for the Protection of Consumers and Competition

(*Tüketicinin ve Rekabetin Korunmasi Genel Müdürlügü*), the Turkish Standards Institute (*Türk Standartlari Enstitüsü*), the General Directorate of Measures and Standards (*Ölçüler ve Standartlar Genel Müdürlügü*), the General Directorate of Basic Health Services (*Temel Saglik Hizmetleri Genel Müdürlügü*), the Health Protection Institute (*Hifzisihha Ensitüsü*), the Public Professional Institutions (*Meslek Kuruluslari*) and the Consumer Establishments of Municipalities.

Organizations of Commercial Establishments

The State is under a duty to take measures to ensure that private enterprises operate in accordance with national economic requirements and social objectives under conditions of security and stability according to Article 48 of the Constitution. Consequently, branches of commercial establishments, such as the Istanbul Chamber of Commerce, the Ankara Chamber of Commerce and the Izmir Chamber of Commerce, have made very effective efforts in the protection of consumers and the settlement of disputes. Nearly all of these establishments have a Consumer Problems Office, which acts as an ombudsman between consumers and the relevant producers. The periodicals, seminars and panels that are organized by these establishments are regarded as milestones in consumer protection. However, the activities of these establishments will be limited in the near future, as Consumer Problems Arbitrators Committees will be established throughout Turkey.

Impact of the Media and Its Organizations

It is easy to say that the media has a spectacular role in the protection of consumers. Most of the newspapers in Turkey, whether large or small, contain a consumer column. The newspapers also educate their readers about where and how to demand their consumer rights. Companies usually do not want to be advertised as "the company cheats" to consumers, so they fulfill the demands forwarded to them through the consumer columns. Turkey's three biggest newspapers, namely, *Hürriyet*, *Milliyet* and *Sabah*, received more than 70,000 complaints in 2003.

Consumer Protection Law Organizations

The CPL established an Advertisement Board, a Consumer Council and a Consumer Problems Arbitrators' Committee for protecting the rights of consumers more effectively. The Advertisement Board determines the principles that must be observed in advertising, and investigates and gives its opinion to the Ministry of Industry and Commerce on sanctions, forbidding the broadcasting of advertisements that conflict with the Law. It consists of twenty-five members chosen by the governmental and non-governmental organizations. The head of the Board is a general director appointed by the Ministry of Industry and Commerce.

Representatives from the governmental and non-governmental organizations form the Consumer Council. There are thirty-three organizations, including the National Education Ministry, the Tourism Ministry and the National Statistics Institute, that are represented on the Council. The main duty of the Council is consultation on the application of the policies designed by the Ministries concerning consumer protection. It has seventy-three members and meets at least once a year.

The Consumer Problems Arbitrators' Committee was formed because of the failings of the judicial system in consumer problems. The Committee consists of five members. According to Article 22 of the CPL, the Ministry of Industry and Commerce must establish at least one Arbitrators' Committee in every province and county to resolve disputes between consumers and sellers. Thus, the new Law allows an optional conciliation system. Under this system, consumers may apply to the Consumer Problems Arbitrators' Committee in relation to disputes not exceeding (in 2004) TL 500-million in value. The decisions of the Council are not binding, but they can be used as evidence in the consumer courts.

Deceptive Advertising and Legislation

General Provisions in the Code of Obligations

Deceptive advertisements can be subject to the provisions of the TCO, as advertisements take place at the beginning of a sale contract. Consumers may believe advertisements or announcements if they contain attractive scenes. Article 28 of the TCO states that:

> "Where a party to a contract has been induced to enter into a contract by the willful fraud of the other party, the defrauded

> party is not bound by the contract unless the other contracting party had or should have had knowledge of the fraud when entering into the contract".

One of the crucial points in this Article is that the deceptive advertisement must be made intentionally in order to be considered as a situation involving fraud. In fact, it is hard to prove the existence of an intention to deceive. The other point is that the deceptive advertisement must be made by the seller. In many instances, advertisements are made by the producers or distributors of goods and not by the sellers. Article 28(1) of the TCO will be applied to the person who made the advertisement.

The second paragraph of the same Article refers to the fraud of a third party. According to the Article, "Where a party to a contract was willfully defrauded by a third person, such party is bound by the contract unless the other contracting party had or should have had knowledge of the fraud when entering into the contract". The consumer may terminate the contract if he can prove that the seller had or should have had knowledge of the fraud when entering into the contract. The consumer is entitled to terminate the contract within one year from the date of discovery of the fraud. The consumer may demand compensation according to Articles 41 *et seq.* of the TCO, such compensation arising from the termination of the contract. It covers not only the loss caused by entering into the contract, but also material and moral damages.

Advertisements Made before the Consumer Protection Law

Concept of Deceptive Advertisement According to the provisions of the TCC, an advertisement is a deceptive advertisement if it contains incorrect information about a product or service. However, an exaggerated advertisement that cannot mislead a consumer cannot be labeled deceptive. Thus, the advertisement must be likely to mislead or be misleading in order to be deceptive. This determination must be made according to an average consumer.

Possible Plaintiffs Article 58 of the TCC lists the possible plaintiffs as:

(1) Anyone who suffers injury as regards his customers, credit, professional reputation, commercial undertaking or other economic interests, or is exposed to such a danger;

(2) Customers whose economic interests have been injured;
(3) Chambers of Commerce and Industry;
(4) Craftsmen's associations;
(5) Exchanges; and
(6) Other professional and economic unions empowered to protect the economic interests of their members according to their statutes, which may bring action according to the provisions of unfair competition.

The injured party or a customer may demand compensation for damage if there is fault on the other side and the payment of moral damages where the conditions indicated in Article 49 of the TCO exist.

A plaintiff other than those stated above may not claim compensation and payment of moral damages according to the provisions of unfair competition, as this right is granted solely to injured persons or customers. However, a consumer organization may still apply for a determination of the existence of unfair compensation, prevention of the unfair competition, removal of the materials displaying the unfair competition and, if the unfair competition is based on untrue or deceitful statements, the rectification of these statements. A consumer organization or other plaintiffs may base their claims on Article 58(3) of the TCC, that is:

> ". . . giving wrong or deceitful information regarding one's own situation, goods and the products of one's work, one's commercial activity or commercial affairs or acting in the same manner regarding third persons and putting them in a situation above their competitors".

However, it should be noted that plaintiffs may still base their claims upon other provisions concerning unfair competition.

Types of Action, Burden of Proof and Defenses Article 58 of the TCC provides for four types of action. An action for the determination of unfair competition[6] is only a claim for determination of the existing situation, which can be used as evidence in other actions. The plaintiff must prove the existence of behavior or advertisements of the defendant that constitute unfair competition. It is the plaintiff's duty to provide evidence, and the defendant must then provide his

6 Commercial Code, Article 58(1)(a).

own evidence to counter the allegations and show that there was nothing in the advertisement that could be interpreted as unfair competition.

An action for the prevention of unfair competition[7] is brought where the court has already decided that unfair competition exists. The plaintiff demands that the opposing party stop the advertisements that constitute unfair competition. The court first rules that there exists subject matter that can be interpreted as unfair competition and then orders the opposing party to stop it immediately.

An action for the removal of materials displaying the unfair competition[8] is where the plaintiff demands the destruction of the advertising materials, such as billboards or posters, that constitute unfair competition. An action for compensation for material and moral damage can be brought by an injured person[9] against the party at fault.[10]

Not all advertisements may cause damage. There are four general conditions for liability concerning damage caused by transactions resulting from advertisements:

(1) An act contrary to the law;
(2) Damage;
(3) A causal relationship; and
(4) Fault.[11]

This action may only be brought before the court if the other party is at fault. The plaintiff must prove the fault of the other party, but the law does not require a special kind or degree of fault for a claim for compensation.[12] If the conditions mentioned above exist, then the plaintiff may claim compensation.

The person claiming compensation must prove the damage according to Article 42(1) of the TCO. The law also provides an optional right for the plaintiff. According to Article 58 of the TCC, the plaintiff may either claim the profits he lost or payment of the value of the advantages obtained by the defendant through the unfair competition. The

---

7 Commercial Code, Article 58(1)(b).

8 Commercial Code, Article 58(1)(c). Compare with Article 25(3) of the Consumer Protection Law.

9 Commercial Code, Article 58(1)(2).

10 Commercial Code, Article 58(1)(d) and (e).

11 Code of Obligations, Article 49.

12 There exists two kinds of fault under the Turkish legal system: where a party acts "intentionally" or where an act is performed "negligently".

plaintiff may only claim compensation for moral damage if the conditions stipulated in Article 49 of the TCO are satisfied.

According to Article 44 of the TCO, the judge may reduce or completely deny any compensation if the injured person has consented to the act or if circumstances for which he is responsible have caused or aggravated the damage, or have otherwise adversely affected the position of the liable party.

A successful claimant may also demand publication of the judgment after it has become final at the expense of the losing party in all of the abovementioned actions. If an act of unfair competition is committed through the press, the actions mentioned under Paragraphs a, b and c of Article 58(1) of the TCC may be brought only against the persons having written the article or provided the advertisement and, in some cases, the editor-in-chief, the advertising manager, the publisher or the printer.

The legal relationship between the consumer and the producer or seller may be defined as either a contractual relationship or a tortious one. The subject here is being evaluated on the basis that the consumers have asserted their claims based on tortious liability for unfair competition according to the provisions of the TCC. The court must then decide whether a tort exists or not.

All acts may lead to a claim for compensation, but there are several conditions required for tortious liability to be upheld. As mentioned before, tortious liability must be compensated if the conditions stated in the law exist. The court, therefore, searches for an act contrary to the law, fault, damage caused by the act and a causal relationship between the act and the damage before ordering compensation.

A defendant facing a claim based on tort may, firstly, try to prove that no act contrary to the law exists. Omissions may also be considered to be contrary to the law. Thus, a producer who neglects to inform consumers can be held responsible according to the good faith principle stated in Article 2 of the CC. Secondly, the producer may try to prove that no casual relationship exists between the act or omission and the injury. The foreseeability and avoidability of the consequences may indicate a causal relationship according to Turkish doctrine.

Damages Recoverable Material and moral damages can be claimed in the above actions. Material damages are damages that can be given a monetary value. The other party's advertisements may cause a consumer's pecuniary assets to be decreased or impede a possible increase in them that may have occurred. A consumer may demand compensation when his economic interests suffer damage due to incorrect information resulting from deceptive advertising.

A question that may come to mind is how can a consumer's economic benefits be effected? Consumers usually trust reliable and powerful brands. One could say that the brand is often the thing that attracts a consumer to a product. The Law does not require a competitive relationship between the plaintiff and the defendant in order to bring the aforesaid actions. Thus, consumers may claim damages from producers if no warning has been given about a product's effects on health.

Statute of Limitations Unfair competition is a special type of tort regulated by the TCC. Article 62 of the TCC states that claims based on the actions described in Article 58 cease after a certain period of time. Normally, the term is one year from the date upon which the party entitled to sue became aware of the circumstances giving rise to a claim but, in any case, this may not be longer than three years from the date upon which the circumstances occurred.

Advertisements Made after the Consumer Protection Law

Legislation The CPL was amended by Law Number 4822 as a result of the efforts to harmonize Turkish legislation with EU law, the amendments coming into force in June 2003. Law Number 4822 expanded the definition of "goods" in order to make the CPL cover electronic products. Distance selling contracts made and/or concluded by electronic means are also brought within the scope of the CPL. Briefly, the concept of goods in the new Law includes any intangible assets that are used in an electronic environment, such as audiovisual products.

However, the general provisions of the TCO and the regulation of unfair competition in the TCC are still in force as general rules that are applicable whenever there are no specific provisions in the law. Plaintiffs may still base their claims upon the provisions concerning unfair competition or Article 28 of the TCO if the provisions of the CPL are not sufficiently clear. The new Law does not contain any definition of "deceptive advertisements", but it states that these kinds of advertisements are prohibited. Thus, the earlier definition of "deceptive advertisements" in the provisions of the TCC is still valid.

Principles of Advertising The CPL contains two main provisions concerning advertisements. The heading of Article 16 is "Commercial Advertisements and Announcements". It is, therefore, hard to say that the scope of this Article is only defective advertisements. The general principle that must be observed in commercial advertisements and announcements is that they "must be true, honest and in conformity with the laws and public morals". Whereas the first paragraph of Article 16 repeats the same principle stated in Articles 19 and 20 of the TCO, the second mentions the types of agreements that are prohibited. Article 16 of the new CPL does not include personal rights, as they are protected under the provisions of the CC:[13]

> "No advertisements or announcements can be made which are deceiving, misleading or exploiting the lack of consumers' experience and knowledge, causing danger to consumers' health and assets, emulating violence and crime, threatening public health or exploiting children, the disabled, the sick or old people.
>
> "Advertisements or announcements related to the same purpose and requirements can be made by means of comparison.
>
> "The person making the advertisements or announcements must prove the concrete claims made by the advertisements or announcements.
>
> "The person making advertisements or announcements on his own behalf and persons and companies in the business of advertisements or announcements should obey this Article."

The CPL places a duty upon the Advertisement Board to establish the principles that must be observed in relation to commercial advertising and announcements. The second paragraph states that the Advertisement Board will determine these principles according to universally accepted rules that are applied in Turkey. The conformity of advertisements with the law and their veracity can be determined easily. The judge determines the honesty and the conformity of advertisements with public morals. However, the Communiqué on Principles and Application Bases Relating to Commercial Advertisements

13 Civil Code, Articles 23, 24 and 24(a).

and Announcements[14] sets forth principles as a guide for judges. The basic principles stated in Article 4 of the Communiqué are as follows:

(1) Advertisements must be true, honest, real and in conformity with the law and general morals;
(2) Every advertisement must obey the general rules that are accepted in business life and by the public in connection with social and economic responsibility awareness;
(3) Advertisements may not contain any determination as to applications and situations that may compromise human security and that do not observe security rules;
(4) In whatever shape or form, it must be clearly understood that there is an advertisement — no subliminal advertisements are allowed; and
(5) Advertisements must be prepared regarding the average consumer's perception level and the probable effect upon the consumer.

The principles constitute the legal and moral bases of the framework of consumer protection. Furthermore, Articles 5 and 6 of the Communiqué define being in conformity with morals, honesty and truth.

Sanctions against Deceptive Advertising With regard to the general situation concerning deceptive advertisements and their consequences, Article 25 of the CPL states that an advertisement or an announcement that infringes the requirements of the law can be:

(1) Stopped;
(2) Corrected in the same way in which it was made; or
(3) Its creators fined.

However, there is an opinion in legal doctrine[15] stating that consumers may claim damages caused by advertisements according to the amended Articles 4 and 5 of the CPL. According to this opinion, advertisements usually contain a promise of quality, and if the product does not match the promised quality, the consumer may demand compensation according to the nature of the defect.

---

14 Communiqué on Principles and Application Bases Relating to Commercial Advertisements and Announcements, dated 21 December 1995, *Official Gazette*, Number 22500.

15 I. Yilmaz Aslan, *Tüketici Hukuku* (Bursa, 1996) at p. 262.

Possible Plaintiffs Consumers are allowed to bring a complaint regarding deceptive advertisements, but not an action in court. The Ministry of Industry and Commerce has the right to order the removal or correction of an advertisement or impose a fine upon the advertisers. In the case of non-compliance with these orders, it can bring the matter to court to stop or correct an advertisement.

Sanctions and Procedures Consumers can make a written application to the Advertisement Board demanding that an advertisement be stopped or corrected or that the advertisers be fined even when no damage exists. The Board has the competence to reject or forward the request to the Ministry, which has the authority to order that the advertisement or announcement be stopped or corrected in the same way in which it was made. The Ministry may fine the infringing party up to TL 4,497,500,000. Article 25 of the new CPL states that if the advertisement or announcement is made countrywide, the fine will be multiplied by ten. However, it should be noted that the Ministry is not obliged to impose a fine or other sanctions based on the request of the Advertisement Board, but is autonomous in its decision-making.

Statute of Limitations All claims attracting fines must be made within a year from the day of infringement. However, claims concerning defective goods are subject to a two-year limitation period, as contained in Article 4 of the CPL. Claims for damage arising due to defective goods are subject to a three-year limitation period.

Amendments Made by Law Number 4822

Unfair Provisions in a Contract

The amended Law states that unilateral contract provisions inserted into a contract, without negotiation with the consumer, which distort the contractual balance against the consumer and which violate the principle of good faith are considered unfair and have no binding effect upon a consumer. The new Law also expressly states that provisions in "form contracts", such as credit card application forms, are assumed to be "non-negotiated contracts". With this provision, consumers are protected against form contracts unilaterally prepared by sellers and imposed upon them. Additionally, in order to protect the consumer and in parallel with EU Directive Number 93/13, in the case of a dispute concerning the unfairness of a standard term, the burden of proving that a particular provision is not unfair rests with the seller.

Purchases with Installment Payments

Pursuant to the amended Law, consumer contracts stipulating payment of the purchase price in installments must include:

(1) Both the consumer's and the seller's full addresses;
(2) The price of the goods in Turkish Lira, including the applicable customs;
(3) The total sale price;
(4) The amount of interest;
(5) The annual rate of interest;
(6) The amount of the installment payments; and
(7) The legal consequences upon default by the consumer.

In the event that future installments are to be secured by a promissory note, then a separate promissory note must be drawn for each such installment and such promissory notes must be drawn in the name of the seller and not as a bearer instrument.

Distance Selling Contracts

The new Law defines a distance selling contract as any contract concerning the delivery of goods or the performance of services that is concluded in a written, audiovisual, telephonic or electronic environment or by using any other means of communication without physically meeting the customer. The new Law provides that, before the conclusion of a distance selling contract, the consumer must be provided with certain information, and the contract may not be concluded before the consumer confirms in writing that he has received such information.

The new Law is similar in many respects to its counterpart in the EU, namely, the Distance Selling Directive.[16] For instance, Article 9A of the CPL defines distance selling contracts in the same manner as Article 2 of the EU Distance Selling Directive. Furthermore, both the new Law and the EU Distance Selling Directive provide that, before

16 Directive 97/7/EC.

the conclusion of a distance selling contract, the consumer must be provided with certain information, and the contract may not be concluded before the consumer confirms in writing that he has received such information. Also, the seller must execute the order within a maximum of thirty days from the day following the day upon which the consumer forwarded his order to the seller. However, under the CPL, this duration may be extended for a maximum of ten days provided that the consumer is given advance written notification.

There are, however, a number of differences between the distance selling provisions of the new Law and the EU Distance Selling Directive. For example, pursuant to the new Law, the seller must prove that the goods or services were not defective when delivered. However, the question of defective goods is not separately regulated under the Distance Selling Directive. Under EU law, this issue is governed by the Product Liability Directive,[17] pursuant to which the injured person must prove actual damage, as well as the defect in the product and a causal relationship between the damage and the defect. In other words, the distance selling provisions of the new Law regarding the burden of proof are more favorable to consumers than the EU Distance Selling and Product Liability Directives.

Consumer Loans

The amended Law also stipulates that consumer loan contracts must be concluded in writing, and a copy of such contract must be given to the consumer. In addition, the loan conditions may not be altered to the detriment of the consumer during the contract term. Pursuant to the new Law, a consumer loan contract must include at least:

(1) The amount of the loan;
(2) The total amount of debt, including interest and other terms;
(3) The annual rate of interest;
(4) The payment dates;
(5) Requested guarantees;
(6) The interest rate upon default (not to exceed thirty per cent annually);
(7) The consequences of default of the debtor;
(8) The terms regarding payment of the debt before the due dates; and

17 Directive 85/374/EEC.

(9) Clarification regarding the applicable rate of foreign exchange in the event that the loan is provided in foreign currency.

Credit Cards

Disputes between banks and consumers concerning credit card transactions have been included within the scope of the CPL. Certain rights are provided under the amended Law in favor of consumers in order to protect them in such transactions. A loan transaction in which a consumer benefits through purchasing goods or services by a credit card or through withdrawing cash from an existing account is subject to certain provisions applicable to consumer loans. For example, a periodic statement of account sent to the consumer by the bank is considered equivalent to the payment plan of a consumer loan. If a consumer does not pay the minimum payment amount stated in the periodic statement, he shall only pay the default interest; no other obligation can be charged to him.

A creditor must notify the consumer thirty days before an increase in the rate of interest. Such interest rate shall not be applied retroactively. If the consumer pays all of the debt at the latest within sixty days from the notification date and ceases benefiting from the loan, the increased rate of interest shall not be applicable to him. If goods or services are purchased by a credit card, the seller or provider cannot request any payment from the consumer as commission or other similar fee in addition to the purchase price.

Warranty Certificates

The new Law provides that the manufacturers or importers of certain products are required to provide a warranty certificate with their products, and that the warranty period must be at least two years from the delivery of the products to the purchaser. Such warranty period was previously one year. Pursuant to the new Law, a warranty certificate covers the defects in a product during the warranty period. During such period, the seller is required to repair the product free of charge even if certain parts of the product must be replaced. In addition to the right of the purchaser to request that the seller repair a defect in the product, the new Law allows a purchaser to:

(1) Withdraw from the sales contract and demand the return of the purchase price;

(2) Demand replacement of the product; or
(3) Demand a refund of a portion of the purchase price in the event that the purchaser cannot use the product regularly as a result of frequent problems, the seller exceeds the maximum time period allowed for the repair of the product or it is impossible to repair the product in question.

If the purchaser has caused the defect in the product by not using the product in accordance with the user instructions accompanying the product, then the purchaser may not benefit from the rights described above.

After-Sales Services

The scope of after-sales services has been extended to include imported industrial goods, whereas the previous provision of the CPL provided such obligation only for industrial goods sold in Turkey. The Law requires the seller to employ sufficient technical personnel and to store spare parts in an amount to be determined by the Ministry of Industry and Commerce. An importer is also required to provide maintenance and repair services for goods that have been imported by a previous importer, provided that the said goods are still within the utilization term. When determining the goods for which maintenance and repair services shall be supplied, the Ministry must obtain the opinion of the Turkish Standards Institute.

Consumer Complaints Arbitration Committee

The new Law makes it mandatory to submit disputes with a value of less than TL 500-million (currently approximately US $350) to the Consumer Complaints Arbitration Committee. The decisions of the Committee become final upon review by the Consumer Court. In disputes with a value higher than TL 580-million, the Committee's decision may be used as evidence before the Consumer Court.

Miscellaneous

The new Law also provides that:
(1) Commercial advertising must be honest and accurate in consideration of moral and personal rights, and in accordance with the rules determined by the Advertisement Board;

(2) The marketing, importation and exportation of goods that look like food products but are actually not is prohibited, as they may endanger the health and security of consumers — for example, the production of a strawberry-shaped eraser with a strawberry flavor is prohibited as it may be dangerous for children;

(3) The Ministry be granted the authority to supervise price stickers. It is now mandatory to indicate the country of production as well as the country of origin, for example, if a French wine is also produced in Turkey after obtaining the necessary licenses, Turkey must be indicated as the country of production, while France must be identified as the country of origin. Goods priced by the Council of Ministers, or any other public entity or a professional organization, cannot be sold at a higher price. Furthermore, if the sticker price and the price at the register are different, then the lower price shall be applied; and

(4) The obligation to prepare an instruction manual in Turkish for industrial goods has been provided in relation to imported industrial goods, and the Ministry shall determine the minimum content of such instruction manuals and stickers by obtaining the opinion of the Turkish Standards Institute.

Conclusion

The new Law has made substantial amendments to the CPL, which is now more favorable to consumers in certain respects as compared to its counterpart under EU law, including the burden of proof of the defect in distance selling contracts. The Ministry has already issued several regulations and communiqués, which are quite similar to their counterparts in the EU, to regulate certain areas in detail. As a result of the efforts to harmonize Turkish legislation with EU law, it is likely that subsequent regulations and communiqués will also closely follow their European counterparts.

Foreign Product Liability Actions in United States Courts

J.K. Hetrick and Gregg T. Nunziata
Dechert, LLP
Philadelphia, Pennsylvania, United States

Introduction

> "As a moth is drawn to light, so is a litigant drawn to the United States. If he can only get his case into their courts, he stands to win a fortune. At no cost to himself, and at no risk of having to pay anything to the other side. The lawyers there will conduct the case . . . on a 'contingency fee' . . . There is also in the United States a right to trial by jury. These are prone to award fabulous damages. They are notoriously sympathetic and know that the lawyers will take forty per cent. All this means that the defendant can readily be forced into settlement. The plaintiff holds all the cards."[1]

While it may not be literally true that in the United States "the plaintiff holds all the cards", it is understandable why a foreign commentator might see it that way. It is quite correct that in American courts plaintiffs enjoy a panoply of substantive and procedural advantages that they do not possess in civil systems, such as most in Europe and the Far East or, for that matter, in many Common Law systems. In recent decades, American plaintiffs have increasingly learned to profit from these advantages. With these well-publicized successes, foreign plaintiffs naturally began seeking access to American courts.[2]

---

1 *Smith Kline & French Labs* v. *Bloch*, 2 All ER 72, 74 (Eng. 1983).

2 It should be noted that there is not one unitary American court system. Rather, each of the United States has its own individual court system, and these run parallel to the federal court system. Thus, two separate and independent systems exist in every American state run by that individual state and another by the United States Federal Government. When speaking of the "United States" or "American" courts, this chapter will be making generalizations about American law — generalizations that may be more or less true of federal or state courts, and more or less true among the various state courts. When a particular court system is being referred to, this will be made clear in the text.

Lure of the American Forum

It is not one factor that leads foreign plaintiffs to gladly accept the inconvenience of bringing suit across oceans, but rather a broad range of factors. These include the possibility of large damage awards, including punitive damages, the availability of jury trials, liberal pleading rules, broad discovery tools and the option to bring claims on a contingent basis.

Any discussion of product liability litigation in American courts cannot fail to notice the increasingly fabulous damage awards granted by juries in recent years. Damages in America are calculated on two principal bases — compensatory and punitive. Compensatory damages are meant to have a basis in the actual harm suffered.[3] However, the addition and expansion of the concept of "pain and suffering" has muddied the waters somewhat. Compensation for lost wages and similar traditional categories of compensatory damages are clearly tethered to concrete figures. A determination of what is fair compensation for "pain and suffering" lacks a similar anchor.

Departing further from the realm of the quantifiable, the concept of punitive damages allows a jury to impose further damages on top of compensatory damages. In order to qualify for punitive damages, plaintiffs must make a threshold showing of certain egregious behavior on the part of the defendant.[4] This requirement has not always proven particularly daunting in the mass tort setting.

Further assisting plaintiffs in United States courts, judgments of whether to impose liability, and how much to award in damages, generally fall to a jury of laymen. In most contexts, plaintiffs in product liability actions do not even need to clear any meaningful substantive hurdles in order to receive a jury trial. Rather, plaintiffs generally have a "right" to a jury, unless they choose to waive that right.[5] It virtually

3 Restatement (Second) of Torts, Section 903 (2002): "'Compensatory damages' are the damages awarded to a person as compensation, indemnity or restitution for harm sustained by him".

4 Restatement (Second) of Torts, Section 908 (2002): "Punitive damages may be awarded for conduct that is outrageous, because of the defendant's evil motive or his reckless indifference to the rights of others".

5 The American Bill of Rights provides: "In suits of common law, where the value in controversy shall exceed twenty dollars, the right to trial by jury shall be preserved, and no fact tried by a jury, shall be otherwise re-examined in any Court of the United States, than according to the rules of the common law": United States Constitutional Amendment VII. Jury trials are also widely available in state courts.

goes without saying that an injured person or group of people might prefer to place their claims before a panel of their peers, rather than an impartial (and arguably conservative) judge, particularly where (as in a product liability action) their opponent is a large international corporation.

Well before a trial even reaches a jury, plaintiffs enjoy significant advantages through the use of what are, generally speaking, liberal pleading rules. A plaintiff may often not need to spell out a well articulated theory of the case to be able to move forward with the litigation. In most American courts, a plaintiff is only expected to make the barest allegations in order to survive a motion to dismiss.[6] This practice, called "notice pleading", requires only a recitation of the fundamental elements of the claim. The official Federal Rules of Civil Procedure offer the following sample Complaint as an acceptable model. Note that it even allows for lack of certainty with regard to the proper defendant and, needless to say, it is a model of brevity:

> "1. Allegation of jurisdiction.
>
> "2. On 1 June 1936, in a public highway called Boyleston Street in Boston, Massachusetts, defendant C.D. or defendant E.F., or both defendants C.D. and E.F. willfully or recklessly or negligently drove a motor vehicle against plaintiff who was then crossing said highway.
>
> "3. As a result plaintiff was thrown down and had his leg broken and was otherwise injured, was prevented from transacting his business, suffered great pain of body and mind, and incurred expenses for medical attention and hospitalization in the sum of one thousand dollars.
>
> "Wherefore plaintiff demands judgment against C.D. or against E.F. or against both in the sum of _________ dollars and costs."

This means it is comparatively affordable for a plaintiff to start the wheels of a civil action turning. Once a plaintiff has stated a generally pleaded cause of action and survived any motions to dismiss, he finds

---

6 Fed. R. Civ. Pro. Section 8(a) (2003), requiring that a complaint contain only "a short and plain statement of the claim"; *Gavara* v. *Pa. H.R.*, 55 Fed. Appx. 60, 63 (3d Cir. 2000).

himself armed with the considerable powers of American discovery tools. He may now demand that a defendant produce huge volumes of documents, answer written questions and produce witnesses for examination.[7] Following the liberal pleading rules, this process may allow a plaintiff to further develop his case at this stage. Further, bearing the costs of meeting discovery requests can prove extraordinarily expensive for defendants who, in product liability actions, tend to have in their possession or their employ the bulk of relevant documents and witnesses. This expense that defendants must bear provides a strategic advantage to plaintiffs; as soon as litigation begins, costs borne by defendants rise no matter how weak a plaintiff's case.

As litigation continues and costs mount on defendants, the typical product liability plaintiff has had not to pay the slightest sum of money. The United States legal system permits plaintiffs' lawyers to take cases on "contingent fee" arrangements, and they frequently do so. Under such arrangement, the plaintiff pays no costs to his attorneys unless the plaintiff prevails at trial, in which case the lawyers take a substantial share of the judgment — generally thirty-three per cent, and sometimes as much as fifty per cent. Not only are such arrangements uncommon in other legal systems, in many countries they are flatly illegal.

Finally, in contrast to other Common Law systems, a failing plaintiff bears no responsibility for a defendant's legal bills. With no costs up front, no downside risks at the conclusion and a range of advantages throughout the process, it is no surprise that a product liability (or any other) plaintiff would seek access to United States courts.

Jurisdiction

It is clear that plaintiffs may wish to pursue their claims in American courts, but can foreign plaintiffs actually do so? If they can, in which courts may they bring their actions? Initially, the answers to these questions would be yes, they can, and plaintiffs will likely have access to a variety of state and federal courts.

The question of whether a court may hear a plaintiff's case is governed by an inquiry into "jurisdiction", the Common Law equivalent

7 Fed. R. Civ. Pro. Sections 26–37 (2003).

of the Civil Law's concept of "competence". In order to hear a given case, a United States court must have both subject matter and personal jurisdiction. Unless a plaintiff can show that a court has each, the court must decline to hear the case.

Subject matter jurisdiction concerns whether the claim presented is within a category of issues that a particular court has the power to hear. For current purposes, it is sufficient to say that American state courts are courts of general subject matter jurisdiction. With some exceptions not relevant here, a state court can hear claims on any issue, which includes product liability based tort claims.

The federal courts, on the other hand, are courts of limited subject matter jurisdiction. Federal courts only have subject matter jurisdiction in certain classes of cases. One basis for federal subject matter jurisdiction is "diversity" of the parties, where the amount in dispute is in excess of US $75,000.[8] Put simply, the parties are diverse where the plaintiff and defendant are not citizens of the same State. Thus, in any action against a United States company by a foreign plaintiff, diversity of the parties will exist. Assuming the "amount in controversy" is in excess of US $75,000 (a safe assumption in the product liability context), a federal court will have subject matter jurisdiction over a product liability claim by a foreign national against a domestic corporation.

As suggested above, a showing of subject matter jurisdiction alone is not sufficient to bring a claim, as plaintiffs must also show that a court has personal or territorial jurisdiction. Traditionally, a court had personal jurisdiction over its citizens[9] and over those that could be found or who possessed property within the boundaries its authority covered.[10] As this concept evolved with industrialization, courts increasingly found that corporations were subject to jurisdiction in any state where they had "certain minimum contacts . . . such that the maintenance of the suit does not offend traditional notions of fair play and substantial justice".[11] Manufacturers of widely distributed products typically find themselves subject to jurisdiction in numerous fora.

8 28 U.S.C.A. Section 1332 (2003).

9 "Citizen" is used here to refer not solely to national citizenship, but also state citizenship among the various United States, that is, a California court would have jurisdiction over Californians as well as those non-Californians, American and foreign, who could be found in California. Under this test, a Californian court would not have jurisdiction over a New Yorker residing in New York.

10 *Pennoyer* v. *Neff*, 96 U.S. 714, 733 (1877).

11 *International Shoe* v. *Wash.*, 326 U.S. 310 (1945).

The practical effect of the foregoing is that foreign product liability plaintiffs suing American corporations will usually have the ability to hand pick a forum in which to bring a claim from a wide array of American courts, including state or federal district courts. This should only make litigating in the United States more attractive to foreign plaintiffs — not only do they benefit from all the procedural and substantive rules discussed above, they also have the power to select the court and jurisdiction where all of those factors run most strongly in a plaintiff's favor, and where the most favorable substantive law and sympathetic jury may be found. Rather than offend basic notions of American jurisprudence, this fact finds itself buttressed by the axiomatic principle that a plaintiff's choice of forum is entitled to great deference.[12]

Forum Non Conveniens

At this point, it might appear that the prospect of litigating in the United States constitutes a foreign plaintiff's dream come true. Save the last two words, that phrase might be accurate. American courts have developed doctrines that, in fact, make it quite challenging for foreign plaintiffs to convert the ethereal into the actual.

Many of the developments in American law generally, and product liability law particularly, have provoked significant controversy. Fantastic jury awards, punitive damages, damages for "pain and suffering", liberal pleading rules, broad rights of plaintiffs to choose the forum (derisively referred to as "forum shopping"), contingency fees and the absence of fee shifting have all inspired lively criticism and proposals for reform.

While legal and political movements to dampen down litigation have yet to achieve any global reform, product liability cases brought by foreign plaintiffs compose one of the categories of cases in which pro-reform forces have met the most success. The impetus for turning away foreign plaintiffs has come not from the political branches, but from the judiciary itself. Relying on the traditional notion of *forum non conveniens*, the courts in recent decades have routinely dismissed foreign claims.

12 *Piper Aircraft Co.* v. *Reyno*, 454 U.S. 235 at 255-56 (1981); *Dowling* v. *Hyland Therapeutics Div.*, 767 F.Supp. 57, 58 (1991) — "Ordinarily, there is a 'strong presumption' in favor of the plaintiff's choice of forum", and citing *Piper*.

Just because an American court has jurisdiction to hear a claim does not mean that it must do so.[13] Several grounds exist upon which it can decline to adjudicate a dispute, one of these grounds being known as the doctrine of *forum non conveniens*. It holds, essentially, that a court may decline to exercise jurisdiction where, for various reasons, litigation makes more sense — is more convenient — elsewhere.

The Federal Test

The United States Supreme Court has developed a flexible approach, which federal courts employ to evaluate whether a case ought to be dismissed on the ground of *forum non conveniens*. The general framework was first announced in *Gulf Oil Corp.* v. *Gilbert*.[14] As an initial matter, a court must find that there is an adequate available forum elsewhere.[15] This condition is easily satisfied in most cases.[16] If all parties may be brought before a particular court, it is generally considered adequate. That the alternate forum provides different substantive law, a lower likelihood of success or less significant available remedies does not render an alternative forum inadequate.[17]

Once a court satisfies itself that an acceptable alternative forum exists, according to the federal approach, it must weigh a variety of private and public considerations before reaching the decision of

---

13 *Gulf Oil Corp.* v. *Gilbert*, 330 U.S. 501, 504 (1947), noting that where a court is shown to have jurisdiction and the power to hear a case "that does not settle the question of whether it must do so". This is in contrast to Civil Law courts which, if competent, must hear the case before it. *Forum non conveniens* does not exist in those systems.

14 *Gulf Oil Corp.* v. *Gilbert*, 330 U.S. 501 (1947).

15 *Piper Aircraft Co.* v. *Reyno*, 454 U.S. 235 at 241 (1981), indicating that a court can only begin a *forum non conveniens* analysis "when an alternative forum has jurisdiction to hear the case"; *Perusahaan Umum Listrik Negara Pusat* v. *M/V Tel Aviv*, 711 F.2d 1231, 1238 (1983) — "The balancing analysis is predicated on the finding that there exists an adequate and available alternative forum". However, *see Islamic Republic of Iran* v. *Pahlavi*, 467 N.E.2d 245 (N.Y. 1984), holding that the availability of an alternative forum is not an absolute precondition to dismissal on the ground of *forum non conveniens*.

16 Lonny S. Hoffman, "*Forum Non Conveniens* — State and Federal Movements", SF13 Ali-Aba 135, 143 (November 2000) — "this first step in the test has not proven to be a significant threshold to cross".

17 *Piper Aircraft Co.* v. *Reyno*, 454 U.S. 235 at 254 (1981).

whether to hear the case or send it back from whence it came.[18] The private considerations include:

> "... relative ease of access to sources of proof; availability of compulsory process for attendance of unwilling, and the cost of obtaining attendance of unwilling, witnesses; possibility of viewing of the premises, if viewing would be appropriate to the action; and all other practical problems that make trial of a case easy, expeditious, and inexpensive. There may also be questions as to the enforceability of a judgment if one is obtained. The court will weigh the relative advantages and obstacles to a fair trial".[19]

The court in *Gulf Oil* held that a plaintiff's choice of forum ought to be disturbed only where a weighing of the factors strongly favors the defendant's position.[20] It also made clear that courts should not permit plaintiffs to choose a forum to harass a defendant, noting that the loose jurisdictional hurdles present an "open door" that "may admit those who seek not simply justice, but perhaps justice blended with some harassment.[21]

As indicated above, under the federal approach, a court may also consider a multitude of public factors. The court in *Gulf Oil* explained these factors as follows:

> "Administrative difficulties follow for courts when litigation is piled up in congested centers instead of being handled at its origin. Jury duty is a burden that ought not to be imposed on the people of a community which has no relation to the litigation. In cases which touch the affairs of many persons, there is reason for holding the trial in their view and reach rather than in remote parts of the country where they can learn of it by report only. There is a local interest in having localized controversies decided at home. There is an appropriateness, too, in having the trial of a diversity case in a forum that is at home with the state law that must govern

---

18 *Gulf Oil Corp.* v. *Gilbert*, 330 U.S. 501, at 508–09 (1947).

19 *Gulf Oil Corp.* v. *Gilbert*, 330 U.S. 501, at 508 (1947).

20 *Gulf Oil Corp.* v. *Gilbert*, 330 U.S. 501 (1947), holding that "unless the balance is strongly in favor of the defendant, the plaintiff's choice of forum should rarely be disturbed".

21 *Gulf Oil Corp.* v. *Gilbert*, 330 U.S. 501, at 507 (1947).

the case, rather than having a court in some other forum untangle problems in conflicts of laws, and in law foreign to itself."[22]

The Supreme Court returned to the question of *forum non conveniens* in *Piper Aircraft Co.* v. *Reyno*. In *Piper*, the court first encountered a product liability suit brought by a foreign plaintiff against domestic corporations. The case involved an action brought by the representative of the estates of British subjects who perished in an airplane crash in Scotland. The pilots and all the decedents were British, and the plane was owned and operated by British companies. The only connection the suit had to the United States was the fact that the manufacturers of the plane and its propellers were American companies. In *Piper*, the court faced a plaintiff who "candidly admits that the action . . . was filed in the United States because its laws regarding liability, capacity to sue, and damages are more favorable to [her] position than are those of Scotland".[23] It used this opportunity to significantly limit foreign plaintiffs' ability to take advantage of favorable American law.

The primary question presented in *Piper* was whether a plaintiff could defeat a motion to dismiss on the ground of *forum non conveniens* where he could demonstrate such a dismissal would result in an unfavorable change in substantive law. The court answered, in clear terms, in the negative. "The possibility of a change in substantive law should ordinarily not be given conclusive, or even substantial, weight in the *forum non conveniens* inquiry."[24] In its decision, the court made clear that this ruling consciously limited the access of foreign plaintiffs to United States courts. It explained that if it had reached a contrary result, "American courts, which are already extremely attractive to foreign plaintiffs, would become even more attractive. The flow of litigation into the United States would increase and further congest crowded courts".[25] Henceforth, a change in substantive law would only be given substantial weight in those cases where "the alternative forum is so inadequate or unsatisfactory that it is no remedy at all".[26]

22 *Gulf Oil Corp.* v. *Gilbert*, 330 U.S. 501, at 508–09 (1947).
23 *Piper Aircraft Co.* v. *Reyno*, 454 U.S. 235 at 240 (1981).
24 *Piper Aircraft Co.* v. *Reyno*, 454 U.S. 235 at 247 (1981).
25 *Piper Aircraft Co.* v. *Reyno*, 454 U.S. 235 at 252 (1981).
26 *Piper Aircraft Co.* v. *Reyno*, 454 U.S. 235 at 254 (1981).

Not content with this clear statement that the advantages of litigation in the United States would not, in themselves, keep foreign plaintiffs in the United States, the court went one step further and announced that the *forum non conveniens* analysis would cut particularly sharply against foreign plaintiffs. As stated above, American courts had long held that a plaintiff's choice of forum should receive a great deal of deference, thus they have been extremely reluctant to dismiss cases on the ground of *forum non conveniens*. The court in *Gulf Oil* described *forum non convenience* as applicable in only "rather rare cases".[27] Indeed, as suggested above, the courts have held that the mere fact that a particular forum is chosen by a plaintiff speaks to its presumptive convenience.[28] In *Piper*, the court explicitly broke with this tradition with regard to foreign plaintiffs. It held that (at least in federal court) foreign plaintiffs are simply not entitled to the same degree of deference. The court reasoned:

> "When the home forum has been chosen, it is reasonable to assume that this choice is convenient. When the plaintiff is foreign, however, this assumption is much less reasonable. Because the central purpose of any *forum non conveniens* inquiry is to establish that the trial is convenient, a foreign plaintiff's choice deserves less deference."[29]

Thus, the court in *Piper* upheld the lower court's decision to grant the defendants' motion to dismiss on the ground of *forum non conveniens* and, in the process, significantly impaired the ability of foreign plaintiffs to maintain their actions in United States courts.

State Approaches

While a *forum non conveniens* analysis in state court would have to proceed under the relevant state's particular laws and precedents, in reality, the analysis tends to be very similar to the federal approach. For example, the California Supreme Court explicitly adopted the framework of *Gulf Oil* in 1954.[30] Recently, that court reaffirmed the

---

27 *Gulf Oil Corp.* v. *Gilbert*, 330 U.S. 501 (1947).
28 *Piper Aircraft Co.* v. *Reyno*, 454 U.S. 235 at 255–256 (1981).
29 *Piper Aircraft Co.* v. *Reyno*, 454 U.S. 235 at 255–256 (1981).
30 *Price* v. *Atchinson, Topeka & Santa Fe Ry. Co.*, 268 P.2d 457 (Cal. 1954).

essential *Gulf Oil* framework.[31] This approach seems to be the most common, but the doctrine may have slight variations and, in a handful of states, the doctrine may not exist at all.[32] Thus, the practitioner is urged to investigate the statutes and case law of the individual state.

Recent Examples and Trends

Courts in the United States have increasingly relied on *forum non conveniens* to keep foreign product liability actions out of United States courts, so much so, that this has become the expected result.[33] Recent cases dismissed on the ground of *forum non conveniens* include actions regarding injuries suffered due to use of tampons, pesticides, blood products for the treatment of hemophilia and breast implants.[34] Following *Piper*, courts have found that a foreign court provides an adequate forum, even where the substantive foreign law offers plaintiffs significantly diminished prospects of recovery.[35] For example, a state court found that a US $10,000 recovery limit does not render a foreign forum inadequate;[36] nor does a requirement of massive filing fees, the presence of a heavily congested and

31 *Stangvik* v. *Shiley, Inc.*, 819 P.2d 14 (Cal. 1991).

32 Daniel J. Dorward, "The *Forum Non Conveniens* Doctrine and the Judicial Protection of Multinational Corporations for Forum Shopping Plaintiffs", 19 U. Pa. J. Int'l Econ. L. 141, 164–65 (1998); David W. Robertson and Paula Speck, "Access to State Courts in Transnational Personal Injury Cases: *Forum Non Conveniens* and Antisuit Injunctions", 68 Tex. L. Rev. 937, 950–51 (1990).

33 Douglas W. Dunham and Eric F. Gladbach, "*Forum Non Conveniens* and Foreign Plaintiffs in the 1990s", 24 Brook. J. Int'l L. 665, 666, concluding "that the clear trend in the 1990s has been for American courts to dismiss actions brought by foreign plaintiffs under product liability theories of recovery".

34 *Kilvert* v. *Tambrands, Inc.*, 906 F.Supp. 790 (S.D.N.Y. 1995); *Proyectos Orchimaex de Costa Rica* v. *E.I. DuPont de Neours & Co.*, 896 F.Supp. 1197 (M.D. Fla. 1995); *Dowling* v. *Hyland Therapeutics Div*, 767 F.Supp. 57 (S.D.N.Y. 1991); *In re Silicone Gel Breast Implants Prod. Liab. Litig.*, 887 F.Supp. 1469 (N.D. Ala. 1995).

35 *Proyectos Orchimaex de Costa Rica* v. *E.I. DuPont de Neours & Co.*, 896 F.Supp. 1197, at 1201 (M.D. Fla. 1995) — "In general, a court engaged in an inquiry concerning the existence of an alternative forum should not hinge its decision based on the possibility of an unfavorable change of law", and citing *Piper*.

36 *Wolf* v. *Boeing Co.*, 810 P.2d 943, 948-49 (Wash. Ct. App. 1991), applying Washington *forum non conveniens* law, which is very similar to the federal approach.

backlogged judicial system and far less favorable tort remedies.[37] Some courts have allowed dismissal on the ground of *forum non conveniens* where the suit abroad might be time barred by the foreign country's statute of limitations.[38] Perhaps most remarkable is that a court even upheld a dismissal on the ground of *forum non conveniens* where, due to political conflicts, no alternative forum was actually available at the time.[39]

Despite the apparent trend indicating that United States courts will dismiss product liability claims brought by foreign plaintiffs, domestic defendants cannot count on such a result. As discussed above, a *forum non conveniens* analysis invokes a multi-factored balancing test. Under no situation can the expected result be the anticipated result. The nature of *forum non conveniens* resists guiding precedent. Such approaches are not without criticism. As Justice Black wrote in a spirited dissent to *Gulf Oil*, where the federal approach was first announced:

> "The broad and indefinite discretion left to federal courts to decide the question of convenience from the welter of factors which are relevant to such a judgment, will inevitably produce a complex of close and indistinguishable decisions from which accurate prediction of the proper forum will become difficult, if not impossible."[40]

Further, the court in *Gulf Oil* directly indicated that trial courts ought to have broad discretion in making a determination on the ground of *forum non conveniens*.[41] This analytical problem persists, as Justice Scalia has written: "The discretionary nature of the doctrine, combined with the multifariousness of the factors relevant to its

---

37 *In re Union Carbide Corp. Gas Plant Disaster at Bhopal, India*, 634 F.Supp. 842, 847–852 (S.D.N.Y. 1986).

38 Lonny S. Hoffman, "*Forum Non Conveniens* — State and Federal Movements", SF13 Ali-Aba 135, 144 (November 2000).

39 *Islamic Republic of Iran*, 467 N.E.2d 245, applying New York *forum non conveniens* law, which is indistinguishable from the federal approach.

40 *Gulf Oil Corp.* v. *Gilbert*, 330 U.S. 501, 516 (1947).

41 *Gulf Oil Corp.* v. *Gilbert*, 330 U.S. 501, 508 (1947) — "Wisely, it has not been attempted to catalogue the circumstance which will justify or require either grant or denial of remedy. The doctrine leaves much to the discretion of the court to which plaintiff resorts, and experience has not shown a judicial tendency to renounce one's jurisdiction so strong as to result in many abuses."

application . . . make uniformity and predictability of outcome almost impossible."[42] A motion to dismiss on the ground of *forum non conveniens* will encounter various odds of success, depending on which judge entertains it and what specific facts make up the case at issue.

Recent examples of cases where courts have rejected a *forum non conveniens* argument include several that cannot easily be reconciled with the broader trend discussed above. For example, a recent federal court decision found that Bolivia could not provide an adequate alternative forum due to excessive corruption in its judicial system.[43] Just a year earlier, another federal court had reached the opposite conclusion regarding Guatemala.[44] Similarly, a 1995 federal court ruling found that India could not offer an adequate alternative forum due to extreme congestion in the legal system,[45] despite the fact that a different federal court reached the opposite conclusion a decade earlier. Although, as mentioned above, some courts have granted motions to dismiss on the ground of *forum non conveniens* even where an action might be time barred in the foreign jurisdiction, other courts have found that no alternative forum exists where claims would be time barred.[46] In the words of Justice Scalia, "In such a regime, one can rarely count on the fact that jurisdiction will be declined".[47]

Dismissals — With a Catch

Even if defendants could virtually count on a dismissal on the ground of *forum non conveniens*, they should still take pause. Recent trends indicate that a favorable result on a motion to dismiss on the ground of *forum non conveniens* may come with strings attached.[48] Prior to entering an order dismissing a case on the ground of *forum non*

42 *Am. Dredging Co.* v. *Miller*, 510 U.S. 443, 455 (1994).

43 *Eastman Kodak Co.* v. *Kavlin*, 978 F.Supp. 1078, 1085 (S.D. Fla. 1997).

44 *Polanco* v. *H.B. Fuller Co.*, 941 F.Supp. 1512, 1525 (D. Minn. 1996).

45 *Bhatnagar* v. *Surrendra Overseas LTD*, 52 F.3d 1220, 1225-30 (3d. Cir. 1995).

46 *Silicone Gel Breast Implants*, 887 F.Supp. at 1475.

47 *Am. Dredging Co.* v. *Miller*, 510 U.S. 443, 455 (1994).

48 *Silicone Gel Breast Implants*, 887 F.Supp. at 1474 — "the court may consider — or even condition its decision on — concession by a party, such as waiving statutes of limitations or objections to process, personal jurisdiction, or admissibility of evidence, or agreeing that a judgment would be enforceable".

conveniens, courts have required defendants to make various concessions including agreeing to submit to process in foreign courts,[49] agreeing to accept any judgment reached by that court[50] and waiving statute of limitations defenses.[51]

In short, a defendant should not expect to receive a *forum non conveniens* dismissal, and will need to muster the very best argument to succeed — and even then, there may be a price to be paid.

49 *Kilvert* v. *Tambrands, Inc.*, 906 F.Supp. 790, at 798 (S.D.N.Y. 1995).
50 *Ministry of Health* v. *Shiley*, 858 F.Supp. 1426, 1442 (C.D. Cal. 1994); *In re Silicone Gel Breast Implants Prod. Liab. Litig.*, 887 F.Supp. 1469, at 1479 (N.D. Ala. 1995).
51 *Kilvert* v. *Tambrands, Inc.*, 906 F.Supp. 790, at 798 (S.D.N.Y. 1995).

Federalism in American Product Liability Law: Do Similar Problems Lie Ahead for the European Union?

Jonathan M. Hoffman
Martin Bischoff LLP
Portland, Oregon, United States

Introduction

Federalism has been defined as "the mode of political organization that unites separate polities within an overarching political system by distributing power among general and constituent governments in a manner designed to protect the existence and authority of both".[1] United States Senator Charles S. Robb once observed that the quickest way to empty a room is to shout "federalism", and the public's eyes "glaze over at mere whispers of the word".[2]

In the United States, product liability lawsuits may be filed in either state or federal court, depending on a variety of factors, most notably whether there is diversity of citizenship between plaintiffs and defendants. In other words, if the plaintiff is a citizen of one state and the defendant is a citizen of another state, diversity of citizenship exists. If there is complete diversity, that is, no plaintiff is a citizen of the same state as any defendant, and the requisite amount in controversy exists (presently United States $75,000), the plaintiff may bring suit in federal, as well as state, court.[3] If suit is filed in state court, diversity exists and the defendant is not a citizen of the state where suit is filed, the defendant can remove the action to federal court, as long as the requisite amount in controversy exists.[4]

1 Daniel J. Elazar, *American Federalism: A View From the States 2* (3rd ed. 1984).

2 John Kincaid, "Foreword: the New Federalism Context of the New Judicial Federalism", 26 Rutgers L.J. 913 (1995).

3 28 U.S.C. Section 1332.

4 28 U.S.C. Section 1441(b).

Federal v. State Jurisdiction

A variety of tactical issues determine whether a plaintiff wants to pursue the claim in state or federal court, just as the defendant may or may not want to remove a case from state to federal court. A plaintiff who wants to remain in state court may add a non-diverse defendant to prevent removal. A defendant can nevertheless remove the action on a showing that joinder of the non-diverse defendant is fraudulent, that is, that there is no legitimate claim against that defendant and that it was joined solely to prevent removal.[5]

To add to the complexity, issues in the case may be governed by state or federal law, regardless of the court in which suit is pending. For example:

(1) The federal statute of repose for product liability actions against the manufacturer of a general aviation aircraft applies to such a claim in both state and federal court, unless applicable state law imposes a shorter period;[6]

(2) State and federal law may impose conflicting duties upon the manufacturer, in which case, under the Supremacy Clause of the United States Constitution, federal law determines whether the federal law pre-empts a conflicting state law;[7] and

(3) State law determines the rules under which a defendant may be liable for punitive damages, but federal law establishes constitutional due process limitations used to determine whether an award of punitive damages is excessive.[8]

Given the variety of state laws, the differences between state and federal law and the differences between state and federal courts, it is not surprising that inconsistencies occur between state and federal courts over a wide range of issues.

In the United States, a disturbing trend may be developing in product liability law. Increasingly, state and federal courts apply similar

---

5 *Badon* v. *RJR Nabisco Inc.*, 236 F.3d 282 (5th Cir. 2000).

6 General Aviation Revitalization Act 1994, 49 U.S.C. Section 40101 (1994).

7 *Crosby* v. *National Foreign Trade Council*, 530 U.S. 363, 120 S.Ct. 2288, 147 L.Ed.2d 352 (2000); *Geier* v. *American Honda Motor Co., Inc.*, 529 U.S. 861, 120 S.Ct. 1913, 146 L.Ed.2d 914 (2000).

8 *BMW of North America, Inc.* v. *Gore*, 517 U.S. 559, 116 S.Ct. 1589, 134 L.Ed.2d 809 (1996); *Honda Motor Co.* v. *Oberg*, 512 U.S. 415, 114 S.Ct. 2331, 129 L.Ed.2d 336 (1994).

or even identical rules of law to render diametrically opposed decisions. That these problems persist in the United States, despite over two centuries of experience with a federal system, raises the question whether Europe's new venture into federal product liability law — with European Union (EU) rules superimposed over inconsistent laws of Member States — may portend analogous if not parallel difficulties down the road.

Procedural and Evidentiary Examples

Two recent examples illustrate cases in which state and federal courts in the United States reached contrary results on pivotal issues by applying state and federal civil procedure and evidence codes, even though the text of the state and federal codes was identical. The first concerns the interpretation of state and federal rules. This is particularly important in American jurisprudence because it directly affects what a jury may hear and decide. In product liability cases, where there is often a catastrophically injured plaintiff seeking to recover on an implausible factual or legal theory of liability, the plaintiff may simply want to get the case before a jury. Conversely, defendants often rely upon procedural and evidentiary rules to keep such cases from coming before a jury at all. Thus, the interpretation of the summary judgment rule and the admissibility of expert testimony are issues of tremendous significance in product liability litigation in the United States. State and federal courts frequently differ on the interpretation of these rules, even when the text of the rule is identical.

Summary Judgment

The *Celotex* trilogy defines the federal standard for summary judgment under Federal Rule 56(c). In *Celotex Corp.* v. *Catrett*,[9] the United States Supreme Court rejected the view that the non-moving party bears the burden of responding to a summary judgment motion only once the moving party has come forward with evidence of the absence of any genuine issue of material fact:

> "In our view, the plain language of Rule 56(c) mandates the entry of summary judgment, after adequate time for discovery

---

9 *Celotex Corp.* v. *Catrett*, 477 U.S. 317, 106 S.Ct. 2548, 91 L.Ed.2d 265 (1986).

> and upon motion, against a party who fails to make a showing sufficient to establish the existence of an element essential to that party's case, and on which that party will bear the burden of proof at trial. In such a situation, there can be 'no issue as to any material fact', since a complete failure of proof concerning an essential element of the non-moving party's case necessarily renders all other facts immaterial. The moving party is 'entitled to a judgment as a matter of law' because the non-moving party has failed to make a sufficient showing on an essential element of her case with respect to which she has the burden of proof . . . but unlike the Court of Appeals, we find no express or implied requirement in Rule 56 that the moving party support its motion with affidavits or other similar materials negating the opponent's claim. On the contrary, Rule 56(c), which refers to 'the affidavits, if any', suggest the absence of such a requirement.[10]

A number of state courts have expressly rejected *Celotex* and reached the opposite conclusion on the same issue, even though the applicable state rule of civil procedure was identical to Federal Rule 56.[11] Likewise, another component of the *Celotex* trilogy, *Anderson* v. *Liberty Lobby, Inc.*,[12] held that when the substantive law required the plaintiff to prove an essential element of the claim by clear and convincing evidence, the clear and convincing standard should also apply to a summary judgment motion. Under this standard, "the appropriate summary judgment question will be whether the evidence in the record could support a reasonable jury finding that the plaintiff has shown actual malice by clear and convincing evidence or that the plaintiff has not". Here, too, some recent state court decisions have refused to follow the federal decision despite identical summary judgment rules under applicable state law.[13]

---

10 *Celotex Corp.* v. *Catrett*, 477 U.S. 317, at 323–324, 106 S.Ct. 2548, at 2552, 91 L.Ed.2d 265 (1986).

11 *Cole* v. *Gohmann*, 727 N.E.2d 1111 (Ind. App. 2000); *Krantz* v. *BT Visual Images, LLC*, 89 Cal. App. 4th 164, 107 Cal. Rptr.2d 209 (2001).

12 *Anderson* v. *Liberty Lobby, Inc.*, 477 U.S. 242, 106 S.Ct. 2505, 91 L.Ed.2d 202 (1986).

13 *Huckabee* v. *Time Warner Entertainment Co.*, 19 S.W.3d 413 (Tex. 2000); *Bartlett* v. *Mirabal*, 128 N.M. 830, 999 P.2d 1062 (N.M.App. 2000).

Although most states have adopted codes of civil procedure that purport to be modeled on the Federal Rules, the differences are often substantial.[14] In many states, including those mentioned above, however, state and federal courts reach inconsistent conclusions even though the text of the respective summary judgment rules is the same. Thus, differences in outcomes cannot be explained simply by textual differences. Moreover, federal tort cases applying the *Celotex/Anderson* interpretation of Rule 56 are typically diversity cases governed by state substantive law pursuant to the *Erie* doctrine.[15] Inconsistent interpretations of identical summary judgment rules in state and federal courts can produce dramatically inconsistent results in cases that are supposed to be treated in the same way in state and federal courts.

Expert Testimony

In a trilogy of cases decided in the past decade, the United States Supreme Court has interpreted Federal Rule of Evidence 702 to require trial judges to act as "gatekeepers" to ensure the reliability and relevance of proffered expert testimony.[16] Notably, the cases in which the court acted were product liability cases. Although some state courts followed suit, other state courts refused to follow the United States Supreme Court's interpretation of Federal Rule 702 even when applying their own identical versions of the same rule.[17] Moreover, even state courts that purport to apply the *Daubert* interpretation of Rule 702 increasingly reach conclusions completely at odds with their federal counterparts. In an extreme example, state and federal courts in the same state reached the opposite result on the same issue, in the same type of product liability case, and even involving the same manufacturer.

---

14 John B. Oakley and Arthur F. Coon, "The Federal Rules in State Courts: A Survey of State Court Systems of Civil Procedure", 61 Wash. L. Rev. 1367 (1986).

15 *Erie Ry. Co.* v. *Tompkins*, 304 U.S. 64, 58 S.Ct. 817, 82 L.Ed. 1188 (1938).

16 *Kumho Tire Co., Ltd.* v. *Carmichael*, 526 U.S. 137, 119 S.Ct. 1167, 143 L.Ed.2d 238 (1999); *General Electric Co.* v. *Joiner*, 522 U.S. 136, 118 S.Ct. 512, 139 L.Ed.2d 508 (1996); *Daubert* v. *Merrell Dow Pharmaceuticals, Inc.*, 509 U.S. 579, 589, 113 S.Ct. 2786, 125 L.Ed.2d 469 (1993).

17 *Logerquist* v. *McVey*, 196 Ariz. 470, 477, 1 P.3d 113, 120 (2000); *Goeb* v. *Tharaldson*, 615 N.W.2d 800, 811 (Minn. 2000); *State* v. *Copeland*, 130 Wash.2d 244, 922 P.2d 1304, 1314 (1996); *Anderson* v. *Combustion Engineering, Inc.*, 256 Wis.2d 389, 389, 647 N.W.2d 460, 462 (Wis.App. 2002).

Hall v. *Baxter Healthcare, Inc.*[18] and *Jennings* v. *Baxter Healthcare, Inc.*[19] are two silicone breast implant cases from the same state. The state and federal courts reached opposite conclusions on the same issue regarding admissibility of expert testimony, despite applying the identical text of state and federal Rule of Evidence 702. The United States District Court excluded the testimony of all of the plaintiffs' experts relating to whether silicone was capable of causing systemic autoimmune disease in women. It reached this conclusion because the treating physician who testified failed to satisfy the "*Daubert* factors" that applied to such testimony.[20] On essentially the same factual foundation, the Oregon Supreme Court, which had earlier agreed with *Daubert*,[21] held that it was reversible error to exclude a physician's opinion that silicone caused the plaintiff's complaints.

In both cases, the plaintiffs attempted to establish causation by having treating physicians offer a causation opinion based on differential diagnosis. In *Hall*, the federal court rejected such a showing based on the following reasoning:

> "Differential diagnosis is a patient-specific process of elimination that medical practitioners use to identify the 'most likely' cause of a set of signs and symptoms from a list of possible causes. However, differential diagnosis does not, by itself, prove the cause, even for the particular patient. Nor can the technique speak to the issue of general causation. Indeed, differential diagnosis assumes that general causation has been proven for the list of possible causes it eliminates."[22]

---

18 *Hall* v. *Baxter Healthcare, Inc.*, 947 F.Supp. 1387 (D.Or. 1996).

19 *Jennings* v. *Baxter Healthcare, Inc.*, 331 Or. 285, 14 P.3d 596 (2000).

20 *Daubert* v. *Merrell Dow Pharmaceuticals, Inc.*, 509 U.S. 579, 589, 113 S.Ct. 2786, 125 L.Ed.2d 469 (1993). In connection with the type of scientific evidence at issue, the Court "suggested" that trial courts consider: (1) Testing; (2) Publication and peer review; (3) Known or potential error rate; and (4) General acceptance.

21 *State* v. *O'Key*, 321 Or. 285, 307 n. 29, 899 P.2d 663 (1995). Furthermore, in another earlier case, the state court had held that, when interpreting a rule of the state evidence code virtually identical to the federal rule of evidence, it is appropriate to consider the federal cases interpreting the rule: *State* v. *Carlson*, 311 Or. 201, 208, n. 8, 808 P.2d 1002, 1007, n. 8 (1991).

22 *Hall* v. *Baxter Healthcare, Inc.*, 947 F.Supp. 1387, at 1413 (D.Or. 1996).

Use of differential diagnosis in lieu of the "*Daubert* factors" received a far more hospitable reception in state court. In *Jennings*, the Oregon Supreme Court found reversible error in the trial court's exclusion of the treating doctor's opinion on causation, which was based on differential diagnosis. The court simply noted that the expert "eliminated other potential causes of the plaintiff's conditions through differential diagnosis, which is a generally accepted form of scientific inquiry".[23] The state court did not discuss *Hall* in reaching its contrary conclusion.

In fairness, a number of other courts have grappled with the admissibility of differential diagnosis causation testimony in recent years, and the criteria that determine admissibility of such testimony continue to be a work in progress.[24] Regardless of its decision, the state court should have identified and confronted the divergence between its own proffered interpretation of Rule 702 and its federal counterpart, and should have considered whether its interpretation fostered or undermined the policies that led to the adoption of uniform evidence codes in the first place.[25] Unfortunately, the state court did not look to any of the then-reported federal cases addressing the admissibility of differential diagnosis under Federal Rule 702.

In many instances, this divergence between state and federal court rulings comes despite the fact that both courts purport to apply the same rule — or at least the identical text of a state and federal rule. When a state court interprets the rule in a manner inconsistent with that of an identical federal rule, it undermines the uniformity and consistency that the drafters probably intended.[26]

---

23 *Jennings* v. *Baxter Healthcare, Inc.*, 331 Or. 285, at 308, 14 P.3d 596, at 608 (2000).

24 *Turner* v. *Iowa Fire Equipment Co.*, 229 F.3d 1202 (8th Cir. 2000); *Heller* v. *Shaw Indus., Inc.*, 167 F.3d 146, 156 (3d Cir. 1999); *In re Paoli R.R. Yard PCB Litig.*, 35 F.3d 717, 755, 758 (3rd Cir. 1994); *Westberry* v. *Gislaved Gummi AB*, 178 F.3d 257, 265 (4th Cir. 1999); Jack E. Karnes, "Establishing the Standard for a Physician's Patient Diagnosis Using Scientific Evidence: Dealing with the Split of Authority Among the Circuit Courts of Appeal", 15 B.Y.U. J.Pub.L. 1 (2000).

25 *Coastal Tankships, U.S.A., Inc.* v. *Anderson*, 87 S.W.3d 591 (Tex.App. 2002), rev. denied, 16 January 2003.

26 *State* v. *Farzaneh*, 468 N.W.2d 638, 641 (N.D. 1991): "Because the Uniform Rules of Evidence were conformed to the Federal Rules of Evidence for purposes of uniformity between State and Federal evidence law . . . [and] [b]ecause of the similarities between our rule and the federal rule, we find it prudent to consider federal precedent on this issue."; *Knowles* v. *Panopoulos*, 66 Ill.2d 585, 590, 363 N.E.2d 805, 6 Ill.Dec. 858 (1977).

With respect to the foregoing examples regarding Federal Rules 56 and 702, state courts could conceivably justify their divergent holdings on the basis that they need not interpret a state rule of procedure or evidence in the same manner as federal courts interpret the same federal rule. Also, if state and federal courts diverge on a minor technical issue, such as the presumptive length of depositions, that divergence would merely be of academic interest. However, in the above cited examples, state and federal courts diverge on issues that might well determine the outcome of the respective cases. In such situations, the state court ought to consider whether a decision to advance distinctive state policies should be made by courts or by those responsible for drafting the state rules. Such a decision should explicitly weigh not only the state's policy interests, but also the interest in achieving consistent results in similar cases, regardless of whether cases are brought in state or federal court. After all, the *Erie* rule in diversity cases "is rooted in part in a realization that it would be unfair for the character or result of a litigation materially to differ because the suit had been brought in a federal court", and in reaction to the "forum shopping" which had grown up for a century in response to the pre-*Erie* rule of *Swift* v. *Tyson*.[27]

Divergence When State and Federal Court Apply the Same Law

As seen below, it is even more troubling that, in other contexts, state and federal courts have reached starkly inconsistent conclusions on the same issue, not only when they interpret similar state and federal rules, but when they apply the very same rule of law. Two examples of this are punitive damages and federal pre-emption.

Punitive Damages

In recent years, the United States Supreme Court has imposed constraints on punitive damages awards based on the Due Process

27 *Swift* v. *Tyson*, 16 Pet (41 U.S.) 1, 10 L.Ed. 865 (1842), holding that federal Common Law overrode contrary state law in a diversity case, discussed in *Hanna* v. *Plumer*, 380 U.S. 460, 466-468, 85 S.Ct. 1136, 1138, 14 L.Ed.2d 8 (1965).

Clause of the Fourteenth Amendment.[28] One of these constraints is to limit the power of one state court to punish a defendant for conduct in other states. In *BMW* v. *Gore*, the court stated:

> "We think it follows from these principles of state sovereignty and comity that a State may not impose economic sanctions on violators of its laws with the intent of changing the tortfeasors' lawful conduct in other States. Before this Court Dr. Gore argued that the large punitive damages award was necessary to induce BMW to change the nationwide policy that it adopted in 1983. However, by attempting to alter BMW's nationwide policy, Alabama would be infringing on the policy choices of other States. To avoid such encroachment, the economic penalties that a State such as Alabama inflicts on those who transgress its laws, whether the penalties take the form of legislatively authorized fines or judicially imposed punitive damages, must be supported by the State's interest in protecting its own consumers and its own economy. Alabama may insist that BMW adhere to a particular disclosure policy in that State. Alabama does not have the power, however, to punish BMW for conduct that was lawful where it occurred and that had no impact on Alabama or its residents. Nor may Alabama impose sanctions on BMW to deter conduct that is lawful in other jurisdictions.[29]

Most recently, in *State Farm Mut. Auto Ins. Co.* v. *Campbell*,[30] the United States Supreme Court amplified and extended its holding in *BMW*, reversing a US $145-million punitive damages bad faith award that had been upheld by the Utah Supreme Court. However, in the year preceding *State Farm*, state and federal courts had applied the due process constraint on punitive damages in clearly inconsistent fashion in several product liability cases, even those involving the same defendant.[31]

---

28 *Cooper Industries, Inc.* v. *Leatherman Tool Group, Inc.*, 532 U.S. 424, 121 S.Ct. 1678, 149 L.Ed.2d 674 (2001); *BMW of North America, Inc.* v. *Gore*, 517 U.S. 559, 116 S.Ct. 1589, 134 L.Ed.2d 809 (1996); *Honda Motor Co.* v. *Oberg*, 512 U.S. 415, 114 S.Ct. 2331, 129 L.Ed.2d 336 (1994).

29 517 U.S. at 573, 116 S.Ct. At 1597, footnotes omitted.

30 *State Farm Mut. Auto Ins. Co.* v. *Campbell*, 538 U.S., 123 S.Ct. 1513 (2003).

31 *Sand Hill Energy, Inc.* v. *Ford Motor Co.*, 83 S.W.3d 483 (2002), pet. for cert. filed sub nom. *Ford Motor Co.* v. *Smith*, 71 USLW 3519 (21 January 2003) (NO 2–1096).

In *White* v. *Ford Motor Co.*,[32] a Nevada federal district court jury rendered a verdict in a wrongful death case against Ford for US $2,305,435 in compensatory damages and US $150,884,400 in punitive damages. The district court remitted the punitive damages to US $69,163,037.10. On appeal, Ford argued that the trial court erred in refusing to give a requested instruction that the jury may only consider the defendant's wrongful conduct that had an impact on the citizens of Nevada and that the jury may not award any punitive damages for the purpose of punishing the defendant relative to the sale of vehicles in other states, or for the purpose of punishing or deterring the defendant's conduct outside the State of Nevada. The Ninth Circuit agreed that the failure to give this instruction was error that required a new trial.

The evidence at trial focused on the number of vehicles Ford sold nationally and the number of parking brake failures reported nationally. The national evidence was not limited by any jury instructions or admonitions to limit its relevance to reprehensibility of the defendant's conduct. The plaintiff's closing argument sought damages to punish Ford for its conduct toward consumers in all states, not just Nevada. The district court determined that Ford's concern about extraterritoriality was inconsequential, even though many states do not recognize a post-sale duty to warn and that at least five states would not permit punitive damages in this type of case. It further reasoned that Ford's conduct was "universal market conduct performed centrally, [and] it was not peculiar to or necessarily performed in any given state".

The Ninth Circuit reversed, pointing out that the distinction offered by the district court was no different than that used by the Alabama court in *BMW* v. *Gore*, which the Supreme Court had rejected. Even if Ford's conduct were unlawful in every state, the extraterritoriality concern would remain because there are important variations and policies for punishment even if each state regards the conduct as unlawful. Nevada's imposition of a much greater sanction than another state would impose for such unlawful conduct amounted to the imposition of its regulatory policies on the entire nation.

This federalism concern applies strongly to the case at hand. Nevada is free, in the absence of federal legislation to the contrary, to choose a policy that may sacrifice some innovation in favor of safety,

---

32 *White* v. *Ford Motor Co.*, 312 F.3d 998 (9th Cir. 2002).

and Alaska is free to choose a policy that may sacrifice some safety in favor of innovation. Alternatively, Alaska may think it gets more rather than less safety by limiting the penalties for innovations and economies, even though some turn out to have unanticipated risks. Neither state is entitled, in the federal republic, to impose its policy on the other. If Nevada imposes an award based on vindicating a national interest in safety, as the jury was encouraged to do in this case and as the district court expressly permitted, then it may deter not only conduct tortious in other states, but also innovations and economies of production that other states have purposely tailored their laws not to discourage so strongly. Measured by Alaska legislative policy, Nevada's policy would be overly deterrent.[33] Accordingly, the case was remanded for a new trial on punitive damages.

By way of contrast, in *Romo* v. *Ford Motor Co.*,[34] the California Court of Appeal upheld an award of US $290-million in punitive damages against Ford for an accident arising out of the rollover of a 1978 Ford Bronco. A third of the roof consisted of steel, and the rear two-thirds was made of fiberglass. The steel roof collapsed, killing Romo. The fiberglass roof broke loose, striking and killing one occupant. Two were ejected and injured. One occupant remained in the car and was also injured.

On review, the Court of Appeal analogized the conduct in question as tantamount to involuntary manslaughter which, when viewed in the context of a mass-produced vehicle sold to the public, "certainly is seriously reprehensible conduct". The court found that the defendant had ignored its own internal safety standards while leaving the Bronco with the appearance of incorporating a roll bar into the vehicle's roof structure. Ford declined to test the strength of the Bronco's roof before placing the vehicle in production. When it did test the roof strength in conjunction with a redesign of the Bronco for 1980, the defendant concluded that the roof, in fact, failed to meet its own standards. Ford modified the roof for the 1980 Bronco, but did nothing to remedy the structural inadequacies of the tens of thousands of 1978 Broncos already on the road. The court also found that the amount of punitive damages was not excessive for a defendant that had daily after-tax profits of US $20-million and a net worth of US $25-billion,

---

33 *White* v. *Ford Motor Co.*, 312 F.3d 998, at 1018 (9th Cir. 2002).

34 *Romo* v. *Ford Motor Co.*, 99 Cal. App. 4th 1115, 122 Cal. Rptr.2d 139 (Cal. App. 2002), rev. den. (23 October 2002), pet. for cert. filed, 71 USLW 3519 (21 January 2003) (NO 2–1097).

of which US $14-billion was cash on hand. The defendant earned well over US $100-million in profit from the 1978 Bronco and had the use of that profit for more than two decades without being penalized in any case for punitive damages arising from its design.[35]

The court acknowledged the great disparity between the compensatory award of approximately US $6-million (reduced to slightly under US $5-million by reason of comparative fault) and the punitive damages award. However, the court concluded that the importance of this factor was somewhat reduced because wrongful death compensatory damages do not fully reflect the harm to the victims. The court also concluded that it was inappropriate to compare the conduct involved with civil fines for similar conduct. Such a comparison "is appropriate when the conduct to be punished cannot result in imprisonment if committed by an individual, but is inappropriate when the malicious conduct could result in substantial imprisonment if committed by an individual instead of a corporation". The court rejected out of hand the argument later accepted by the Ninth Circuit in *White* that the imposition of punitive damages violated the extraterritorial constraints imposed by the United States Supreme Court in *BMW* v. *Gore*. The court noted:

> ". . . here, by contrast, the interest California seeks to protect — individual human lives — is neither unique to California nor limited to its own citizens: any 1978 Bronco operated on California highways creates the same risks to its occupants no matter where the vehicle was sold nor where its occupants reside".[36]

Ultimately, though, it is clear that, as things presently stand, the Due Process Clause of the Fourteenth Amendment prevents extraterritorial conduct from serving as the basis for increasing a punitive damages award in federal court in the Ninth Circuit, but not in a state court within the same circuit.

---

35 *Romo* v. *Ford Motor Co.*, 99 Cal. App. 4th 1115, at 1149, 122 Cal. Rptr.2d 139, at 164 (Cal. App. 2002), rev. den. (23 October 2002), pet. for cert. filed, 71 USLW 3519 (21 January 2003) (NO 2–1097).

36 *Romo* v. *Ford Motor Co.*, 99 Cal. App. 4th n. 3, at 1115, 122 Cal. Rptr.2d, n. 3 at 166 (Cal. App. 2002), rev. den. (23 October 2002), pet. for cert. filed, 71 USLW 3519 (21 January 2003) (NO 2–1097).

Federal Pre-Emption

Following the advent of the airbag and its gradual introduction into motor vehicles, claims arose in state and federal courts alleging that vehicles not equipped with airbags were defective in design. Manufacturers contended that Federal Motor Vehicle Safety Standard (FMVSS) 208 pre-empted any claim alleging that an automobile was defective in design because it lacked an air bag, as the Regulation gave manufacturers a choice between installing air bags or providing passive restraints utilizing a motorized shoulder belt. Significantly, virtually every federal court that had considered the issue held such claims to be pre-empted, either under express pre-emption[37] or under ordinary pre-emption principles.[38] By contrast, virtually every state court that had addressed the issue had reached precisely the opposite result, finding no pre-emption.[39]

Ultimately, in *Geier* v. *American Honda Motor Co., Inc.*,[40] the United States Supreme Court held that "no airbag" claims were pre-empted by FMVSS 209. However, until the Supreme Court stepped in, such claims were actionable in state court, but not in federal court, even though the decisive issue and controlling law was exactly the same in every forum.

Equal Opportunity Activism

It should come as little surprise that state and federal courts seem to be pursuing conflicting agendas on issues such as those discussed above. It is a concern, if not a surprise, that both state and federal courts seem to be more politicized than ever before. In many states,

---

37 *Harris* v. *Ford Motor Co.*, 110 F.3d 1410, 1413-1415 (9th Cir. 1997).

38 *Montag* v. *Honda Motor Co.*, 75 F.3d 1414, 1417 (10th Cir. 1996); *Pokorny* v. *Ford Motor Co.*, 902 F.2d 1116, 1121–1125 (3d Cir. 1990); *Taylor* v. *General Motors Corp.*, 875 F.2d 816, 825–827 (11th Cir. 1989); *Wood* v. *General Motors Corp.*, 865 F.2d 395, 412–414 (1st Cir. 1988).

39 *Drattel* v. *Toyota Motor Corp.*, 92 N.Y.2d 35, 43-53, 677 N.Y.S.2d 17, 699 N.E.2d 376, 379-386 (1998); *Minton* v. *Honda of America Mfg., Inc.*, 80 Ohio St.3d 62, 70–79, 684 N.E.2d 648, 655–661 (1997); *Munroe* v. *Galati*, 189 Ariz. 113, 115–119, 938 P.2d 1114, 1116–1120 (1997); *Wilson* v. *Pleasant*, 660 N.E.2d 327, 330–339 (Ind. 1995); *Tebbetts* v. *Ford Motor Co.*, 140 N.H. 203, 206–207, 665 A.2d 345, 347–348 (1995).

40 *Geier* v. *American Honda Motor Co., Inc.*, 529 U.S. 861, 120 S.Ct. 1913, 146 L.Ed.2d 914 (2000).

popularly elected judges have resulted in expensive political campaigns. Presidential selection and confirmation of federal judges has become a hot political issue as well. The public is increasingly aware of the political ramifications of judicial decisions, as exemplified by the Supreme Court's most controversial case in recent years, *Bush* v. *Gore*.[41] At the state level, the election of judges, even when running as "non-partisan" candidates, has become increasingly politicized, leading one state appellate jurist to comment:

> "[I]n the decade of the 1990s, special interest groups throughout the country realized that social, political, business, and environmental issues decided by elected state supreme court judges were too important to ignore. The outcome of court decisions, the groups reasoned, could and should be influenced through support for candidates who were likely to rule favorably on the issues important to those groups.
>
> "As a result of those realizations, supreme court elections in many states . . . have become hotly contested battles, almost indistinguishable from the rest of the American partisan political process. State supreme court elections are now complete with large campaign contributions, independent expenditure from special interest groups, massive television and print advertising and some judicial candidates, mostly non-incumbents, indicating willingness to test the speech restrictions mandated by judicial conduct rules. As a result, constitutional scholars, historians, social commentators, the American Bar Association (ABA) and watchdog groups are now voicing grave concern that state supreme court elections are being transformed into purely political affairs at odds with the independent and impartial role that judges and courts must perform under America's three-branch system of government."[42]

Furthermore, outside the domain of tort law, the Supreme Court has been dramatically altering the relationship between state and federal law in a manner not seen since the New Deal. The court is applying the

---

41 *Bush* v. *Gore*, 531 U.S. 98, 121 S.Ct. 525, 148 L.Ed.2d 388 (2000).

42 Paul J. DeMuniz, "Politicizing State Judicial Elections: A Threat to Judicial Independence", 38 Will. L. Rev. 367, 368 (2002), footnotes omitted.

rubric of federalism to limit the federal government's power over state government. Thus, in *Alden* v. *Maine*,[43] the court held that state governments could not be sued in state court, even on federal claims, without their consent. In *Florida Prepaid Postsecondary Education Expense Board* v. *College Savings Bank*,[44] the court held that a federal law authorizing suits against states for patent violations was invalid under Clause 5 of the Fourteenth Amendment. Most recently, in *Federal Maritime Commission* v. *South Carolina State Ports Authority*,[45] the court held that a state government cannot be "sued" in a federal agency proceeding that is adjudicatory in nature.

One commentator has described these recent decisions as "radical changes in pre-existing jurisprudence".[46] Another critic describes the extent of these decisions:

> "Indeed, a large number of decisions in the last few terms on issues such as federalism, congressional enforcement of the Fourteenth Amendment, abortion, religion, free expression, capital punishment, and affirmative action should be at least troubling to any proponent of principled judicial restraint. Of course, the Court's recent and highly controversial decision in *Bush* v. *Gore*, ruling five to four in favor of ending recounts in the disputed 2000 presidential election, has also been widely criticized as an extravagant, unprincipled, and partisan decision. Notably, commentators across the political spectrum have criticized the Court in recent years for its general "arrogance", "hubris", "contempt for the competing views of the political branches", and "strategic concern for [the Court's] own institutional prerogatives", as well as for its displays of political "feuding", constituency-serving, results-oriented judging, excessive "partisan[ship]", and lack of "respect for the dignity and authority of the law".[47]

---

43 *Alden* v. *Maine*, 527 U.S. 706, 119 S.Ct. 2240, 144 L.Ed.2d 636 (1999).

44 *Florida Prepaid Postsecondary Education Expense Board* v. *College Savings Bank*, 527 U.S. 627, 119 S.Ct. 2199, 144 L.Ed.2d 575 (1999).

45 *Federal Maritime Commission* v. *South Carolina State Ports Authority*, 535 U.S. 743, 122 S.Ct. 1864, 152 L.Ed.2d 962 (2002).

46 Louise Weinberg, "Of Sovereignty and Union: The Legends of Alden", 76 N.D.L. Rev. 1113, at 1117 (2001).

47 Jack Wade Nowlin, "The Judicial Restraint Amendment: Populist Constitutional Reform in the Spirit of the Bill of Rights", 78 N.D.L. Rev. 171, 174–174 (2002), footnotes omitted.

If federalism were the principal bone of contention, one might expect the more conservative federal bench to defer consistently to the primacy of state law and for the more liberal state courts to defer to federal law. However, no such pattern has emerged. Rather, the more liberal state courts consistently resist defendants' claims of federal pre-emption in product liability cases, for example, the "no airbag" pre-emption cases predating *Geier*. Conversely, the purported "new federalists" of the Supreme Court have no qualms about breaking new ground in the opposite direction. Thus, in *Bush* v. *Gore*, and notwithstanding the court's traditional practice that it will defer to state courts on the interpretation of state law,[48] the court determined that the Florida Supreme Court had infringed upon the state legislature's authority by establishing rules for counting ballots where the voter's intent was unclear:

> "This inquiry does not imply a disrespect for state courts but rather a respect for the constitutionally prescribed role of state legislatures. To attach definitive weight to the pronouncement of a state court, when the very question at issue is whether the court has actually departed from the statutory meaning, would be to abdicate our responsibility to enforce the explicit requirements of Article II."[49]

One might infer that federalism is simply a device used to justify an alternative form of result-oriented judicial activism. As one article suggests, "claims of federalism are often nothing more than strategies to advance substantive positions or, alternatively, that people declare themselves federalists when they oppose national policy, and abandon that commitment when they favor it".[50]

Judicial Restraint

At first blush, it is especially troubling if state and federal courts render starkly inconsistent decisions on the same issue, such as the test

48 *Mullaney* v. *Wilbur*, 421 U.S. 684, 95 S.Ct. 1881, 44 L.Ed.2d 508 (1975), cited in *Bush* v. *Gore*, 531 U.S. 98, at 114, 121 S.Ct. 525, at 535, 148 L.Ed.2d 388 (2000), Rehnquist CJ concurring.

49 *Bush* v. *Gore*, 531 U.S. 98, at 115, 121 S.Ct. 525, 148 L.Ed.2d 388 (2000).

50 Edward L. Rubin and Malcolm Feeley, "Federalism: Some Notes on a National Neurosis", 41 UCLA L. Rev. 903, 948 (1994).

for the constitutionality of punitive damages and whether state law is pre-empted by a particular federal statute or regulation. However, at least this sort of problem, if sufficiently serious, can be alleviated by the Supreme Court, as it eventually did in *Geier*. Unfortunately, such a resolution came only after over a decade of litigation and millions of dollars of expense for plaintiffs and defendants alike.

In some ways, the courts' divergence over evidentiary and procedural rules is an even more vexing problem than their conflict over rules of substantive federal law, such as pre-emption and punitive damages. When courts twiddle with uniform rules of evidence and civil procedure to accomplish their view of a "fair" result, they may overlook the significant policy concerns that motivated the legal community to draft these codes in the first place. This battle has been traced back nearly two centuries, to populist desires to reform a system of justice considered by the public to be controlled by aristocratic judges and lawyers. Some of the early impetus for codification of the Federal Rules of Evidence came in the early nineteenth century along with the rise of Jacksonian democracy. Jacksonians sought "to professionalize the administration of justice" and were increasingly hostile toward "lawyers and the aristocracy they were thought to serve through their use of feudal English precedents".[51] The battle to establish a unified evidence code continued for well over a century, through the tortuous, but ultimately unsuccessful, effort to adopt the ABA Model Code from its publication in 1942, followed by the adoption of the Federal Rules of Evidence and the adoption of parallel codes in many states.

Adoption of the Federal Rules of Civil Procedure was a similarly monumental project. From the earliest years of the Republic, Congress sought to legislate consistency between the procedures of federal courts and those of the states in which they sat. The Process Act of 1789 provided that, in actions of law, procedures in federal courts should be the same as in each state, "as are now used or allowed in the Supreme Courts of the same".[52] From 1789 until adoption of the Federal Rules of Civil Procedure in 1938, a succession of efforts were made to achieve procedural uniformity between the federal and state courts in each state, without much overall success. As early as 1911, the ABA adopted a resolution "favoring a uniform system of federal

---

51 21 Wright and Graham, *Fed. Practice and Procedure*, Section 5005 at 62 (1977).
52 4 Wright and Miller, *Fed. Practice and Procedure*, Section 1092 at 11 (2002).

procedure under rules prepared by the Supreme Court for use in the federal courts; it was also contemplated that the rules would serve as models for state adoption".[53] When the Federal Rules were finally adopted over two decades later and became effective in 1938, they became a model for subsequent state procedure.[54] Nevertheless, there has been increasing balkanization of procedural practice, both among the federal district courts[55] and between state and federal courts.[56]

If some semblance of uniformity between state and federal procedure and evidence rules on important issues is to be achieved, much of the effort needs to be directed to the states. Under well-established federal law, in federal court, the Federal Rules of Civil Procedure trump a contrary state rule.[57]

No doubt there are good reasons for tailoring rules of civil procedure to unique features of state law rather than adopting them wholesale from the federal rules. State courts decide many kinds of cases that are not seen in federal courts, and few would claim that a uniform "one size fits all" system of procedures is appropriate for all state and federal courts. It is quite a different proposition to say that when a state and a federal rule are identical, the respective courts ought to blithely interpret such rule as they wish, without regard to the potential for inconsistent outcomes of similar cases in different courts within the same state. As Lord Mansfield stated centuries ago, "We must act alike in all cases of like nature",[58] a proposition that Judge Friendly described as "the most basic principle of jurisprudence".[59] One need not take sides as to who is right and who is wrong to see that this principle may soon be in as much trouble as it was in the era of *Swift* v. *Tyson*, when application of federal Common Law in diversity

---

53 4 Wright and Miller, *Fed. Practice and Procedure*, Section 1003 at 19 (2002).

54 4 Wright and Miller, *Fed. Practice and Procedure*, Section 1005 at 32 (2002).

55 Carl Tobias, "Local Federal Civil Procedure for the Twenty-First Century", 77 N.D. Rev. 533 (2002).

56 John B. Oakley and Arthur F. Coon, "The Federal Rules in State Courts: A Survey of State Court Systems of Civil Procedure", 61 Wash. L. Rev. 1367 (1986).

57 *Hanna* v. *Plumer*, 380 U.S. 460, 466–468, 85 S.Ct. 1136, 1138, 14 L.Ed.2d 8 (1965).

58 *Rex* v. *Wilkes*, 98 Eng. Rep. 327, 335 (1770). The same thought was expressed by Cardozo: "It will not do to decide the same question one way between one set of litigants and the opposite way between another": B. Cardozo, *The Nature of the Judicial Process* 33 (1921), cited in Henry J. Friendly, "Indiscretion About Discretion", 31 Emory L. J 747, 758 (1982).

59 Henry J. Friendly, "Indiscretion About Discretion", 31 Emory L. J 747, 758 (1982).

cases led to rampant forum shopping for nearly a century, until it was ended by the *Erie* decision.

Certainly, one may question whether it is a desirable or necessary feature of the American judicial system to achieve uniformity, and the rhetoric of those who advocate procedural uniformity is sometimes dubious, implying that uniformity has some metaphysical benefit in and of itself.[60] Ultimately, however, it is difficult to justify a system under which two identical cases, pending in state and federal court in the same state, should result in different outcomes based on differing rules of evidence or procedure. The courts which make decisions resulting in these different outcomes rarely acknowledge explicitly that they are doing so, let alone attempt to justify why doing so is appropriate. Ultimately, whether state courts reach opposite conclusions on identical issues on matters of substantive law or procedural law, one should strive for a system under which such differences in outcomes are minimized, or at least that the courts directly confront the implications of such decisions.

Implications for the European Union

What, if any, implications do America's problems with federalism have for the EU? At first blush, it is perilous to draw conclusions too hastily. After all, given the United States system of trial by jury and the relative ease of recovery of punitive damages, American cases concerning federal due process constraints on punitive damages, evidence law and summary judgment may be irrelevant in the EU.

However, there is likely to be tension between the Product Liability Directive of 1985 (the Directive), which is binding on all Member States, and the "special liability systems" of those states. Given the recent ruling of the European Court of Justice (ECJ) barring Member States from establishing or maintaining any product liability system of general application in addition to the Directive,[61] juxtaposed

60 Thomas O. Main, "Procedural Uniformity and the Exaggerated Role of Rules: A Survey of Intra-State Uniformity in Three States That Have not Adopted the Federal Rules of Civil Procedure", 46 Vill. L. Rev. 311, 312–317 (2001).

61 Case C-520, *Commission of the European Communities* v. *French Republic* (2002); Case C-154-00, *Commission of the European Communities* v. *Hellenic Republic* (2002); Case C-183-00, *Commission of the European Communities* v. *Medicina Asturiana* (2002).

against the Directive's lack of exclusivity and preservation of the rules of Member States concerning contractual and non-contractual liability, it would not be surprising for the courts of different Member States to reach different outcomes on identical cases, despite the existence of the EU's supposedly "uniform" product liability law.

In the United States, the debate to delineate between the powers of the states and the national government was resolved in the Constitutional Convention over 200 years ago, but disagreements continue to exist as to the intersection between "states' rights" and national power. In the EU, the debate is still in its earliest stages, but is expressed more in terms of how much autonomy Member States should have, how that autonomy should best be preserved and how to reconcile Member State autonomy with effective governance at the EU level.[62]

There are other reasons why the American experience with federalism may offer limited lessons for the EU. One is that America's system is derived from English Common Law, whereas most of the EU Member States are Civil Law countries. Furthermore, from the inception of the Republic, American courts assumed and exercised the power of judicial review, that is, the power to invalidate legislative acts deemed to violate the constitution — a power even their English counterparts were loath to exercise.[63] To some degree, what is occurring in the United States may arise from the fact that American courts have historically been more activist and powerful in extending and modifying the law than their counterparts both in the United Kingdom and in continental Europe. Thus, such a clash between courts is probably more likely under the American model than with a more restrained European judicial system.

However, conflicts among the Member States may be a more significant problem in the EU than in the United States, particularly if

62 Ernest A. Young, "Protecting Member State Autonomy in the European Union: Some Cautionary Tales from American Federalism", 77 N.Y.U.L.Rev. 1612, 1618 (2002).

63 The American concept of judicial review most likely emanates from an English case, *Dr. Bonham's Case*, 77 Eng. Rep. 638, K.B. 1610. Although the concept did not take hold in England, it was accepted in the colonies before the American Revolution and served as a justification for colonial resistance to some of the English legislation, such as the Writs of Assistance that led to the revolution itself: Bernard Bailyn, *Pamphlets of the American Revolution*, (Harvard Univ. Press, 1965) at pp. 411–412. After the adoption of the United States Constitution, American courts quickly adopted the concept that a legislative act contrary to the Constitution was invalid: *Hayburn's Case*, 2 U.S. (2 Dall.) 409 (1972); *Marbury* v. *Madison*, 5 U.S. (1 Cranch) 137 (1803).

the Directive remains non-exclusive and if the ECJ permits Member States to continue to maintain their own special liability rules. The risk is that the court in one Member State might adjudge a product defective under its own liability rules, even though the same product characteristic might not be deemed to constitute a defect by the courts of another Member State. In the United States, this occurs all the time, without fanfare, primarily because such decisions are made by juries rather than judges. One question would be whether the application of the current EU system, with local autonomy, could create an appearance of local favoritism if, for example, the courts of one Member State applied standards that tended to favor that State's manufacturers at the expense of the manufacturers of another Member State. It was a similar concern — the risk of favoritism toward local residents at the expense of non-residents, or at least the appearance of such favoritism — that caused America's founders to give federal courts jurisdiction over diversity cases in the first place.[64]

It could well be that the EU's new venture into product liability law will proceed more smoothly and successfully than it has in the United States. This could occur because the EU is molding a better-designed system, or simply because Europeans are less litigious than Americans. In either event, there will be much to learn from each other's experiences.

64 *Burgess* v. *Seligman*, 107 U.S. (17 Otto) 20, 34, 2 S.Ct. 10, 27 L.Ed. 359 (1883) — "the very object of giving to the national courts jurisdiction . . . in controversies between citizens of different states was to institute independent tribunals, which . . . would be unaffected by local prejudices and sectional views . . ."; Henry J. Friendly, "The Historic Basis of Diversity Jurisdiction", 41 Harv. L. Rev. 483 (1928).

Recent Developments Regarding American Personal Injury Law

Sheldon Karasik
Karasik & Associates, LLC
New York, United States

Introduction

This chapter will review important developments regarding American personal injury law. After providing a snapshot of recent court cases in this area, case studies will be discussed concerning issues relating to asbestos, toxic mold, lead paint and chemical contamination. In the process, the critical impact that burgeoning liability scenarios have on corporate defendants and their insurers will be traced, including the issues raised by the corporate bankruptcies that have occasionally ensued.

Before turning to these matters, two important preliminary considerations require attention. First, it is important to distinguish a "personal injury" claim from a "product liability" claim. Second, it is critical to appreciate the fundamental systemic differences between the American system of jurisprudence and that of Europe. In this latter regard, there are two key elements of distinction, namely, the bifurcated, federal character of the system itself, and its reliance on the role of the jury as fact finder. The complex interplay between these two elements has lead to a system of personal injury tort liability that is viewed by many as being dangerously out of control.

What Is a "Personal Injury" Claim?

Within the American legal system, historically, there have been two types of civil liability: that arising in contract and that in tort. Contract liability is outside the scope of this chapter and, broadly speaking, deals with liability arising out of business arrangements and agreements. Contractual harm is distinct from tortious harm and is ordinarily financial rather than physically injurious. Within the area of tort liability, there again have traditionally been two subdivisions: personal injury and property damage. The focus of this review will be on only one of these, personal injury. Under that rubric, there are again two types of injuries: bodily injury, including compensation for "pain and suffering", medical expenses and lost income, and psychological injury, such as intentional infliction of emotional distress.

Personal injury can be caused by many types of tortious conduct. For example, a truck driver can intentionally or negligently drive his vehicle in such a manner as to kill pedestrians crossing the road. Alternatively, a dangerous product being transported in that same truck can explode when the truck stops short, killing pedestrians by the force of the explosion. In the first instance, there is a traditional claim for personal injury; in the second, there is a personal injury caused by a product. Both result in personal injuries, but only the latter gives rise to a product liability claim. Thus, claims for product liability are a subset of personal injury claims, which themselves can be caused by products or almost anything else.

A garden variety personal injury claim can differ from a product liability claim in many ways, but chiefly because the latter is often governed by principles of strict liability, while the former is usually governed by principles of negligence. This means that to succeed in a non-product personal injury claim, a plaintiff must usually demonstrate the breach of a duty of care owed by the defendant to the plaintiff; in other words, that the defendant was careless in his regard for the plaintiff, that is, fault. On the other hand, to succeed in a product liability case, the plaintiff only needs to show that the product in question, for example, asbestos tiles, was unreasonably dangerous, and not necessarily that any specific carelessness on the part of its manufacturer (or anyone else) was to blame for that condition. This is because often some specific statute governs the level of safety required from a certain product and, if the statute is violated, liability attaches.

However, it is not always true that non-product personal injury cases require proof of negligence. For example, in New York, there is a statute[1] that provides that if a worker falls from a scaffolding, ladder, hoist or other height on a construction site in the course of his duties, then those who own, operate and maintain such devices are strictly liable for injuries that result. Also, conversely, some products may not be governed by a safety statute (or provision of Common Law) in a given state, or anywhere in the United States. In *James* v. *Meow Media, Inc.*,[2] for example, on 1 December 1997, Michael Carneal walked into the lobby of Heath High School in Paducah, Kentucky and shot several of his fellow students, killing three and wounding many others. The parents and estate administrators of Carneal's victims — Jessica James, Kayce Steger and Nicole Hadley (collectively referred to as "James") — appealed from the judgment of a district court dismissing their case for failing to state claims upon which relief could be granted.

They had sued several video game, movie production and Internet content-provider firms. According to James' complaint, Carneal regularly played video games, watched movies and viewed Internet sites produced by the defendant firms. These activities, the parents argued, desensitized the shooter to violence and caused him to kill. They claimed that distribution of this material to impressionable youth constituted negligence. In addition, they alleged strict product liability. The firms argued that they owed no duty to protect third parties from how players or viewers processed the ideas and images, and that the killer's independent decision to kill constituted a superseding cause. They also contended that they had not distributed "products" under Kentucky law. On the negligence claim, the appellate court found that the firms did not owe a duty to protect the decedents, noting, among other things, that individuals were generally entitled to assume that third parties will not commit intentional criminal acts. It further concluded that even if it were to find a duty, the parents probably had not alleged sufficient facts to establish proximate causation. On the product liability issue, it held that the video game cartridges and the like were not sufficiently "tangible" to constitute products.

1 Labor Law, Section 240.

2 *James* v. *Meow Media, Inc.*, 300 F.3d 683 (6th Cir. 2002).

In *Trull* v. *Volkswagen of America, Inc.*,[3] on the other hand, the case was based on allegations of defective design of a car, where one boy was injured and another killed. The court stated:

> "Plaintiffs' claim of liability was that the 1986 Vanagon had been defectively designed and was unreasonably dangerous because it was not equipped with lap/shoulder belts in each of the rear seats. The only passenger body restraints were lap belts. The jury, in answer to specific questions, found that VW was not liable in strict liability but was liable in negligence. It awarded Nathaniel Trull the sum of US $8,917,335.27. It awarded the estate of Benjamin Trull US $1,290,980.70".

The manufacturer contended that the verdicts were inconsistent, and that the finding of liability based on negligence was nullified by the finding that the manufacturer was not liable on the strict liability claim. In its jury instructions, the district court explained the elements of strict liability and negligence separately. The court noted that the manufacturer did not object until after the jury was discharged, thus waiving its right to object to any foreseeable combination of proper responses to the questions on the verdict forms, and held that, therefore, in the context of this case, there was no plain error in the judgment because New Hampshire law, which governed the case, did not prohibit such a verdict. The appellate court found that there was a plethora of evidence from which the jury could have found that the manufacturer was negligent, and that the negligence was the proximate cause of the enhanced injuries suffered by the father's sons. The appellate court found that the district court did not abuse its discretion in denying the motion for a remittitur, that is, a request that the trial judge review the reasonableness of the jury's award of damages.

On the other hand, while some product liability claims are "strict liability" (usually, they are based on the presence of a design defect rendering the product unreasonably dangerous), it is also possible to impose liability on a product manufacturer who fails to warn about the

3 *Trull* v. *Volkswagen of America, Inc.*, 311 F.3d 58 (1st Cir. 2002).

dangers of its product. This is, essentially, negligence-based product liability. As the court explained in *Freas* v. *Prater Constr. Corp.*:[4]

> "This court recently set forth a manufacturer's duty in the context of a plaintiff's claim of failure to warn or adequately warn premised on either negligence or strict liability. This court, after examining Section 388 and Section 402A of Restatement (Second) on Torts (1965), at 300–301 and 347, held that:
>
> "In a product liability case where a claimant seeks recovery for failure to warn or warn adequately, it must be proven that the manufacturer knew, or should have known, in the exercise of ordinary care, of the risk or hazard about which it failed to warn. Further, there will be no liability unless it be shown that the manufacturer failed to take the precautions that a reasonable person would take in presenting the product to the public. This court held that the standard imposed on a manufacturer in a negligence claim grounded on an inadequate warning is the same as that imposed in a strict liability claim based on inadequate warning. It was determined that Section 388 and Section 402A are actually two sides of the same standard. Both impose liability on a manufacturer for the failure to warn foreseeable users of a product's hazardous or unreasonably dangerous condition. While Section 388 of the Restatement sets forth a manufacturer's duty to warn those who may be exposed to hazards in the use of its product, Comment g to Section 388 further explains that the duty can be discharged if the manufacturer exercises reasonable care to give those who are to use the chattel the information which the supplier possesses, and which he should realize to be necessary to make its use safe for them and those in whose vicinity it is to be used. Likewise, Comment j to Section 402A references failure to warn and adds, in relevant part, that:
>
> "Directions or warning. In order to prevent the product from being unreasonably dangerous, the seller may be required to give directions or warning, on the container, as to its use. Where warning is given, the seller may reasonably assume

---

4 *Freas* v. *Prater Constr. Corp.*, 573 N.E.2d 27 (Ohio 1991).

that it will be read and heeded; and a product bearing such a warning, which is safe for use if it is followed, is not in a defective condition, nor is it unreasonably dangerous."

James and *Trull* highlight the fact that product liability claims can be propounded and tried simultaneously with garden variety negligence claims, and the overlapping issues that can result when this occurs.

The concept of strict product liability is alien to the law of many nations. As the court stated, for example, in *Gonzalez* v. *Chrysler Corp.*:[5]

"Although Mexico apparently recognizes strict liability against the defendant users of a dangerous product, it does not recognize strict liability against the manufacturer or designer of a dangerous product. See Article 19 C.C.D.F.; Symposium, Part-Five, "A Serious Accident Occurs in the Mexican Plant: Problems of Corporate and Product Liability", 4 U.S.-MEX. L.J. 125, 128 (1996) ("There is no cause of action under Mexican law for an injured party to sue a remote manufacturer or vendor, unless the plaintiff is in privity of contract with the defendant or can prove the manufacturer's or the vendor's negligence. Product liability is a distinctly United States concept . . . Mexican law does have a doctrine of strict liability, but not of product liability. Under Mexico's strict liability, the defendant is normally the user (whether owner, agent or bailee) of an inherently dangerous mechanism, instrument, apparatus or substance who, with its use, injures the plaintiff") (citation omitted). Similarly, Scotland at the time of the pertinent events in *Piper Aircraft* did not have strict liability for the design or manufacture of dangerous products. See David M. Walker, *The Law of Delict in Scotland*, 614-615 (2d ed. 1981) ("Product liability came to Scotland with the Consumer Protection Act of 1987, but this was more than a decade after the operative facts in Piper.")."

The European Community recently took steps toward the adoption of a strict product liability system, but the European system still discourages a rabid plaintiff bar by the lack of contingency fees and punitive damages, forcing the losing party to pay the winner's

5 *Gonzalez* v. *Chrysler Corp.*, 301 F.3d 377 (5th Cir. 2002).

attorney fees, restricting discovery filings and the absence of civil juries. What is more, the general social climate in Europe is one that tends to downplay confrontation and thereby discourages litigation generally, whereas the opposite is true in the United States. Dow Chemical Company, for example, estimates that it faces 100 times greater exposure to liability-related expenses in the United States as compared to Europe. Yet, Dow still, of course, does business (profitable business) in the United States because it is the world's largest and most dynamic economy and simply too big to ignore.

However, even in the United States, strict product liability is a relatively recent innovation. It began with the landmark ruling of the California Supreme Court in *Greenman* v. *Yuba Power Products*,[6] which was then embraced by Section 402A of the American Law Institute's Restatement (Second) of Torts (1965), with the provision that:

> ". . . one who sells any product in a defective condition unreasonably dangerous to the user or consumer or to his property is subject to liability for physical harm thereby caused to the ultimate user or consumer, or to his property [even though] the seller has exercised all possible care in the preparation and sale of his product".

An infamous example of the rampant expansion of this doctrine by activist judges came in *Lovelace* v. *Astra Trading Corp.*,[7] where the court ruled that bystanders injured by such "defective" products also had a cause of action against the manufacturer. Other such instances are too numerous to list.

Different legal rules may govern product liability and negligence claims. For example, in *Masters* v. *Hesston Corp.*,[8] a farmer lost part of his right arm and injured his left hand when his right hand was caught in a hay baler's feed rolls. The district court determined that the statute of repose barred the farmer's strict product liability claim (in other words, the plaintiff had waited too long to file such a claim), but went forward to review the negligence claim on the merits. The district court then excluded the farmer's expert's testimony as to the negligence claim, and the appellate court determined that the district court did not err or abuse its discretion, ruling that the farmer failed in

---

6 *Greenman* v. *Yuba Power Products*, 377 P.2d 897 (Cal. 1962).

7 *Lovelace* v. *Astra Trading Corp.*, 439 F.Supp. 753 (S.D. Miss. 1977).

8 *Masters* v. *Hesston Corp.*, 291 F.3d 985 (7th Cir. 2002).

his burden of showing that an alteration exception to the statute of repose applied. Regarding the negligence claim, the expert's opinion that the manufacturer breached the standard of care was held not to have been reached through a reliable methodology.

One key aspect of a product liability case that distinguishes it from an ordinary negligence case is that the plaintiff must show that the offending product was "introduced into the stream of commerce" in order to take advantage of strict liability provisions. Another key feature of a strict liability case is that the plaintiff is saddled with a significant technical burden; obviously, to show a "design defect" requires that the plaintiff avail himself of expensive expert testimony to establish such a flaw. Of course, the plaintiff must also show that the product in question is, because of the flaw, "unreasonably" unsafe to use. In other words, proving a defect exists is meaningless if the product nonetheless performs satisfactorily, and merely a small element of danger may not suffice to carry the plaintiff's burden. These are factors that serve to counterbalance, to at least some limited extent, the enormous benefit of not having to show "negligence" on the part of the defendant in building the product with such a flaw. A key element of a negligence defense, for example, is that the harm caused was not "foreseeable". This defense is inoperative in the strict product liability context. However, the defenses of "assumption of the risk" and "misuse", including alteration and modification, are available, as is the doctrine of "comparative fault" in many jurisdictions.

A negligence case may offer other advantages to a plaintiff. In New York, for example, in a negligence action based on personal injuries, a defendant may not serve interrogatories and also seek to depose the plaintiff without leave of the court, but the defendant is free to do so in a strict product liability action. A plaintiff who fears extensive discovery, therefore, may wish to trade a heavier burden of proof for protection from that intrusion. However, there are many instances where additional benefits attach to a strict liability case. For example, in *Gander* v. *FMC Corp.*,[9] the jury awarded a plaintiff US $2-million for harm from a defective coal conveyor, but also found the plaintiff ninety per cent at fault. Under applicable Missouri law, had the case been based in negligence, the plaintiff would only have recovered US $200,000, since the doctrine of comparative fault

9 *Gander* v. *FMC Corp.*, 892 F.2d 1373 (8th Cir. 1990).

would have applied. However, that state does not apply comparative fault to strict liability cases, and the plaintiff recovered the full amount of the verdict. *Gander* emphasizes the extreme complexity that results from federalism, and the need to closely understand (and monitor) all prevailing applicable legal systems. Indeed, distinctions between negligence and strict liability can expand or seem to vanish depending on the court in which they are addressed. Thus, in *Barron* v. *Ford Motor Co. of Canada*,[10] the court stated that "there might seem to be all the difference in the world between negligence and strict liability, but in a product liability case this often is not true". The court explained that "the plaintiff must either prove that the product was defective or that it was unreasonably dangerous, and in determining whether a product is defective or unreasonably dangerous the court weighs costs and benefits just as it would do in a negligence case". It noted that:

> ". . . the difference between the two grounds of liability bites when the defendant is being sued for a product defect created by a component that he had bought, and he could not be sued for negligence because he used all due care in buying, inspecting, and installing it, so that he was without blame yet is liable nonetheless if liability is strict".

Also, a negligence case makes the defendant more unappealing to the jury, hence conceivably more worthy of scorn and significant financial sanction. As the court noted in *Greenland* v. *Ford Motor Co.*,[11] "every plaintiff lawyer wants to show negligence of the manufacturer, even if he is suing under a theory which does not require negligence", since while "fault may not be required for a plaintiff's judgment, it may obviously affect the amount the jury awards" and, therefore, "the case is prepared in the same manner regardless of the theories of liability or defenses which are involved".

Product liability claims existed as well under the Common Law before statutory standards were established, and issues can arise in applying that Common Law. In *Densberger* v. *United Techs. Corp.*,[12] for example, appellees claimed that the manufacturer was liable for the crash of an army helicopter, causing either death or injury due to defective fuel tanks made by the manufacturer. The appellate court

---

10 *Barron* v. *Ford Motor Co. of Canada*, 965 F.2d 195 (7th Cir. 1992).

11 *Greenland* v. *Ford Motor Co.*, 347 A.2d 159 (N.H. 1975).

12 *Densberger* v. *United Techs. Corp.*, 283 F.3d 110 (2nd Cir. 2002).

held that, contrary to the manufacturer's claims, the Connecticut Product Liability Act (CPLA) did not pre-empt all Common Law theories of product liability. Rather, as the exclusive basis for product liability claims under Connecticut law, the CPLA barred separate Common Law causes of action in product liability cases.

Because the CPLA did not expressly prohibit post-sale liability for negligent failure to warn, the negligence-based Common Law duty survived and was cognizable under the statute. As to the manufacturer's claim that there could be no duty to warn claim since the army knew of the dangers at issue, the court held that a reasonable jury could have concluded from the evidence that the manufacturer knew or should have known that the helicopter could become uncontrollable in an asymmetric condition when equipped with the auxiliary tanks, and that the army did not have similar knowledge. However, there are cases where a warning is specifically prescribed. For example, in *West* v. *Mattel, Inc.*,[13] a child was injured by swallowing and choking on a figurine included in a toy set sold by the manufacturer. The toy set's box contained a choking hazard warning that complied with federal requirements set forth at 16 C.F.R. Section 1500.19. The manufacturer argued that the plaintiffs' claims were pre-empted by Section 1500.19(h) because imposition of liability would necessarily be predicated on a failure to give adequate warnings.

The court found that pre-emption extended to Common Law claims that were based on the inadequacy of the warning label; thus, Section 1500.19(h) pre-empted the plaintiffs' claims that the toy set was defectively marketed because it was not sold with adequate warnings or instructions and that the manufacturer was negligent in failing to warn or adequately warn of the choking dangers. However, the court ruled that there was no pre-emption of claims:

(1) That the toy set was defectively designed;
(2) That the manufacturer was negligent for failing to develop toys that were not likely to cause choking;
(3) For negligent infliction of emotional distress; and
(4) For breach of implied warranties of merchantability and fitness.

It was not clear that those theories required an alteration of the toy set's warning.

13 *West* v. *Mattel, Inc.*, 2003 U.S. Dist. LEXIS 2928 (S.D. Tex. 2003).

One of the developing areas of product liability being exploited by the plaintiff bar is liability for alleged harm caused by users of various "diet" medications, which supposedly suppress the desire to eat, but may also inflict various side effects. In *Watson* v. *Wyeth Co.*,[14] for example, the plaintiff alleged damage as a result of taking a drug called Pondimin (a.k.a. Fenfluramine and/or Phentermine or Fen-Phen). Wyeth sought to remove the case to federal court from state court (obviously hoping for a more receptive environment) and argued that there was true diversity of citizenship to support such jurisdiction because the other defendants, who would allegedly destroy diversity, had been fraudulently joined by the plaintiff as a tactic to avoid removal and remain in the comfortable confines of state court.

The federal court concluded that the drug manufacturers had carried their burden of proving that the non-consenting drug manufacturers were fraudulently joined because the plaintiff had not provided any reliable evidence to suggest that the drug that they manufactured caused any of the plaintiff's symptoms. Thus, the plaintiff could not have had any real intent to pursue the non-consenting drug manufacturers. The doctor was also fraudulently joined, since the plaintiff's claims were prescribed according to La. Rev. Stat. Ann. Section 9:5628. Thus, there was no possibility that the plaintiff could have succeeded against the doctor in state court.

Why Is American Tort Liability Spiraling Out of Control?

America's system of jurisprudence is designed to prevent the accumulation of dictatorial power in the hands of a few. The unintended consequence of this system, however, is to place alleged tortfeasors between the proverbial rock and hard place. On the one hand, each one of the fifty American states has its own constitution, its own Supreme Court and its own peculiar systems of Common Law and statutory law. This negates the accumulation of power in the federal courts, but the downside is the particularly American concept of "forum shopping". In other words, a cause of action that may be rejected in Philadelphia may nonetheless rise, phoenix-like, in Phoenix. On the other hand, power is further divided within each state system between the judge and a jury of lay persons, who have proven

14 *Watson* v. *Wyeth Co.*, 2003 U.S. Dist. LEXIS 1367 (E.D. La. 2003).

remarkably willing to travel down a garden path laid by an aggressive, resourceful and ever-expanding plaintiff bar. Indeed, it is often the case that corporate America looks not to the court system to provide any relief from snowballing liability and its consequences, but rather to legislation outlawing or restricting the causes of action themselves. Recent examples of what appears to be the "runaway train" character of American tort litigation spring all too readily to mind.

The Mafia Priesthood?

A vivid illustration of the extreme lengths to which plaintiffs' attorneys are willing to stretch their creative initiative can be seen in their use of the federal Racketeer Influenced and Corrupt Organizations Act (RICO), designed to combat organized crime and the Mafia, as a bludgeon in tort litigation because the act sanctions conspiratorial activity and imposes treble damages and attorneys' fees. Thus, the front page of the 1 April 2002 issue of the *National Law Journal* newspaper carried a story, under the headline "RICO Long Shot", discussing a multi-million dollar RICO suit by alleged victims of sexual harassment — against a group of Catholic bishops.

The Delicious Conspiracy

A second equally vivid example was the lawsuit filed on 20 November 2002 in federal court in Manhattan on behalf of McDonalds restaurant customers who claim that the eatery's high-fat, addictive and warningless menu has made them obese, diabetic and subject to high blood pressure. Plaintiffs characterized McDonald's food as "a very insipid, toxic kind of thing" when ingested regularly by young children. The plaintiffs include a Bronx teen who ate every meal at McDonald's for three years while living in a homeless shelter. Another is a thirteen-year-old boy from Staten Island who says that he ate food at McDonald's three to four times a week and is now five foot four and 278 pounds. McDonald's has already settled a lawsuit with a vegetarian, agreeing to pay US $10-million to charity as recompense for clandestinely adding beef flavoring to the oil in which its French fries were cooked. This action was met in some circles with guffaws, but they quickly dissipated when it was remembered that not long ago a different patron was able to recover several million dollars in monetary damages when she spilled a cup of the company's coffee on her lap, claiming that the coffee was "too hot".[15]

A plethora of imitator suits naturally followed, some successful and some not. The outgrowth of this system is a powerful plaintiffs' bar with a formidable political lobby in Washington D.C. and state capitals, which has been successful in preventing the enactment of legislation that might limit compensatory or punitive damage awards, much less the causes of action themselves. The additional American wrinkle is the concept of federalism, which means that even if one forum, say New York, obviates a cause of action or limits damage awards, this does not mean that another forum, say California, may not countenance innovations in the opposite direction.

15 On 17 August 1994, a state court jury in Albuquerque, New Mexico awarded eighty-one-year-old Stella Liebeck US $160,000 in compensatory damages and US $2.7-million in punitive damages after she was burned by coffee purchased from a drive-through window at a McDonald's restaurant. According to news reports, Mrs. Liebeck contended that, for taste reasons, McDonald's served coffee about twenty degrees hotter than other fast food restaurants and, in spite of numerous complaints, had made a conscious decision not to warn customers of the possibility of serious burns. The jury's verdict received worldwide attention: Andrea Gerlin, Wall St. J. Europe, 2 September 1994, 1994 WL-WSJE 2037634; *Greene* v. *Boddie-Noell Enters.*, 966 F.Supp. 416 (W.D. Va. 1997). The plaintiffs' bar put the following spin on the case (48 Rutgers L. Rev. 673): "As of 11 November 1995, 600 stories had reported the McDonald's spilled coffee case on NEXIS in the CURNWS file. The McDonald's coffee case resulted in a punitive damages award to a woman who spilled coffee on her lap and sued McDonald's because the coffee was too hot: Wash. Post, 18 October 1995, at A18. The vast majority of these stories decried the verdict as outrageous, often reporting half-truths and quarter-truths about the case. Unreported, however, was the seriousness of the burns and McDonald's prior knowledge of hundreds of similar incidents. Carl Bogus writes: We will almost certainly hear more about the recent case of the woman who won a US $2.9-million jury verdict against McDonald's after burning herself with a cup of hot coffee. However, do not expect to hear that McDonald's coffee is heated between 180 and 190 degrees Fahrenheit, while coffee made at home is between 130 and 140 degrees; that over the past ten years, McDonald's received 700 reports of patrons burning themselves with its superheated coffee; or that the eighty-one-year-old plaintiff was hospitalized for eight days and underwent skin graft operations for third-degree burns. Don't expect to hear as well that the court reduced the US $2.9-million jury verdict for punitive damages to US $480,000".

Unsafe at Any Warning

Shattering both the rule and record books, on 3 October 2002, a Los Angeles California jury awarded US $750,000 in compensatory damages plus US $100,000 in pain and suffering against Philip Morris to a woman named Betty Bullock who had been smoking since the age of seventeen and had contracted lung cancer. The jury then moved on to earth-shakingly consider punitive damages, having found that Philip Morris intentionally misrepresented the adverse health impacts of smoking. In 2000, a Florida jury had awarded US $145-billion in punitives to a class of thousands of plaintiffs on similar allegations against three defendants, a verdict which is still being appealed. However, the *Bullock* jury broke new ground, awarding the jaw-dropping sum of US $28-billion to one plaintiff against one defendant. On 5 August 2002, the California Supreme Court had ruled that statements made by tobacco companies during their negotiations with the government from 1988 to 1998 could not be used against them in litigation, and Philip Morris is naturally appealing the *Bullock* verdict on this and numerous other grounds, including the fact that Bullock admitted that she had been urged to quit by her doctor and her daughter but had ignored their advice, saying "this is my business, I'm an adult".

A law professor was quoted as saying "juries all around the country are sending a message that this conduct was not only totally inexcusable but that it was so outrageous that there is no amount of money that would be enough to punish the people who perpetrated it". The tobacco giant received an early Christmas present from the trial judge, however, when, on 23 December, the judge reduced the award to just 0.1 per cent of what the jury had awarded, US $28-million, and Bullock accepted rather than face a new trial, saying she was "very ill" and "does not want to fight anymore". The largest single punitive award against Philip Morris had been US $3-billion, and the amount had been reduced by ninety-seven per cent to just US $100-million on appeal. Criticizing the trial judge, Bullock's counsel stated:

> "Philip Morris earns over US $14-million per day from selling cigarettes in the United States [The judge] has fined [the company] two days of its earnings. In California, a motorist who drives in the carpool lane without any passengers is fined US $271, which is two days' pay for the average Californian. If two days' pay is a proper fine for a traffic

> violation, then two days' pay is not the proper fine for [the company] in killing so many Americans over a fifty-year period. This is not a real punishment for Phillip Morris."

Though malignant, reasoning of this kind is obviously effective in the jury room and was not sufficiently combated by Phillip Morris' counsel. Bullock's counsel does not mention, of course, that:

(1) His client is not dead;
(2) Only his client would benefit from a larger award, not "so many Americans" who were not parties to the action;
(3) The jury was not imposing a "fine" prescribed by law but rather was freely exercising arbitrary discretion; or
(4) His client willfully accepted the risks of tobacco smoking, whereas authorized carpool lane users do not willfully accept the behavior of unauthorized users.

Unsafe at Any Speed

On another front, a record US $290-million punitive damages award was recently upheld by the California Supreme Court in *Romo* v. *Ford Motor Co.*,[16] where a family sued the car maker for defective design of a vehicle. Counsel for Ford, not surprisingly, was quoted as saying "there's never been a greater need for tort reform than now (the cost of the United States civil legal system is in excess of US $165-billion annually, while federal class action filings are up by a factor of three over the past decade, state class actions by a factor of ten)". However, the plaintiff attorney who two months ago won a US $271-million judgment against a gas company in an explosion burn case, *Johnson* v. *Equitable Resources Inc.*,[17] stated that "these juries are saying 'enough is enough, corporate America'".

Physician, Heal Thyself

It would be far from surprising to find a person allegedly injured by asbestos, toxic mold or lead paint to be involved simultaneously in two different sets of legal proceedings: one to hold someone responsible for the dangerous exposure and a second to seek retribution from a doctor who mistreated the resulting illness. Malpractice liability is another

16 *Romo* v. *Ford Motor Co.*, 2002 Cal. LEXIS 7254 (23 October 2002).
17 *Johnson* v. *Equitable Resources Inc.*, Number 1-CI-00130 (Knott Co. Ky. Cir. Ct.).

area of exploding growth for plaintiffs. On 5 February 2003, an editorial entitled "The Doctor is Out" appeared in the *New York Times*. The editorial noted the prospect of thousands of doctors walking off their jobs in New Jersey to protest skyrocketing malpractice premiums that reach US $100,000 per year for some specialists. The physicians blame million-dollar "jackpot" jury verdicts and urge the legislature to adopt a US $250,000 cap on non-economic (that is, "pain and suffering") damages. New Jersey already has a cap in place, under which, for actions filed on or after 27 October 1997, no defendant is liable for any punitive damages in any action for an amount in excess of five times the liability of that defendant for compensatory damages, or US $350,000, whichever is greater.[18]

New York, by contrast, has no statutory limit on damages, and the editors of the *Times* stated that the New Jersey proposal was "far too simplistic a prescription". The *Times* urged lawmakers not to "demonize" trial lawyers, since "tort reform alone is hardly the answer". The *Times* recommended that "the insurance industry should be required to present the same sort of detailed justification for malpractice increases as is not required for auto insurance hikes". The *Times* suggested that a "tiny minority of inept doctors" might be responsible for most malpractice cases, and urged licensing reform to weed them out. It urged lawmakers to appoint a specialized commission to study the problem.

California, on the other hand, already has a cap like the one doctors propose in New Jersey.[19] Non-economic damages, defined as compensation for pain, suffering, inconvenience, physical impairment, disfigurement and other non-pecuniary injury, are limited to US $250,000. The cap applies whether the case is for injury or death, and it allows only one US $250,000 recovery in a wrongful death case.[20] There is authority, however, for allowing separate caps for the patient and a spouse claiming loss of consortium.[21] The cap on non-economic damages has been held to be constitutional.[22]

In Pennsylvania, the story is different yet again. There, generally, the state does not impose a cap on compensatory damages. However,

18 N.J. Stat. Ann. Section 2A:15–5.14 (b).

19 Cal. Civ. Code Section 3333.2 (West 1997).

20 *Yates* v. *Pollock*, 194 Cal. App. 3d 195, 239 Cal. Rptr. 383 (1987).

21 *Atkins* v. *Strayhorn*, 223 Cal. App. 3d 1380, 273 Cal. Rptr. 231 (1990).

22 *Fein* v. *Permanente Medical Group*, 38 Cal. 3d 137, 695 P.2d 665, 211 Cal. Rptr. 368 (1985), also upholding the modification of the collateral source rule.

physician members of the Medical Professional Liability Catastrophe Loss Fund are, in effect, subject to limited liability because of state-sponsored excess insurance. Effective from 25 January 1997, punitive damages against individual physicians shall not exceed 200 per cent of the compensatory damages, but shall not be less than US $100,000 unless a lower verdict for compensatory damages is returned by the trier of fact.[23] The threatened New Jersey walkout is only one instance in an ongoing series of such threats and actual walk-outs by physicians across the country protesting higher malpractice premiums that insurers say are justified by escalating jury verdicts against negligent doctors.

In *Schriever* v. *Maddox*,[24] the plaintiff was hit in the arm by a flying piece of metal while at work. She was treated by one doctor and returned to work the next day, but it turned out that the treating physician had failed to diagnose a ruptured tendon. A second doctor, working at the company, removed her stitches and also failed to diagnose the underlying condition. By the time it was correctly diagnosed (by an orthopedic surgeon), it was too late for restorative surgery. This resulted in a fifteen per cent loss of movement in the affected arm. The plaintiff brought suit and won a jury award of US $533,000 — she dismissed her employer and its doctor before trial. She admitted at trial that she had worked continuously after the incident until she left work permanently to care for her children, and her complaint made no claim for lost wages, as to which no evidence was submitted at trial. However, nevertheless, the court charged the jury on lost wages and the jury returned a general verdict.

On appeal, the case was remanded for a new trial on damages only. The plaintiff argued that the error was harmless, since no request had been made for damages, but the court held that the award was so large on its face that it might have included such an amount. This illustrates how quickly, and how badly, a matter can get out of control from the defendant's perspective; even though a new trial was ordered, the plaintiff will obviously have considerable additional settlement leverage as the parties seek to avoid the expense of such proceedings.

A stark contrast can be perceived between the *Schriever* award and that involved in *Buckholtz* v. *MacNeal Hospital*.[25] There, the plaintiff's

23 40 Pa. Cons. Stat. Ann. Section 1301.812-A(g) (West Supp. 1997).

24 *Schriever* v. *Maddox*, 2003 Ga. App. LEXIS 191 (Ct. App. 3rd Div. 11 February 2003).

25 *Buckholtz* v. *MacNeal Hospital*, 2003 Ill. App. LEXIS 99 (App. Ct. 1st Dist. 31 January 2003).

father died in the hospital due to blood complications after doctors performed surgery despite being unable to insert a necessary catheter into the man's vein. The jury's award, at US $801,642.57 (for loss of companionship), does not seem to place the loss of a father in appropriate proportion to the fifteen per cent loss of movement in an arm. On appeal, the court affirmed the award as against the treating physician, but dismissed the hospital, holding that the doctors were not its agents, but rather independent contractors for whom the hospital could not be held vicariously liable. The doctor had sought remittitur on the grounds that the award was "astounding" and could only be construed as punitive damages, not permitted under Illinois law in such a case. However, the defendants had perhaps made a tactical error, since they had chosen to focus their defense not on an effort to minimize the daughter's suffering, but rather on proving that the father was "so ill that his death was momentarily imminent". The court held that there was sufficient evidence for the jury to find that the father was "strong, independent, and determined to continue to enjoy life with his family".

Buckholtz, in turn, can be contrasted with *Cramer* v. *Benedictine Hospital*,[26] where the estate of a severely retarded thirty-year-old man who grabbed a corn cob from the garbage and swallowed it whole sued for wrongful death when he developed complications resulting from his treatment. Here, the jury awarded the estate US $1-million. Yet, the court held that the award "deviated materially from what would constitute reasonable compensation" and ordered remittitur. The court held that the plaintiff could only recover for pain and suffering before his death, and ruled that the six days between that event and his trauma meant that the award should be reduced by two-thirds to US $350,000.

On the other hand, in *Zygmunt* v. *Berkowitz*,[27] the decedent's wife and children brought an action when the husband and father died as the result of failure to diagnose unstable angina. Here, the jury awarded the wife US $637,500 for the husband's lost earnings, but nothing to the children for "loss of guidance". The court reversed the latter decision as contrary to the evidence and ordered a new trial on that issue. In another novel development, a plaintiff child in Illinois received a US $9-million settlement for "reduced life expectancy"

---

26 *Cramer* v. *Benedictine Hospital*, 2003 NY. App. Div. LEXIS 339 (3rd Dept. 23 January 2003).

27 *Zygmunt* v. *Berkowitz*, 2003 NY. App. Div. LEXIS 516 (2nd Dept. 31 January 2003).

due to negligent medical care provided to the child's mother, one of the first such awards in the country.[28]

Jocular Jurists

Perhaps compounding the issue of runaway juries are incidents from the bench which hardly serve to emphasize the gravity of ballooning tort judgments, such as a dissenting opinion in verse entered in the Pennsylvania Supreme Court's divided decision in *Porreco* v. *Porreco*,[29] which appears below in its entirety (it was not the first time that the justice in question issued such an opinion). Not only is this an actual judicial opinion, but, in a Common Law jurisdiction, it could constitute the actual law itself.

"A groom must expect matrimonial pandemonium
When his spouse finds he's given her a cubic zirconium
Instead of a diamond in her engagement band
The one he said was worth twenty-one grand.

"Our deceiver would claim that when his bride relied
On his claim of value, she was not justified
For she should have appraised it; and surely she could have,
However, the question is whether a bride-to-be would have.

"The realities of the parties control the equation,
Also, here they're not comparable in sophistication;
The reasonableness of her reliance we just cannot gauge
With a yardstick of cqual cxpcricncc and age.

"This must be remembered when applying the test
By which the 'reasonable fiancée' is assessed.
She was 19, he was nearly 30 years older;
Was it unreasonable for her to believe what he told her?

"Given their history and Pygmalion relation,
I find her reliance was with justification.
Given his accomplishment and given her youth,
Was it unjustifiable for her to think he told the truth?

---

28 *Townsend* v. *Little Company of Mary Hospital and Health Care*, Number 0 L 3555 (Cook Co. Ill. Cir. Ct., 16 December 2002).

29 *Porreco* v. *Porreco*, 2002 Pa. LEXIS 2468 (27 November 2002).

"Or for every prenuptial, is it now a must
That you treat your betrothed with presumptive mistrust?
Do we mean reliance on your beloved's representation
Is not justifiable, absent third party verification?

"Love, not suspicion, is the underlying foundation
Of parties entering the marital relation;
Mistrust is not required, and should not be made a priority.
Accordingly, I must depart from the reasoning of the majority."

Substantive Areas of Liability for Personal Injury Claims

Asbestos

Review of recent developments in the area of asbestos liability helps to illustrate the often murky distinction between "products" and "personal injury" claims, as well as the significance of insurance issues in determining the ultimate funding of these claims and the role of bankruptcy courts in dealing with the impact on American business that the onslaught of such claims has wrought. It also highlights how a type of exposure that was thought to be contained can break free of its confines by means of creative plaintiff attorneys and unanticipated sources of liability.

Contours of the Catastrophe

On 8 February 2002, a New York City jury awarded the family and estate of a man who died at age fifty-one of mesothelioma resulting from asbestos exposure in the course of his work as an auto mechanic the astounding sum of US $53-million.[30] The award was allocated among thirty-six defendants, including the "big three" auto makers. Suits against the auto makers concerning asbestos containing automobile parts are now on the rise, and since 1 January 2000, at least two dozen companies have filed for bankruptcy protection due to asbestos liabilities.

30 *Estate of Brown* v. *AC&S et al.*, Number 12658–00, Sup. Ct. NY. Cnty.

On 10 March 2003, the United States Supreme Court handed down its opinion in *Norfolk & Western Railway Company* v. *Freeman Ayers*.[31] In that case, former employees of the railway sued for negligent exposure to asbestos, which caused them to contract asbestosis. The case was based on the Federal Employers' Liability Act (FELA), which provides that "every common carrier by railroad while engaging in interstate commerce shall be liable in damages to any person suffering injury while he is employed by such carrier in commerce". Generally, a cause of action in tort is based on state law, and enters federal court only based on diversity of citizenship between the parties, but there are exceptions if a federal statute, such as the FELA, is involved.

While *Freeman* was tried and appealed in West Virginia state courts, it could be appealed from that state's highest court to the United States Supreme Court because federal law was at issue. Generally speaking, an ordinary state court tort decision could not be appealed to the United States Supreme Court. The employees claimed damages, not only for bodily injury, but for psychological harm, namely, the consequences of their fear of developing cancer. The trial judge charged the jury that they could compensate the employees for this fear if they found it had been proven, an intermediate appellate court affirmed this and the state Supreme Court refused to hear the case. However, the United States Supreme Court agreed to do so, and upheld the trial court ruling, creating a great incentive for plaintiffs to file cases under the FELA and perhaps presaging a new avalanche of asbestos and other personal injury litigation.

Bankruptcies Follow

On 21 October 2002, it became international news that Swiss-Swedish electrical engineering giant ABB Ltd. may place its United States subsidiary, Stamford, Connecticut-based Combustion Engineering Inc. (CEI), into Chapter 11 bankruptcy proceedings as a result of the latter's massive asbestos liability. CEI has some 14,000 employees. Traded on the New York Stock Exchange, shares of ABB fell by forty per cent in value, trading as low as US $1.39 as against a fifty-two-week high of over US $2.17. The company announced that targets for both

31 *Norfolk & Western Railway Company* v. *Freeman Ayers*, 2003 U.S. LEXIS 1956 (10 March 2003).

operating profit and margin would not be met, and Moody's downgraded the company's debt from Baa2 to Baa3.

According to CEI's filings with the SEC, in the first quarter of 2002, there were approximately 14,300 new asbestos bodily injury claims filed against the subsidiary, and 13,500 existing claims were settled at a cost of US $51-million, more than fifty per cent without payment. This was a decrease of five per cent from the previous year as to the number of filed claims, but an increase of nearly a third in annual settlement costs. Defense costs were in excess of US $10-million per year. The company maintains reserves of US $940-million for claims and US $590-million for defense costs. There are approximately 94,000 pending claims. As to insurance, the company stated:

> "Our management has considered the financial viability and legal obligations of Combustion Engineering's insurance carriers and concluded that, except for those insurers that have become or may become insolvent, the insurers will continue to fund their portion of the claims costs relating to asbestos litigation settlements. Accordingly, the expected amounts of insurance recoveries are recognized on an undiscounted basis. Combustion Engineering will fund defense costs. Over time, as available coverage under Combustion Engineering's insurance policies is utilized against asbestos claims payments, the portion of the cost of resolving asbestos claims that will be recovered under Combustion Engineering's insurance policies will be reduced."

Cash payments by the company to resolve claims annually were as follows:

Date	Costs	Expected Insurance Reimbursement
1999	US $67-million	n/a
2000	US $125-million	US $43-million
2001	US $136-million	US $48-million

For 2002, CEI was on pace to exceed US $200-million in claim payouts. The company's book value was only a little over US $800 million. Thus, market fears began to spread that plaintiff claims would soon find a way to reach the parent entity, as has been done many times in the past. CEI also has a hazardous waste site in Windsor, Connecticut, and ABB spent US $6-million to remediate radiological contamination there in 2001.

Use of Indirect Channeling Injunctions

Section 524(g) of the Bankruptcy Code contains a specific provision that provides for what is known as a "channeling injunction" to issue from the bankruptcy court, providing immunity to an asbestos debtor from future claims where the debtor, as part of a bankruptcy proceeding, establishes a qualifying trust to compensate asbestos claimants. The injunction does not "discharge" the claims, but it rather "channels" them to payment from a single source, namely, the trust. Insurance contributions, of course, may be an important or even critical component of such a trust. These injunctions, therefore, may be written to protect not only the debtor, but also its insurers. In fact, it is really only by resort to such a device that all parties can hope to achieve full and permanent relief from asbestos claims.

Outside bankruptcy, of course, a settlement with only one claimant or group of claimants does not prevent another injured party from stepping forward to assert additional claims; even if a class action is filed, there remains the possibility for injured persons to "opt out" of the class action and later bring their own lawsuit. By barring unknown future claims and establishing a fixed liability, the channeling injunction becomes a very valuable legal mechanism for defendants. The trust created to pay the claims must be approved not only by the court, but also by seventy-five per cent of the proposed members of the class to whom it will pay claims.[32]

One of the more interesting twists on a bankruptcy filing necessitated by asbestos liabilities involved Halliburton Corporation. On 18 December 2002, Halliburton (formerly run by the current United States Vice-President) announced an agreement, in principle, to

32 *In re Joint Eastern and Southern Districts Asbestos Litigation*, 878 F.Supp. 473 (E.D.N.Y. and S.D.N.Y. 1995); *In re Hillsborough Holdings Corp.*, 197 B.R. 372 (M.D.Fla. 1996); *In re Dow Corning Corp.*, 244 B.R. 721 (E.D.Mich. 1999); *In re Eagle Pitcher Industries Inc.*, 203 B.R. 256 (S.D. Ohio 1996).

achieve a global settlement of more than 300,000 outstanding asbestos claims it was facing. Halliburton offered to pay approximately US $4-billion (consisting of around US $2.8-billion in cash, US $100-million in notes and 60-million Halliburton shares valued at around US $1.2-billion) into a trust fund under an agreement with more than seventy-five per cent of the existing plaintiffs, which would ostensibly allow the company to impose a "cram-down" settlement on the entire group. Halliburton shares rose four per cent on the news.

Halliburton stated that it had received about 546,000 asbestos claims since 1976, of which 328,000 were still open, and that another half a million claims were expected by 2017. Most of the claims involve Dresser Industries (now known as DII), which, along with the other major litigation target, Brown and Root Inc. (now known as KBR), will retain the rights to the first US $2.3-billion of insurance proceeds.

In the first few months of 2002, Halliburton lost several major asbestos verdicts to the tune of US $150-million. Then, on Valentine's Day, Halliburton's subsidiary, Harbison-Walker Refractories Co., filed for bankruptcy in the Western District of Pennsylvania. The bankruptcy court issued a stay covering two-thirds of the outstanding litigation, and this stay has been repeatedly extended with the consent of the plaintiffs as the settlement was negotiated. Halliburton sought to impose the bankruptcy stay against certain litigation pending against Dresser in addition to that involving Harbison because of the shared insurance assets that had now become subject to the bankruptcy court's jurisdiction, a move designed to keep Halliburton's own corporate name unsullied by any bankruptcy proceedings.[33]

On 14 March 2002, Halliburton announced an eleven cent per share first-quarter charge due to a write-off of receivables which occurred when the Delaware Supreme Court held that primary coverage provided by Highlands Insurance Company (formerly a Halliburton subsidiary) and applicable to approximately 30,000 of the claims would be unavailable, costing the company about

33 Use of bankruptcy of a subsidiary to clean up broader parental exposure in this manner is a burgeoning practice in bankruptcy: *A.H. Robbins* v. *Piccinin*, 788 F.2d 994 (4th Cir. 1996) ("actions related to the bankruptcy proceedings against the insurer or against officers or employees of the debtor who may be entitled to indemnification under such policies or who qualify as an additional insured under the policy are to be stayed"); *In re Johns Manville Corp.*, 26 B.R. 420 (S.D.N.Y. 1983).

US $80-million. Halliburton said that it had more than US $2-billion in additional coverage. In July 2002, Halliburton had stated that it expected to recover US $1.6-billion from insurance coverage and would need US $2.2-billion in cash to settle the asbestos cases, and took a US $391-million after-tax charge for the second quarter related to the legal exposure over the course of the next fifteen years.

Historical Perspective

Beginning in the 1970s, when injuries caused by exposure to asbestos first came to light, claims were brought by construction workers on building sites where asbestos-containing materials (ACMs) were installed, usually for fireproofing purposes. These claims were handled in state forum, administrative proceedings under each state's applicable "workers' compensation" statute, which prevent employees from suing employers for bodily injury incurred on the job, requiring them instead to submit such claims for processing to the employer's workers' compensation insurer. However, such statutes do not provide for any compensation for "pain and suffering", the bread and butter of the plaintiffs' bar, and accordingly it was not long[34] before they began to assert claims against the manufacturers of the ACMs for product liability — claims which, as it happened, offered the convenient benefit in many states of a "strict liability" standard not dependent on proof of negligence. Thus, although asbestos is not, per se, a product, the individuals harmed by exposure to products containing asbestos began to successfully assert strict liability product claims.

This wave of litigation bankrupted many of the manufacturers, chief among them the now infamous Johns Manville Corporation (JM). JM filed for bankruptcy in 1982, faced with over half a million personal injury claims, a figure expected to quadruple by the time all claims had been received. In addition to the possibility of settling claims for pennies on the dollar, a bankruptcy filing offers companies the added attraction of litigating what would otherwise be state

34 An example of the earliest proceedings can be found in *UNR Industries, Inc.* v. *Continental Ins. Co.*, 682 F. Supp. 1434 (N.D. Ill. 1988) ("UNR Industries, Inc., its predecessors and owned affiliated companies manufactured asbestos products beginning in the 1920s. Most production ceased by 1963 and all production stopped by 1970. In December 1966, the first product liability claim involving injury from exposure to asbestos products was filed.").

claims in a federal forum, since bankruptcy protection is offered only under federal law and in federal court. Generally speaking, state courts are far more plaintiff-friendly than are their federal counterparts.

It was originally thought that this wave of litigation would dissipate as the main manufacturers declared bankruptcy and the prospects of large, quick settlements concomitantly diminished, but the opposite has in fact occurred, with new claims being filed at an increasing rate approaching 100,000 per year. On 10 April 2002, the front-page story in the *New York Times* reported that "at least 90,000 new claims were filed last year alone" and noted that Dow, Halliburton and 3M had all lost multi-million dollar lawsuits in the past year. Viacom, chiefly an entertainment company, faced over 100,000 accrued claims owing to its purchase of former producer Westinghouse. The ultimate cost of the corpus of asbestos litigation could be as high as US $275-billion. An 18 April 2002 story in the *Times* business section reported that Honeywell "appears to have misinformed analysts and shareholders about how much of a US $53.5-million verdict it is responsible for paying in the case of a man who died of a cancer caused by asbestos".

The article continued as follows:

> "When the judgment was announced on Feb. 8 in a Manhattan court, Honeywell's stock dove as much as 11 per cent during the day, shaving US $3-billion off its market value. Honeywell's shares quickly rebounded after the company said it had been found liable for less than US $1.1-million of the verdict, a figure that made its way into Wall Street analysts' reports. However, the company's statement immediately raised questions among lawyers who had followed the case but were not involved in it. Those lawyers, who included both plaintiff and defense attorneys, said the company's true responsibility was much greater.
>
> "Honeywell now says that it must pay at least US $11-million of the judgment, according to Peter M. Kreindler, its general counsel. Mr. Kreindler said Honeywell planned to appeal the verdict and had not misled investors about its size. The company does not face financially significant liability from asbestos cases, he said, and has US $2-billion in asbestos insurance.

> "Although US $11-million is minor for a company Honeywell's size, investors are nervous about Honeywell's asbestos liabilities. Last winter, investors punished the stocks of several major companies like Halliburton and 3M after a series of multimillion-dollar asbestos verdicts. The companies generally say that they do not expect the litigation to damage their financial health, but most have not discussed their liabilities in detail.
>
> "Honeywell faces about 50,000 asbestos injury claims, including nearly 1,000 claims from people suffering from the cancer in this case, mesothelioma. The North American Refractories Company, a former unit of AlliedSignal, which merged with Honeywell in 1999, made bricks that contained asbestos. That business faces an additional 116,000 asbestos claims and filed for bankruptcy in January."

Numerous factors may explain the increase in filings. Many claimants may feel the need to establish a place in line among the creditors waiting to be paid in bankruptcy proceedings before assets are depleted. In addition, there may be fear of federal legislation that would limit legal rights to protect manufacturers and jobs (something made more likely under the pro-business administration of President George W. Bush). There have also been a number of rulings overturning class action filings on the grounds that individual cases of extreme bodily injury require individual trials on the merits, thus necessitating hundreds of new individual filings by parties who formerly thought themselves members of classes.

Asbestos also highlights another key feature of the American judicial system: forum shopping. For example, although Mississippi has only one per cent of the total United States population, twenty per cent of all asbestos cases have been filed there, a clear indication that the plaintiffs' bar feels the state's juries are highly sympathetic to their cause. In turn, the reality of a sympathetic forum gives rise to an additional concern, namely, the possibility of a third wave of litigation against very peripheral players in the asbestos product line, such as a landlord who owns an asbestos-contaminated building, fostered by an aggressive and creative plaintiffs' bar and a judiciary keen on seeing sick people compensated rather than denied benefits due to bankruptcy filings. Obviously, there are serious concerns about the fairness of holding liable peripheral players whose ability to learn about the dangers of asbestos, or indeed even its presence in their buildings, was minimal at the time of installation.

Court Decisions

Although, so far, this is essentially an unrelenting onslaught of negative developments for defendants (and their insurers), it must be noted that the possibility still exists to win significant victories in litigation that will have the effect of limiting exposure to monumental liability. A good recent example is the Louisiana Supreme Court's decision in *Bonnette* v. *Conoco Inc.*[35] The matter was a class action in which the plaintiff group claimed exposure to asbestos waste located in soil they purchased from the defendant. The trial court awarded damages for increased risk of disease, fear of disease, punitive damages and property damage. Each adult plaintiff received US $12,500 for mental anguish and US $10,000 for risk of disease, while each child received US $20,000 for each category. Each plaintiff received US $7,500 in punitive damages, and property owners received an award ranging from US $1,000 to US $2,000 for property damage. The intermediate appellate court affirmed.[36]

On appeal, the divided Supreme Court (there was a lengthy dissent by a single justice) reversed in large part. It held that, since none of the plaintiff experts showed any "significant" actual exposure to asbestos, the awards for risk of disease were invalid. It also held that a generalized fear of disease did not establish "genuine and serious mental distress" and struck down that award as well. Punitive damages were also vitiated, since the defendant had acted in compliance with state environmental regulations in effect during the period of pollution. The court upheld the property damage awards based on the potential stigma associated with the contamination.

The court admitted that "for the entire period of time that the asbestos contaminated soil remained on the plaintiffs' properties they were exposed to some asbestos fiber count which exceeded the normal ambient air", but concluded that this exposure was slight, and that, accordingly, the increased risk of disease was also slight. It asked "whether Louisiana law permits the recovery of compensatory damages for a 'slight' exposure to asbestos" and answered in the

35 *Bonnette* v. *Conoco Inc.*, 2003 La. LEXIS 119 (28 January 2003).
36 At 801 So. 2d 501 (2001).

negative. Rather, the court said, a "significant" exposure was required. Further, the court held that:

> "... in order for plaintiffs to recover emotional distress damages in the absence of manifest physical injury, they must prove their claim is not spurious by showing the particular likelihood of genuine and serious mental distress arising from special circumstances".

Where plaintiffs do not seek medical treatment or attempt remediation, the court stated, "we cannot say they suffered from genuine and serious mental distress that guarantees their claim for mental distress damages is not spurious".

It need hardly be pointed out that the wave of bankruptcies sweeping the asbestos industry highlights the importance, from the plaintiffs' perspective, of triggering insurance coverage maintained by these insolvent firms. Therefore, insurance issues become significantly intertwined in the personal injury litigation and, accordingly, they too must be carefully monitored and understood.

In *Continental Casualty Co.* v. *Rapid American Corp.*,[37] New York's highest court dealt with a coverage dispute between an insurer and a manufacturer of asbestos who faced numerous claims, and laid out the critical legal issues. The court held in favor of the insured as to the carrier's duty to defend under a standard Comprehensive General Liability (CGL) policy containing a "pollution exclusion". The trial court granted summary judgment to the carrier, holding that it had no duty to defend since asbestos fibers were "pollution" excluded from coverage; but an appellate panel reversed, and the state's highest court, the Court of Appeals,[38] upheld the reversal.

First, the court addressed the carrier's argument that there had been no "occurrence" under the policy because either:

(1) The exposure was not "unintended and unexpected" and was, therefore, excluded from the definition of "occurrence"; or
(2) The exposure did not occur within the policy period, but rather long before the policy's inception.

---

37 80 N.Y.2d 640, 609 N.E.2d 506, 593 N.Y.S. 2d 966 (1993).

38 Although the highest court in the United States is the Supreme Court, and most states follow suit by naming their own highest courts "Supreme", New York is a bizarre anomaly: in New York State the "Supreme" court is the lowest trial court, while the highest court is called the Court of Appeals.

The court rejected both of these arguments. First, the court held that even though the insured had been subjected to numerous judgments for punitive damages, which required findings that the insured knew the risks posed by the ACMs it produced but willfully disregarded those risks, the court held that, whether or not such knowledge was present constituted a factual issue for trial on indemnity and could not suffice to avoid the duty to defend.

Second, the court noted that, although the question of when an asbestos bodily injury occurs has been "hotly contested" throughout the country, with different results in different states,[39] the court stated that, in New York, courts would apply an "injury-in-fact" approach, "which rests on when the injury, sickness, disease or disability began". The parties then disputed whether or not this would lead to an "occurrence" within the policy period, with the carrier relying heavily on the fact that the insured had already invoked coverage under earlier policies. The court rejected this argument as well, ruling that no waiver of right to claim under the instant policy was implied. The court then turned to the pollution exclusion, and held that the clause was ambiguous as to asbestos and, therefore, to be construed against the carrier; the ambiguity arose as to whether a "discharge into the atmosphere" occurred, as required by the exclusion, when asbestos fibers are released and inhaled by workers.

In *Aetna Casualty and Surety Co.* v. *The Wallace & Gale Co.*,[40] asbestos coverage issues were raised in the context of a bankruptcy proceeding in federal court in Maryland. The defendant was an insulation contractor that supplied ACMs from the 1930s to the 1970s. The court held that there was a duty to defend under various CGL policies from a litany of carriers (written from the 1960s to the 1980s), and that a plan of reorganization for the defendant debtor was approved, calling for the creation of a trust fund into which the

---

39 The court identified at least four different competing theories: (1) Exposure to asbestos; (2) Manifestation of disease; (3) Onset of disease; and (4) Any of the above — the "continuous trigger theory". Thus, in *J.H. France Refractories Co.* v. *Allstate Ins. Co.*, 14 Phila. 291 (Phila. Cnty Common Pleas 1986), vacated and remanded 372 Pa. Super. 575, 539 A.2d 1345, affirmed in part and reversed in part 534 Pa. 29, 626 A.2d 502 (1993), the state trial court expressed dismay on discovering that "four Federal Circuit Courts of Appeal have construed this concept three contrary ways" and concluded that "the fact that these courts have divergent holdings further persuades [the court] to construe the policies broadly in favor of the insured".

40 *Aetna Casualty and Surety Co.* v. *The Wallace & Gale Co.*, 275 B.R. 223 (S.D. Md. 2002).

coverage would be paid, if any. The court then turned to the litigation of coverage rights. This involved dealing with a thorny and now classic problem: allocation of coverage to many policies from various insurers over nearly a half a century of accruing injury — an issue that has received radically different treatment according to the state whose law governs the claim.

The insurers argued for a "time-on-the-risk"[41] approach, meaning that, for periods during which the insured "went bare" (that is, was self-insured), the *pro rata* share of each insurer would be reduced *pro tanto*. Some carriers also sought to impose aggregates on policies that did not facially contain them, on the theory that their "completed operations" clauses set limits on exposures. Other carriers asserted that no "occurrence" took place because the asbestos injuries complained of were "expected or intended" by the insured. To complicate matters, the underlying bodily injury claimants intervened in the proceedings on the side of the defendant, urging the court to rule that "each insurer should be fully responsible for Wallace & Gale's liability for bodily injury claims up to the limits of each policy" and that none of the policies should be construed to contain applicable aggregate limits.

Cross-motions for summary judgment were filed, and the court's resulting ruling was a mixed bag for the insurers. The court held that if a claimant was first exposed to asbestos in the course of employment, then the policy in force at that time would respond, as well as each subsequent policy, for "all sums" that the insured became liable to pay on that account. The court rejected penalizing the insured for going bare, stating that "the fact remains that there is no explicit or unambiguous policy provision allowing the insurers to allocate the loss so as to deprive the policyholder of full coverage", citing the contrary authority, which relies on the "all sums" clause to impute full indemnification.

The court also rejected the "expected and intended" and "known loss" defenses, stating that to construe these defenses as the carriers suggested would "defeat the whole idea of purchasing liability

41 The most salient alternative to the "time-on-the-risk" or "horizontal" approach is the infamous "vertical spike", in which the insured is permitted to run his entire exposure up through all the levels of coverage in any given triggered year, irrespective of whether there are years in which no, or less, coverage was obtained. Both schools of thought have substantial currency among American courts, and there are all manner of compromises.

insurance", which is to guard against claims that can be "anticipated" — thus, something more than mere predictability was required, namely, that the defendant "subjectively expected or intended to produce bodily injuries while it was installing the asbestos-related materials". The court did not rule down-the-line for the policyholder, but the court also determined that if initial exposure occurred after operations were concluded or if exposure that began during operations continued after operations were complete, then the aggregate limits of any policy that came into effect after operations were complete would apply.

The nuts and bolts of asbestos liability are illustrated in *Hoerner* v. *Anco Insulations*,[42] by the jury for the husband's exposure to ACMs in the workplace from 1957 to 1982. The husband suffered from only "mild" asbestosis with "relatively slow progression of actual fibrosis". The trial judge then "divided the US $475,000 into 21 virile shares, one for each of the twelve party defendants cast in judgment and one for each of the nine non-party settling defendants cast in judgment", resulting in a virile share amount of US $22,6109.05, and the judge accordingly reduced the award by nine one-third virile shares to account for the settlement to US $263,889.39.

The court upheld the plaintiff's general theory of liability even though the plaintiff "worked on hundreds of job sites, some of them as short as hours or days" and, therefore, the identification of responsible defendants was highly daunting. The court held that no requirement exists compelling the plaintiff in an asbestos case to prove that this exposure to asbestos from a specific source is the proximate cause of his disease. However, the court did exculpate eight of the twenty-one defendants for failure to show causation, and accordingly increased the trial court's final award. As to damages, the court upheld the jury's award for mental suffering based on the plaintiff's "fear of cancer" believing that it was reasonable for a jury to consider an asbestos victim's cancer phobia as part of his damages.

Insurance issues also arose in the case. Home Insurance Co. issued a single US $1-million excess policy to one of the defendants and two

42 *Hoerner* v. *Anco Insulations*, 2002 La. App. LEXIS 123 (23 January 2002), where a couple was awarded US $475,000. The jury assigned liability as follows: US $150,000 for physical pain and suffering; US $150,000 for physical disability; US $150,000 for mental pain and suffering; US $20,000 for medical expenses; and US $5,000 for loss of consortium. Nothing was awarded for lost wages, although the plaintiff had asserted that he retired at age fifty-six due to physical exhaustion caused by his disease.

of its executive officers, who had been sued personally. Home asserted that since the total award was within the primary coverage, it should have been dismissed from the case rather than being allocated a virile share. The court stated:

> "The Louisiana Supreme Court has held that under the exposure theory applicable in Louisiana, primary insurance policies issued to a defendant in consecutive years during which the plaintiff in an asbestos case was exposed may be stacked horizontally. Thus, a single insurer that issued primary policies to a defendant in an asbestos case in consecutive years is liable for an amount up to the limits of all the policies issued for relevant years added together. Moreover, excess insurers are not required to make indemnity payments until all applicable primary limits are exhausted."

The court concluded that the total amount of available primary coverage from 1971 to 1974 was US $500,000 and, therefore, no liability could attach to Home.

Fidelity & Casualty Insurance Company was cast in judgment for a dissolved insured, and settled with the plaintiffs before trial. Accordingly, the trial judge reduced the plaintiffs' award by a virile share attributable to Fidelity. However, the plaintiffs appealed! The trial court stated:

> "Although it is somewhat inconsistent with their argument that the jury properly found [the dissolved company] liable, [plaintiffs] argue that the record evidence indicates that [the injured plaintiff] was not exposed to products manufactured by [the dissolved company] during [the year in which Fidelity wrote coverage]."

Therefore, the plaintiffs argued that there should be no discount to their award on account of the Fidelity settlement. The trial court rejected this rather opportunistic argument.

As asbestos claims have proceeded, in addition to driving many manufacturers into bankruptcy, mounting claims have also begun to exhaust product liability aggregates in the manufacturers' CGL insurance policies. As a result, certain plaintiff attorneys have begun attempting to draft complaints alleging not strict product liability, but some form of ordinary negligence, thereby triggering the per occurrence limits of the non-products CGL coverage. Although some courts have expressed disfavor for such creative pleading, for example, in *LaFleur v. Hollier Floor Covering*,[43] other courts have seemed to countenance it, for example, *Rogers* v. *Johnson & Johnson Products, Inc.*[44]

This issue, which arises in the insurance context, brings one back to one of the basic starting points addressed in the introduction: the interplay between personal injury and products claims. Indeed, the theory behind recasting an asbestos claim as one for negligence, such as an improper failure to warn, can be applied to other dangerous products. What may, in fact, be seen will be complaints alleging both products and non-products claims. This will allow plaintiffs to advance strict liability and negligence claims and, at the same time, target both products and non-products CGL coverage, the

43 *LaFleur v. Hollier Floor Covering*, 774 So. 2d 359 (La. 3rd Cir. App. 2000). The court stated: "The plaintiffs' allegations include the failure to test and properly remove the asbestos containing sheet vinyl and non-compliance with state and federal regulations concerning the removal of asbestos containing sheet vinyl. [The insured] urges this court to conclude that these acts and omissions are outside the confines of the asbestos exclusion. We find no merit to the arguments presented by [the insured]. The petition alleges negligence in the handling of material containing asbestos fibers and damage resulting from the mishandling of that material. The characterization of several different acts of negligence is of no consequence because each act relates to the asbestos exposure and nothing else.".

44 *Rogers* v. *Johnson & Johnson Products, Inc.*, 523 Pa. 176, 565 A.2d 751 (1989). The court held: "Nor can we agree with the Superior Court's tacit conclusion that a plaintiff who has presented a malfunction case will always be precluded from proceeding on an alternate theory of negligence. It is altogether possible that a plaintiff's injuries could be caused jointly by a defective product and also by third party negligence so long as the negligence does not constitute a supervening cause of the malfunction. Given the occurrence of a malfunction, the [alleged] negligence assumes legal significance only if it was a superseding cause. . . . Questions of proximate causation should normally be left to the finder of fact." *See also Hartford Mutual Ins. Co.* v. *Moorhead*, 396 Pa. Super. 234 (1990), appeal denied 527 Pa. 617, 590 A.2d 757 (1991) (when a claim is brought under the auspices of a "negligent failure to warn", it is appropriate to view the complaint as one charging improper conduct, and not one of making a defective product, despite arguable similarities between such claims); *Pennsylvania National Mutual Cas. Ins. Co.* v. *Kaminski Lumber Co., Inc.*, 397 Pa. Super. 484 (1990) (rejecting insurer's contention that failure to warn claims are excluded from coverage because they are, "in essence", claims of product liability); *Devich* v. *Commercial Union Ins. Co.*, 867 F.Supp. 1230 (W.D.Pa. 1994) aff'd, 66 F.3d 310 (3d Cir. 1995) (interpreting *Moorhead* as standing for the proposition that an insurer must accept a claim as pled rather than attempting to justify its decision to deny coverage by attempting to re-characterize the claim within the terms of a policy exclusion).

latter, of course, offering the inviting prospect of per occurrence (non-aggregate) CGL insurance coverage.

Legislative Initiatives

Corporate defendants are far from sanguine about the prospects for litigation victories or insurance proceeds to insulate them from crushing liability exposures. Hence, they have turned in a concerted manner to an effort to resolve the matter via legislation.

Supported by former asbestos manufacturers, over the past two decades, six different United States Congressmen (Hart 1981, Fenwick 1981, Miller 1982/1983, Williams 1985, Brickman 1991 and Hyde 1999/2000) have proposed bills seeking to control the floodtide of asbestos litigation to protect the manufacturers from bankruptcy. In addition, there was the Asbestos Workers' Recovery Act proposal of 1984 to 1985, and the activity of two special select congressional committees, the Committee for Equitable Compensation and the Ad Hoc Committee on Asbestos Litigation. None of these efforts have come to legislative fruition.

Thus, in *Ortiz* v. *Fibreboard Corp.*,[45] the United State's highest court stated:

> "Like *Amchem Products, Inc.* v. *Windsor*, 521 U.S. 591, 138 L.Ed.2d 689, 117 S.Ct. 2231 (1997), this case is a class action prompted by the elephantine mass of asbestos cases, and our discussion in *Amchem* will suffice to show how this litigation defies customary judicial administration and calls for national legislation. To date Congress has not responded. In 1967, one of the first actions for personal asbestos injury was filed in the United States District Court for the Eastern District of Texas against a group of asbestos manufacturers. In the 1970s and 1980s, plaintiffs' lawyers throughout the country, particularly in East Texas, honed the litigation of asbestos claims to the point of almost mechanical regularity, improving the forensic identification of diseases caused by asbestos, refining theories of liability, and often settling large inventories of cases."

---

45 *Ortiz* v. *Fibreboard Corp.*, 527 U.S. 815, 119 S.Ct. 2295, 144 L.Ed.2d 715 (1999).

The most recent bill to be considered by the House of Representatives[46] was known as the Fairness in Asbestos Compensation Act. The legislation, sponsored by two well-known arch-conservative legislators, including the current Chairman of the House Judiciary Committee and the current United States Attorney General, contained a highly restrictive definition of an asbestos-related injury that, according to some analysts, would exclude two-thirds of pending cases. It would also have established a bureaucratic mechanism within the United States Department of Justice, partly funded with taxpayers' dollars, to adjudicate and pay the remaining claims. In 2000, the Judiciary Committee favorably reported the bill by a narrow margin of eighteen to fifteen, but it was opposed by the Department of Justice and died in the Senate.

Most recently pending in the United States House of Representatives was a bill[47] seeking to halt claimants who show no manifest asbestos disease or life-threatening effects of asbestos exposure from filing claims against bankrupt asbestos companies (the bill is an amendment to the United States Bankruptcy Code).[48] The sponsor of this bill, a Republican Utah congressman named Christopher Cannon, is also working with a group called the Asbestos Alliance on drafting yet another piece of major asbestos legislation. The group's website[49] states the current status of the legislation: "The Asbestos Alliance is currently discussing our proposed legislative solution to the asbestos litigation crisis with Members of Congress." The site states that the proposal would:

(1) Establish objective medical criteria for asbestos-related impairment;
(2) Liberalize statutes of limitations and other technical rules to remove the incentive for premature filings;
(3) Eliminate the consolidations that create "bet-the-company" situations, which lead to shotgun settlements with thousands of people who are not sick; and
(4) Eliminate abusive forum shopping, which today concentrates thousands of claims in jurisdictions that have no connection whatever with those claims.

---

46 H.R. 1283.

47 H.R. 4696.

48 Currently, forty-four other bills are pending in the United States Congress that touch in some way on asbestos, including the Ban Asbestos in America Act, which is self-explanatory.

49 www.asbestossolution.org.

The Asbestos Alliance is a subgroup of the National Association of Manufacturers, which describes itself as follows:

> "The National Association of Manufacturers — 18-million people who make things in America — is the nation's largest industrial trade association. The NAM represents 14,000 members (including 10,000 small and mid-sized companies) and 350 member associations serving manufacturers and employees in every industrial sector and all 50 states. Headquartered in Washington, DC, the NAM has 10 additional offices across the country."

Several insurance companies are also apparently supporting the bill, though with little publicity so far. The Cannon Bill, potentially the seventh in a long line of failures, may or may not be introduced for consideration in the near future. The Utah Congressman is currently seeking co-sponsors to support the legislation and is not releasing any draft. The plaintiffs' bar will undoubtedly produce stiff opposition to any bill that is ultimately proposed and seems to have a perfect batting average so far.

Toxic Mold: the "New Asbestos"

Contours of the Catastrophe

Mold litigation is exploding in the United States, and some hopeful plaintiff attorneys have labeled it "the new asbestos". Mold growths form on certain types of construction materials when they become moist due to improper water seals. Recently, scientific evidence demonstrated that some mold growths can be hazardous to human health, and a deluge of negligence suits followed. These actions roughly parallel the wider phenomenon of "sick building syndrome", which results when modern office buildings, hermetically sealed, lack proper ventilation systems so that microbes and out-gassing chemicals cannot escape and form an allegedly toxic brew. In June 2001, a Texas jury awarded US $32-million to a family for damage to their home allegedly caused by mold.[50]

The most important reporter on insurance law in the United States is *Insurance Pleadings*, produced by the LEXIS/NEXIS subsidiary

50 *Ballard* v. *Fire Ins. Exchange*, Number 99-05252, Tex. Dist. Ct. Travis County.

Mealey's.[51] Mealey's now devotes an entire separate paid specialty publication to the burgeoning area of toxic mold litigation. Already, these cases are cutting a broad swath across the legal landscape due to plaintiff creativity, which may have wide-ranging permutations. Thus, for example, in *Segal* v. *State Farm Ins. Co.*,[52] an insured brought an action against her homeowner's carrier alleging that, as a result of the company's negligent failure to properly handle her claim for water damage to her home, toxic molds were allowed to propagate, giving rise to an additional claim for personal injuries, including liver failure. The trial court dismissed the case for failure to prosecute because the plaintiff was having difficulty lining up expert medical testimony to establish causation, but the appellate panel reversed, finding that the delay was due only to attorney error, which could have been addressed through sanctions rather than dismissal.

The American mass media is full of horror stories about the dangers of mold contamination. As just one example, *Time* magazine ran a major mold piece on 24 June 2001, among other things, attributing a woman's breast cancer to the mold infestation of her US $300,000 home. Those seeking legal representation for mold-related issues do not have far to travel on the Internet. A website called www.moldlawyer.com provides a handy directory of plaintiff mold counsel for each of the fifty states, with nearly a hundred listings in New York State alone. The site also offers links to mold experts and removal contractors, as well as information about self-testing by homeowners. Another such site is www.injuryboard.com, which does not limit itself to toxic mold, but rather purports to offer educational materials (and lawyer referrals) regarding a whole host of potential personal injury causes of action.

Recent Litigation

Rivera v. *Phipps Houses Services*[53] provides a good case study of American federalism and plaintiff creativity at work in the context of toxic mold infestation. There, tenants sued their landlord for failing to correct water penetration problems that led to the growth of toxic

51 www.mealeys.com.

52 *Segal* v. *State Farm Ins. Co.*, 2001 Cal. App. LEXIS 1475 (2nd App. Dist. 25 October 2001).

53 *Rivera* v. *Phipps Houses Services*, 2001 U.S. Dist. LEXIS 8939 (S.D.N.Y. 29 June 2001).

molds. The plaintiffs sought to proceed in federal rather than state court, but lacked diversity of citizenship between the parties or any specific federal cause of action. Instead, the plaintiffs asserted that, since federal housing standards (for example, pertaining to bans on racial discrimination) had been incorporated into the tenants' leases, and since those leases had been drafted in connection with federally subsidized housing programs, the federal court should agree to hear the plaintiffs' state-law based breach of contract claims. However, the *Rivera* court refused to do so, holding that there was no private right of action under any of the applicable federal standards, and it deferred to the state forum since landlord-tenant law is traditionally a matter for state courts.

The Supreme Court of Delaware recently upheld a cause of action for mold contamination in *New Haverford Partnership* v. *Stroot.*[54] There, a jury awarded the plaintiff US $1-million for personal injuries and US $5,000 for property damage when a landlord failed to repair leaks which gave rise to mold propagation. This award was reduced by twenty-two per cent for the jury's allocation of contributory negligence to the plaintiff. The plaintiff "suffered frequent headaches, sinus problems, chest pains and body aches", as well as the aggravation of her sinus and asthma conditions. The plaintiff produced expert testimony concerning causation and damage. According to the court:

> "Plaintiffs offered the opinions of several experts to support their claims. Dr. Yang, a mycologist and microbiologist, inspected Haverford Place, took bulk samples and air samples, and interviewed residents. He opined that there was excessive and atypical mold growth in the apartment buildings; that it was caused by long term leaks; and that the widespread mold contamination posed a health risk to tenants. Dr. Johanning, a physician board-certified in environmental and occupational medicine, gathered similar data at Haverford Place. He also took blood samples from plaintiffs. Based on his analysis of this data, Johanning opined that the high concentration of toxic mold at Haverford Place significantly and permanently increased the severity of Stroot's asthma. He also opined that Stroot's cognitive deficits, diagnosed by Dr. Gordon, were caused by exposure to

54 *New Haverford Partnership* v. *Stroot*, 772 A.2d 792 (Del. 2001).

> excessive and atypical molds. Johanning testified that Watson developed an allergy to Penicillium and permanent upper respiratory problems as a result of her exposure to the same molds. Dr. Gordon, a neuropsychologist who has studied cognitive defects associated with exposure to atypical molds, evaluated Stroot and concluded that she suffers from significant cognitive impairment in the areas of attention, concentration, memory and executive functions. Gordon opined that these problems are permanent and were proximately caused by Stroot's exposure to atypical molds. Dr. Rose, a physician who is board-certified in pulmonary, occupational and environmental medicine, examined Stroot and opined that Stroot developed osteopenia as a result of her increased steroid usage while at Haverford Place. Dr. Rose also opined that Stroot's steroid usage increased her risk of developing tuberculosis."

The landlord defendant challenged the sufficiency of this evidence. The court stated:

> "Landlord argues that the opinions of plaintiffs' experts were deficient in several respects: i) Lynn is not a property manager and is not familiar with the standard of care in Delaware; ii) Gordon did not scientifically eliminate other possible causes of Stroot's cognitive deficits; iii) neither Lynn, Yang, or Johanning took air pressure readings or otherwise determined the air flow within the apartment; iv) none of the experts had a scientific basis on which to conclude that the excessive mold found in 1994 also was present in 1992; and v) none of the experts had a proper foundation on which to base an opinion on causation. In addition, landlord complains that evidence of mold in two apartments not inhabited by plaintiffs was prejudicial and not scientifically connected to the mold levels in plaintiffs' apartments. Finally, landlord contends that the trial court abused its discretion in refusing to order the production of Stroot's psychiatric records."

Although the landlord sought to exclude the plaintiff's expert testimony from the jury's consideration, he was not successful.

Stroot highlights that, because this is a new field, the science is not well settled; compelling scientific studies usually require years of evidence-gathering before receiving the seal of approval from recognized authorities. In the case of mold, there have been no long-term group studies and much evidence is anecdotal. Mold can propagate in virtually any moist environment, giving rise to the possibility of a wide cross-section of suits in both commercial and residential settings and concerning both new and old buildings. However, as illustrated by *Stroot*, the most common cases involve apartment buildings. Even here, however, the range of potential defendant insureds is broad and may include architects, realtors, owners, management companies, contractors, city inspectors and homeowner associations.

Centex-Rooney Construction Co. v. *Martin County*[55] involved a US $14-million judgment against a construction manager for a county courthouse project, and the manager's sureties.[56] Following completion of the construction, water leaks and mold growth were discovered. Several employees were diagnosed with work-related asthma, and thereafter the County filed suit against several defendants, including Centex, the sureties, the project architect and the concrete and masonry construction company, for breach of contract and negligence, alleging improper design and construction. The appellate panel noted that: "Centex claims that the scientific principle underlying Dr. Morey's and Dr. Hodgson's expert testimony, studies linking exposure to the toxic molds found in the buildings with health risks, was not generally accepted in the scientific community". However, the court nonetheless affirmed the jury verdict because "Dr. Morey and Dr. Hodgson each testified about numerous publications accepted in the scientific community recognizing the link between exposure to the highly unusual toxigenic molds and adverse health effects".

If a large multi-story apartment building is contaminated with toxic mold, a plethora of lawsuits may result. A plaintiff who is not a citizen of the United States, or who is suing an out-of-state defendant, may choose to bring his case in either federal or state court. Groups of plaintiffs may join together under the aegis of a single attorney, or there may be a multitude of individual suits. Alternatively, plaintiffs may seek class certification. Even if many lawsuits

---

55 *Centex-Rooney Construction Co.* v. *Martin County*, 706 So. 2d 20 (4th Dist. Fla. App. 1997).

56 The sureties were Seaboard Surety Company, St. Paul Fire & Marine Insurance Company and American Insurance Company.

proceed separately, the plaintiffs' bar may be organized and sharing documents, expert witnesses and strategies.

In defending toxic mold cases, there are many important considerations. First, remediation is highly complex and expensive. In *Centex-Rooney*, for example, the court noted:

> "Because health complaints continued, the County retained Dr. Morey, another expert in indoor air quality, for a second opinion on the courthouse's and office building's indoor air quality issues. The results of Dr. Morey's air and bulk sample testing in the buildings indicated a significant presence of two highly unusual and toxigenic molds. He reported the presence of these molds to the advisory committee and recommended that the County obtain a medical opinion to advise the building's occupants about the potential risks associated with the molds. When Dr. Morey's follow-up testing revealed the same results, he advised the County to remove the moldy ceiling tiles, wallboards, carpet, and other moldy material from the buildings, using hazardous waste disposal techniques."

Second, experts are few and, therefore, also expensive. Third, cases dealing with new, complex issues and long tail injuries with a multitude of plaintiffs are difficult and time-consuming to try. Accordingly, companies need to prepare in advance to meet the challenges posed by such cases, organizing, investigating, creating banks of "corporate knowledge" and preparing to manage the actual litigation at every phase.

Closely related to and indeed the underpinning for toxic mold litigation is the "sick building" syndrome. This doctrine was turned ironically against the courts themselves in *Schmidt* v. *County of Norfolk*,[57] where the county courthouse, which housed a probate and family court, was ninety-nine years old, with additions of between fifty and twenty-seven years old. The plaintiffs contended that the condition and layout of the courthouse interfered with the public's right to obtain justice and impeded the employees in performing their jobs. The defendants admitted problems, including overcrowding, security issues, fire code violations and health concerns, including

57 *Schmidt* v. *County of Norfolk*, 2002 Mass. Super. LEXIS 327 (Sup. Ct. 15 August 2002).

the lack of ventilation. After a bench trial in which both sides presented expert testimony, the court found that a serious health hazard was posed to the employees and the public by the lack of ventilation in the original part of the courthouse. Moreover, mold litigation against a courthouse in Polk County Florida resulted in a jury verdict of over US $25-million against Reliance Insurance Company. A similar action was filed against the courthouse in DuPage County, Illinois.

Other recent awards of note include the following:

(1) A homeowner settled a mold-related bad faith lawsuit against his insurer, during trial, for US $1.5-million;[58]

(2) A homeowners' group settled, for US $1.3-million, toxic mold claims against builders and contractors;[59] and

(3) A federal jury in California awarded US $18-million — all but US $500,000 of that amount in punitive damages — to a homeowner against an insurer that declined coverage for mold damage, but the trial judge reduced the award to US $3-million and the case is on appeal.[60]

Whether toxic mold litigation proves to be the next asbestos is still, however, an open question.

Lead Paint

Contours of the Catastrophe

In recent years, a body of scientific evidence has shown that children who eat lead paint chips, and even children who merely spend time in rooms containing decaying lead paint dust which they breathe, develop learning disabilities and even serious motor-neural diseases.

---

58 *Blum* v. *Chubb Custom Insurance Co.*, Number 99–3563 (Nueces Co., Texas, Dist. Ct.).

59 *Club at Wood Ranch* v. *Roberts Group*, Number 21522 (Ventura Co., Cal., Super. Ct.).

60 *Anderson* v. *Allstate Insurance Co.*, Number 0-907 (E.D. Cal.). Lastly, mold cases also raise some interesting insurance issues. Generally speaking, mold exclusions have been upheld and, in fact, in *Cooper* v. *American Family Mutual Ins. Co.*, Number CV-00-1097, Mealey's 9 April 2002 (D.Az.), not only did the carrier prevail in a coverage action for mold damages on the basis of an exclusion, but it then moved to recover attorneys' fees from the insured in the amount of US $15,657 on the basis that the attempt to seek such coverage by the insured (who had been reimbursed for water damage to drywall and flooring caused by water but not additional damage caused by mold) was frivolous.

These cases differ from asbestos or toxic mold claims in that they are not "latent" or "long tail" injuries which reveal themselves only many years in the future in the form, especially, of cancer. Rather, blood levels of lead can be shown to be elevated almost instantly on exposure, and some experts are prepared to predict permanent brain damage on that basis alone. This litigation has not initially focused on the manufacturers of lead paint, as in asbestos, but rather on the owners of the buildings where the paint is present, more similar to the mold scenario. However, like asbestos and unlike mold, lead paint cases focus on buildings constructed a long time ago, lead paint having been eliminated from new construction as asbestos has been. Mold, on the other hand, is particularly prevalent in modern construction, as drywall materials are highly susceptible, and can occur in any construction where there is water penetration.

General Accident Insurance Company v. *Idbar Realty Corp.*[61] illustrates key differences between a lead paint injury and an asbestos injury. In *Idbar Realty*, the court faced the question of whether lead paint poisoning diagnosed in 1984 could be covered under insurance policies issued in 1987. The court rejected the contention that New York had adopted an "injury in fact test for prolonged exposure situations" in cases that did not involve latent injuries, such as asbestosis. It said that lead paint poisoning was not a "latent" injury similar to asbestosis, but rather could manifest itself shortly after ingestion began. Furthermore, the court held that, under New York law, an "injury in fact" could occur in more than one policy period, and noted that there was evidence that the lead paint injury increases in severity as more paint is ingested. Thus, the court said, if there are "separate onsets, aggravations, increases in severity, increases in persistence or manifestations of symptomatology", then each affected policy would be triggered, citing generally various authorities, but no reported cases from New York (the court did note one Kings County Supreme Court case, unreported). On appeal, the ruling was modified.

The Second Department held that "because it cannot be determined on the record before this court whether any injury occurred during the effective dates of the subject insurance policies, the declaration that General Accident had duty to indemnify the

61 *General Accident Insurance Company* v. *Idbar Realty Corp.*, 163 Misc. 2d 809, 622 N.Y.S. 2d 417 (Suffolk Cnty. 1994).

defendants-landlords was premature".[62] In *U.S. Liability Ins. Co.* v. *Farley*, the insurer "failed to present proof that [the affected] children did not suffer additional bodily injuries during the policy period" and the court, therefore, held the insurer to its duty to defend, clearly implying that had the insurer been able to prove the absence of additional bodily injury during the policy period, it would have been able to avoid its duty to defend. Farley cited only non-lead paint cases (including, ironically, an asbestos case) to support its holding, a good indication that authority on point in this area is relatively sparse.[63]

Just as with toxic mold, the World Wide Web abounds in specialized sites designed to help potential plaintiffs identify liability issues and locate counsel. For example, there is a large and elaborate site at www.leadpoisoninginfocenter.com, where potential clients can "learn more about legal rights from a lead poisoning lawyer". Likewise, the broader injury lawyer network contains www.injury-lawyer-network.com/lead-paint-poisoning.htm, a specialized page for lead claims, and a host of consultants and abatement contractors are but a mouse click away.

As with asbestos, the news on lead paint is not entirely bleak. As noted above, the initial target of lead paint suits were the landlords who owned the contaminated buildings. However, as it became apparent that many of these defendants were without the wherewithal (or insurance) to fully pay compensation, or where the owner was a government entity, a spate of suits against the manufacturers has erupted, with governments in the State of Rhode Island and the cities of Milwaukee and Chicago, among many others, filing civil complaints seeking reimbursement for expensive lead paint remediation efforts. However, the lead paint industry has so far never lost or settled one of these actions. The key problem for the plaintiffs lies in identifying which of the numerous corporations that previously manufactured lead paint produced the specific product that harmed the

62 *General Accident Insurance Company* v. *Idbar Realty Corp.*, 229 AD 2d 515, 646 N.Y.S. 2d 138 (2nd Dept. 1996), citing the intervening *U.S. Liability Ins. Co.* v. *Farley*, 215 A.D.2d 371, 626 N.Y.S. 2d 238 (2nd Dept. 1995).

63 Further evidence, if any is needed, of the dearth of authority may be gleaned from *U.S. Liability Ins. Co.* v. *Selman*, 70 F.3d 684 note 6 (1st Cir. 1995), where the federal court, applying Massachusetts law, could cite only *Farley* and *Idbar Realty* for the view that "courts have found in similar cases that each ingestion of lead paint leads to a discrete injury". Thus, it appears not only that New York authority is rather sparse, but that New York is relatively rich in authority compared to other jurisdictions.

claimants at issue. Although some work is now underway to classify all lead paints based on chemical composition and attribute them to specific manufacturers, plaintiffs' first attempt to deal with this burden was to avoid it entirely, by arguing for a "market share theory" of liability, under which each manufacturer would pay that portion of a judgment that its product sales bore in relation to the lead paint market.

Recent Litigation

In *Jackson* v. *Chetram*,[64] parents won a jury verdict on behalf of their child against the owner of their residential building, which they alleged had poisoned the child through poorly maintained lead paint. The jury found that they sustained damage in the amount of US $3,390,000 (US $1,600,000 for future loss of earnings, US $500,000 for past pain and suffering, US $1,125,000 for future pain and suffering and US $165,000 for future medical costs), and the defendant sought remittitur. The trial court granted those branches of the defendant's motion which were to set aside the verdict as against the weight of the evidence as to future loss of earnings and future medical costs, and to reduce the verdict as to damages awarded for past pain and suffering and future pain and suffering, as excessive to the extent of directing a new trial on these issues, unless the plaintiffs stipulated to reduce the verdict as to past pain and suffering from US $500,000 to US $150,000 and, as to future pain and suffering, from US $1,125,000 to US $500,000, and to the entry of an amended judgment in the principal sum of US $650,000. The plaintiffs appealed, but the appeals panel affirmed. It stated:

> "The Supreme Court properly set aside the award for future loss of earnings as the calculation by the plaintiffs' expert was based on the speculative premise that the infant plaintiff would only obtain a ninth-grade education. Opinion evidence must be based on facts in the record or personally known to the witness. The infant plaintiff, who was in the fifth grade at the time of the trial, had never been left back a grade and had tested above her grade level in reading. The plaintiffs' own expert testified that a child who is capable of reading at his or her proper grade level is able to graduate

64 *Jackson* v. *Chetram*, 751 N.Y.S.2d 551 (2nd Dept. 2002).

> from high school. In the absence of evidence to support the expert's underlying assumption that the infant plaintiff would only obtain a ninth-grade education, his opinion as to future loss of earnings was of no probative value."

This result can be contrasted with *McIntyre* v. *Phila. Hous. Auth.*,[65] where the jury awarded US $250,000 in a suit brought by the grandparents of a child injured by lead paint exposure (US $125,000 each was awarded on negligence and breach of implied warranty of habitability claims). The defendant landlord alleged that a breach of warranty claim could not be countenanced in addition to a separate tort claim, and the appellate panel agreed, holding that, to rule otherwise, would result in a "complete erosion" of the distinction between tort and contract actions. Since there was only one kind of damages, the net effect would be to award tort damages in a contract action.

Pennsylvania's highest court recently handed down an important decision on lead paint insurance issues. In *Lititz Mut. Ins. Co.* v. *Steely*,[66] the trial court held that the insurer had a duty to defend a lead paint injury case notwithstanding a general pollution exclusion, but the appellate panel reversed, finding that lead paint was unambiguously a "pollutant" within the meaning of the exclusion. The Supreme Court reversed again and upheld the duty to defend, stating that "it appears that of those jurisdictions that have decided the issue, a majority have found that the pollution exclusion clause does not bar coverage" (citing New Jersey, Connecticut, New York and law review authority). The court agreed that "the definition of 'pollutant' unambiguously encompasses lead-based paint", but it found that the question of "discharge or dispersal" of a pollutant was more complicated. The court focused on the fact that the deterioration of lead paint is gradual, and concluded that the "natural, plain and ordinary meaning" of discharge was limited to sudden and immediate events, or at least gave rise to ambiguity to be construed against the insurer.

Insurers scored a victory on the same issue, however, in *Hale* v. *American Family Mut. Ins. Co.*,[67] further illustrating the significance of federalism, though the case has yet to reach the highest court. In *Hale*, the court held that a general pollution exclusion clause barred a lead paint claim. Summary judgment to the carrier was affirmed on

65 *McIntyre* v. *Phila. Hous. Auth.*, 2003 Pa. Commw. LEXIS 16 (8 January 2003).
66 *Lititz Mut. Ins. Co.* v. *Steely*, 785 A.2d 975 (Pa. 2001).
67 *Hale* v. *American Family Mut. Ins. Co.*, 639 N.W.2d 802 (Ct. App. Wisc. 2001).

appeal. The court stated that "lead paint chips, flakes and dust are widely, if not universally, understood to be dangerous and capable of producing lead poisoning; thus, a reasonable landlord understands that lead is a pollutant". Even though there was evidence of internal insurer communications to the contrary, the court held those to be "immaterial" to the question. The court held that, if the child herself had removed the paint chips from the wall, there might not have been a "release" as required under the pollution exclusion clause but, since she picked up the chips from the floor, a "release" had occurred.

On 29 October 2002, the first municipal action against the lead paint industry (by the State of Rhode Island) ended in a mistrial when the jury became hopelessly deadlocked over the question of whether lead paint was a "nuisance" in their state. Some members of the jury were convinced that it was landlords, not manufacturers, who were responsible for incidents of lead paint poisoning because it was their lack of maintenance that exposed the victims. Other members believed that, since there was overwhelming evidence that the lead paint industry knew full well about the potential health hazards of their product many years before they ceased manufacturing it, they should be held accountable for the problem. Currently, the case is enmeshed in post-trial motion practice and there may well be a second trial on the merits.

The Rhode Island matter began with the filing of an omnibus complaint setting forth a smorgasbord of claims; pre-trial motion practice then whittled this list down to the single charge of "nuisance", and the trial was bifurcated. In the first phase, a jury was to decide whether lead paint was or was not a "nuisance" in Rhode Island. If the answer was affirmative, a second trial was to address the damage that had accrued and the compensation to be paid, and by which lead paint companies, several having been sued along with the industry trade association. The plaintiff was represented at trial by both the Attorney General of the State of Rhode Island (an elected official who had made the case part of his political platform) and private counsel.

At the eleventh hour before trial, the defendants sought to derail the case by filing motions with the United States and Rhode Island Supreme Courts, but were rebuffed. The case then moved before the jury in the first week of September 2002, and the plaintiff called a litany of scientific experts, including medical doctors, to testify as to the hazards of lead paint. During the week, the City of Chicago announced that it, too, would file a lead paint lawsuit, and the Attorney

General was defeated in primary elections in his bid to become the state's next governor. During the second week, this testimony from the plaintiff continued, and the jury had to be partially sequestered as political rallies against the lead paint industry were held around the courthouse, including a display of children's shoes to mark each allegedly poisoned child.

In the third week, the defense scored a victory on cross-examination when a key plaintiff witness admitted that Rhode Island public health laws do not require the removal of lead paint from buildings, only treatment. In the fourth week, a second victory was won by the lead defendants as they successfully precluded reference by witnesses to any evidence of incidents of lead poisoning from the first phase of trial. The State then rested its case and the defense moved, unsuccessfully, to dismiss. It then called surprisingly few witnesses of its own and rested its case, apparently confident of its prospects and wishing to send a message of invulnerability to the plaintiff bar across the country. Indeed, the defense began its assault by asserting that blood sampling methodology was defective in Rhode Island (using finger pricks instead of venous withdrawals) and, therefore, sought to discount the data. Here, the defense failed to convince the judge. The defense was no doubt unpleasantly surprised, therefore, when the jury returned after its deliberations and announced that it was hopelessly deadlocked. For the first time, a plaintiff was able to convince at least a few jurors that the lead industry, not landlords, should be held responsible for lead paint contamination.

Chemical Contamination

Contours of the Catastrophe

In 1980, the United States Government enacted the Comprehensive Environmental Response Cleanup and Liability Act (CERCLA), which provides for strict liability of owners for properties contaminated by hazardous chemicals, and establishes a private right of action supported by an award of attorneys' fees to the prevailing plaintiff. Ever since then, an era of aggressive personal injury and property damage litigation (and not only or even mostly under the aegis of CERCLA, but also under state Common Law) has begun. Hundreds of waste sites across the country have been named on the federal government's National Priorities List, and thousands of civil lawsuits have been filed against these and other facilities.

Recent Litigation

International Issues The potential scope of environmental claims was evident in *Flores* v. *Southern Peru Copper Corp.*[68] In that case, the plaintiffs, residents of Ilo, Peru, sued a Peruvian company in New York to take advantage of propitious United States environmental tort law, alleging jurisdiction under the Alien Tort Claims Act (ATCA).[69] They alleged that the defendant's mining and refinery operations produced toxic chemicals that migrated off-site and caused asthma and lung disease. The court dismissed the case for lack of subject matter jurisdiction, holding that the ATCA requires a showing of "harm to human life, health and development" that violates "well-established, universally recognized norms of international law".

The ATCA was originally enacted in 1789 and was rarely ever invoked for the first two centuries of its existence; but, then, enter the creative plaintiffs' bar of the last two decades. It began with a ruling in New York's Second Circuit in 1980 that allowed the ATCA to be invoked to combat a case of torture, and this opened the floodgates. Soon after, courts began identifying other similar acts offensive to the international conscience, which could support jurisdiction in United States federal courts under the ATCA. The court in *Flores* recognized that the ATCA could be the basis for an international environmental claim — a case involving oil exploration-related pollution in Ecuador is currently on appeal to the Second Circuit, and a similar case in Texas had found subject matter jurisdiction, but then dismissed on grounds of *forum non conveniens*.

Complex Statute of Limitations Issues Special rules have been developed in environmental cases to save plaintiffs from the ill-effects of statutes of limitations. In *Town of Sturbridge* v. *Mobil Corporation*,[70] a municipality sued a gasoline company for polluting the local drinking wells. The defendant argued that the applicable three-year statute of limitations barred the claim. As to property damage claims the court agreed, but as to negligence claims it did not. It stated that the "discovery rule" for chemical contamination would operate to toll the statute of limitations for personal injury claims "until the plaintiff

---

68 *Flores* v. *Southern Peru Copper Corp.*, 2002 U.S. Dist. LEXIS 13013 (S.D.N.Y. 16 July 2002).

69 28 U.S.C.S. Sections 1331 and 1350.

70 *Town of Sturbridge* v. *Mobil Corporation*, 195 F.Supp. 2d 330 (D. Mass. 2002).

knows or reasonably should have known that it had been harmed by the defendant's conduct". In other words, the plaintiff knew about the presence of chemicals, and this knowledge was sufficient to trigger the statute of limitations for property damage, since it was the presence itself (that is, the pollution) which caused the harm. However, the court held that there was a genuine issue of material fact as to what the plaintiff knew about potential personal injury resulting from the contamination, such that the issue had to be passed on to plenary trial.

In *Freier* v. *Westinghouse Electric Corporation*,[71] a statute of limitations issue also arose. *Freier* involved the leaching of toxic substances from a landfill in Cheektowaga, New York, and the same "triable issues of fact" conclusion was reached, reversing the district court's ruling to the contrary. The plaintiffs sued various companies that delivered waste materials to the landfill, alleging that various cancers had resulted from exposure to the material. New York has a specific statute of limitations applicable to injuries resulting from exposure to toxic substances (other than wrongful death and survivorship claims), which provides a three-year period that begins to run when the injury was discovered, or reasonably should have been discovered, or one year after the discovery of the injury's cause if that occurs up to five years after the discovery of injury.

However, to extend the period beyond three years, the plaintiff must show scientific or medical evidence "sufficient to ascertain the cause of his injury had not been discovered, identified or determined within the three-year period". CERCLA, on the other hand, provides a uniform standard for determining the accrual dates of claims of personal injury and establishes a "federally required commencement date" to start the running of the applicable statute of limitations period, which date is defined as "the date plaintiff knew or reasonably should have known that the personal injury or property damages were caused or contributed to by the hazardous substance or pollutant or contaminant concerned". The court then held that, although the plaintiffs' wrongful death and survivor claims would have been barred under state law (because wrongful death claims must be brought two years from the date of death and survivor claims three years from the date of injury), they were saved by CERCLA pre-emption of the state statute applicable to such claims. In essence, the court held that CERCLA's provisions meant that New York law had to apply the

71 *Freier* v. *Westinghouse Electric Corporation*, 303 F.3d 176 (2nd Cir. 2002).

same statute of limitations methodology to wrongful death claims as it did to first party personal injury tort claims, as specified above.

The defendants had challenged this pre-emption as unconstitutional, that is, arguing that the federal government lacked the power to instruct states about their statutes of limitations, but the court upheld it under the Commerce Clause, that is, the provision of the federal Constitution authorizing the federal government to regulate interstate commerce. Defendants then argued that media and government reports on site contamination were sufficient to give plaintiffs a "reasonable suspicion" of danger such that claims should have been filed earlier, and the district court embraced this view, but the appellate panel rejected it and held that there was merely a factual dispute for plenary trial.

In *Lessord* v. *GE*,[72] landowners complaining of contamination argued that their action was timely under N.Y. C.P.L.R. Section 214-c(2) because the evidence showed that, regardless of when the landowners' property first became contaminated, they did not have knowledge of such contamination until less than two years before they filed the complaint. Under N.Y. C.P.L.R. Section 214-c(4), the landowners claimed that their action was timely because they did not know that the cause of the contamination of the stream on their property was storm water runoff from one of the manufacturing sites until investigations were conducted by the State. There was some evidentiary support for the landowners' allegations that they were unaware of the contamination in the stream until 1999, and that it was not until 2000 at the earliest that there was solid evidence as to which manufacturing site was a possible source of that contamination. Consequently, the court concluded that issues of fact existed concerning when the landowners discovered, or reasonably should have discovered, both the injury at issue in their claims against the two manufacturers that moved to dismiss, and the cause of that injury.

Class Action Issues One of the most formidable plaintiff weapons in chemical contamination cases is the use of a class action. Once a class is certified by a court, a cash settlement almost always results, since the risks of proceeding to trial against so many plaintiffs can be catastrophic. In *In re MTBE Product Liability Litigation*,[73] the court

72 *Lessord* v. *GE*, 2002 U.S. Dist. LEXIS 24839 (W.D.N.Y. 2002).
73 *In re MTBE Product Liability Litigation*, 209 F.R.D. 323 (S.D.N.Y. 2002).

refused to certify a class alleging contamination of their well water via gasoline and, specifically, the known carcinogen methyl tertiary butyl ether (MTBE). When gasoline is spilled, the chemical properties of MTBE cause it to separate from the other components of the liquid and to travel through soil further and faster than any of those components. There are four key elements of a successful class certification:

(1) Numerosity, that is, there are so many affected persons that having each one sue individually is impracticable;
(2) Commonality, that is, all the affected are seeking to invoke the same legal principles to vindicate their claims;
(3) Ascertainability, that is, the full membership of the class can be determined by applying objective criteria; and
(4) Typicality, that is, all the affected persons have suffered the same type of injury.

The court held that the proposed class failed to satisfy the typicality requirement (though it satisfied each of the other three) because various different causes had lead to gasoline leakages and because some of the plaintiffs could identify a specific gas station responsible for the leakage while others could not, and would seek to rely on the "market share" theory of liability to apportion damages. Further, some of the proposed class members had personal injury claims, while others sought only injunctive relief.

Regulatory Statutes The ability to defend against a CERCLA claim was probed in *United States* v. *Domenic Lombardi Realty, Inc.*,[74] where the realtor's motion presented the following issues:

(1) Whether CERCLA was a constitutional congressional enactment under the Commerce Clause;[75]
(2) Whether the presence of contaminated soil on the property involved constituted a "release" or "threatened release" as defined in CERCLA; and
(3) Whether the realtor may properly avail itself of the protection afforded by CERCLA's "innocent landowner" defense.[76]

---

74 *United States* v. *Domenic Lombardi Realty, Inc.*, 204 F.Supp. 2d 318 (DRI 2002).

75 United States Constitution, Article I, Section 8, Clauses 1 and 3.

76 42 U.S.C.S. Section 9601(35)(B).

The district court adopted the report and recommendation of the magistrate insofar as the magistrate concluded that CERCLA was a constitutional enactment under the Commerce Clause and that the presence of PCB-contaminated soil on the property constituted a "release" as defined by CERCLA, but declined to adopt the magistrate's suggestion to grant EPA's motion for summary judgment because there remained disputed issues of material fact regarding whether the innocent landowner defense afforded defendant protection from CERCLA liability. The district court reasoned that the defendant must be given an opportunity to develop its innocent landowner defense at trial and that only partial summary judgment was appropriate.

The federal government was hoist with its own petard in *Hoery* v. *United States*,[77] where the questions were:

(1) Whether the continued migration of toxic chemicals from defendant United States' property to the plaintiff property owner's land, allegedly caused by chemical releases by the United States, constituted continuing trespass and or nuisance under Colorado law; and
(2) Whether the ongoing presence of those toxic chemicals on the owner's property constituted continuing trespass and or nuisance under Colorado law.

The owner brought suit under the Federal Tort Claims Act (FTCA) against the United States, asserting claims for, *inter alia*, continuing trespass and nuisance. The owner claimed that the United States negligently released toxic chemicals from a military base into the ground, which contaminated his nearby residential property. The court held that the alleged migration and ongoing presence of toxic chemicals on the owner's property each constituted a continuing trespass and nuisance under Colorado law. The alleged tortious conduct of the United States included its failure to abate and to remove the toxic chemicals it placed beneath the owner's property. This tortious conduct was not limited to the initial release of the chemicals from the base.

---

77 *Hoery* v. *United States*, 2003 Colo. LEXIS 116 (Co. 2003).

Jurisdiction In *Plaza Speedway, Inc.* v. *United States*,[78] the speedway, which was located next to an army base, sued the army in 1997 alleging that the army had contaminated the speedway's groundwater and soil through the use of jet fuels and chemicals on the base. The speedway had filed an administrative claim on 13 October 1995, which the army failed to address. The army contended that the district court lacked subject matter jurisdiction over the speedway's action because it filed its administrative claim outside the FTCA's two-year statute of limitations. On appeal of the district court's judgment and award for the speedway, the Tenth Circuit held that the district court failed to take several facts into consideration that led to the conclusion that when the speedway was notified, on 23 August 1993, of the presence of contaminants in its well, it had reason to suspect the source might have been the army's property. These facts included the speedway's knowledge that its property was tested in 1993, that it knew the army used jet fuel, solvents and chemicals, and that the speedway's only neighbor was the army. Therefore, the judgment for the speedway was reversed and the case was remanded with instructions to dismiss for lack of subject matter jurisdiction.

Conclusion

This chapter has highlighted what many believe to be the increasingly "out of control" nature of American personal injury law. Since this development is the natural outgrowth of the judicial system itself, as well as the country's socio-political environment, unfortunately for both corporate America and the American consumers who ultimately bear the costs of litigation outrages, efforts to reform the system have so far met with very little success. Any meaningful solution must come from the political arena, since the problems are entrenched within the social fabric and innate to American jurisprudence.

78 *Plaza Speedway, Inc.* v. *United States*, 311 F.3d 1262 (10th Cir. 2002).

Air Carriers' Liability for Passenger Injuries Resulting from Hijackings

D. Bradley Kizzia
Strasburger & Price, LLP
Dallas, Texas, United States

Introduction

11 September 2001 is a day no one will soon forget. This horrific day started at 8:48 a.m. when American Airlines flight 11, a Boeing 767, crashed into the north tower of the World Trade Center in New York City.[1] Eighteen minutes later, at 9:06 a.m., United Airlines flight 175 crashed into the south tower of the World Trade Center. Thirty-seven minutes later, at 9:43 a.m., American Airlines flight 77 crashed into the west side of the Pentagon.[2] Finally, at 10:37 a.m., United Airlines flight 93 crashed eighty miles southwest of Pittsburgh, Pennsylvania. The four hijackings rank as the "worst and most audacious terror attack[s] in American history".[3]

The September 11th hijackings were the first commercial domestic airline hijackings in over ten years.[4] The weapons of choice for the September 11th hijackers were box cutters. Despite anecdotal information about lax security, there have actually been few hijackings of American commercial airlines that involved a lethal weapon passing

1 Serge Schmemann, "Hijacked Jets Destroy Twin Towers and Hit Pentagon", *New York Times*, 12 September 2001, at http://www.nytimes.com/2001/09/12/nyregion/12PLANhtml.

2 "Morning of Mayhem", *New York Times*, 12 September 2001, at A14.

3 Serge Schmemann, "Hijacked Jets Destroy Twin Towers and Hit Pentagon", *New York Times*, 12 September 2001, at http://www.nytimes.com/2001/09/12/nyregion/12PLANhtml.

4 D. Bradley Kizzia, "Liability of Air Carriers for Injuries to Passengers Resulting from Domestic Hijackings and Related Incidents", 46 J. Air L. & Com. 147 (1980). In 1987, a discharged airline employee used his credentials to circumvent passenger screening, carried a pistol on board and shot the pilot and co-pilot, causing the plane to crash.

through the pre-boarding screening system since the United States Civil Aviation Security Program was fully implemented in January 1973.[5]

"Hijacking" has been defined as "the unlawful seizure and diversion of aircraft to unscheduled destinations".[6] For the purposes of this chapter, "skyjacking" and "hijacking" will be considered synonymous and will be used interchangeably. The same will apply to "skyjacker" and "hijacker". For the purposes of criminal prosecution, "air piracy" is defined as a "seizure of control, by force or violence or threats of force or violence, or by any other form of intimidation" of an aircraft.[7] According to the Federal Aviation Administration (FAA), a "successful" hijacking is one in which the perpetrator forces an American aircraft to make an unscheduled landing in another country.[8] When making reference to a "successful" hijacking, this chapter utilizes the Federal Aviation Administration definition of such incidents. However, whether or not a skyjacker diverts an aircraft to a non-scheduled stop in a foreign country is not determinative of the air carrier's liability for injuries that may have been incurred by its passengers. The recorded hijacking attempts against United States air carriers since January 1973 do not include incidents in which persons were prevented from doing so by detection of weapons or explosives in the pre-boarding screening procedures. Only those incidents where the would-be skyjacker manages to board the aircraft are officially categorized as attempted hijackings.[9]

This chapter will focus on the potential liability of commercial airlines, which includes commercial operators engaging in intra-state common carriage covered by the Code of Federal Regulations.[10] A common carrier holds its services out to the general public to carry for

5 Department of Transportation, Federal Aviation Administration, Semi-annual Report to Congress on Effectiveness of the Civil Aviation Program, 1 January–30 June 1979 (1979), submitted pursuant to the Federal Aviation Act, 49 U.S.C. Section 1341 (1976), as amended, Pub. L. Number 93–366 (1979).

6 *United States* v. *Cyzewski*, 484 F.2d 509, 511 (5th Cir. 1973).

7 49 U.S.C. Section 1472(i)(2) (1976).

8 Department of Transportation, Federal Aviation Administration, Semi-annual Report to Congress on Effectiveness of the Civil Aviation Program, 1 January–30 June 1979 (1979), submitted pursuant to the Federal Aviation Act, 49 U.S.C. Section 1341 (1976), as amended, Pub. L. Number 93-366 (1979).

9 Semi-annual Report to Congress on Effectiveness of the Civil Aviation Program, 1 January–30 June 1979 (1979), submitted pursuant to the Federal Aviation Act, 49 U.S.C. Section 1341 (1976), as amended, Pub. L. Number 93–366 (1979), at p. 4.

10 Code of Federal Regulations, Title 14, Part 121.7 (1980).

hire at a uniform rate all persons who apply, so long as there is room on board.[11] A private carrier does not offer its services to the general public and reserves the right to refuse carriage to anyone.[12]

The liability of air carriers for injuries to passengers on international flights to, from or stopping over in the United States is governed by the Warsaw Convention,[13] as modified by the Montreal Agreement (hereinafter, the Warsaw Convention, as modified by the Montreal Agreement, will be referred to as the "Warsaw system"). The Warsaw Convention creates both a presumption of liability on the part of the carrier for injury or death arising out of international transportation (subject to certain defenses) and a concomitant limitation of liability (subject to certain exceptions) to 125,000 Poincare francs (about US $8,300) per passenger.[14] On 14 May 1966, the United States announced the approval by the Civil Aeronautics Board (CAB)[15] of the arrangement known as Agreement CAB 18900, which provides, *inter alia*, that the parties thereto agree to include in their tariffs to be filed with the CAB a "special contract: by which the carrier would waive its defense of due care provided by Article 20(1) of the Convention and also raise its limitation of liability under the Convention to US $75,000".[16] Together, the Agreement (signed by each airline), the requisite tariff, filed pursuant to the Agreement on 16 May 1966, the Notice to Passengers included within the ticket informing the passenger of the change in the regime of the Warsaw

11 *Jackson* v. *Stancil*, 116 S.E.2d 817 (N.C. Supp. 1960).

12 *Sleezer* v. *Lang*, 102 N.W.2d 435 (Neb. 1960); M. McClintock, *Aircraft Hijacking: Its Civil and Criminal Ramifications* (1971) at p. 65; McClintock, "Skyjacking: Its Domestic Civil and Criminal Ramifications", 39 J. Air L. & Com 29, 42–43, notes 56–57 (1973).

13 49 U.S.C. Section 40105 (1997). The Warsaw Convention is officially entitled "Convention for the Unification of Certain Rules Relating to International Transportation by Air", opened for signature on 12 October 1929, declaration of adherence by the United States deposited at Warsaw, Poland on 31 July 1934, proclaimed on 29 October 1934, 49 Stat. 3000–26 T.S. 876 (1934).

14 *Dunn* v. *Trans World Airlines, Inc.*, 589 F.2d 408, 410 (9th Cir. 1978).

15 Department of State Press Release, Numbers 100 and 111, 54 Dept. State Bull. 955 (1966).

16 Fed. Reg. 7,302 (1966); *Day* v. *Trans World Airlines Inc.*, 528 F.2d 31 (2d Cir. 1975), cert. denied, 429 U.S. 890 (1976); *Karfunkel* v. *Campagnie Nationale Air France*, 427 F. Supp. 971 (S.D.N.Y. 1977).

Convention (and of its applicability) and the CAB order constitute what has been called the "Montreal Agreement".[17]

The Montreal system has not changed the test of the Warsaw Convention, but rather "impose[s] on international aviation involving the United States a . . . system of liability that is essentially contractual in nature".[18]

The Warsaw Convention contains specific articles which attempt to regulate liability of international air carriers in a uniform manner by establishing a presumption of liability,[19] by limiting liability[20] and by establishing defenses against liability.[21] The Montreal Agreement, which became effective on 16 May 1966, provided two major modifications to the Warsaw scheme of air carrier liability by raising the carrier's limitation of liability for the death, wounding or other bodily injury of a passenger and by imposing a system of absolute liability.[22]

While hijackings of international flights have given rise to a number of lawsuits by passengers to recover damages for injuries suffered, only two hijackings of American domestic flights have resulted in a reported court decision,[23] despite the fact that the majority of hijackings involving American carriers have occurred on domestic flights. Of the twenty-eight hijacking incidents involving United States air carriers since 1 January 1978, twenty-two were hijackings of domestic flights. Seventeen out of the twenty such

---

17 L. Kreindler, *Aviation Accident Law*, Sections 12A.01–12A.07 (1978).

18 *See* generally, Lowenfeld and Mendelssohn, "The United States and the Warsaw Convention", 80 Harv. L. Rev. 497 (1967).

19 Warsaw Convention, Articles 17, 18 and 19.

20 Warsaw Convention, Articles 22 and 24.

21 Warsaw Convention, Articles 20 and 21.

22 *Burnett* v. *Trans World Airlines, Inc.*, 368 F. Supp. 1152, 1154–55 (D.N.M. 1973); *Husserl* v. *Swiss Air Transport Co.*, 351 F. Supp. 702, 706 (S.D.N.Y. 1972), aff'd, 485 F.2d 1240 (2d Cir. 1973).

23 *Smith* v. *America West Airlines, Inc.*, 44 F.3d 344 (5th Cir. 1995) and *National Airlines, Inc.* v. *Edwards*, 336 So.2d 545 (Fla. 1976). *Ashley* v. *American Airlines, Inc.*, 738 F. Supp. 783 (S.D.N.Y.) involved a flight from the Virgin Islands to New York, which was hijacked by an escorted prisoner and taken to Cuba.

skyjackings since 1 January 1979 occurred on domestic flights.[24] Twelve of the thirteen successful skyjackings since January 1973 involved domestic flights. "International transportation" is "any transportation in which according to the contract made by the parties, the place of departure and the place of destination, whether or not there be a break in the transportation . . . are situated . . . within the territories of two High Contracting Parties . . ." to the Warsaw Convention.[25] The Warsaw Convention applies to "all international transportation of persons, baggage, or goods performed by aircraft for hire".[26] A domestic flight of an American carrier is one that is scheduled to begin and end in the United States. FAA statistics normally do not distinguish between domestic and international flights because screening procedures and security measures mandated by the FAA do not differentiate between domestic and international flights.

Under the Warsaw system, a "hijacking" is within the term "accident" as used in Article 17 of the Warsaw Convention, and is sufficient to raise the presumption of liability under Article 17.[27] *Karfunkel* v. *Compagnie Nationale Air France*[28] was brought in New York against the defendant airline to recover for damage suffered by passengers during a hijacking on the Common Law theories of negligence and false imprisonment. The court held that the flight fell within international transportation and was subject to the provisions of the Warsaw Convention. The case was dismissed for lack of subject

24 Department of Transportation, Federal Aviation Administration, Semi-annual Report to Congress on Effectiveness of the Civil Aviation Program, 1 January–30 June 1979 (1979), submitted pursuant to the Federal Aviation Act, 49 U.S.C. Section 1341 (1976), as amended, Pub. L. Number 93–366 (1979) at pp. 2–4; Department of Transportation, Federal Aviation Administration, Semi-annual Report to Congress on the Effectiveness of the Civil Aviation Program, 1 July–31 December 1978 (1979) at pp. 2–4; Department of Transportation, Federal Aviation Administration Semi-annual Report to Congress on the Effectiveness of the Civil Aviation Program, 1 January–30 June 1978 (1978) at pp. 7–8.

25 Warsaw Convention, Article 1(2).

26 Warsaw Convention, Article 1(1).

27 *Karfunkel* v. *Compagnie Nationale Air France*, 427 F. Supp. 971 (S.D.N.Y. 1977); *Krystal* v. *British Overseas Airways Corp.*, 403 F. Supp. 1322 (C.D. Cal. 1975); *Burnett* v. *Trans World Airlines, Inc.*, 368 F. Supp. 1152 (D.N.M. 1973); *Husserl* v. *Swiss Air Transport Co.*, 351 F. Supp. 702, 707–08 (S.D.N.Y. 1972), aff'd, 485 F.2d 1240 (2d Cir. 1973); *People ex rel Compagnie Nationale Air France* v. *Gilberto*, 383 N.E.2d 977 (Ill. 1978); *Rosman* v. *Trans World Airlines, Inc.*, 34 N.Y.2d 385, 358 N.Y.S.2d 97, 314 N.E.2d 848 (1977).

28 *Karfunkel* v. *Compagnie Nationale Air France*, 427 F. Supp. 971 (S.D.N.Y. 1977).

matter jurisdiction because, under the Warsaw Convention, New York was not one of the locations that suit could be brought against Air France to recover for damages incurred on the Tel Aviv to Paris flight. Article 28(1) of the Warsaw Convention provides in part that an action for damages must be instituted in a court "of the domicile of the carrier or of his principal place of business, or where he has a place of business through which the contract has been made, or before the court at the place of destination".

This chapter is concerned with the liability of an airline for passenger injuries or death resulting from an incident of domestic air hijacking or related crime, since the full screening of passengers and their carry-on items was instituted in 1973.[29] The analysis is divided into two parts. The first part of the analysis focuses on an airline's liability for domestic hijackings prior to the September 11th tragedies. Specifically, the first part examines:

(1) Airline liability under a theory of negligence;
(2) Possible airline defenses of contributory negligence and assumption of the risk;
(3) Airline liability for mental or emotional injuries; and
(4) Airline hijackings and conflict of laws.

The second part of the analysis focuses on the new federal legislation that resulted from the September 11th tragedies. Specifically, the second part addresses:

(1) The September 11th Victims Compensation Fund Act of 2001; and
(2) The Aviation and Transportation Security Act of 2001.

Skyjacking Threat Since January 1973

In 1973, the first year of mandatory screening of all passengers and their carry-on baggage, the number of attempted hijackings of air carriers in the United States dropped to one from twenty-seven in

29 Department of Transportation, Federal Aviation Administration, Semi-annual Report to Congress on Effectiveness of the Civil Aviation Program, 1 January–30 June 1979 (1979), submitted pursuant to the Federal Aviation Act, 49 U.S.C. Section 1341 (1976), as amended, Pub. L. Number 93–366 (1979) at p. 9.

1972.[30] Furthermore, during the six-year period from 1 January 1973 to 31 December 1978, there were a total of twenty-five hijacking attempts perpetrated against United States carriers as contrasted with the twenty-seven hijacking attempts in 1972, the last year prior to implementation of the 100 per cent screening system. Although there were thirty-one hijackings of American airliners during the sixty-one-month period between January 1973 and 30 June 1979, none involved real firearms or high explosives smuggled through the passenger screening system.[31] By contrast, of the forty-six hijackings of foreign air carriers that occurred during the thirty-month period between 1 January 1977 and 30 June 1979, at least thirty-one of the incidents occurred because of inadequate passenger screening employed by foreign airlines in countries outside the United States, which permitted real weapons or explosives to be carried on board the aircraft.[32] Many foreign airports employ less than adequate security measures. American commercial air carriers are required to employ the minimum preflight screening measures even when serving foreign airports.[33]

On the surface, these statistics are impressive. However, statistics often hide the truth. For example, on 24 January 1980, a passenger successfully smuggled a .25 caliber handgun aboard a Delta Airlines plane bound from Los Angeles to New York.[34] The passenger then successfully hijacked the Delta airliner and diverted it to Havana,

---

30 Department of Transportation, Federal Aviation Administration, Semi-annual Report to Congress on Effectiveness of the Civil Aviation Program, 1 January–30 June 1979 (1979), submitted pursuant to the Federal Aviation Act, 49 U.S.C. Section 1341 (1976), as amended, Pub. L. Number 93–366 (1979), at p. 20 (Exhibit 1).

31 Department of Transportation, Federal Aviation Administration, Semi-annual Report to Congress on Effectiveness of the Civil Aviation Program, 1 January–30 June 1979 (1979), submitted pursuant to the Federal Aviation Act, 49 U.S.C. Section 1341 (1976), as amended, Pub. L. Number 93–366 (1979) at p. 1.

32 Department of Transportation, Federal Aviation Administration, Semi-annual Report to Congress on the Effectiveness of the Civil Aviation Program, 1 July–31 December 1978 (1979) at p. 7; Department of Transportation, Federal Aviation Administration, Semi-annual Report to Congress on Effectiveness of the Civil Aviation Program, 1 January–30 June 1979 (1979), submitted pursuant to the Federal Aviation Act, 49 U.S.C. Section 1341 (1976), as amended, Pub. L. Number 93–366 (1979) at p. 6.

33 However, when a foreign airport fails to meet acceptable security measures, 49 U.S.C. Section 44907 (1997) governs.

34 *Dallas Morning News*, 26 January 1980, at p. 1, column 1; *New York Times*, 27 January 1980, at p. 18, column 5.

Cuba.[35] Further, since 1973, there have been several successful hijackings of commercial airliners by passengers armed with knives or other weapons.[36] Then, there is 11 September 2001. All four of the planes hijacked on September 11th were performed by passengers armed with "box cutters" and "bombs allegedly contained in their checked baggage",[37] although proof of the latter allegations has apparently never materialized.

As evidenced by the September 11th hijackings and these other incidents, it is apparent that airline passengers continue to face the risk of a harrowing experience in which their lives and property are placed in actual jeopardy. While, in theory, a passenger who has suffered serious physical and/or emotional damage as a result of an attempted or successful hijacking or act of sabotage could bring a tort action against the hijacker or saboteur,[38] in reality, such a suit would not be worthwhile in the vast majority of cases. Normally, hijackers do not have recoverable assets.[39] The same would seem applicable to saboteurs. Those that are apprehended and are not completely destitute are further subject to the expense of defending against a criminal prosecution, which may likely result in imprisonment. Furthermore, if the hijacking is successful, the perpetrator may no longer be subject to the jurisdiction of American courts. However, the United States is party to the Hague Convention for the Suppression of Unlawful Seizure of Aircraft 1970,[40] which provides for the mandatory punishment or extradition of all skyjackers taken into custody in a signatory state. While 85.4 per cent of skyjackers escaped prosecution in 1969, only 28.1 per cent did so in 1972. In the case of sabotage, the saboteur

35 *Dallas Morning News*, 26 January 1980, at p. 1, column 1; *New York Times*, 27 January 1980, at p. 18, column 5.

36 D. Bradley Kizzia, "Liability of Air Carriers for Injuries to Passengers Resulting from Domestic Hijackings and Related Incidents", 46 J. Air L. & Com. 147 (1980) at pp. 147–150.

37 Serge Schmemann, "Hijacked Jets Destroy Twin Towers and Hit Pentagon", *New York Times*, 12 September 2001, at http://www.nytimes.com/2001/09/12/nyregion/12PLANhtml; "Morning of Mayhem", *New York Times*, 12 September 2001, at A14.

38 Such an action might be brought for assault or battery. Additionally, an action for intentional infliction of mental distress or false imprisonment might lie against a hijacker: *Karfunkle* v. *Compagnie Nationale Air France*, 427 F. Supp. 971, 977 (S.D.N.Y. 1977).

39 Barrett, "Terrorism and the Airline Passengers", 128 New L.J. 499 (1978); Comment, "Aircraft Hijacking: Criminal and Civil Aspects", 22 U. Fla. L. REV 72, 90 (1969).

40 T.I.A.S. Number 7192 (1970).

may never be known. Eighty-four per cent of serious bomb threats made against United States aircraft during the first six months of 1979 were transmitted telephonically.[41]

Prior to the Aviation and Transportation Security Act of 2001,[42] a suit against the United States Government for injuries arising out of a domestic skyjacking or similar incident would likely prove equally fruitless, not because of the inability to recover on a judgment awarded, but because of an inability to state a claim on which relief can be granted.[43] In the first place, the duty to screen passengers for weapons was expressly placed on the airlines.[44] Secondly, such an action against the federal government would have to be brought under the Federal Tort Claims Act,[45] which does not apply to a claim "based on an act or omission of an employee of the Government, exercising due care, in the execution of a statute or regulation",[46] nor to a claim "based on the exercise or performance or the failure to exercise or perform a discretionary function or duty" on the part of a government agency or employee.

Both of these limitations would pose significant barriers to actions by airline passengers against the federal government to recover damages for injuries received during a hijacking or act of sabotage because the federal government's former role in preventing hijackings was

41 Department of Transportation, Federal Aviation Administration, Semi-annual Report to Congress on Effectiveness of the Civil Aviation Program, 1 January–30 June 1979 (1979), submitted pursuant to the Federal Aviation Act, 49 U.S.C. Section 1341 (1976), as amended, Pub. L. Number 93-366 (1979) at p. 7.

42 49 U.S.C. Section 114 (2001).

43 An argument in favor of government liability might be an analogy to principles of law concerning government liability for the negligent operations of its air traffic controllers: M. McClintock, *Aircraft Hijacking: Its Civil and Criminal Ramifications* (1971) at p. 80; McClintock, "Skyjacking: Its Domestic Civil and Criminal Ramifications", 39 J. Air L. & Com 29, 51–53 (1973). *See* generally Comment, "Government Liability — Air Traffic Controllers — Duty of Care", 33 J. Air. L & Com. 185 (1967). For a study of the plaintiff's rights to bring an action against a governmental entity for injuries arising out of an airport attack, *see* Comment, "Deterring Airport Terrorist Attacks and Compensating Their Victims", 125 U.Pa. L. Rev 1134 (1977).

44 49 U.S.C. Section 44901(a) (1997); 14 C.F.R. Section 108.11(a) (2001).

45 28 U.S.C. Sections 1346 (b), 2671–80 (1997).

46 28 U.S.C. Section 2680(a) (1997).

primarily regulatory.[47] The regulatory functions of government agencies are the types of activities exempted by the foregoing exceptions.[48] On the other hand, if a federal officer (not involved in policy formulation), such as an FBI agent, assumes an operational role in a particular emergency situation, like a hijacking, the employee's negligent handling of the situation may result in government liability for resulting injuries, as was the result in *Downs* v. *United States*.[49]

For the passenger who is injured on a United States domestic flight, an alternative to suit against the hijacker or against the federal government is an action for negligence against the airline involved. In certain circumstances, prior to 11 September 2001, an injured passenger could recover in such a suit against an airline, particularly if the principles of negligence per se or *res ipsa loquitur* were applied. However, the passage of the Aviation and Transportation Security Act of 2001 may significantly alter an airline's potential liability from that date forward.

47 The current federal role in the airline security program of regulation, assistance and enforcement is embodied in 49 U.S.C. Section 44903 (Supp. 2001). The United States Supreme Court has decided that immunized discretion of federal employees "includes determinations made by executives or administrators in establishing plans, specifications or schedules of operations" [footnote omitted]. "Where there is room for policy judgment and decision there is discretion": *Dalehite* v. *United States*, 346 U.S. 15, 35 (1953).

48 *Downs* v. *United States*, 522 F.2d 990, 996 (6th Cir. 1975); *Starr* v. *FAA*, 589 F.2d 307, 313 (7th Cir. 1978) (courts will defer to discretion granted to the Federal Aviation Administration by Congress to determine the type and scope of air safety rules, even if on its own the court may have adopted different standards).

49 *Downs* v. *United States*, 522 F.2d 990, at 997 (6th Cir. 1975) 522. The *Downs* case would appear to be limited to an incident in which a government agent intervenes, on behalf of the government, in a hijacking already in progress. In case of the agent's negligence, the airline may be jointly liable for resulting injuries to passengers. In *Downs*, only a small passenger airliner was involved. A Pacific Southwest airliner was involved in an attempted hijacking on 5 July 1972, where one passenger was killed and two were subsequently killed, and FBI agents were involved: *New York Times*, 5 July 1971, at p. 1, column 5. It is not known whether any claims or lawsuits resulted from this incident.

Airline Liability Pre-Aviation and Transportation Security Act

Treaties or statutes can affect an airline's liability for hijackings. The Warsaw system operates as a treaty and, therefore, the supreme law of the land; thus, it pre-empts local law and provides exclusive, though virtually certain, relief to injured passengers on international flights.[50] In *Husserl* v. *Swiss Air Transport Co.*,[51] the court stated that, under Article 24 of the Warsaw Convention:

> ". . . any action, however founded, seeking recovery for injuries comprehended by Article 17 [bodily injuries] and caused by an accident occurring in a place specified by Article 17 [on board the aircraft or in the course of embarking or disembarking] can be brought only subject to the conditions and limits established by the Warsaw system. To this extent at least . . .. the treaty provides for the exclusive relief available for injury sustained in international transportation".

Those types of injury not comprehended by the Warsaw system "should be governed exclusively by the substantive law which would be applicable if the treaty did not exist".[52] The Warsaw system limits only those claims for injury comprehended by Article 17.[53] On the other hand, in the absence of a statute establishing a different rule, negligence on the part of an airline must be established in order to hold the airline liable for damages incurred as a result of a hijacking or related crime perpetrated against a domestic flight.[54] This would

50 *United States* v. *Belmont*, 301 U.S. 324 (1937); *Burnett* v. *Trans World Airlines*, 368 F. Supp. 1152 (D.N.M. 1973); *Husserl* v. *Swiss Air Transport Co.*, 351 F. Supp. 702, 706 (S.D.N.Y. 1972), aff'd, 485 F.2d 1240 (2d Cir. 1973); *Bradfield* v. *Trans World Airlines, Inc.*, 88 Cal. App.3d 681, 684, 152 Cal. Reptr. 172, 175 (1979); *Schedlmayer* v. *Trans International Airlines*, 416 N.Y.S.2d 461, 463 (1979).

51 *Husserl* v. *Swiss Air Transport Co.*, 388 F. Supp. 1238, at 1246 (S.D.N.Y. 1975).

52 *Husserl* v. *Swiss Air Transport Co.*, 388 F. Supp. 1238, at 1247 (S.D.N.Y. 1975).

53 *Husserl* v. *Swiss Air Transport Co.*, 388 F. Supp. 1238, at 1248 (S.D.N.Y. 1975).

54 *Arrow Aviation, Inc.* v. *Moore*, 266 F.2d 488 (8th Cir. 1959); *Noel* v. *United Aircraft Corp.*, 204 F. Supp. 929, 940 (D. Del. 1962); *Ness* v. *West Coast Airlines, Inc.*, 90 Idaho 111, 410 P.2d 965 (1965); *Griffith* v. *United Airlines, Inc.*, 416 Pa. 1, 203 A.2d 796, 799 (1964); M. McClintock, *Aircraft Hijacking: Its Civil and Criminal Ramifications* (1971) at p. 68; McClintock, "Skyjacking: Its Domestic Civil and Criminal Ramifications", 39 J. Air L. & Com 29, 42 (1973); Tompkins, "The Aftermath of a Hijacking—Passenger Claims and Insurance", 39 J. Air. L. & Com. 381, 384 (1973).

generally require the plaintiff passenger to prove that the airline was under a duty to exercise care towards him, that by acting, or failing to act, in a certain manner the duty was breached by the airline, that the breach of duty was a proximate cause of the plaintiff passenger's injuries and that, as a result of those injuries, the plaintiff passenger suffered certain identifiable damage.

Contrastingly, an injured passenger on an international flight who brings suit to recover under the Warsaw system needs to show an injury, proximate cause and damage.[55] In *Orr* v. *New Orleans Pub. Serv. Inc.*,[56] it was held that the mere showing of injury to a fee-paying passenger and his failure to reach his destination safely establishes a *prima facie* case of negligence and imposes on the carrier the burden to overcome the *prima facie* case.[57] Passengers seeking recovery for injuries during hijackings of American carriers engaged in international transportation must generally bring their actions under the provisions of the Warsaw Convention, as amended by the Montreal Agreement. Article 17 of the Warsaw Convention provides:

> "The carrier shall be liable for damage sustained in the event of the death or wounding of a passenger or any other bodily injury suffered by a passenger, if the accident which caused the damage so sustained took place on board the aircraft or in the course of any of the operations of embarking or disembarking."[58]

Some jurisdictions would also require a showing that the plaintiff passenger was not guilty of contributory negligence.[59] In the context of international flights and the governing Warsaw system, the Article 20(1) provision that the "carrier shall not be liable if he proves that he and his agents have taken all necessary measures to avoid the damage or that it was impossible for him or them to take such measures" has been waived by carriers flying to and from the United States under the Montreal Agreement.[60]

---

55 *Husserl* v. *Swiss Air Transport Co.*, 388 F. Supp. 1238 n. 4 (S.D.N.Y. 1975).

56 *Orr* v. *New Orleans Pub. Serv. Inc.*, 349 So.2d 417, 419 (La. App. 1977).

57 *See also Campbell* v. *New Orleans Pub. Serv., Inc.*, 369 So.2d 733, 735 (La. App. 1979) (requiring carrier to "convincingly" overcome plaintiff passenger's *prima facie* case).

58 49 Stat. 3018 (1936).

59 W. Prosser, *Law of Torts*, Section 65, at p. 416 (4th ed. 1971).

60 *Karfunkel* v. *Compagnie Nationale Air France*, 427 F. Supp. 971, 975 (S.D.N.Y. 1977).

Scope of Duty and Determination of Breach

In the context of a domestic flight, the duty of an airliner to its passengers is defined by state law,[61] although federal law[62] governs the operation, control and safety of carriers.[63] The federal regulatory statute provides that "a remedy under this part is in addition to any other remedies provided by law".[64] An airline is a common carrier, and like all common carriers, it bears a very high standard of care as to its passengers.[65] Congress has recognized this policy[66] and provides in part:

> "(a) The Administrator of the Federal Aviation Administration shall promote safe flight of civil aircraft in air commerce by prescribing . . ..
>
> "(d) When prescribing a regulation or standard under subsection (a) or (b) of this section or any of Sections 44702–44716 of this title, the Administration shall —
>
> "(1) consider —
>
> "(A) the duty of an air carrier to provide service with the highest possible degree of safety in the public interest."

In characterizing the scope of this duty, courts have held that a carrier's duty to its passengers requires the exercise of the "highest degree of care",[67] the "highest degree of vigilance, care, and precaution",[68]

---

61 *Braniff Airways, Inc.* v. *Nebraska State Board of Equalization and Assessment*, 347 U.S. 590, 597 (1954).

62 49 U.S.C. Sections 44901–44938 (1997).

63 *Manfredonia* v. *American Airlines, Inc.* 15 Av. Cas. 17, 368 (N.Y. Sup. Ct. 1979), citing *City of Burbank* v. *Lockheed Air Terminal*, 411 U.S. 624, 638 (1973).

64 49 U.S.C. Section 40120(c) (1997).

65 *Delta Airlines* v. *Gibson*, 550 S.W.2d 310, 312 (Tex. Civ. App. — El Paso 1977, no writ); W. Prosser, *Law of Torts*, Section 34, at pp. 180–181 (4th ed. 1971).

66 49 U.S.C. Section 44701 (1997).

67 *Cattaro* v. *Northwest Airlines, Inc.*, 236 F. Supp. 889 (E.D. Va. 1964); *Letsos* v. *Chicago Transit Auth.*, 254 N.E.2d 645 (Ill. App. 1969); *Quigley* v. *Wilson Line of Mass.*, 154 N.E.2d 77, 79 (Mass. 1958); *Southeastern Aviation, Inc.* v. *Hurd*, 209 Tenn. 639, 355 S.W.2d 436 (1962); *Virginia* v. *United Airlines*, 248 S.E.2d 124, 130 (1978).

68 *Orr* v. *New Orleans Pub. Serv. Inc.*, 349 So.2d 417, 419 (La. App. 1977).

"utmost care",[69] and a "high degree of care".[70] The high risks of air travel and the control exercised by the airline are viewed as justification for the higher standard.[71] It is a traditional principle that the greater the danger, the greater the care required.[72] However, arguably the greater amount of care is only what is reasonable care under the circumstances. The primary rationale for the higher standard of care imposed on common carriers is the degree of control exercised over the passenger during the transportation.[73] The feeling is that "[a]irline passengers are completely at the mercy of the carrier and are entitled to assume that the highest degree of care is being taken for their safety".[74] On the other hand, it has been consistently held that a common carrier is not an insurer of the safety of its passengers.[75] "A carrier does not, by its contract to transport safely, insure safe arrival".[76]

At Common Law, the general rule in tort is that a private person has no duty to protect other persons from the criminal acts of third persons.[77] Hence, a party's nonfeasance does not normally result in liability being imposed on him. Nonfeasance, that is, the failure to undertake measures to protect another from harm, is distinguished from misfeasance, which involves active misconduct causing positive injury to another.[78] An exception has long existed in tort law

---

69 *Bullock* v. *Tamiami Trail Tours, Inc.*, 266 F.2d 326, 332 (5th Cir. 1959); *Roberts* v. *Trans World Airlines*, 225 Cal. App. 2d 344, 37 Cal. Rptr. 291 (1964); *Exton* v. *Cent. R.R.*, 62 N.J.L. 7, 42 A. 486,489 (1899).

70 *McCoy* v. *Chicago Transit Auth.*, 69 III 2d 280, 371 N.E.2d 625 (1977); Smith v. West Suburban Transit Lines, Inc., 27 Ill. App.3d 220, 326 N.E.2d 449, 451 (1975); *Griffith* v. *United Air Lines, Inc.*, 416 Pa. 1, 203 A.2d 796, 799 (1964).

71 M. McClintock, *Aircraft Hijacking: Its Civil and Criminal Ramifications* (1971) at p. 66; McClintock, "Skyjacking: Its Domestic Civil and Criminal Ramifications", 39 J. Air L. & Com 29, 43 (1973).

72 *Tom* v. *Days of '47, Inc.*, 16 Utah 2d 386, 401 P.2d 946 (1965); *Ziser* v. *Colonial Western Airways, Inc.*, 162 A. 591 (N.J. 1932).

73 Comment, "Deterring Airport Terrorist Attacks and Compensating the Victims", 125 U. Pa. L. Rev. 1134, 1159 (1977).

74 *Widmyer* v. *Southeast Skyways, Inc.*, 584 P.2d 1, 5 (Alaska 1978).

75 *Ness* v. *West Coast Airlines, Inc.*, 90 Idaho 111, 410 P.2d 965, 967 (1965); *Orr* v. *New Orleans Pub. Serv., Inc.*, 349 So.2d 417 (La. App. 1977); *Quigley* v. *Wilson Line of Mass.*, 154 N.E.2d 77, 79 (Mass. 1958); *Griffith* v. *United Airlines, Inc.*, 416 Pa. 1, 203 A.2d 796, 799 (1964).

76 *Higgins* v. *New Orleans Pub. Serv., Inc.*, 347 So.2d 944, 946 (La. App. 1977).

77 W. Prosser, *Law of Torts*, Section 56, at p. 340 (4th ed. 1971).

78 W. Prosser, *Law of Torts*, Section 56, at p. 339 (4th ed. 1971).

where certain special relationships combined with special conditions and circumstances have resulted in the imposition of liability for failure to undertake protective measures to prevent harm from befalling another due to the criminal act of a third person.[79] Thus, the special relationship which exists between a common carrier and its passengers has been held to impose a duty on the carrier to protect its passengers from the harmful acts of third persons, including employees, other passengers and strangers.[80]

However, even "where the highest degree of care characterized the relationship, the criminal acts of third parties impose no liability unless there are present special circumstances that create in the minds of reasonable men an apprehension of danger".[81] A carrier will generally be held liable for the injuries to a passenger that are caused by the assault or other misconduct of a third person only where the carrier has reason to anticipate the incident, that is, where the danger is known to the carrier or should have been known to the carrier, but the carrier nevertheless fails to exercise a degree of care and vigilance practicable under the circumstances to prevent the injury.[82]

In *Quigley* v. *Wilson Line of Massachusetts, Inc.*,[83] the Massachusetts Supreme Court declared that a carrier's liability rests on the duty that is imposed by law "to anticipate that which is reasonably foreseeable and to prevent that which is reasonably preventable in the way of violent injury to its passengers".[84] In *Bullock* v. *Tamiami Trail Tours, Inc.*,[85] the federal appellate court applied Florida law and held that "[i]f the injury could have been reasonably anticipated in time to have

79 W. Prosser, *Law of Torts*, Section 56, at p. 341 (4th ed. 1971).

80 *Kenney* v. *Southeastern Pa. Transp. Auth.*, 581 F.2d 351 (3d Cir. 1978); *Bullock* v. *Tamiami Trail Tours, Inc.*, 266 F.2d 326 (5th Cir. 1959); *McCoy* v. *Chicago Transit Auth.*, 69 Ill. 2d 280, 371 N.E.2d 625 (1977); Restatement (Second) of Torts, Section 302B.

81 *Cornpropst* v. *Sloan*, 528 S.W.2d 188, 192 (Tenn. 1975), overruled on a different point by *McClung* v. *Delta Square Ltd. Pshp.*, 937 S.W.2d 891, 899 (Tenn. 1996), interpreting the rule of *Railroad* v. *Hatch*, 116 Tenn. 580, 94 S.W. 671 (1906).

82 *Kenan* v. *Houstoun*, 150 Fla. 357, 7 So.2d 837, 838 (1942); *McCoy* v. *Chicago Transit Auth.*, 69 Il.2d 280, 371 N.E.2d 625, 628 (1977); *Letsos* v. *Chicago Transit Auth.*, 47 Ill.2d 437, 265 N.E.2d 650, 653 (1970); *Railroad* v. *Hatch*, 116 Tenn. 580, 94 S.W. 671 (1906); *Fuller* v. *Southwestern Greyhound Lines, Inc.*, 331 S.W.2d 455 (Tex. Civ. App. — Austin 1960, writ ref'd n.r.e.).

83 *Quigley* v. *Wilson Line of Massachusetts, Inc.*, 154 N.E.2d 77 (Mass. 1958).

84 *Quigley* v. *Wilson Line of Massachusetts, Inc.*, 154 N.E.2d 77, at 80 (Mass. 1958).

85 *Bullock* v. *Tamiami Trail Tours, Inc.*, 266 F.2d 326 (5th Cir. 1959).

prevented its occurrence, the carrier is subjected to the highest degree of care to its passengers either to protect him from or to warn him of the danger".[86] In this regard, the Restatement (Second) of Torts provides, in Section 302B, comment e, that there are situations that arise when one party is under a special responsibility toward another, such that he is required, as a reasonable person, to anticipate and guard against the criminal misconduct of others. Section 314A(1)(a) states that, because of the special relationship, a common carrier is under a duty to take reasonable action to protect its passengers against unreasonable risk of physical harm.

Despite some state court decisions that have indicated that a carrier's liability for criminal attacks on its passengers might be predicted only on some action or conduct of the particular assailant that gave advance notice to the carrier of the probability of danger,[87] it is highly unlikely that an argument by a defendant airliner that a hijacking incident was not an anticipated danger would succeed in precluding its liability for resulting injuries to its passengers. For one thing, use of the hijacker behavioral profile should alert airline personnel to potentially dangerous individuals. It has been held that it is knowledge of the "conditions" which are likely to result in danger to a passenger,[88] or it is the "nature" of the threat which should be anticipated,[89] as opposed to the particular threat of a particular offender, that gives rise to the duty on the part of the carrier to prevent the criminal assault. Additionally, knowledge of prior criminal assaults or violence has been held to invoke the carrier's duty to act to prevent potential assaults or acts of violence.[90] Comment f to Section 344 of the Restatement (Second) of Torts states that:

> "[i]f the place or character of [a party's] business or his past experience, is such that he should reasonably anticipate careless or criminal conduct on the part of third persons,

---

86 *Bullock* v. *Tamiami Trail Tours, Inc.*, 266 F.2d 326, at 331 (5th Cir. 1959).

87 *Cornpropst* v. *Sloan*, 528 S.W.2d 188, 193 (Tenn. 1975), overruled on a different point by *McClung* v. *Delta Square Ltd. Pshp.*, 937 S.W. 2d 891, 899 (Tenn. 1996).

88 *Neering* v. *Illinois Cent. R.R.*, 383 Ill. 366, 50 N.E.2d 497, 503 (1943); *Haynes* v. *Chicago Transit Auth.*, 59 Ill. App.3d 97, 376 N.E.2d 680, 682–83 (1978).

89 *Fuller* v. *Southwestern Greyhound Lines, Inc.*, 331 S.W.2d 455, 458 (Tex. Civ. App. — Austin 1960, writ ref'd n.r.e.).

90 *Haynes* v. *Chicago Transit Auth.*, 59 Ill. App. 3d 997, 376 N.E.2d 680, 683 (1978); *Mancha* v. *Field Museum of Natural History*, 5 Ill. App.3d 699, 283 N.E.2d 899 (1972); *Amoruso* v. *New York City Transit Auth.*, 207 N.Y.S.2d 855 (1960).

either generally or at some particular time, he may be under a duty to take precautions against [such conduct] . . .".

The frequency of attempted skyjackings and related criminal acts, along with the fact that extensive pre-flight screening of all passengers is conducted (as required by law), leaves little doubt that hijacking attempts and similar acts of crime are to be reasonably anticipated. Furthermore, skyjacking and sabotage are viewed as "inevitable corollaries to modern techniques of air transport".[91]

Pre-Flight Screening

From the foregoing, it can be concluded that American commercial air carriers have a Common Law duty to protect their passengers against attempted hijackings and similar threatening acts by implementing security measures designed to prevent such criminal activity. The duty aspect of the plaintiff passenger's action in negligence is further enhanced by the fact that the United States Congress expressly placed the obligation to screen embarking passengers and their carry-on items for weapons on the air carriers, at least prior to 11 September 2001.[92] The express purpose was "to protect persons and property aboard aircraft operating in air transportation . . . against acts of criminal violence and aircraft piracy".[93] Pursuant to the legislative mandate, the FAA promulgated regulations, one of which generally prohibits an air carrier from allowing "any person to have . . . a deadly or dangerous weapon, either concealed or unconcealed, accessible to him while aboard an aircraft being operated by" the air carrier.[94] An air carrier may not "knowingly permit any passenger to transport . . . a loaded firearm in checked baggage".[95]

In light of this regulation and the clear intent and purpose of the Air Transportation Security Act of 1974[96] (to protect passengers engaging in commercial air travel from hijacking and similar crimes),

91 *Evangelinos* v. *Trans World Airlines, Inc.*, 550 F.2d 152, 159–60 (3d Cir. 1977), where skyjacking and sabotage, as threats posed to passengers boarding or on board an aircraft, were viewed as part of terrorism, that is, "a risk which accompanies international air travel".

92 49 U.S.C. Section 44901(a) (1997).

93 49 U.S.C. Section 44903(b) (1997).

94 14 C.F.R. Section 108.11(a) (2001).

95 14 C.F.R. Section 108.11(c) (2001).

96 49 U.S.C. Section 44903 (1997).

it is submitted that a passenger who has suffered injuries arising out of a hijacking incident, in which the hijacker managed to smuggle a weapon on board, can bring a claim for negligence against the airline involved.[97] On the other hand, Section 288A of the Restatement (Second) of Torts recognizes "excused violations" where the actor, in the exercise of reasonable care, is unable to comply. Furthermore, negligence per se would probably not apply to cases where a saboteur or extortionist places a bomb in checked baggage that is taken aboard and successfully diverts the route of the aircraft or causes the device to detonate. Although the Air Transportation Security Act of 1974 makes it a federal crime to place or attempt to place an explosive or incendiary device aboard a commercial aircraft,[98] the law does not expressly place the obligation for preventing such an occurrence on airlines.[99]

In *Manfredonia* v. *American Airlines*,[100] it was held that a breach of a federal statute or regulation may provide grounds for a cause of action for damages in a state court arising from injury sustained thereby.[101] The case involved an airline passenger who was assaulted in flight by an intoxicated fellow passenger. While, on the issue of Common Law negligence, the defendant airline was determined not to be liable for failing to exercise proper care in protecting the plaintiff passenger from injury, the appellate court remanded after ruling that a cause of action on behalf of the injured passenger is implied for violation of the FAA regulation which forbids the service of alcoholic beverages to an intoxicated person. The court declared that a breach of a statute may provide a basis for an action for damages if:

---

97 *Chumney* v. *Nixon*, 615 F.2d 389 (6th Cir. 1980) (existence of the right to maintain a civil action for damages due to assault aboard an aircraft may be implied from a federal criminal statute designed to protect airline passengers); *Galella* v. *Onassis*, 353 F. Supp. 196, 227 (S.D.N.Y. 1972); *Martin* v. *Herzog*, 228 N.Y. 164, 126 N.E. 814 (1920); Tompkins, "The Aftermath of a Hijacking — Passenger Claims and Insurance", 39 J. Air. L. & Com. 381, 386 (1973); Restatement (Second) of Torts, Section 228B (1965).

98 49 U.S.C. Section 46505, note 12 (1997).

99 14 C.F.R. Section 108.11(c) (2001), which requires air carriers to implement a system designed, *inter alia*, to prevent the carriage of any explosive or incendiary device in checked baggage.

100 *Manfredonia* v. *American Airlines*, 15 Av. Cas. 17,638 (N.Y. App. Div. 1979).

101 *Manfredonia* v. *American Airlines*, 15 Av. Cas. 17,638, at 17,642 (N.Y. App. Div. 1979); *Cort* v. *Ash*, 422 U.S. 66, 78 (1975).

"(1) the regulation was intended to protect a particular class of persons;

"(2) there was an intention to create or deny a private right;

"(3) the right would be consistent with the goal of the statute; and

"(4) the cause of action is one traditionally left to state law."[102]

Assuming that a commercial air carrier has a duty to protect its passengers from the threat of skyjackings and related criminal acts of third parties by preventing potential skyjackers and saboteurs from taking aboard its aircraft weapons and explosives or incendiary devices, it follows that the air carrier's failure to detect such criminal instruments during the pre-boarding screening procedures would constitute a breach of that duty.[103] In *Airline Motor Coaches, Inc.* v. *Carver,*[104] the Texas Supreme Court stated in a portentous decision that:

> ". . . it could well be negligence to permit a passenger to bring in with him what is obviously an open can of gasoline, or an uncrated dog. Even when the luggage admitted is legitimate, negligence may arise . . . where the luggage somehow comes to create a dangerous situation of which the carrier's agents knew or would have known if they had fulfilled their duty . . . of properly inspecting or policing the vehicle".

In *Herman* v. *Trans World Airlines, Inc.,*[105] the lower court considered a claim by a passenger for damages due to extreme fright and emotional injury arising out of a hijacking of an international flight. Although the decision was based on the provisions of the Warsaw system, the Common Law duty of air carriers to protect their passengers

---

102 *Manfredonia* v. *American Airlines*, 15 Av. Cas. 17,638 (N.Y. App. Div. 1979); *Rauch* v. *United Instruments*, 548 F.2d 452, 457 (3d Cir. 1976); *In re Paris Air Crash of 3 March 1974*, 399 F. Supp. 732 (C.D. Cal. 1975).

103 *Virginia* v. *United Airlines, Inc.*, 248 S.E.2d 124, 130 (Va. 1978).

104 *Airline Motor Coaches, Inc.* v. *Carver*, 226 S.W.2d 830, 833 (Tex. 1950).

105 *Herman* v. *Trans World Airlines, Inc.*, 40 A.D.2d 850, 337 N.Y.S.2d 827 (1972), rev'd on other grounds, 34 N.Y.2d 385, 358 N.Y.S.2d 97 (1974).

from assaults was noted.[106] In *Edwards* v. *National Airlines, Inc.*,[107] a state appellate court in Florida held that a cause of action upon which relief could be granted was stated by a passenger who, in a claim based in part on negligence, alleged consequential damages arising out of a 1971 hijacking of a domestic flight to Cuba. The ruling of the appellate court was subsequently reversed by the Florida Supreme Court because the injuries alleged were too remote.[108] The hijackers were armed, and the plaintiff contended that the airline, as a carrier, breached its duty to take extreme precautions to prevent hijackings by screening its passengers for weapons and explosives.[109] Whether the penetration of the screening system was due to a failure to utilize recognized measures or equipment or to an inadequate search or inspection of the hijacker's person and apparel or of his carry-on baggage, or due to a malfunction of the mechanical or electronic detection devices, the airline could be culpable.[110] In *Southeastern Airlines* v. *Hurd*,[111] it was decided that an air carrier owes its passengers the highest degree of care with respect to service and maintenance of its equipment. It has been held that:

> "[A] passenger who pays his fare to a common carrier expects safe transportation to his destination and a carrier is required to do all that human care, vigilance, and foresight can reasonably do to transport its passengers safely, consistent with its mode of conveyance and the practical operation of its business."[112]

106 *Herman* v. *Trans World Airlines, Inc.*, 40 A.D.2d 850, 337 N.Y.S.2d 827, at 830 (1972).

107 *Edwards* v. *National Airlines, Inc.*, 307 So.2d 244 (Fla. App. 1974), rev'd on other grounds, 336 So.2d 545 (Fla. 1976).

108 *National Airlines, Inc.* v. *Edwards*, 336 So.2d 545 (Fla. 1976).

109 *National Airlines, Inc.* v. *Edwards*, 336 So.2d 545, at 546 (Fla. 1976).

110 *Virginia* v. *United Airlines, Inc.*, 248 S.E.2d 124, 130 (Va. 1978); M. McClintock, *Aircraft Hijacking: Its Civil and Criminal Ramifications* (1971) at pp. 69–70; McClintock, "Skyjacking: Its Domestic Civil and Criminal Ramifications", 39 J. Air L. & Com 29, 42 (1973); Barrett, "Terrorism and the Airline Passengers", 128 New L.J. 499, at 502 (1978); 49 U.S.C. Section 41702 (1997), which imposes a duty on air carriers to provide safe and adequate interstate air transportation.

111 *Southeastern Airlines* v. *Hurd*, 355 S.W.2d 436 (Tenn. 1962).

112 *Letsos* v. *Chicago Transit Auth.*, 118 Ill. 2d 26, 254 N.E.2d 645, 647 (1969), rev'd, 47 Ill.2d 437, 265 N.E.2d 650 (Ill. 1970). The reversal was on factual grounds. *See also* *Lutz* v. *Chicago Transit Auth.*, 36 Ill. App.2d 79, 183 N.E.2d 579, 581 (1962).

Because of the high standard of care that an air carrier owes its passengers, and given the carrier's duty to prevent weapons or explosive devices from being taken aboard its aircraft by embarking passengers, one approach would be to find the airline negligent if it could have prevented the skyjacking but failed to do so.[113] In at least one jurisdiction, the trial court would, on a showing by a plaintiff passenger of the occurrence of a skyjacking or related crime, shift the burden to the air carrier to prove that the incident was not the result of its negligence.

This shifting of the burden of going forward with the evidence is similar to the rebuttable presumption of breach of duty owed that is used by some jurisdictions when a negligence claim is based on the doctrine of *res ipsa loquitur. Res ipsa loquitur* is utilized in cases where the mere fact that a particular harm has occurred may itself tend to establish a breach of duty owed.[114] The majority of American courts regard *res ipsa loquitur* merely as one form of circumstantial evidence that permits an inference of negligence.[115] Although the theory of *res ipsa loquitur* generally may not be applicable to cases involving the liability of common carriers for injuries to their passengers inflicted by third parties, an argument can be put forth that the principle of *res ipsa loquitur* should be available to an injured passenger in a hijacking case, at least in the context of determining whether an airline is negligent for allowing weapons or explosive devices to be taken aboard its aircraft.[116] W. Prosser sets out three conditions usually necessary for the application of the principle of *res ipsa loquitur*:

> "(1) the event must be of a kind which ordinarily docs not occur in the absence of someone's negligence;

---

113 *Campbell* v. *New Orleans Pub. Serv., Inc.*, 369 So.2d 733 (La. App. 1979); *Higgins* v. *New Orleans Pub. Serv., Inc.*, 347 So.2d 944 (La. App. 1977); *Orr* v. *New Orleans Pub. Serv., Inc.*, 349 So.2d 417 (La. App. 1977).

114 *Ten Ten Chestnut St. Corp.* v. *Quaker State Bottling Co.*, 186 Pa. Super Ct. 585, 142 A.2d 306 (1958); *Coca Cola Bottling Co. of Helena* v. *Mattice*, 219 Ark. 428, 243 S.W.2d 15 (1951); *Johns* v. *Penn R. Co.*, 226 Pa. 319, 75 A. 408 (1910).

115 *Bell &. Koch, Inc.* v. *Stanley*, 375 S.W.2d 696 (Ky. 1964); *Gardner* v. *Coca Cola Bottling Co.*, 267 Minn. 505, 127 N.W.2d 557 (1964); W. Prosser, *Law of Torts*, Section 40, at pp. 229–229 (4th ed. 1971).

116 W. Prosser, *Law of Torts*, Section 39, at p. 24 (4th ed. 1971).

"(2) it must be caused by an agency or instrumentality within the exclusive control of the defendant;

"(3) it must not have been due to any voluntary act or contribution on the part of the plaintiff."[117]

For instance, in the aforementioned hijacking of the Delta airliner to Cuba, the method used by the hijacker to get the firearm through the screening checkpoint has never been conclusively determined.[118] Under *res ipsa loquitur*, the mere fact that the handgun was taken aboard the aircraft would tend to establish a breach of the duty of high care owed by the airline to its passengers. In the first place, because it was mandatory, at least prior to 2002, that all passengers and their carry-on items be screened by the air carriers, and in light of the sophisticated mechanisms available to detect such firearms, it would seem that an incident of this type would not normally occur in the absence of the carrier's negligence.[119] According to Prosser, "[a]ll that is needed is evidence from which reasonable men can say that on the whole it is more likely that there was negligence associated with the cause of the event than that there was not".[120] On the other hand, the airline might attempt to prove that it had done everything possible to avert such an occurrence.

Secondly, the passenger screening station and the detecting devices employed were in the exclusive control of Delta at the time that the hijacker passed through on his way to board the aircraft with the handgun.[121] To establish exclusive control by the defendant, it is enough to show that the defendant has the right or power of control and the opportunity to exercise it, or that the defendant is under a duty that cannot be delegated to another, or that the defendant shares the duty and the responsibility at the time of the negligence.[122] In *Husserl*

---

117 *See also* Goldin, "The Doctrine of *Res Ipsa Loquitur* in Aviation Law", 18 So. Cal. L. Rev. 15, 124 (1945); Restatement (Second) of Torts, Section 328D (1965).

118 Speculation has suggested that the handgun was concealed in a baby's metal seat carrier: *New York Times*, 27 January 1980, at p. 18, column 5.

119 *Shaw* v. *Pacific Greyhound Lines*, 50 Cal. App. 2d 153, 323 P.2d 391 (1958); *Southeastern Aviation* v. *Hurd*, 355 S.W.2d 436 (Tenn. 1962); *Newberger* v. *Pokrass*, 33 Wis.2d 569, 148 N.W.2d 80 (1967).

120 W. Prosser, *Law of Torts*, Section 39, at p. 218 (4th ed. 1971).

121 *Gadde* v. *Michigan Consolidation Gas Co.*, 377 Mich. 117, 139 N.W.2d 722 (1966); *Whitney* v. *Northwest Greyhound*, 242 P.2d 257 (Mont. 1952).

122 W. Prosser, *Law of Torts*, Section 39, at p. 220 (4th ed. 1971).

v. *Siviss Air Transport Co.*,[123] the court held that injuries to a passenger sustained during a hijacking of an international flight are compensable under the Warsaw system and stated that "the carrier is best qualified initially to develop defensive mechanisms to avoid such incidents, since it physically controls the aircraft and access to it".[124]

Thirdly, it does not appear likely that any passenger on the previously discussed Delta flight that was hijacked to Cuba, who may have suffered severe traumatic damage resulting from the incident, would have contributed to his injuries by his own conduct.[125] Thus, the three elements essential to the invocation of *res ipsa loquitur* would appear to be present in a skyjacking incident such as the Delta hijacking, where a hijacker succeeded in penetrating the airline's pre-flight screening system with a firearm. While *res ispa loquitur* is not applicable against multiple defendants where it is inferable that only one has been negligent, in the case of joint tortfeasors, for example, where an injured passenger brings suit against the airline and the skyjacker, *res ispa loquitur* may be applied against the carrier.[126]

In addition to the use of devices designed to detect firearms and other weapons, an air carrier has the authority to refuse transportation to a would-be passenger when, in the reasonable judgment of the carrier, the passenger might endanger the flight.[127] While, generally, every citizen has the public right of transit through navigable airspace,[128] the passenger's right to demand air transportation is qualified by the duty of the air carrier to observe proper safety standards.[129] An air carrier must refuse to transport a person who does not consent to a search of his person and luggage.[130] The fact that a carrier can exclude a passenger who might be inimical to the safety of

---

123 *Husserl* v. *Siviss Air Transport Co.*, 351 F. Supp. 702 (S.D.N.Y. 1972).

124 *Husserl* v. *Siviss Air Transport Co.*, 351 F. Supp. 702, at 707 (S.D.N.Y. 1972).

125 *Dallas Morning News*, 26 January 1980, at p. 1, column 1; *Simmons* v. *F. W. Woolworth Co.*, 163 Cal. App.2d 709, 329 P.2d 999 (1958); *Vistica* v. *Presbyterian Hosp.*, 67 Cal.2d 465, 432 P.2d 193, 62 Cal. Rptr. 577 (1967).

126 *Capital Transit Co.* v. *Jackson*, 149 F.2d 839 (D.C. Cir. 1945); *Pickwick V. Stages Corp.* v. *Messinger*, 44 Ariz. 174, 36 P.2d 168 (1934).

127 49 U.S.C. Section 44902(b) (1997).

128 49 U.S.C. Section 40103(a)(2) (1997).

129 *Aller* v. *Chicago & S. Air Lines, Inc.*, 4 CAB 113, 117 (1943).

130 14 C.F.R. Section 108.9(b) (2001).

the other passengers does not alter its status as a common carrier.[131] Nevertheless, even given the existence of this authority and the availability of sophisticated weapon detecting devices, the airlines may maintain that it does not necessarily follow that the fact of an armed hijacker on board a commercial aircraft is due to the air carrier's negligence.

In support of the airlines' position, the law certainly does not require air carriers to exercise all care that is within the human mind's conceptual capabilities or that which will free passengers from all possible dangers.[132] The airline may be bound only to undertake action which is "practicable"[133] or that which is "compatible with the normal operation of its business".[134] Hence, if the minimum prescribed security measures and screening devices are the fullest extent of what is practicable for a particular airline, then the fact that an offender is able to circumvent the screening system employed, or that screening devices that are developed do not have the capabilities to detect certain types of weapons or explosives,[135] may not render the airline negligent.

There are indications that the mechanisms presently utilized for screening passengers and their carry-on items are effective and that any breakdowns in the system are due primarily to the carelessness of personnel at passenger screening checkpoints. FAA officials have pointed to human error as the primary reason for security slip-ups. The converse is not true, that is, the carrier may not be absolved from liability by ineffective screening mechanisms, if more sophisticated devices are available. As previously noted, since 100 per cent screening was instituted in January 1973, only one firearm has been carried by a skyjacker through a screening station. Although knives or other weapons (not firearms or explosives) were employed in several attempted hijackings since January 1973, knives are capable of being

---

131 M. McClintock, *Aircraft Hijacking: Its Civil and Criminal Ramifications* (1971) at p. 65; McClintock, "Skyjacking: Its Domestic Civil and Criminal Ramifications", 39 J. Air L. & Com 29, 43 n. 57 (1973); *Williams* v. *Trans World Airways*, 369 F. Supp. 797 (S.D.N.Y. 1974), holding that an airline is authorized to refuse transport to an individual who was a fugitive from justice and considered dangerous. *See also Mason* v. *Belieu*, 543 F.2d 215 (6th Cir.), cert. denied, 429 U.S. 852 (1976).

132 *Kasanof* v. *Embry-Riddle Co.*, 26 So.2d 889 (Fla. 1946).

133 *Orr* v. *New Orleans Pub. Serv., Inc.*, 349 So.2d 417 (La. App. 1977).

134 *Virginia* v. *United Airlines*, 248 S.E.2d 124, 130 (Va. 1978).

135 The weapon detectors designed to react to metal fail to detect non-metallic weapons, such as explosives, acids, plastic or glass.

discovered on a would-be passenger's person by the metal detector[136] and in the passenger's carry-on luggage by the x-ray machine.[137]

Furthermore, the x-ray machines in current use have the capacity to permit detection of explosives carried in luggage.[138] With the exception of the gasoline smuggled aboard four United States airliners, no high explosive device has penetrated the pre-flight passenger screening system since the system's implementation. Five explosive or incendiary devices were detected at screening stations in 1977, three in 1978 and three during the first half of 1979.[139] Therefore, it is arguable that screening mechanisms in current use will probably detect most instrumentalities intended to effectuate skyjackings if those devices are properly employed at pre-boarding check points.

Nevertheless, even if it were to be conceded that the screening mechanisms presently deployed are less than adequate to meet the newly rising threat of hijackings and related crimes, it has been held that an air carrier has the "duty to exercise such means as were available to it to avoid or minimize the danger to its passengers",[140] and that "[a] failure to do anything which could have been done . . . to prevent the injury renders the carrier liable".[141] The fact that an air carrier has complied with FAA regulations will not absolve it of negligence if the high standard of care would require greater precautionary measures.[142]

There are at least four types of explosive detection mechanisms that have completed development or have been in the final stages of

136 *United States* v. *Flum*, 518 F.2d 39 (8th Cir. 1975).

137 Department of Transportation, Federal Aviation Administration, Semi-annual Report to Congress on Effectiveness of the Civil Aviation Program, 1 January–30 June 1979 (1979), submitted pursuant to the Federal Aviation Act, 49 U.S.C. Section 1341 (1976), as amended, Pub. L. Number 93–366 (1979), at p. 5.

138 Barrett, "Terrorism and the Airline Passengers", 128 New L.J. 499, at 502 (1978).

139 Department of Transportation, Federal Aviation Administration, Semi-annual Report to Congress on Effectiveness of the Civil Aviation Program, 1 January–30 June 1979 (1979), submitted pursuant to the Federal Aviation Act, 49 U.S.C. Section 1341 (1976), as amended, Pub. L. Number 93–366 (1979) at pp. 1 and 28 (Exhibit 9).

140 *Ness* v. *West Coast Airlines*, 90 Idaho 111, 410 P.2d 965, 968 (1965).

141 *Bullock* v. *Tamiami Trail Tours, Inc.*, 266 F.2d 326, 330 (5th Cir. 1959).

142 *Stromsodt* v. *Parke-Davis & Co.*, 257 F. Supp. 991 (D.N.D. 1966). However, *see* Aviation and Security Act of 2001, 49 U.S.C. Section 114(a) (2001).

evaluation.[143] The FAA has made specially trained explosive detection dog teams available to airlines at twenty-nine airports across the country.[144] It has been proposed that all embarking passengers be submitted to the "sniffer" dog test in addition to the metal-detecting device to prevent explosives from being carried onto aircraft on the persons of skyjackers.

Screening of checked luggage has also long been advocated to reduce the possibility that bombs will be smuggled aboard aircraft in that manner.[145] Although even prior to 31 December 2002, an air carrier was required to submit an acceptable plan to the FAA designed in part to prevent "the carriage of any explosive or incendiary device in checked baggage",[146] air carriers are now required to screen checked luggage. They have long been required to prevent unauthorized cargo and baggage from being loaded aboard aircraft.[147] Hence, a plaintiff passenger may be able to establish a breach of the air carrier's duty to detect weapons and explosives, despite the deficiencies of the particular devices or measures utilized by the airline, by showing that more sophisticated mechanisms or more reliable procedures were available to the airline. An assumption is made that some screening devices may be better and some security measures safer or more reliable than those minimally required by the FAA. On the other hand, if the air carrier, in the exercise of its high degree of care, could not have prevented a particular stratagem employed by an offender to get weapons or explosives on board an aircraft, then there was no breach of duty, no negligence and, at least in the context of a domestic flight, no liability on the part of the air carrier.

---

143 The basic characteristics of the devices are x-ray absorption, thermal neutron activation, nuclear magnetic resonance and vapor characterization: Department of Transportation, Federal Aviation Administration, Semi-annual Report to Congress on Effectiveness of the Civil Aviation Program, 1 January–30 June 1979 (1979), submitted pursuant to the Federal Aviation Act, 49 U.S.C. Section 1341 (1976), as amended, Pub. L. Number 93-366 (1979) at p. 34 (Exhibit 15).

144 In recent evaluations, the "K-9" teams maintained a level of explosive detection surety of approximately ninety-eight per cent and a false alert rate of about four per cent.

145 Eight explosive devices were discovered on board commercial aircraft during the six and a half-year period between 1 January 1973 and 30 June 1979: Department of Transportation, Federal Aviation Administration, Semi-annual Report to Congress on Effectiveness of the Civil Aviation Program, 1 January–30 June 1979 (1979), submitted pursuant to the Federal Aviation Act, 49 U.S.C. Section 1341 (1976), as amended, Pub. L. Number 93–366 (1979) at p. 26 (Exhibit 7).

146 14 C.F.R. Section 108.9 (2001).

147 14 C.F.R. Section 108.13(b) and (c) (2001).

Further, the high duty of care imposed on air carriers may require the deployment of armed security guards at screening check points, boarding areas and/or aboard the aircraft. Such actions might be necessary to prevent a potential hijacker from forcing his way through or around passenger screening stations and onto waiting aircraft, and to satisfy the airline's duty to exercise all available means to minimize danger to its passengers in some jurisdictions[148] or to exercise all means practicable in other jurisdictions.[149] Federal regulations, as laid down by the FAA, require only that an airline "as part of its security program, provide for law enforcement support . . . to assist passenger screening operations" for flights at certain airports that are not required to maintain security forces.[150] It has been held that a common carrier normally has no duty to provide armed guards to protect its passengers.[151] A carrier is not required to furnish a security force sufficient to prevent all violence or danger posed by other passengers or strangers when such threats are not reasonably expected.[152]

On the other hand, a carrier is required to furnish a force of security guards sufficient to protect its passengers from foreseeable assaults by other passengers or strangers. Nevertheless, the fact that a carrier has taken such steps to increase security may not be enough to preclude its liability as a matter of law.[153] In light of the carrier's high standard of care, it may be held liable for injuries to passengers resulting from the negligence of law enforcement officers hired by the carrier where the officer's negligence constituted a breach of the carrier's duty to protect its passengers.[154]

In independent contractor cases, the general rule of tort law is that one who employs an independent contractor is not liable for the negligent conduct of the latter, even if the independent contractor's negligence occurs while it is acting within the scope of the contract.[155] However, an exception to this no liability rule is recognized in the context of non-delegable duties. If the obligor's duty is non-delegable as a matter of law, for example, where the specific

---

148 *Ness* v. *West Coast Airlines*, 90 Idaho 111, 410 P.2d 965, 968 (1965).

149 *Orr* v. *New Orleans Pub. Serv., Inc.*, 349 So.2d 417, 419 (La. App. 1977).

150 14 C.F.R. Section 108.15(a) (2001); 14 C.F.R. Section 107.13(b) (2001).

151 *Higgins* v. *New Orleans Pub. Serv., Inc.*, 347 So.2d 944, 946 (La. App. 1977).

152 *Dilley* v. *Baltimore Transit Co.*, 39 A.2d 469 (Md. 1944).

153 *Kenny* v. *Southeastern Pa. Transp. Auth.*, 581 F.2d 351, 354 (3d Cir. 1978).

154 *Quigley* v. *Wilson Line of Mass.*, 338 Mass. 125, 154 N.E.2d 77, 80 (1958).

155 W. Prosser, *Law of Torts*, Section 71, at p. 468 (4th ed. 1971).

obligation is imposed on the specific party, or its class, by statute, the employer cannot relieve himself from liability by hiring an independent contractor to perform the obligation.[156] In *Quigley* v. *Wilson Line of Massachusetts*,[157] where the defendant carrier employed security officers to patrol its station to deter criminal activity, the court declared that:

> "[e]ven if the hired police officers . . . were acting as independent contractors . . . the defendant common carrier was not thereby relieved from its liability for the negligence of those officers in not adequately protecting the plaintiff against a foreseeable risk".[158]

It has been held that the duty of a carrier to transport its passengers in safety is non-delegable.[159]

A very significant issue that may arise in hijacking-related suits for damages by passengers against air carriers is the question of the liability of airlines for the emotional injuries suffered by passengers, for example, resulting from hijackings in which the skyjacker claims possession of a bomb or wields a toy pistol that appears to be real, but is in fact not armed. This question is particularly relevant since the implementation of a pre-boarding screening system applicable to all passengers and their carry-on items, which has proven highly effective in preventing firearms and explosive devices from being carried aboard commercial aircraft. According to the FAA, only one firearm and no explosive device has penetrated the pre-flight screening system since the system's institution in January 1973. Between 1 January 1973 and 10 September 2001, there were at least thirty-two United States hijacking incidents in which the hijacker passed through normal screening procedures.[160] Of these thirty-two, twenty-one involved unarmed skyjackers who, once aboard, feigned possession of a weapon or explosive device.

---

156 *Chicago, K & W R.R.* v. *Hutchinson*, 25 P. 576 (Kansas 1891); *Snyder* v. *Southern Cal. Edison Co.*, 44 Cal. 2d 793, 285 P.2d 912 (1955).

157 *Quigley* v. *Wilson Line of Massachusetts*, 338 Mass. 125, 154 N.E.2d 77 (1958).

158 *Quigley* v. *Wilson Line of Massachusetts*, 338 Mass. 125, 154 N.E.2d 77, at 80 (1958).

159 *Eli* v. *Murphy*, 39 Cal. 2d 598, 248 P.2d 756 (1952).

160 Department of Transportation, Federal Aviation Administration, Semi-annual Report to Congress on Effectiveness of the Civil Aviation Program, 1 January–30 June 1979 (1979), submitted pursuant to the Federal Aviation Act, 49 U.S.C. Section 1341 (1976), as amended, Pub. L. Number 93–366 (1979) at p. 1.

An issue antecedent to the problem of damages is whether there is a breach of a duty owed in a case where an unarmed skyjacker seizes control of an air carrier by claiming possession of an explosive device or weapon and threatens to kill someone on board or detonate the explosive device if his demands are not met. At least three seizures of American commercial airliners in 1980 involved such circumstances.[161] Six such incidents occurred in 1979.[162] Two other hijacking incidents on United States air carriers in 1979 involved skyjackers who threatened to destroy the aircraft they were on with explosives or incendiary devices that they did not actually possess. One had in his possession a pocket knife, the other wielded a bottle of rum.[163] Even if it can be concluded that an air carrier's duty to exercise a high degree of care to protect its passengers from hijackings and similar crimes imposes upon it the obligation to prevent weapons and explosive devices from being taken aboard its aircraft, it does not necessarily follow that all hijackings manifest a breach of this duty. Exercising "extraordinary care and diligence"[164] may not prevent a hijacking in which the offender forces his way through the screening station with weapon drawn. The same would seem to be true in the context of an unarmed skyjacker where no amount of pre-flight searching would necessarily prevent the crime.

On the other hand, an argument could be made that the proper use of the hijacker behavioral profiles could detect these "bluff-artists" who are nonetheless hijackers despite the fact that they possess no real weapon. Furthermore, although the metal detector may not be activated by a toy pistol or an artificial explosive device, the x-ray machine or a thorough physical search could discover such items. Of course, these latter measures would not be effective against a potential hijacker who does not even possess a simulated weapon or device.

---

161 *Miami Herald*, 17 August 1980, at p. 1, column 5; *Washington Post*, 11 August 1980, at p. 11, column 5; *Washington Post*, 13 July 1980, at p. 6, column 2.

162 Department of Transportation, Federal Aviation Administration, Semi-annual Report to Congress on Effectiveness of the Civil Aviation Program, 1 January–30 June 1979 (1979), submitted pursuant to the Federal Aviation Act, 49 U.S.C. Section 1341 (1976), as amended, Pub. L. Number 93–366 (1979) at pp. 2–4.

163 Department of Transportation, Federal Aviation Administration, Semi-annual Report to Congress on Effectiveness of the Civil Aviation Program, 1 January–30 June 1979 (1979), submitted pursuant to the Federal Aviation Act, 49 U.S.C. Section 1341 (1976), as amended, Pub. L. Number 93–366 (1979) at pp. 2–4.

164 *Yellow Cab Co. of Atlanta* v. *Carmichael*, 33 Ga. App. 364, 368, 126 S.E. 269, 271 (1925).

However, confidence in effective screening procedures coupled with the perpetrator's failure to display any type of weapon or device (simulated or otherwise) might justify a more aggressive response to a would-be hijacker. Hence, it is plainly not ridiculous to consider that an air carrier, in the exercise of a high degree of care, could detect or otherwise appropriately respond to potential skyjackers and, therefore, prevent skyjackings perpetrated by those who carry no weapon or explosive on board the aircraft with them.

Protective Measures after Boarding

The carrier's duty to exercise a high degree of care to protect its passengers is not limited in its applicability to the measures utilized by the airline to prevent passengers from boarding its aircraft with weapons or explosive devices. The high standard of care also defines the scope of the air carrier's obligation to its passengers after everyone has boarded and while the aircraft is in flight. The carrier may be "required to exercise the highest degree of care, foresight, prudence, and diligence reasonably demanded at any time by the conditions or circumstances then affecting the passenger and the carrier".[165] It is necessary, therefore, to donate some attention to the conduct or actions taken by airline personnel during the course of a skyjacking or similar crime. Of course, if an air carrier is found to be negligent for allowing the hijacking to occur in the first instance, for example, by permitting a weapon to penetrate the screening system, then the exercise of even extraordinary care by the airlines during the course of the crime would not absolve its liability for the initial negligence.

In this regard, it should be noted that a pilot in command is given wide discretion in an emergency situation to make decisions and take whatever action he deems necessary under the circumstances.[166] Under the doctrine of sudden emergency, the pilot of an air carrier is not required by law to exercise a higher standard of care than "ordinary care" — that of a reasonably prudent man under similar circumstances.[167] Thus, a pilot or a crew member generally is not chargeable

165 *Whitman* v. *Red Top Sedan Service, Inc.*, 218 So.2d 213, 216 (Fla. App. 1969).

166 14 C.F.R. Section 121.559(a) (2001).

167 M. McClintock, *Aircraft Hijacking: Its Civil and Criminal Ramifications* (1971) at p. 74; *contra Massato* v. *Public Serv. Coordinated Transp.*, 71 N.J. Super. 39, 176 A.2d 280, 284 (1961) (carrier's duty of high care is not diminished in case of sudden emergency).

with negligence, and an airline is not liable, if he acts in an emergency situation according to his best judgment even if, in retrospect, his actions were not the most reasonable[168] or constituted an error in judgment, so long as the error was not positive negligence.[169] However, if the situation of emergency arises because of the negligence of the airline or one of its employees, for example, where an armed hijacker slips through a screening checkpoint undetected, the doctrine of sudden emergency is inapplicable, and the airline's liability is not shielded by the circumstances of imminent danger.[170]

Additionally, in *Downs* v. *United States*,[171] it was held that the extent to which "an actor will be excused for errors in judgment under [emergency] circumstances, is qualified by the training and experience he may have, or be expected to have, in coping with the danger or emergency with which he is confronted".[172] In *Downs*, survivors of two victims of an aircraft hijacking brought suit against the United States alleging that the negligent handling of the situation provoked the hijacker to kill his hostages. The court decided that where one trained to handle dangerous situations, as was the FBI agent in that case, is required "to make a judgment which may result in the death of innocent persons, he is required to exercise the highest degree of care commensurate with all facts within his knowledge".[173] Because United States airline flight crews are required to take part in an FAA program to learn in-flight and ground anti-hijack procedures and anti-hijack defensive tactics,[174] the standard articulated in *Downs* may provide a second limitation on the sudden emergency doctrine as it is applicable to airline personnel during a hijacking incident.

It has been suggested that an air carrier may be negligent for failing to resist a hijacker, that is, for passively acquiescing to the offender's demands.[175] For the air carrier's employees to assume that

---

168 *Chapman* v. *United States*, 194 F.2d 974 (5th Cir.), cert. denied, 344 U.S. 821 (1952).

169 Jackson v. *Stancil*, 116 S.E.2d 817 (N.C. 1960); *Murphy* v. *Neely*, 179 A. 439 (Pa. 1935).

170 *Jackson* v. *Stancil*, 116 S.E.2d 817 (N.C. 1960).

171 *Downs* v. *United States*, 522 F.2d 990 (6th Cir. 1975).

172 *Downs* v. *United States*, 522 F.2d 990, at 1002 (6th Cir. 1975).

173 *Downs* v. *United States*, 522 F.2d 990, at 1003 (6th Cir. 1975).

174 Department of Transportation, Federal Aviation Administration, Semi-annual Report to Congress on Effectiveness of the Civil Aviation Program, 1 January–30 June 1979 (1979), submitted pursuant to the Federal Aviation Act, 49 U.S.C. Section 1341 (1976), as amended, Pub. L. Number 93–366 (1979) at p. 13.

175 M. McClintock, *Aircraft Hijacking: Its Civil and Criminal Ramifications* (1971) at p. 70.

a hijacker is, in fact, armed with a dangerous weapon or explosive device is tantamount to an assumption that the airline has been negligent in allowing the hijacker to penetrate the screening system. Although it may seem inequitable that an air carrier should escape liability by assuming its own negligence, this is an argument for imposition of strict liability. In light of the grave risk, that of the loss of a large number of lives, it would not seem unreasonable to accede to the demands of a skyjacker who may very well possess a bomb.

It is conceded that there may arise circumstances where it would not be consistent with the air carrier's high duty of care to automatically accede to the dictates of a skyjacker, for example, where the airline personnel know or should know that he is not armed. Perhaps an airline's employees should be required to demand some proof from the skyjacker that he is, in fact, in possession of a dangerous weapon or explosive device. The purpose of such a requirement would be to detect those would-be hijackers who do not even possess a simulated weapon or bomb. Six of the ten attempted hijackings perpetrated aboard United States air carriers in 1979 involved hijackers who claimed to possess an explosive or incendiary device. Five of these hijackers had nothing even resembling such a device in their possession, yet two succeeded in diverting airliners out of the United States.[176] One hijacker successfully forced an Air Florida jetliner to Cuba by claiming a bar of soap in a box was a bomb.[177]

It is conceded further that there is case law to support the position that a person has no duty to his business invitees to acquiesce to the criminal demands of a third party intruder in order to protect the business invitee from physical harm or death.[178] However, to acknowledge that there may be no duty to acquiesce is distinguished from asserting that it constitutes negligence to acquiesce. Furthermore, it is

176 Department of Transportation, Federal Aviation Administration, Semi-annual Report to Congress on Effectiveness of the Civil Aviation Program, 1 January–30 June 1979 (1979), submitted pursuant to the Federal Aviation Act, 49 U.S.C. Section 1341 (1976), as amended, Pub. L. Number 93-366 (1979) at pp. 2–4.

177 *Washington Post*, 11 August 1980, at p. 11, column 5.

178 *Boyd* v. *Racine Currency Exch.*, Inc., 56 Ill. 2d 95, 306 N.E.2d 39 (1973); *Noll* v. *Martan*, 347 Pa. 213, 32 A.2d 18 (1943); *contra Genovay* v. *Fox*, 50 N.J. Super. 538, 143 A.2d 229, rev'd on other grounds, 29 NJ 436, 149 A.2d 212 (1959); *Sinn* v. *Farmers' Deposit Savings Bank*, 300 Pa. 85, 150 A. 163 (1930); Restatement (Second) of Torts, Sections 75 and 83 (1965), which states the principle that a person defending himself or his property may be liable for harm to third persons if his acts create an unreasonable risk of harm to such persons.

submitted that any cases holding that a businessman need not accede to the criminal demands of an intruder to save the lives of business invitees do not arise out of the special legal relationship between the common carrier and its passengers. In *Boyd* v. *Racine Currency Exch., Inc.*,[179] a wrongful death action was brought by the widow of a customer killed by an armed robber when a teller at a currency exchange refused to comply with his demands for money even though the robber threatened to kill the customer if his demands were not met. The court found no duty to accede to the robber's demands.

Moreover, the contention that an air carrier is negligent where it acquiesces to the demands of a hijacker is inconsistent with the general principle of law that a common carrier must always choose the course of action least likely to expose its passengers to harm.[180] This rule may be limited by holdings in other cases to the effect that common carriers owe their passengers the "highest degree of care consistent with the practical operation of the plane".[181] Thus, an air carrier may be justified, despite a hijacker's demands, in refusing transport to Iran if the aircraft were incapable of transoceanic flight. In *Downs* v. *United States*, the court ruled that a person trained to handle dangerous situations is:

> ". . . under a duty in a hijacking situation, to choose a course of action which would maximize the hostages' safety and to attempt a capture of the hijacker only if possible by means compatible with the greater interest. . . . [T]he means employed to effect any capture should be consonant with that which would provide the maximum assurance possible that hostages would not be harmed as a result".[182]
>
> "Applying this standard, the FBI agent was held to have been negligent for choosing to use force when there existed "a better-suited alternative to protecting the hostages' well-being. That choice was not to intervene forcibly but to continue the 'waiting game'". While the *Downs* court announced that a "waiting game" is preferable to use of force in a hijacking situation, it left open the question of whether, in

179 *Boyd* v. *Racine Currency Exch., Inc.*, 56 Ill. 2d 95, 306 N.E.2d 39 (1973).

180 *Spalt* v. *Eaton*, 118 N.J.L. 327, 192 A. 576, 578 (1937); *Harpell* v. *Public Serv. Coordinated Transp.*, 20 N.J. 309, 120 A.2d 43, 47 (1956).

181 *Southeastern Aviation* v. *Hurd*, 209 Tenn. 639, 355 S.W.2d 436, 446 (1962).

182 *Downs* v. *United States*, 522 F.2d 990, at 1001–1002 (6th Cir. 1975).

a case where a "waiting game" is not an option, full acquiescence to the hijacker's demands is preferable to use of force.

Hence, unless some opportunity presents itself that would allow for the hijacker to be subdued without exposing the passengers to a greater risk of danger, it was arguable before September 11 that most circumstances surrounding an air hijacking or related incident would suggest that acquiescence to the hijacker's demands would constitute the course of action least likely to expose its passengers to danger. It has been held that a carrier has no obligation to physically intervene in an assault on one passenger by another.[183] If an airline's employees take action to physically overpower a hijacker, although they are privileged to do so, the airline may be held to be negligent if its other passengers are exposed to harm.[184] This reasoning would probably not apply to an incident where a bomb has been placed on an air carrier. In such a case, the carrier's duty to protect its passengers would require the carrier to act to inspect any package that it reasonably believes to contain explosives[185] and, in such a case, it would be liable for any injuries incurred by innocent passengers.[186] Where one undertakes an act that he has no duty to perform, the act generally must be performed with ordinary care.[187] Of the ten skyjacking incidents involving United States air carriers in 1979, seven were thwarted when the hijacker was physically subdued, five times by FBI agents or police and twice by airline personnel with the assistance of passengers. One hijacker was shot and killed by policemen from Sydney, Australia.[188]

Proximate Cause

Assuming that a plaintiff passenger can establish that, by its actions or omissions, the airline has breached a duty owed to the passenger,

183 *Higgins* v. *New Orleans Pub. Serv., Inc.*, 347 So.2d 944, 946 (La. App. 1977).

184 *Watson* v. *Chicago Transit. Auth.*, 52 Ill. 2d 503, 288 N.E.2d 476, 478 (1972); *Spalt* v. *Eaton*, 118 N.J.L. 327, 192 A. 576, 578 (1937).

185 *State* v. *Morris*, 42 Ohio St. 2d 307, 329 N.E.2d 85, 93–94 n.1 (1975).

186 *Miller* v. *Mills*, 257 S.W.2d 520 (Ky. 1953).

187 *Northwest Airlines* v. *Glenn L. Martin Co.*, 224 F.2d 120 (6th Cir. 1955).

188 Department of Transportation, Federal Aviation Administration, Semi-annual Report to Congress on Effectiveness of the Civil Aviation Program, 1 January–30 June 1979 (1979), submitted pursuant to the Federal Aviation Act, 49 U.S.C. Section 1341 (1976), as amended, Pub. L. Number 93–366 (1979) at pp. 2–4.

before liability can be imposed, it must be shown that the air carrier's negligence was a proximate cause of the injuries incurred by the plaintiff passenger. The basic issue in this regard is whether the hijacker's criminal acts break the chain of causation so completely as to supercede the air carrier's negligence as the proximate cause of the injury to the passenger.[189] The general rule is that, because a common carrier is not an insurer of the safety of its passengers, it is not responsible for the consequences of felonious acts perpetrated by persons not in its employ nor under its control,[190] even if the carrier's negligence has created a condition that serves to facilitate the subsequent independent criminal acts of the third persons.[191]

However, the subsequent criminal act of a third person does not automatically relieve the party that is guilty of an earlier negligent or wrongful act from responsibility. The general exception to the aforementioned rule is that:

> ". . . the subsequent independent act, in order to break the causal connection, must be one, the intervention of which was not probable or foreseeable by the first wrongdoer. . . . [W]hen the intervening cause of an injury is of such nature as could reasonably have been anticipated, . . . the earlier negligent act, if it contributed to the injuries may be regarded as the proximate cause".[192]

As stated in Section 448 of the Restatement (Second) of Torts:

> "The act of a third person in committing an intentional tort or crime is a superceding cause of harm to another resulting therefrom, although the actor's negligent conduct created a situation which afforded an opportunity to the third person to commit such a tort or crime, unless the actor at the time of his negligent conduct realized or should have realized the likelihood that such a situation might be created, and that a

---

189 W. Prosser, *Law of Torts*, Section 44, at p. 270 (4th ed. 1971).

190 *Wing Hang Bank, Ltd.* v. *Japan Air Lines Co.*, 357 F. Supp. 94 (S.D.N.Y. 1973); *Terre Haute, Indianapolis and E. Traction Co.* v. *Scott*, 197 Ind. 587, 150 N.E. 777 (1926).

191 *Neering* v. *Illinois Cent. R.R.*, 383 Ill. 366, 50 N.E.2d 497, 503 (1943).

192 *Neering* v. *Illinois Cent. R.R.*, 383 Ill. 366, 50 N.E.2d 497, at 503–504 (1943); *Werndli* v. *Greyhound Corp.*, 365 So.2d 177, 178 n.1 (Fla. App. 1978); *Kenny* v. *Southeastern Pa. Transp.*, 581 F.2d 351 (3rd Cir. 1978); W. Prosser, *Law of Torts*, Section 44, at p. 275 (4th ed. 1971).

> third person might avail himself of the opportunity to commit such a tort or crime."

Once it has been determined that it is an air carrier's duty to anticipate and guard against hijackings and similar crimes, and this duty is breached, it follows that the occurrence of the very incident that the airline was under a duty to prevent will not supercede the airline's liability.[193] The point that air carriers are bound by their high standard of care to anticipate and to guard against potential hijackings and related crimes has been made previously in this chapter. Moreover, as has also been noted, at least prior to 11 September 2001, Congress expressly placed on the airlines the duty to screen all passengers and their carry-on items for weapons and explosives to protect passengers and their property against acts of criminal violence and aircraft piracy.[194] It is submitted, therefore, that an airline may be held liable for injuries suffered by its passengers during a skyjacking, or similar crime, by its failure to adequately screen the potential hijacker prior to boarding or due to some subsequent negligent act in not properly responding to the hijacker and threat after boarding. In this situation, the air carrier has made a substantial contribution to those injuries even though the injuries would not have occurred but for the hijacker's acts.[195]

On the other hand, the injuries for which a plaintiff passenger seeks compensation must not be too remote. In *National Airlines, Inc.* v. *Edwards*,[196] a passenger on an American airliner that was hijacked to Cuba brought suit against the air carrier to recover for illness and injuries that resulted in mental and physical disability and loss of wage-earning capacity that the passenger allegedly sustained as a result of being forced to consume Cuban food and drink. The plaintiff apparently had to claim that her injuries resulted in part from the consumption of Cuban food because Florida adheres to the impact doctrine in claims for damages due to mental and emotional injuries. The Florida Supreme Court reversed the appellate court, and reinstated an order of dismissal rendered by the trial court, on the grounds that the damages alleged to be the result of the airline's negligence were too remote as a matter of law in that they were not the natural and

---

193 W. Prosser, *Law of Torts*, Section 44, at p. 275 (4th ed. 1971).

194 49 U.S.C. Section 44903(b) (1997).

195 W. Prosser, *Law of Torts*, Section 44, at p. 273 (4th ed. 1971).

196 *National Airlines, Inc.* v. *Edwards*, 336 So. 2d 545 (Fla. 1976).

probable consequences of the tortious act and did not ordinarily and naturally flow therefrom.[197] The court cited *Taylor Imported Motors, Inc.* v. *Smiley*,[198] and *Kwoka* v. *Campbell*[199] in support of its opinion.

Contributory Negligence

In some states, the defense of contributory or comparative negligence may be available to airlines.[200] In such a jurisdiction, a passenger suffering injuries during a hijacking or similar incident would be unable to recover, or his recovery might be diminished, if his own negligence proximately contributed to his own injuries. Contributory negligence, where applicable, is a complete bar to recovery in a case brought in negligence.[201] In jurisdictions where comparative negligence is applied, a passenger's conduct may mitigate against his recovery as opposed to barring recovery.

The question of whether or not a passenger was guilty of contributory negligence might arise where a passenger voluntarily acts to subdue a hijacker and is injured as a result. A plaintiff passenger who has increased the risk of harm to himself over what the risk would have been had he exercised reasonable care may be held to have exculpated a negligent airline.[202] On the other hand, courts have held that where a plaintiff is confronted with imminent peril to himself or to a third person, for example, another passenger, he may assume extraordinary risks in attempting to protect himself or a third person from the danger without being guilty of contributory negligence.[203] An application of this rule to the context of airline hijackings would limit the availability of the contributory or comparative negligence defense for the air carriers.

---

197 *National Airlines, Inc.* v. *Edwards*, 336 So. 2d 545 (Fla. 1976).

198 *Taylor Imported Motors, Inc.* v. *Smiley*, 143 So.2d 66 (Fla. App. 1962).

199 *Kwoka* v. *Campbell*, 296 So.2d 629 (Fla. App. 1974).

200 W. Prosser, *Law of Torts*, Section 65, at p. 416 (4th ed. 1971).

201 *La Com* v. *Pacific Gas & Electric Co.*, 132 Cal. 2d 889, 281 P.2d 894 (1955); compare *State* v. *Henson Flying Serv., Inc.*, 60 A.2d 675 (Md. App. 1948); *Bradfield* v. *Trans World Airlines, Inc.*, 88 Cal. Ap. 3d 681, 152 Cal. Rptr. 172 (1979), holding that comparative negligence is available as a defense in actions based on the Warsaw Convention.

202 *Northwest Airlines* v. *Glenn L. Martin Co.*, 224 F.2d 120 (6th Cir. 1955).

203 *Aylor* v. *Intercountry Construction Corp.*, 381 F.2d 930 (DC. Cir. 1976); *Thompson* v. *Van Wagener*, 25 Utah 2d 383, 483 P.2d 427 (1971); *Eckert* v. *Long Island R.R.*, 43 N.Y. 502 (1871); W. Prosser, *Law of Torts*, Section 33, at p. 168 (4th ed. 1971).

Assumption of Risk

One who becomes a passenger on an air carrier engaged in a domestic flight normally assumes the risks of those perils incident to air travel that cannot be averted even by the carrier's exercise of the highest degree of care.[204] In light of this principle, it has been suggested that an assumption of the risk[205] defense may be asserted by an air carrier in response to an action for injuries resulting from a skyjacking incident.[206] To establish a defense of assumption of the risk, a carrier would have to show that the passenger knew of and appreciated the risk of hijacking before contracting for passage.[207] Thus, the air carrier could probably utilize such a defense only if a hijacking warning were printed on the passenger ticket, which is the contract of carriage between the passenger and carrier. In this way, the passenger could be held to have voluntarily entered into the contract of carriage fully knowing and appreciating the risk involved, but still electing to encounter the possible danger by boarding the plane.[208]

Without notice and warning, the assumption of the risk defense would fail because the passenger, as one to whom the high duty of care is owed, has a right to assume that it will be performed and is not required to anticipate the airline's negligent acts or omissions.[209] Even if an airline did have an adequate warning of the hijacking danger printed on its tickets, making the determination that the risk of losing passengers is outweighed by the potential liability, any provisions that would exclude or limit liability may be held to be imposed by adhesion and against public policy.[210] The Warsaw Convention's limitations on air carrier liability are effectuated through the contract

---

204 *Wilson* v. *Colonial Air Transp., Inc.*, 180 N.E. 212 (Mass. 1932); compare *Husserl* v. *Swiss Air Transp. Co.*, 351 F. Supp. 702 (S.D.N.Y. 1972) (brought under Article 17 of the Warsaw Convention, which provides that the carrier "shall be liable" for any bodily injuries occurring on international flights).

205 W. Prosser, *Law of Torts*, Section 68, at p. 439 (4th ed. 1971).

206 M. McClintock, *Aircraft Hijacking: Its Civil and Criminal Ramifications* (1971) at p. 72.

207 Restatement (Second) of Torts, Section 469 (1965).

208 M. McClintock, *Aircraft Hijacking: Its Civil and Criminal Ramifications* (1971) at p. 73; A. Toothman, *Legal Problems of Skyjacking*, 251, 257 (1969).

209 *Northwest Airlines* v. *Glenn L. Martin Co.*, 224 F.2d 120 (6th Cir. 1955).

210 *Deutsche Lufthansa Aktiengesellschaft* v. *CAB*, 479 F.2d 912 (DC. Cir. 1973); *Lisi* v. *Alitalia-Linee Aeree Italiane*, 253 F. Supp. 237 (S.D.N.Y.), aff'd, 370 F.2d 508 (2d Cir. 1966); aff'd by an equally divided court, 390 U.S. 455 (1968); Restatement (Second) of Contracts, Section 195 (1981).

between an airline and its passengers as expressed by the ticket.[211] Article 3(1) of the Warsaw Convention requires that a ticket state that the transportation is subject to the Convention liability rule, while Section (2) provides that a carrier must deliver a passenger ticket to a passenger if it is to avail itself of the Convention's liability limitations.[212]

Furthermore, courts have recognized that, in situations where statutes have been enacted to protect a particular class of persons against their own inability to protect themselves, the fundamental purpose of such statutes would be defeated if a member of the protected class were held to assume the risk.[213] Furthermore, some jurisdictions have abandoned assumption of the risk as a bar to recovery in negligence cases.[214] In such cases, courts have generally concluded that where a statute has been enacted to protect a particular class of plaintiffs, they cannot assume the risk of violation of the statute, either expressly or by implication. Therefore, a plaintiff passenger who suffers injuries arising out of the skyjacking of a United States carrier, in which the hijacker has carried a concealed weapon or explosive device through the passenger screening station and aboard the aircraft without detection, may not be held to have assumed the risk in light of the protective purpose of the legislation and regulations pursuant thereto requiring airlines to "prevent or deter the carriage aboard its aircraft of any explosive or incendiary device or weapon in carry-on baggage or on or about the persons of passengers".[215] On the other hand, an airline's assumption of the risk defense is more apt to prevail in a case arising out of a hijacking in which the skyjacker was not armed, because there would be no violation of statute by the airline in such a case.

Compensable Injuries

Since pre-flight screening of all airline passengers and their carry-on items was implemented in January 1973, there has been only one

211 *In re Air Crash in Bali, Indonesia*, 462 F. Supp. 1114 (C.D. Cal. 1978), rev'd on other grounds, 684 F.2d 1301 (9th Cir. 1982).

212 Warsaw Convention, Article 3.

213 *Narramore* v. *Cleveland C.C. & St. L. R. Co.*, 96 F 298 (6th Cir.), cert. denied, 175 U.S. 724 (1899); *Suess* v. *Anouherd Steel Products Co.*, 180 Minn. 21, 230 N.W. 125 (1930). Restatement (Second) of Torts, Section 496F (1965).

214 *Farley* v. *MM Cattle Co.*, 529 S.W.2d 751 (Tex. 1975).

215 14 C.F.R. Section 108.9(a) (2001); 49 U.S.C. Section 46505 (1997).

skyjacking attempt aboard a United States air carrier that involved a hijacker armed with a firearm that penetrated the screening system.[216] There have been several incidents in which some lesser weapon, for example, a knife, was used. Overall though, excluding the September 11th tragedies, the number of passengers who have actually sustained direct bodily injuries at the hands of skyjackers on American airliners since January 1973 has been small. On 4 April 1979, a female hostage received cuts on her throat from the knife of a would-be hijacker.[217] No other airline passengers sustained bodily injuries in the course of the twenty-eight hijacking incidents on United States air carriers in 1978 and 1979.[218] On the other hand, between 1974 and 30 June 1979, criminal acts perpetrated against United States civil aviation resulted in a total of 116 deaths and 120 injuries, which, of course, include persons other than passengers.[219] Leading up to 11 September 2001, there had been no hijackings aboard a domestic carrier since 1991.

The question of whether a passenger on a hijacked or similarly threatened airliner can recover for any mental anguish, emotional trauma, nervous shock or fright has become a particularly critical issue since January 1973. There is no question that an innocent

216 Department of Transportation, Federal Aviation Administration, Semi-annual Report to Congress on Effectiveness of the Civil Aviation Program, 1 January–30 June 1979 (1979), submitted pursuant to the Federal Aviation Act, 49 U.S.C. Section 1341 (1976), as amended, Pub. L. Number 93–366 (1979) at p. 1; *New York Times*, 27 January 1980, at p. 18, column 5.

217 Department of Transportation, Federal Aviation Administration, Semi-annual Report to Congress on Effectiveness of the Civil Aviation Program, 1 January–30 June 1979 (1979), submitted pursuant to the Federal Aviation Act, 49 U.S.C. Section 1341 (1976), as amended, Pub. L. Number 93–366 (1979), at p. 3.

218 Department of Transportation, Federal Aviation Administration, Semi-annual Report to Congress on Effectiveness of the Civil Aviation Program, 1 January–30 June 1979 (1979), submitted pursuant to the Federal Aviation Act, 49 U.S.C. Section 1341 (1976), as amended, Pub. L. Number 93–366 (1979), at pp. 2-4; Department of Transportation, Federal Aviation Administration, Semi-annual Report to Congress on the Effectiveness of the Civil Aviation Program, 1 July–31 December 1978 (1979) at pp. 2–4; Department of Transportation, Federal Aviation Administration Semi-annual Report to Congress on the Effectiveness of the Civil Aviation Program, 1 January–30 June 1978 (1978) at pp. 7–8.

219 Department of Transportation, Federal Aviation Administration, Semi-annual Report to Congress on Effectiveness of the Civil Aviation Program, 1 January–30 June 1979 (1979), submitted pursuant to the Federal Aviation Act, 49 U.S.C. Section 1341 (1976), as amended, Pub. L. Number 93–366 (1979) at p. 9.

passenger can recover damages for any bodily injuries proximately caused by an airline's negligence. By contrast, some objections against permitting recovery for negligently inflicted mental distress have been advanced, among them, that it cannot be measured in terms of money, that it is too remote and that increased litigation will result.[220] These objections would seem to have no special application to suits arising out of airline hijackings. Furthermore, modern courts have largely dismissed these arguments because "[m]ental suffering is no more difficult to estimate in financial terms, and no less a real injury than physical pain. . . . It is the business of the courts to make precedent where a wrong calls for redress, even if lawsuits must be multiplied".[221] The only valid objection to allowance of recovery for mental or emotional injury is considered to be the danger of vexatious suits and fictitious claims because mental anguish is viewed as being easily simulated.

One result of these concerns was the development of the "impact" doctrine, or the theory that requires the presence of physical "impact" at the time of the incident giving rise to the psychiatric injury to insure that the alleged mental distress is legitimate.[222] In *Burnett* v. *Trans World Airlines, Inc.*,[223] it was held that mental anguish alone is not compensable under the Warsaw system's provision that the air carrier shall be liable for bodily injuries received by its passengers. However, the court also decided that an injured passenger could recover for bodily injuries even though not caused by physical contact and that "emotional distress . . . directly precipitated by bodily injury [is] considered as a part of the bodily injury itself for which damages are recoverable".[224] It was similarly held in *Roman* v. *Trans World Airlines, Inc.*[225] that an airline is liable under the Warsaw system for "palpable, objective bodily injuries including those caused by the psychic trauma of the hijacking, and for damages flowing from those bodily injuries [including mental suffering], but not for the trauma as such or for the non-bodily or behavioral manifestations of that trauma". In support of the *Roman* v. *Trans World Airlines, Inc.*

220 W. Prosser, *Law of Torts*, Section 33, at p. 327 (4th ed. 1971).
221 W. Prosser, *Law of Torts*, Section 33, at pp. 327–328 (4th ed. 1971).
222 *Purcell* v. *St. Ry.*, 48 Minn. 134, 50 N.W. 1034 (1892).
223 *Burnett* v. *Trans World Airlines, Inc.*, 368 F.Supp. 1152 (D.N.M. 1973).
224 *Burnett* v. *Trans World Airlines, Inc.*, 368 F.Supp. 1152, 1158 (D.N.M. 1973).
225 *Roman* v. *Trans World Airlines, Inc.*, 34 N.Y..2d 385, 358 N.Y.S.2d 97, 314 N.E.2d 848 (1974).

decision, the Supreme Court held, in *Eastern Airlines* v. *Floyd*,[226] that "purely mental" injuries are not compensable under the Warsaw Convention.

Clearly, where, as a result of a defendant's negligence, the plaintiff suffers physical injury, courts will order compensation for purely mental or emotional elements of the accompanying or consequential damage, such as fright at the time of the injury.[227] Moreover, with the recent trend toward the abandonment of the impact requirement in a majority of jurisdictions,[228] a plaintiff generally may recover for mental and emotional injuries suffered as a result of another's negligence, even where there has been no physical impact, if the party seeking recovery was subjected to fear of physical injury as a direct result of the tortious conduct. The reason for the retreat from the impact requirement was expressed in *Battalla* v. *State*:[229]

> "It is fundamental to our Common Law system that one may seek redress for every substantial wrong. . . . In many instances, just as in impact cases, there will be no doubt as to the presence and extent of the damage and the fact that it was proximately caused by defendant's negligence. In the difficult cases, we must look to the quality and genuineness of proof, and rely to an extent on the contemporary sophistication of the medical profession and the ability of the court and jury to weed out the dishonest claims. Claimant should, therefore, be given an opportunity to prove that her injuries were proximately caused by defendant's negligence."

It has been held that there may even be recovery for mental or emotional suffering in the absence of the fear of potential physical injury to the person directly subjected to the negligent act of another, provided that the psychic injury is genuine, substantial and proximately caused by the defendant's negligence.[230]

---

226 *Eastern Airlines* v. *Floyd*, 499 U.S. 530 (1991).

227 *Baltimore & O.R. Co.* v. *McBride*, 36 F.2d 841 (6th Cir. 1930); *Steitz* v. *Giford*, 280 N.Y. 15, 19 N.E.2d 661 (1939).

228 W. Prosser, *Law of Torts*, Section 33, at p. 168 (4th ed. 1971) at 332; Restatement (Second) of Torts, Section 313 (1965).

229 *Battalla* v. *State*, 10 N.Y.2d 237, 219 N.Y.S.2d 34, 176 N.E.2d 729, 740–42 (1961).

230 *Johnson* v. *State*, 37 N.Y.2d 378, 383–84, 372 N.Y.S.2d 638, 642–43, 334 N.E.2d 590, 593 (1975). However, *see Mason* v. *Belieu*, 543 F.2d 215 (6th Cir.), cert. denied, 429 U.S. 852 (1976) (wife held not entitled to recover for mental distress suffered when

In *Kalish* v. *Trans World Airlines*,[231] an airline passenger was held entitled to recover for emotional injuries incurred when she was allegedly trampled by other passengers who were trapped in a burning aircraft. The court held that, due to the circumstances of the case, the plaintiff passenger was not required to prove physical impact:

> "[A]ny person in plaintiff's predicament would anticipate and be terrified, on a sustained basis, by the possibility of suffering very serious injury or death while a captive in a burning aircraft. Such anticipation, anxiety and anguish would not be suffered in split-seconds, but over a prolonged period of twenty minutes or more which heightened plaintiff's natural horror and the consequential psychic traumatic effects of the situation. Each second was an eternity. This was . . . a real life terror-in-the-sky emergency which, undoubtedly, had an overwhelming, engulfing, terror-stricken impact on plaintiff as a captive passenger . . . The obvious mental anguish which all passengers including plaintiff must have suffered over their possibility of being destroyed in a crash or by an explosion in mid-air beggars [sic] normal imagination unless one has actually been the victim of such events. This court concludes that the assault against the plaintiff's emotional senses of these circumstances was so pervasive as to be tantamount to the infliction of physical blows on her body, and was the same as if she had suffered additional, actual body injuries".[232]

The reasoning of the court in *Kalish* is very easily applicable to an air carrier hijacking case, which is also a "terror-in-the-sky emergency", such that it is "obvious" that passengers would suffer mental anguish and anxiety over the possibility of being destroyed in a crash or by an explosion in mid-air. Under *Kalish*, and other similar cases, a passenger on an air carrier that is hijacked may recover, *inter alia*, for any mental anguish, emotional trauma, nervous shock and fright even without proof of physical injury or impact in a jurisdiction that does not adhere to the "impact" rule.

---

airplane prevented husband from boarding scheduled flight despite airline's failure to give wife valid explanation when husband did not arrive on flight) and *Cohen* v. *Varig Airlines*, 62 A.D.2d 234, 405 N.Y.S.2d 44, 49–50 (1978) (plaintiffs were held not entitled to recover for alleged mental and emotional suffering due to lost luggage).

231 *Kalish* v. *Trans World Airlines*, 89 Misc. 2d 153, 390 N.Y.S.2d 1007 (1977).

232 *Kalish* v. *Trans World Airlines*, 89 Misc. 2d 153, 390 N.Y.S.2d 1007, at 1011 (1977).

Furthermore, because courts have determined "impact" to be sufficient in minor contacts with the person that could not be responsible for the real injury, a plaintiff passenger may be able to recover for mental and emotional injuries arising out of skyjackings and related crimes, even in jurisdictions that follow the "impact" rule. Sufficient impact has been found in a slight blow,[233] a trivial jolt or jar,[234] a forcible seating[235] and a fall caused by fainting.[236] Moreover, it has been held that "shock to the nerves and nervous system", by itself, constitutes physical harm that is enough to satisfy the requirement of impact.[237]

Nevertheless, in the absence of an application of the rule in *Kalish* that the circumstances of the injury provide a sufficient guarantee that the claim for mental anguish is genuine, most courts will require evidence of physical consequences or manifestations of the psychiatric injury before damages will be awarded.[238] In a jurisdiction that follows the impact doctrine, some physical contact, however slight, will be required before recovery for mental distress will be allowed. In *Burnett* v. *Trans World Airlines, Inc.*, 368 F. Supp. 1152 (D.N.H. 1973), the court rejected an argument that the hijacking itself and the subsequent division of the aircraft constituted bodily injury in spite of the fact that the abduction of the passengers was apparently an actionable interference with the person of the passenger. Because of the divergent positions assumed by numerous states on the issue of compensation for persons suffering mental or emotional injuries, the determination of choice of law questions may dispose of current and future suits by passengers of air carriers for injuries resulting from skyjackings. The assumption is made that bodily injuries to airline passengers on hijacked United States flights will be the exception and not the rule.

---

233 *Space* v. *Lynn & B.R.R.*, 172 Mass. 488, 52 N.E. 747 (1898).

234 *Zelinsky* v. *Chimes*, 196 Pa. Super. 312, 175 A.2d 351 (1961) ("any degree of physical impact, however slight"); *Kasey* v. *Suburban Gas Heat of Kennewick, Inc.*, 60 Wash.2d 468, 374 P.2d 549 (1962) (shock explosion); *Boston* v. *Chesapeake & O.R. Co.*, 223 Ind. 425, 61 N.E.2d 326 (1945).

235 *Driscoll* v. *Gaffey*, 207 Mass. 109, 92 N.E. 1010 (1910).

236 *Comstock* v. *Wilson*, 257 N.Y. 231, 177 N.E. 431 (1931).

237 *Vanoni* v. *Western Airlines*, 247 Cal. App.2d 793, 56 Cal. Rptr. 115 (1967), which allowed recovery for fright due to the negligent operation of the airliner.

238 *Robb* v. *Pennsylvania R.R.*, 58 Del. 454, 210 A.2d 709 (1965); *Daley* v. *La Croix*, 384 Mich. 4, 179 N.W.2d 390 (1970); *Niederman* v. *Brodsky*, 436 Pa. 401, 261 A.2d 84 (1970); Restatement (Second) of Torts, Section 33 (1965).

In addition to claiming for bodily injuries and mental distress, a plaintiff passenger might also seek to recover for lost work time, delay or substitute travel expenses incurred or loss of a business deal or contract.[239] However, domestic airlines are able to avoid or limit liability for delays in completion of flights in accordance with tariffs filed with and approved by the CAB.[240]

Conflict of Laws

For choice of law purposes, the ideal case would involve a plaintiff passenger and defendant airline who are both domiciled in the state in which the hijacker boarded and the plaintiff's injury occurred. In such a case, there would probably be no doubt as to which state's substantive law would apply. Should a domestic hijacking result in litigation, however, it is likely that the case would involve a passenger and airline with different domiciles, and a situation where the hijacker boarded the aircraft in one state and the passenger suffered injury in another state. In the January 1980 Delta hijacking, the Atlanta-based air carrier was flying from Los Angeles, California to New York City with passengers boarding in Los Angeles, Dallas, Texas and Atlanta, Georgia, when it was hijacked while in North Carolina's air space. The hijacker smuggled the handgun aboard the aircraft in Atlanta, Georgia.[241]

State substantive laws applicable to a passenger's suit for damages arising out of a hijacking of a domestic commercial airliner may conflict on several issues in addition to whether persons who have suffered mental or emotional injuries will be compensated:

(1) The interpretation of the doctrine of *res ipsa loquitur*;
(2) The duty of care owed by air carriers to their passengers; and
(3) Whether contributory or comparative negligence and/or assumption of the risk may be asserted by the air carrier in order to bar or reduce the injured passenger's recovery.

---

239 M. McClintock, *Aircraft Hijacking: Its Civil and Criminal Ramifications* (1971) at pp. 57–59; McClintock, "Skyjacking: Its Domestic Civil and Criminal Ramifications", 39 J. Air L. & Com 29, 39–40 (1973).

240 49 U.S.C. Section 41509 (1997); Tompkins, "The Aftermath of a Hijacking — Passenger Claims and Insurance", 39 J. Air. L. & Com. 381, 388 (1973).

241 *Dallas Morning News*, 26 January 1980, at p. 1, column 1.

States even disagree on the choice of law rule that is to be utilized in order to determine the state law that is applicable to the merits of the case.[242] Three frequently employed conflicts theories are:

(1) *Lex loci delicti*, in which the court applies the law of the jurisdiction where the tort occurred;[243]
(2) "Significant contacts", which calls for a determination of which state has the most significant relationship to the issue;[244] and
(3) "Government interest", under which the court compares the law of the state involved and the interests of the litigants to determine the law most "appropriately" applicable to the subject issue.[245]

In this regard, the former strict *lex loci delicti*, "place of injury", rule has largely been abandoned in favor of one of the more flexible rules that permit analysis of the policies and interests underlying the particular issue before the court.[246] In the frequently cited case of *Babcock* v. *Jackson*,[247] the court concluded that:

> "[j]ustice, fairness and the 'best practical result' may best be achieved by giving controlling effect to the law of the

---

242 Douglas, "Air Disaster Litigation Without Diversity", 45 J. Air L. & Com. 411, 424 (1980).

243 The court may look to the place of injury, *In Re Air Crash Disaster at Boston, Massachusetts on 31 July 1973*, 399 F.Supp. 1106, 1115 (D. Mass. 1975), or to the state where the tortious act occurred: *Manos* v. *TWA, Inc.*, 295 F.Supp. 1170, 1176 (N.D. Ill. 1969).

244 Douglas, "Air Disaster Litigation Without Diversity", 45 J. Air L. & Com. 411, 425 (1980). Section 146 of the Restatement (Second) of Conflict of Laws provides: "In an action for a personal injury, the local law of the state where the injury occurred determines the rights and liabilities of the parties, unless, with respect to the particular issue, some other state has a more significant relationship . . . with the occurrence and the parties, in which event the local law of the other state will govern." Section 378 of the Restatement (Second) of Conflict of Laws (1934) states: "The law of the place of the wrong determines whether a person has sustained a legal injury.".

245 Douglas, "Air Disaster Litigation Without Diversity", 45 J. Air L. & Com. 411, 425 (1980); *In re Paris Air Crash of 3 March 1974*, 399 F.Supp. 732 (C.D. Cal. 1975).

246 *Lowe's North Wilkesboro Hardware, Inc.* v. *Fidelity Mut. Life Ins. Co.*, 319 F.2d 469, 473 (4th Cir. 1973); *Griffith* v. *United Air Lines, Inc.*, 416 Pa. 1, 203 A.2d 796, 805 (1964); *George* v. *Douglas Aircraft Co.*, 332 F.2d 73 (2d Cir.), cert. denied, 379 U.S. 904 (1964); *Pearson* v. *Northeast Airlines, Inc.*, 309 F.2d 553 (2d Cir. 1962), cert. denied, 372 U.S. 912 (1963); *Schmidt* v. *Driscoll Hotel, Inc.*, 249 Minn. 376, 82 N.W.2d 365 (1957); *Kilberg* v. *Northeast Airlines, Inc.*, 9 N.Y.2d 34, 211 N.Y.S.2d 133, 172 N.E.2d 526 (1961).

247 *Babcock* v. *Jackson*, 12 N.Y.2d 473, 240 N.Y.S.2d 743, 191 N.E.2d 279 (1963).

> jurisdiction which, because of its relationship or contact with the occurrence or the parties, has the greatest concern with the specific issue raised in the litigation".[248]

The United States Supreme Court has indicated apparent approval of the trend to depart from the "place of the injury" rule to give consideration to the extent of the interests of the states having contact with the legal issue and with the parties. In *Richards* v. *United States*, the law of the place where the act or omission occurred was applied even though the injury occurred in another state.[249]

It is submitted that in a suit brought by a passenger who seeks recovery from an airline for injuries received during a domestic skyjacking carried out by a hijacker who succeeded in smuggling a weapon or explosive device aboard, the liability of the airline should normally be resolved by the law of the state where the hijacker boarded the aircraft, even though the actual injuries may have been sustained while the airliner was within the territorial auspices of another state. This rule would avoid having to deal with the problem of determining over which state's territory the passenger's injury occurred, a problem that would be particularly troublesome in the case of alleged mental or emotional distress because the injury may result from the entire traumatic event, which could encompass flight over several states.

Furthermore, application of the law of the state where the hijacker penetrated the screening system is consistent with the rule that whether a person has been negligent is normally determined by reference to the law of the state where he acted and the standards of conduct in existence there.[250] Moreover, an analysis of the policies and interests of the respective states with regard to hijackings and their prevention would favor application of the law of the state where the hijacker smuggled his weapon past the pre-flight screening checkpoint. Federal regulations prohibit an airline from allowing a passenger to board its aircraft with a dangerous weapon or explosive

---

248 *Babcock* v. *Jackson*, 12 N.Y.2d 473, at 481, 240 N.Y.S.2d 743, at 749, 191 N.E.2d 279, at 283 (1963).

249 *Richards* v. *United States*, 369 U.S. 1, at 12–13 (1962).

250 H. Goodrich, *Conflicts of Laws*, Section 94, at p. 173 (4th ed. 1964); *Vrooman* v. *Beech Aircraft Corp.*, 183 F.2d 479 (10th Cir. 1950); *Farmer* v. *Standard Dredging Corp.*, 167 F. Supp. 381 (D. Del. 1958).

device,[251] and state courts impose liability on carriers for failure to protect their passengers from foreseeable harm.[252] Since the federal regulations and the Common Law duty of protection seek to regulate activity that poses particular danger to the public, the state in which the pre-flight screening procedures are effectuated has a clear interest in their reasonable performance. If the protection afforded the public by the regulation is to be effective, it must be effective at the source of the danger, for example, the screening checkpoint.

Therefore, considering the purpose of the regulations, the state where the hijacker boards the aircraft has a greater relation to the occurrence of a hijacking than does a state wherein the actual injury was sustained by the passenger, despite the latter state's interest in providing compensation to those injured within its boundaries. Accordingly, the law of the state where the aircraft was boarded by the hijacker should normally govern suits for damages brought by passengers against airlines for injuries suffered during in-flight hijackings of domestic carriers.[253] On the other hand, in a case where the issue of the air carrier's negligence arises solely out of the actions taken by the carrier's employees during the course of an in-flight skyjacking, for example, where the hijacker is not armed and the air carrier's employees take no action to determine such, an analysis of each state's relationship to the occurrence may lead to a different result and an application of the law of the state where the injury, if any, occurred.

Federal Legislation — Post September 11th Tragedies

September 11th Victim Compensation Fund Act

The September 11th Victim Compensation Fund Act of 2001 encompasses part of the United States Congress' legislative reaction to the September 11th tragedies. In general, this Act allows for qualified victims to obtain compensation for physical injuries or death that

251 14 C.F.R. Section 108.9(a) (2001).

252 *Letsos* v. *Chicago Transit Auth.*, 47 Ill. 437, 441, 265 N.E.2d 650, 653 (1976).

253 *People ex rel Compagnie Nationale Air France* v. *Gilberto*, 74 Ill. 2d 90, 383 N.E.2d 977, 981 (1978) (applicability of the Warsaw Convention "depends on the place where the 'accident', rather than the resulting injuries occurred, and the 'accident'. . . consisted of the hijacking itself").

resulted from the September 11th terrorist-related aircraft crashes.[254] Qualified victims under this statute are individuals or deceased individuals' representatives:

> ". . . who [were] present at the World Trade Center (New York, New York), the Pentagon (Arlington, Virginia), or the site of the aircraft crash at Shanksville, Pennsylvania at the time, or in the immediate aftermath, of the terrorist-related aircraft crashes of 11 September 2001; and suffered physical harm or death as a result of such an air crash".[255]

Also, qualified victims include any individual or deceased individual's representative:

> ". . . who was a member of the flight crew or a passenger on American Airlines flight 11 or 77 or United Airlines flight 93 or 175, except that an individual identified by the Attorney General to have been a participant or conspirator in the terrorist-related aircraft crashes of 11 September 2001, or a representative of such individual".[256]

Once an individual qualifies as a victim, he then files a claim asserting factual information relating to physical harm, economic losses and non-economic losses suffered as a result of the September 11th terrorist-related crashes.[257] The individual's claim is then processed by the Special Master, who determines the amount of compensation warranted.[258] Any compensation received from the September 11th Victim Compensation Fund will be reduced by the amount of compensation the victim received or is entitled to receive from "life insurance, pension funds, death benefit programs or payments by Federal,

254 September 11th Victim Compensation Fund Act of 2001, Pub. L. Number 107–42, 115 Stat. 230, 237 (2001).

255 September 11th Victim Compensation Fund Act of 2001, Pub. L. Number 107–42, 115 Stat. 230, 239 (2001).

256 September 11th Victim Compensation Fund Act of 2001, Pub. L. Number 107–42, 115 Stat. 230, 239 (2001).

257 September 11th Victim Compensation Fund Act of 2001, Pub. L. Number 107–42, 115 Stat. 230, 238 (2001).

258 September 11th Victim Compensation Fund Act of 2001, Pub. L. Number 107–42, 115 Stat. 230, 239 (2001).

State, or local governments related to the terrorist-related aircraft crashes of 11 September 2001".[259]

Upon submission of a claim under the September 11th Victim Compensation Fund Act of 2001, the individual "waives the right to file a civil action (or to be a party to an action) in any Federal or State court for damages sustained as a result of the terrorist-related aircraft crashes of 11 September 2001".[260] The statute of limitations for filing a claim with the September 11th Victim Compensation Fund is two years from the promulgation of the applicable regulations.[261]

If an individual decides not to file under the September 11th Victim Compensation Fund, that individual can pursue a civil action for damages arising out of the terrorist-related crashes.[262] However, this suit must be filed in the District Court of the Southern District of New York. Further, the substantive law applicable to such a suit shall be derived from the state law in which the crash occurred, unless such law is inconsistent with or pre-empted by federal law.

Aviation and Transportation Security Act

The Aviation and Transportation Security Act of 2001 encompasses another part of United States Congress' reaction to the September 11th tragedies. This Act was broad in its nature and sweeping in its changes to the current aviation security system. Many of these changes will substantially affect the course of future litigation regarding airline hijackings. The Act created the Transportation Security Administration,[263] which is headed by the Under Secretary of Transportation for Security.[264] In general, the Under Secretary is responsible for "carrying out chapter 449 (49 U.S.C.S. Sections 44901 *et seq.*), relating to civil aviation security, and related research and development activities".[265]

---

259 September 11th Victim Compensation Fund Act of 2001, Pub. L. Number 107–42, 115 Stat. 230, 237–239 (2001).

260 September 11th Victim Compensation Fund Act of 2001, Pub. L. Number 107–42, 115 Stat. 230, 240 (2001).

261 September 11th Victim Compensation Fund Act of 2001, Pub. L. Number 107–42, 115 Stat. 230, 238 (2001).

262 September 11th Victim Compensation Fund Act of 2001, Pub. L. Number 107–42, 115 Stat. 230, 240–241 (2001).

263 Aviation and Security Transportation Act of 2001, 49 U.S.C. Section 114(a) (2001).

264 49 U.S.C. Section 114(b)(1) (2001).

265 49 U.S.C. Section 114(d)(1) (2001).

Specifically, the Under Secretary is now responsible for, and shall provide for, the screening of all passengers and property, including United States mail, cargo, carry-on and checked baggage, and other articles that will be carried aboard a passenger aircraft operated by an air carrier, intrastate air carrier or foreign air carrier.[266] Additionally, the Under Secretary is responsible for hiring, retaining and testing all security screening personnel at all airports in the United States where screening is required.[267] In order to perform all of these functions, the Under Secretary is authorized to acquire all necessary real property, human resources and other resources that are needed to perform his responsibilities.[268]

With regard to in-flight safety, the Act provides that the Under Secretary is responsible for the hiring, training and deploying of federal air marshals.[269] The Under Secretary may require the "deployment of Federal air marshals on every passenger flight of air carriers in air transportation or intrastate air transportation".[270] Further, the Under Secretary "shall provide for deployment of Federal air marshals on every such flight determined by the Secretary to present high security risks".[271]

For airline personnel, the FAA Administrator, in conjunction with the Under Secretary, law enforcement, security and terrorism experts, air carriers and labor organizations representing commercial aviation employees, is responsible for developing a training program for crew members.[272] This program must provide "detailed guidance for a scheduled passenger air carrier flight and cabin crew training program to prepare crew members for potential threat conditions". The Act provides for a sixty-day timetable for the development of this program,[273] and requires air carriers to complete the training of all flight and cabin crews within 180 days after approval of the training program.

The Act also requires the FAA Administrator to issue an order providing for the strengthening of the flight deck door and locks on

266 49 U.S.C. Section 44901(a) (2001).
267 49 U.S.C. Section 114(e) (2001).
268 49 U.S.C. Section 114(j) (2001).
269 49 U.S.C. Section 44917(a) (2001).
270 49 U.S.C. Section 44917(a)(1) (2001).
271 49 U.S.C. Section 44917(a)(2) (2001).
272 49 U.S.C. Section 44918(a) (2001).
273 49 U.S.C. Section 44903 (2001).

passenger aircraft to ensure that the door cannot be forced open from the passenger compartment.[274] Further, the Act requires that such flight deck doors remain locked "while any such aircraft is in flight except when necessary to permit access and egress by authorized persons". The Act prohibits possession of a key to the flight deck door by any member of the flight crew who is not assigned to the flight deck. Finally, the Act limits liability with regard to the September 11th tragedies. The Act provides that:

> ". . . notwithstanding any other provision of law, liability for all claims, whether for compensatory or punitive damages or for contribution or indemnity, arising from the terrorist-related aircraft crashes of 11 September 2001, against an air carrier, air craft manufacturer, airport sponsor . . . shall not be in an amount greater than the limits of liability insurance coverage maintained by that air carrier, aircraft manufacturer, airport sponsor or person".[275]

Terrorism Risk Insurance Act

In recognition of the difficulties encountered by businesses and individuals in obtaining property and casualty coverage after 11 September 2001, Congress has enacted the Terrorism Risk Insurance Act of 2002. The Act creates the Terrorism Insurance Program, a temporary Federal program under which the government will share the risk of insured loss due to acts of terrorism with property and casualty insurance carriers. The Terrorism Insurance Program is established within the Department of the Treasury, with the Secretary of the Treasury charged with administration of the program.[276] The Act requires that insurance carriers doing business in the United States provide property and casualty insurance for acts of terrorism whose terms do not "differ materially" from the terms, amounts and other coverage limitations applicable to losses arising from events other than acts of terrorism.[277]

---

274 Aviation and Security Transportation Act of 2001, Pub. L. Number 107–71, 115 Stat. 597, 605–606 (2001).

275 Air Transportation Safety and System Stabilization Act, Pub. L. Number 107–71, 115 Stat. 597, 646 (2001).

276 Terrorism Risk Insurance Act of 2002, Pub. L. Number 107–297, 116 Stat. 2322 (2002).

277 Terrorism Risk Insurance Act of 2002, Pub. L. Number 107–297, 116 Stat. 2322 (2002).

Insurance carriers will receive Federal reimbursement for a portion of paid losses from coverage offered in accordance with the Act.

In order to be eligible for participation in the program, "an act of terrorism" must be certified by the Secretary of the Treasury and exhibit certain characteristics.[278] Acts covered are those terrorist acts that are violent or dangerous to human life, property or infrastructure, and must be perpetrated by individuals, acting on behalf of a foreign person or interest, as part of an effort to coerce the government or civilian population of the United States.[279] While, generally, the terrorist act must have resulted in damage in the United States, insured losses suffered by an air carrier are covered by the Act regardless of where the loss occurs.[280] Property and casualty insurance losses must exceed US $5-million, and acts committed as part of the course of a war declared by Congress are not covered.[281] The Secretary's certification of an act of terrorism is final and is not subject to judicial review.

The Act also creates a Federal cause of action for claims for property damage, personal injury or death that exist once the Secretary of the Treasury has certified an event as an act of terrorism.[282] This cause of action is the exclusive remedy for such claims relating to terrorist acts. Any amounts awarded in such an action that are attributable to punitive damages are not counted as insured losses under the Act.

Conclusion

The Warsaw system, with its imposition of absolute liability on international air carriers for injuries to their passengers, has provided a regime within which passengers who suffer injuries during hijackings of international flights have not infrequently sought compensatory relief. By contrast, although the majority of hijacking incidents that have involved American air carriers have occurred on domestic flights, and even though the airlines are not protected on domestic flights by the limitations on liability applied to international flights, passengers thereon, for whatever reason, have

278 31 C.F.R. Section 50.5(b) (2003).
279 31 C.F.R. Section 50.5(b) (2003).
280 31 C.F.R. Section 50.5(b)(iii) (2003).
281 31 C.F.R. Section 50.5(b)(2) (2003).
282 Terrorism Risk Insurance Act of 2002, Pub. L. Number 107–297, 116 Stat. 2322 (2002).

generally not utilized the Common Law negligence theory to recover damages for their injuries. This chapter supports the position that a passenger on a domestic flight could, in some circumstances, recover in a negligence action against the airline for injuries resulting from a skyjacking.

An airline has a duty to exercise a high degree of care to protect its passengers from the threat of hijackers. This duty would seemingly require the airline to exercise a high degree of care to prevent any passenger from smuggling a weapon or explosive device aboard its aircraft. While it is unclear whether this duty would be breached in the case where a hijacker takes a weapon onto the aircraft by circumventing or forcing his way through the pre-flight screening station, the airline might have been found negligent where it failed to detect a weapon or explosive device that was carried by a hijacker through the airline's screening checkpoint, at least prior to the federal takeover of that responsibility. If negligence per se is not imposed in the case where a weapon or explosive device has penetrated the screening system, the burden could be shifted to the airline to show that it was not negligent in that it had taken all reasonably practical measures to prevent such a penetration of its security system. This defense should succeed in the case of the hijacker who possesses no real weapon, but perhaps only if the simulated weapon, if any, is shown not to be detectable by the airline's exercise of a high degree of care, and only if it is further shown that the hijacker was not subject to detection through utilization of the behavioral profile.

In the case of an unarmed hijacker who boards having no instrument in his possession with which to promote the hoax, a plaintiff passenger would be hard-pressed to show that the airline was negligent in screening the hijacker prior to boarding. However, the carrier's duty to exercise a high degree of care for the safety of its passengers continues beyond the pre-flight screening station through the entire flight, and at least in the context of the unarmed hijacker, it is arguable that the airline should not readily accede to the hijacker's demands until there is some showing on the part of the hijacker that he is capable of carrying out the threats he has made. Nevertheless, in light of the airline's duty to exercise a high degree of care to provide for the safety of all the passengers on board, acquiescence to a hijacker's demands on the part of the air carrier should constitute a breach of duty only when it is clearly shown that the carrier's employees knew or plainly should have known that the hijacker was unarmed.

Diversion of the aircraft to a foreign country upon the demand of the hijacker would seem more consistent with the airline's duty to protect its passengers than would taking the risk of death or serious injury to its passengers in order to reach a scheduled destination without delay. Thus, in the context of a hijacking carried out by an unarmed hijacker, a plaintiff passenger who has nonetheless suffered severe mental distress and anxiety due to the traumatic hijacking experience, in which the hijacker was perceived to possess the power to cause the deaths of everyone aboard the aircraft, would likely not be able to prove negligence on the part of the airline, either in failure to detect a weapon at the screening checkpoint or in acceding to the demands of the hijacker who has claimed to possess a bomb. Even if the problem of the impact rule could be overcome in this case, such a plaintiff should not be able to recover from the airline for injuries unless a system that would impose liability without fault were implemented. Those who favor adequate compensation for all injuries might support such a proposal.[283]

On the other hand, opponents would consist of those who believe that the function of the law is "to limit the legal consequences of wrongs to a controllable degree" as opposed to establishing a remedy for every wrong.[284] Furthermore, the allocation of the full costs of hijackings and similar criminal offenses should not be placed on the airlines without considering the equities of the burden. "Although protection of the injured passengers is assumed, the requirement that airlines bear the expense of attacks which they may well be powerless to prevent could actually lead to a reduction of air service or to an unreasonable drain on the airline's coffers."[285]

The law is most likely to impose liability in those cases where the air carrier possesses the power but fails to adequately protect its passengers. Between January 1973 and 10 September 2001, twelve of the forty-five attempted hijackings aboard United States carriers involved a firearm, knife or other weapon or explosive material passing undetected through pre-boarding passenger screening systems

283 M. McClintock, *Aircraft Hijacking: Its Civil and Criminal Ramifications* (1971) at p. 70; McClintock, "Skyjacking: Its Domestic Civil and Criminal Ramifications", 39 J. Air L. & Com 29, 44 (1973).

284 *Howard* v. *Lecher*, 42 N.Y.2d 109, 366 N.E.2d 64, 66, 397 N.Y.S.2d 363 (1977).

285 Comment, "Deterring Airport Terrorist Attacks and Compensating the Victim", 125 U. Pa. L. Rev. 1134, 1155 (1977).

that the airlines were obligated to maintain.[286] The airlines may have had the duty and power to prevent these hijackers from boarding their aircraft while armed. It is submitted that, in most jurisdictions, a plaintiff passenger would be able to recover in a negligence action against the airline for any resulting physical or mental injuries arising out of such hijacking cases.

However, since 11 September 2001, the law and circumstances regarding airport and airline security have changed in dramatic respects. The threats and risks have increased, but airline liability exposure and responsibility may have decreased. The Federal Transportation Security Administration has, by law, assumed responsibility for much of airport and airline security, but it will be determined in the future if and how such authority relieves airlines of their legal responsibilities to provide for the safety of their passengers.

286 Department of Transportation, Federal Aviation Administration, Semi-annual Report to Congress on Effectiveness of the Civil Aviation Program, 1 January–30 June 1979 (1979), submitted pursuant to the Federal Aviation Act, 49 U.S.C. Section 1341 (1976), as amended, Pub. L. Number 93–366 (1979) at p. 1.

Siting Transnational Claims in United States Courts

Regina LaPolla
LaPolla Law Firm
New York, United States

Introduction

Even with the specter of tort reform sweeping through the United States, the federal and state court forums in the country remain very attractive to foreign plaintiffs who have been injured by products manufactured or designed in the United States. Tort claims brought in the United States can be prosecuted on a contingency fee basis, where the injured plaintiff has little to no risk of paying any money should he lose. At most, the plaintiff risks being liable for the "costs" of the litigation in jurisdictions where attorneys are ethically constrained from paying costs for a client. In reality, plaintiffs' attorneys rarely seek to recover costs they have advanced on a client's behalf if the case is unsuccessful. This minimal risk is contrasted by litigation-chilling practices, such as "loser pays", where the losing party must pay not only the costs but the attorneys' fees of the successful party. In both federal and state courts, the rules of civil procedure allow for broad and wide-ranging discovery. This allows many cases to be resolved through settlement before ever reaching the trial stage.

Also, tort claims are typically tried before a jury rather than a judge. Juries are well known to be more generous in setting damage awards than judicial officers. Moreover, juries have fairly wide latitude to impose punitive damages. It is, therefore, understandable why so many plaintiffs prefer to litigate their claims in the United States. It is also understandable why so many defendants would rather litigate in almost any forum other than the United States. To balance these competing interests, courts have developed a body of case law addressing when it is appropriate for the court to decline jurisdiction in preference of a foreign forum. This chapter provides a brief overview of the important strategic developments employed by both defense counsel and plaintiffs' counsel in *forum non conveniens*[1] skirmishes.[2]

Choice of Forum

Forum non conveniens

The federal doctrine of *forum non conveniens* is governed by the factors outlined and explained in the Supreme Court's trilogy of cases: *Gulf Oil Co.* v. *Gilbert*,[3] *Koster* v. *Lumbermens Mutual Casualty Co.*[4] and *Piper Aircraft Co.* v. *Reyno*.[5] *Koster* does not establish a separate standard from *Gilbert* for *forum non conveniens* dismissals. *Koster* and *Gilbert* were decided on the same day, and did not explicitly state that one established a stricter standard than the other. Instead, *Koster* is an example of the *Gilbert* factors applied to the facts of that case. Moreover, in *Piper*, the Supreme Court characterized *Gilbert* and *Koster* as establishing a single balancing test for *forum non conveniens*, with the rebuttable presumption that a plaintiff's choice of forum would not be disturbed.[6]

In these decisions, the Supreme Court stated that a plaintiff's choice of forum should rarely be disturbed. However, when an alternative forum has jurisdiction to hear the case, and when trial in the chosen forum would "establish . . . oppressiveness and vexation to a defendant . . . out of all proportion to the plaintiff's convenience", or when the "chosen forum [is] inappropriate because of considerations affecting the court's own administrative and legal problems", a court may, in the exercise of its sound discretion, dismiss the case.[7] To

1 The doctrine of *forum non conveniens* in the federal court system will be the primary focus of this chapter. Although foreign plaintiffs file suit in state courts, defendants typically attempt to remove the action to federal court.

2 This chapter presupposes familiarity with factors used in balancing the considerations when determining whether to dismiss an action based on *forum non conveniens*. For an introduction to those factors and their application, the reader is referred to the Supreme Court's decision in *Piper Aircraft Co.* v. *Reyno*, 454 U.S. 235 (1981).

3 *Gulf Oil Co.* v. *Gilbert*, 330 U.S. 501 (1947).

4 *Koster* v. *Lumbermens Mutual Casualty Co.*, 330 U.S. 518 (1947).

5 *Piper Aircraft Co.* v. *Reyno*, 454 U.S. 235 (1981).

6 *Piper Aircraft Co.* v. *Reyno*, 454 U.S. 235, 241 (1981).

7 *Koster* v. *Lumbermens Mutual Casualty Co.*, 330 U.S. 518, 524 (1947).

guide the trial court in exercising this discretion, the Supreme Court provided a list of "private interest factors" affecting the convenience of the litigants, and a list of "public interest factors" affecting the convenience of the forum.[8] The factors pertaining to the private interests of the litigants included the:

> ". . . relative ease of access to sources of proof; availability of compulsory process for attendance of unwilling, and the cost of obtaining attendance of willing, witnesses; possibility of view of premises, if view would be appropriate to the action; and all other practical problems that make trial of a case easy, expeditious and inexpensive".[9]

The public factors bearing on the question included: the administrative difficulties flowing from court congestion; the "local interest in having localized controversies decided at home"; the interest in having the trial of a diversity case in a forum that is at home with the law that must govern the action; the avoidance of unnecessary problems in conflict of laws, or in the application of foreign law; and the unfairness of burdening citizens in an unrelated forum with jury duty.[10] When confronted with a motion to dismiss claiming *forum non conveniens*, the trial court must first determine if an adequate alternative forum exists. Should it determine that there is an adequate alternative forum, the trial court must then perform a balancing test of the factors enumerated in *Gilbert* to decide whether the litigation should proceed in the United States or the alternative forum.

Forum Shopping and Deference to Plaintiff's Choice of Forum

No discussion of *forum non conveniens* would be complete without an understanding of the unspoken policy that underlies the doctrine and seems to influence many courts' decisions. Before undertaking any *forum non conveniens* analysis, the court must decide how much deference it should give to the plaintiff's choice of forum. It is perfectly acceptable for an attorney to choose a forum that is the most advantageous to his client regardless of which side he is representing.

8 *Gulf Oil Co.* v. *Gilbert*, 330 U.S. 501, 508–509, note 6 (1947).
9 *Gulf Oil Co.* v. *Gilbert*, 330 U.S. 501, 508 (1947).
10 *Gulf Oil Co.* v. *Gilbert*, 330 U.S. 501, 509 (1947).

The Supreme Court in *Piper* noted:

> ". . . [i]n holding that the possibility of a change in law unfavorable to the plaintiff should not be given substantial weight, we also necessarily hold that the possibility of a change in law favorable to defendant should not be considered. Respondent suggests that Piper and Hartzell filed the motion to dismiss, not simply because trial in the United States would be inconvenient, but also because they believe the laws of Scotland are more favorable. She argues that this should be taken into account in the analysis of the private interests. We recognize, of course, that Piper and Hartzell may be engaged in reverse forum-shopping. However, this possibility ordinarily should not enter into a trial court's analysis of the private interests. If the defendant is able to overcome the presumption in favor of plaintiff by showing that trial in the chosen forum would be unnecessarily burdensome, dismissal is appropriate — regardless of the fact that defendant may also be motivated by a desire to obtain a more favorable forum".[11]

Courts that must handle *forum non conveniens* motions more frequently have taken a more pragmatic approach of admitting that both sides to a dispute engage in forum shopping, and allowing those competing concerns to essentially cancel each other. In *Iragorri* v. *United Technologies Corp.*,[12] the court stated:

> "Courts should be mindful that, just as plaintiffs sometimes choose a forum for forum shopping reasons, defendants also may move for dismissal under the doctrine of *forum non conveniens* not because of genuine concern with convenience but because of forum shopping reasons."

Problems arise when a forum is chosen that appears to have little or no legitimate reason supporting its choice. Courts abhor forum shopping, whether it is done by the attorneys for the plaintiff or defendant. Despite the Supreme Court's statement that forum shopping exists on both sides and should not ordinarily influence the trial court's analysis, the unspoken assumption behind the determination of the level of

11 *Piper Aircraft Co.* v. *Reyno*, 454 U.S. 235, 264, note 19 (1981).

12 *Iragorri* v. *United Technologies Corp.*, 274 F.3d 65, 75 (2nd Cir. 2001).

deference to be given to a plaintiff's choice of forum is inextricably intertwined with the notion of forum shopping. Ordinarily, the plaintiff's choice of forum will not be disturbed.[13] In *Iragorri*, the Second Circuit recently re-stated the principle that a court should begin with the assumption that a plaintiff's choice of forum will stand unless the defendant can demonstrate that reasons exist to afford it less deference.[14]

If the court believes that the suit was filed in the United States for no other reason than to take advantage of favorable laws, greater possible damage recoveries and/or more open discovery processes, the case will probably be dismissed under the *forum non conveniens* doctrine.[15]

Indeed, it was the Supreme Court in Piper that condoned the concept that deference to the plaintiff's choice of forum must be examined on a sliding scale:

> "The District Court's distinction between resident or citizen plaintiffs and foreign plaintiffs is fully justified. In *Koster*, the Court indicated that a plaintiff's choice of forum is entitled to greater deference when the plaintiff has chosen the home forum. 330 U.S. at 524. When the home forum has been chosen, it is reasonable to assume that this choice is convenient. When the plaintiff is foreign, however, this assumption is much less reasonable. Because the central purpose of any *forum non conveniens* inquiry is to ensure that the trial is convenient, a foreign plaintiff's choice deserves less deference."[16]

This pronouncement has been put into practical effect by the lower courts, which routinely examine whether there are legitimate valid reasons for the litigation to be situated in the forum where it has been filed. As most recently stated by the Court of Appeals for the Second Circuit:

> ". . . the greater the plaintiff's or the lawsuit's *bona fide* connection to the United States and to the forum of choice and

13 "Unless the balance is strongly in favor of the defendant, the plaintiff's choice of forum should rarely be disturbed": *Gulf Oil Co.* v. *Gilbert*, 330 U.S. 501, 508 (1947).

14 *Iragorri* v. *United Technologies Corp.*, 274 F.3d 65, 70–71 (2nd Cir. 2001).

15 "[D]ismissal may be warranted where a plaintiff chooses a particular forum, not because it is convenient, but solely in order to . . . take advantage of favorable law". Piper Aircraft Co. v. Reyno, 454 U.S. 235, 249, note 15 (1981).

16 *Piper Aircraft Co.* v. *Reyno*, 454 U.S. 235, 255–56 (1981).

> the more it appears that considerations of convenience favor the conduct of the lawsuit in the United States, the more difficult it will be for the defendant to gain dismissal for *forum non conveniens*. . . . On the other hand, the more it appears that the plaintiff's choice of a United States forum was motivated by forum shopping reasons — such as attempts to win a tactical advantage resulting from local laws that favor the plaintiff's case, the habitual generosity of juries in the United States or in the forum district, the plaintiff's popularity or the defendant's unpopularity in the region or the inconvenience and expense to the defendant resulting from litigation in that forum — the less deference the plaintiff's choice commands and, consequently, the easier it becomes for the defendant to succeed on a *forum non conveniens* motion by showing that convenience would be better served by litigating in another country's courts."[17]

To avoid a charge of forum shopping, where the connection between the forum and the subject of the litigation is tenuous, the attorney choosing the forum must be prepared to explain to the court why the chosen forum is the most appropriate and convenient forum. There are some situations where this argument will be stronger than others, for example, if a defendant is not amenable to suit in the plaintiff's home jurisdiction, the plaintiff has no choice but to travel to the defendant's home jurisdiction to institute suit.

Corporate defendants who have been successful in dismissing cases based on *forum non conveniens* will then typically assert, *inter alia*, that the courts in the plaintiffs' home countries do not have jurisdiction to hear the case, to order discovery of documents and witnesses in the United States, to pierce the corporate veil and recover against the parent corporation. Courts in the United States are more aware of these practices and typically condition *forum non conveniens* dismissals upon the defendant at least agreeing to submit to jurisdiction in the alternative forum. Courts have imposed other conditions, including waiving any statute of limitations defense, providing discovery in the alternative forum as would have been available in the United States and case-specific conditions to prevent prejudice to the plaintiff. Such conditional dismissals typically include a right to return to the dismissing court if the defendant

---

17 *Iragorri* v. *United Technologies Corp.*, 274 F.3d 65, 72 (2nd Cir. 2001).

violates the conditions. As the Court of Appeals for the Second Circuit recognized:

> "One of the factors that necessarily affects a plaintiff's choice of forum is the need to sue in a place where the defendant is amenable to suit. Consider, for example, a hypothetical plaintiff residing in New Jersey, who brought suit in the Southern District of New York, barely an hour's drive from the plaintiff's residence, because the defendant was amenable to suit in the Southern District but not in New Jersey. It would make little sense to withhold deference for the plaintiff's choice merely because she did not sue in her home district.[18]

This does not usually require that the plaintiff file suit in his home jurisdiction and have the case dismissed because the defendant is not subject to jurisdiction. Such a requirement would expose the plaintiff to the risk that the statute of limitations would run on his claim. However, the plaintiff's attorney should retain an expert in the law of the plaintiff's home jurisdiction, who will be available to submit affidavits to the court in the defendant's jurisdiction in response to the *forum non conveniens* motion. A plaintiff from outside the United States suing a defendant in either federal or state court should anticipate that the defendant will file a motion to dismiss based on *forum non conveniens* as it is common practice to do so. The plaintiff should be prepared to mount a strong opposition to this anticipated motion before it is filed, as the time to submit papers in response to the motion will likely be insufficient to prepare a strong and adequate response. It is, however, important to note that defendants, in moving to dismiss under *forum non conveniens*, will frequently consent to the jurisdiction of the alternative forum. Because the availability of the alternative forum is determined at the time the suit is dismissed rather than when it is filed, a defendant can "cure" the lack of an alternative available forum by agreeing to submit to the foreign court's jurisdiction after the plaintiff files in the United States, causing the plaintiff to jump through several procedural hoops before finally situating the litigation in a forum where it can proceed.[19]

---

18 *Iragorri* v. *United Technologies Corp.*, 274 F.3d 65, 72 (2nd Cir. 2001).

19 *Satz* v. *McDonnell Douglas Corp.*, 244 F.3d 1279, 1283, note 3 (11th Cir. 2001) (alternative forum need only be available at the time of dismissal); *Veba-Chemie A.G.* v. *M/V Getafix*, 711 F.2d 1243, 1248 (5th Cir. 1983) (holding that, for purposes of *forum non conveniens*, "availability of an alternative forum refers only to the time of dismissal").

Another way to avoid the charge of forum shopping is to include in the complaint a claim for violation of some law of the forum jurisdiction that can be characterized as a "conduct regulating" law. In the recent case of *DiRienzo* v. *Philip Services Corp.*,[20] the Second Circuit reversed the federal district court's dismissal of an action under *forum non conveniens* citing numerous errors in the lower court's reasoning. The majority of the errors assigned to the lower court were based on its failure to give proper credit to the connection the forum had to the lawsuit and its interest in hearing the dispute:

> "It was [defendant] who came to [the plaintiffs] by registering its stock on American exchanges, filing statements with the SEC, and conducting the bulk of its business — including multiple corporate acquisitions — in the United States. Plaintiffs are involved in this lawsuit precisely because of aggressive selling techniques by [defendant] within the United States that targeted United States investors as potential purchasers of its stock.
>
> "Reversal is further warranted in the circumstances presented here because the district court's ruling falls outside the permissible range of decisions, once the interest of the United States in enforcing its securities laws is factored into the equation. A strong public interest favors access to American courts for those who use American securities markets. The fraud on the market theory itself illustrates investors' reliance upon accurate and complete information. For securities markets to function efficiently, securities fraud law must be clear and enforceable. As the statute explaining the need for regulation and control of transactions in securities exchanges and over-the-counter markets states, these transactions are 'affected with a national public interest'.[21] Thus, those laws must also be applied consistently with regard to the significant majority of the putative class who bought their securities on American markets."[22]

---

20 *DiRienzo* v. *Philip Services Corp.*, 294 F.3d 21 (2nd Cir. 2002).

21 Securities Exchange Act of 1934, Section 2, 15 U.S.C. Section 78b.

22 *DiRienzo* v. *Philip Services Corp.*, 294 F.3d 21, 32–33 (2nd Cir. 2002).

Although DiRienzo brought claims under the federal securities laws, other courts have recognized that the home forum of the defendant always has some interest in regulating the defendant's conduct.[23] Thus, if a claim can be included that allows a foreign plaintiff to seek redress against a United States corporation under a conduct regulating law in the United States, it is more likely that the action will not be dismissed.

Once the court has determined the amount of deference that will be given to the plaintiff's choice of forum, it will then turn towards the tests set forth by the Supreme Court. The movant, typically the defendant, bears the burden of making a showing that an adequate alternative forum exists, and that the balance of the private and public interest factors favor dismissal.

Adequate Alternative Forum

The doctrine of *forum non conveniens* presupposes that an adequate alternative forum is available to hear the case. This is a two-part inquiry: availability and adequacy. In *Re Air Crash Disaster Near New Orleans, La.*,[24] an alternative forum is available if all parties are amenable to process and come within the jurisdiction of the forum.[25] An alternative forum is adequate when the parties will not be deprived of all remedies or treated unfairly.[26]

The hurdle of what constitutes an adequate alternative forum is a very easy one for defendants to overcome. There have been very few cases where an alternative forum was found to not exist or to be inadequate. In some of the cases where the alternative forum was found to be inadequate, it was more due to the movant's failure to submit the proper evidence than to the forum.[27] Essentially, if the defendant is

---

23 *Reid-Walen* v. *Hansen*, 933 F.2d 1390, 1400 (8th Cir. 1990) ("defendant's home forum always has a strong interest in providing a forum for redress of injuries caused by its citizens").

24 *Re Air Crash Disaster Near New Orleans, La.*, 821 F.2d 1147, 1165 (5th Cir. 1987) (*en banc*), partially vacated on other grounds, 490 U.S. 1032 (1989).

25 Wright, Miller & Cooper, *Federal Practice and Procedure*, 2nd edition (1986) Section 3828.

26 *Piper Aircraft Co.* v. *Reyno*, 454 U.S. 235, 255 (1981).

27 *El-Fadl* v. *Central Bank of Jordan*, 75 F.3d 668 P.C. Cit. 1996 (reversing and remanding *forum non conveniens* dismissal due to defendant's failure to counter plaintiff's expert submission); *Axordia Northeast, Inc.* v. *Thesseus International Asset Fund, N.V.*, 205 F.Supp. 2d 176 (S.D.N.Y. 2002) (defendants moved for a transfer of

amenable to process and the alternative forum recognizes some claim for compensation that the plaintiff can pursue, the alternative forum will be deemed to be adequate absent a strong showing that an independent judiciary does not exist in the forum.[28]

Allegations of Corruption

Allegations that the court system in a foreign country is corrupt typically fail to render a forum inadequate unless the plaintiff can show that the defendant has been actively involved with the corruption.[29]

---

venue to Kosovo and failed to meet the stricter standard of proof required for a *forum non conveniens* motion; court took judicial notice that Kosovo had recently been in a chaotic state and denied the motion to dismiss); *Estates of Ungar* v. *Palestinian Authority*, 153 F.Supp. 2d 76 (D.R.I. 2001) (motion for *forum non conveniens* dismissal denied when defendants failed to identify an alternative forum).

28 Courts have found that quasi-judicial bodies are not adequate alternative forums: *In re Assicurazioni Generali S.p.A. Holocaust Insurance Litigation*, 228 F.Supp. 2d 348, 355–57 (S.D.N.Y. 2002) (private, non-governmental forum set up by defendants was a "company store" and not an adequate alternative forum); *Rasoulzadeh* v. *Associated Press*, 574 F.Supp. 854, 861 (S.D.N.Y. 1983) (court has "no confidence whatsoever in the plaintiffs' ability to obtain justice at the hands of courts administered by Iranian mullahs").

29 *Blanco* v. *Banco Indus. de Venezuela, S.A.*, 997 F.2d 974, 981 (2nd Cir. 1993) (refusing, despite charges of corruption, to find Venezuelan courts an inadequate alternative forum where parties' contract contained a forum selection clause naming Venezuela as parties' forum of choice); *Mercier* v. *Sheraton Int'l, Inc.*, 981 F.2d 1345, 1351 (1st. 1992) (finding Turkey to be an adequate alternative forum despite plaintiff's claim that Turkish courts had a profound bias against Americans and foreign women), cert. denied, 508 U.S. 912 (1993); *Abdullahi* v. *Pfizer, Inc.*, 2002 U.S. Dist. LEXIS 17436 at *27 (S.D.N.Y. 17 September 2002) ("conclusory allegations of corruption or bias on the part of the foreign forum will not prevent a dismissal on *forum non conveniens* grounds" . . . "[further, none of the submissions allege corruption of the Nigerian judicial process on the part of Pfizer") (on appeal); *Gonzales* v. *P.T. Pelangi Niagra Mitra Int'l*, 196 F.Supp. 2d 482, 487–88 (S.D. Tex. 2002) (plaintiff's general accusations contained in "voluminous proof of corruption in the Indonesian judiciary – including newspaper articles, statements by prominent Indonesian politicians, the results of a survey conducted by the Partnership for Governance Reform in Indonesia, a World Bank report and statements by the United States Government" failed to render Indonesia an inadequate forum); *Aguinda* v. *Texaco, Inc.*, 142 F.Supp. 2d 534, 544 (S.D.N.Y. 2001), aff'd 2002 WL 188015 (2nd Cir. 16 August 2002) (finding State Department reports containing "conclusory assertions as to the relative corruptibility or incorruptibility of Ecuadorian courts, with scant references to specifics, evidence, or application to the instant cases" to be of "little use"); *Torres* v. *Southern Peru Copper Corp.*, 965 F.Supp. 899, 903 (S.D. Tex. 1996) (finding that Peruvian judicial system

Differences in Procedure

Charges that the alternative forum will not offer the same procedural safeguards, access to discovery or remedies are insufficient to render the alternative forum inadequate. Thus, assertions that the alternative forum does not allow contingency fee contracts,[30] does not provide for trial by jury,[31] does not provide the same scope for discovery,[32] does not provide for the same types of damages, including exemplary

---

was not so corrupt as to render Peru an inadequate alternative forum), aff'd, 113 F.3d 540 (5th Cir. 1997); *Banco Mercantil, S.A.* v. *Arencibia*, 927 F.Supp. 565, 567 (D. Puerto Rico 1996) (rejecting claim that courts of Dominican Republic were so corrupt as to provide an inadequate alternative forum); *Chesley* v. *Union Carbide Corp.*, 927 F.2d 60, 66 (2nd Cir. 1991) ("It is not the business of our courts to assume responsibility for supervising the integrity of the judicial system of another sovereign nation. Such an assumption would directly conflict with the principle of comity . . ."). However, *see Eastman Kodak Co.* v. *Kavlin*, 978 F.Supp. 1078, 1086 (S.D. Fla. 1997) (reports of corruption in Bolivia coupled with allegations that the defendants were involved directly with influence peddling in connection with criminal charges filed against certain employees of the plaintiff in Bolivia rendered Bolivia an inadequate forum).

30 *Magnin* v. *Teledyne Continental Motors*, 91 F.3d 1424, 1430 (11th Cir. 1996) ("Magnin also points out, almost in passing, that if the case is tried in France he will not receive a jury trial, nor will he be able to obtain counsel through a contingency fee arrangement, because such fee arrangements are not permitted in France. As cherished as trial by jury is in our law, and as cherished as contingency fee arrangements have become to some plaintiffs and their attorneys, Magnin has not cited us to any Supreme Court or court of appeals decision giving such considerations substantial weight in *forum non conveniens* analysis. The argument is particularly weak in regard to contingency fees. In *Coakes* v. *Arabian American Oil Co.*, 831 F.2d 572, 576 (5th Cir. 1987), the Fifth Circuit held that the ban against contingency fees in England should not significantly influence the *forum non conveniens* determination, and observed that, 'if the lack of a contingent fee system were held determinative, then a case could almost never be dismissed because contingency fees are not allowed in most forums'. The same is pretty much true of trial by jury. As the Supreme Court noted in *Piper Aircraft Co.*, 454 U.S. at 252 n. 18, 102 S.Ct. at 264 n. 18, 'jury trials are almost always available in the United States, while they are never provided in Civil Law jurisdictions', and 'even in the United Kingdom, most civil actions are not tried by a jury'. Yet, there are numerous decisions dismissing cases in favor of a Civil Law jurisdiction forum, and in favor of the United Kingdom as a forum."); *de Melo* v. *Lederle Laboratories*, 801 F.2d 1058 (8th Cir. 1986).

31 *Magnin* v. *Teledyne Continental Motors*, 91 F.3d 1424, 1430 (11th Cir. 1996).

32 *Satz* v. *McDonnell Douglas Corporation*, 244 F.3d 1279, 1283 (11th Cir. 2001); *Doe* v. *Hyland Therapeutics Division*, 807 F.Supp. 1117, 1123-24 (S.D.N.Y. 1992).

and punitive damages,[33] does not recognize all the causes of action that could be asserted in the United States,[34] has very high filing fees[35] or experiences judicial delays[36] will not render the alternative forum inadequate.

Impact of Tort Reform

Courts are in agreement that tort reform in a foreign jurisdiction will not render an alternative forum inadequate as long as it provides reasonable compensation to the plaintiff. The Ninth Circuit reaffirmed this position in the recent case of *Lueck* v. *Sundstrand Corporation*,[37] where the plaintiff challenged New Zealand as an adequate alternative forum due to the tort reform measures it had enacted.

In 1972, the New Zealand legislature passed the Accident Compensation Act, which was amended in 1982, 1992 and 1998[38] to provide coverage, on a no-fault basis, for those who suffer personal injury arising from accidents. The Accident Compensation Act bars civil claims for damages and, instead, provides for benefits from the Accident Rehabilitation and Compensation Insurance Corporation. When originally enacted in 1972, those benefits "included [all] medical and rehabilitative expenses, compensation for eighty percent of lost earnings as long as disability continued, and lump-sum payments

---

33 *Vasquez* v. *Bridgestone/Firestone, Inc.*, 325 F.3d 665 (5th Cir. 2003) ("The fact that Mexico provides a wrongful death cause of action, albeit with severe damage caps makes the country an adequate forum"); *de Melo* v. *Lederle Laboratories*, 801 F.2d 1058 (8th Cir. 1986).

34 *De Melo* v. *Lederle Laboratories*, 801 F.2d 1058 (8th Cir. 1986).

35 *Satz* v. *McDonnell Douglas Corporation*, 244 F.3d 1279, 1283 (11th Cir. 2001) ("The plaintiffs' concerns about Argentine filing fees, the lack of discovery in Argentine courts, and their fear of delays in the Argentine courts do not render Argentina an inadequate forum").

36 *Gschwind* v. *Cessna Aircraft Company*, 161 F.3d 602, 607 (10th Cir. 1998) ("Plaintiff's brief implies that the French system is inadequate because of the delay that might be involved in a French proceeding. According to Plaintiff, the French courts would stay a civil action until the completion of their criminal proceedings. Such a delay does not render the French courts inadequate"). However, *see Bhatnagar* v. *Surrendra Overseas Ltd.*, 52 F.3d 1220, 1227 (3rd Cir. 1995) (finding that Indian forum was inadequate where delays of twenty-five years were possible).

37 *Lueck* v. *Sundstrand Corporation*, 236 F.3d 1137 (9th Cir. 2001).

38 The 1992 amendment included among its changes the renaming of the Accident Compensation Act as the Accident Rehabilitation and Compensation Insurance Act. The 1998 amendments, the Accident Insurance Act, only affect workplace accidents.

of up to $ 27,000 (N.Z.) for non-economic losses . . .".[39] Under the 1992 amendments to the Accident Compensation Act, the compensation for lost earnings remains at eighty per cent of the claimant's former salary, but is capped at NZ $1,179 per week.[40]

The 1992 amendments also eliminated lump sum payments for non-economic losses.[41] Instead, the Accident Compensation Act provides for a quarterly allowance based on the degree of the claimant's disability.[42] Medical expenses continue to be covered.

The plaintiffs in *Lueck* v. *Sundstrand Corporation* asserted that New Zealand offered no remedy for their losses because it had "legislated tort law out of existence" via the Accident Compensation Act scheme.[43]

The Ninth Circuit rejected the plaintiff's characterization that a forum is inadequate if it provides compensation via a regulatory scheme instead of via the judicial system. As stated by the court:

> "[t]he district court was not required to ask whether Plaintiffs could bring this lawsuit in New Zealand, but rather, whether New Zealand offers a remedy for their losses. The district court did not abuse its discretion in finding that an adequate remedy is available in New Zealand".[44]

Interpreting the Supreme Court's decision in *Piper*, the Ninth Circuit continued:

> "[t]he effect of Piper Aircraft is that a foreign forum will be deemed adequate unless it offers no practical remedy for the

---

39 Richard S. Miller, "An Analysis and Critique of the 1992 Changes to New Zealand's Accident Compensation Scheme", 52 Md. L. Rev. 1070 (1993) (citing 1982 Act, Parts V–VII).

40 Richard S. Miller, "An Analysis and Critique of the 1992 Changes to New Zealand's Accident Compensation Scheme", 52 Md. L. Rev. 1070, 1074 (1993) (citing 1992 Act, Sections 39(1), 48 and 70).

41 Richard S. Miller, "An Analysis and Critique of the 1992 Changes to New Zealand's Accident Compensation Scheme", 52 Md. L. Rev. 1070, 1074–75 (1993).

42 Richard S. Miller, "An Analysis and Critique of the 1992 Changes to New Zealand's Accident Compensation Scheme", 52 Md. L. Rev. 1070, 1075 (1993) (citing 1992 Act, Section 54).

43 One of the flaws in the plaintiff's argument, which the Ninth Circuit seized upon, was that accident victims could still sue for damages for mental distress not resulting from physical injury. Suits seeking punitive or exemplary damages were also allowed. *Lueck* v. *Sundstrand Corporation*, 236 F.3d 1137, 1142 (9th Cir. 2001).

44 *Lueck* v. *Sundstrand Corporation,* 236 F.3d 1137, 1143 (9th Cir. 2001).

> plaintiff's complained of wrong. A New Zealand remedy is unquestionably available here".[45]

The Ninth Circuit also referred to other court opinions which found that adequate compensation was available under the Accident Compensation Act. The court cited the opinions in *In Re Silicone Gel Breast Implants Product Liability Litigation*[46] and *Stonnell* v. *Int'l Harvester Co.*[47] However, the circuit courts are split on whether the limitation on damages available under a tort reform or legislative scheme can be so *de minimis* that they render the alternative forum inadequate.

In *Irish Nat. Ins. Co., Ltd.* v. *Aer Lingus Teoranta*,[48] an insurer brought suit against an airline that had carried and damaged goods shipped on the airline by an insured. The goods were shipped from Ireland to the United States. The complaint alleged that the goods left the insured's factory and were delivered to the airline in good order in Ireland. When the goods arrived in the United States, however, they were badly damaged. If the suit was brought in Ireland, the insurance company would be limited in its recovery to US $260. The actual damage incurred was in excess of US $125,000. The defendant moved to dismiss on the grounds of *forum non conveniens*. The district court granted the motion with a statement in its opinion that:

> ". . . the real purpose for bringing this action in New York does not appear to be to vindicate this forum's interest in improving New York as a point of entry, but rather to avoid the possibility that application of Irish law will result in a

45 *Lueck* v. *Sundstrand Corporation*, 236 F.3d 1137, 1144 (9th Cir. 2001).

46 *Re Silicone Gel Breast Implants Product Liability Litigation*, 887 F.Supp. 1469, 1475 (N.D. Ala. 1995) (which dismissed wrongful death and personal injury actions against breast implant manufacturers by New Zealand residents based on a finding that the plaintiffs could either "use the court system or pursue administrative remedies" under the Act).

47 *Stonnell* v. *Int'l Harvester Co.*, 132 Ill. App. 3d 1043, 478 N.E.2d 518 (Ill. App. Ct. 1985) (which dismissed the wrongful death claim of a New Zealand resident arising out of an accident that occurred in New Zealand using a tractor manufactured in Great Britain which had been designed by the United States defendant, because the parents of the decedent could receive compensation under the Accident Compensation Act even if it was less than what they may have been able to recover in the United States); *Lueck* v. *Sundstrand Corporation*, 236 F.3d 1137, 1145 (9th Cir. 2001).

48 *Irish Nat. Ins. Co., Ltd.* v. *Aer Lingus Teoranta*, 1984 U.S. Dist. LEXIS (E.D.N.Y. 6 January 1984).

smaller recovery for plaintiff as a result of law in that forum with respect to the limitation of liability provisions of the Warsaw Convention".[49]

The plaintiff appealed the dismissal to the Second Circuit. In a unanimous opinion, the Second Circuit reversed the dismissal. Judge Van Graafeiland began his opinion with the telling statement:

> "The doctrine of *forum non conveniens* ostensibly is invoked to determine in which of two jurisdictions a case should be tried. In some instances, however, invocation of the doctrine will send the case to a jurisdiction which has imposed such severe monetary limitations on recovery as to eliminate the likelihood that the case will be tried. When it is obvious that this will occur, discussion of convenience of witnesses takes on a Kafkaesque quality — everyone knows that no witnesses ever will be called to testify. This appears to be such a case."[50]

The court then focused on the assertion of the defense counsel, which was accepted by the trial court, that the action was brought in the United States merely to avoid the limitation on damages. Rather than adopt the negative view that the plaintiff was engaged in forum shopping, the Second Circuit stated:

> "If the foregoing statements are true, the real issue before the district court was not whether the case should be tried in Ireland, but whether it would be tried at all. Nevertheless, feeling bound by this Court's decision in *Alcoa Steamship Co., Inc.* v. *M/V Nordic Regent*, 654 F.2d 147, 159 (2d Cir.1978) (en banc), cert. denied, 449 U.S. 890, 66 L. Ed. 2d 116, 101 S. Ct. 248 (1980), the district court proceeded to weigh the merits of a trial in Ireland against a trial in America just as if the former were likely to occur. Although the procedure smacks somewhat of a legal charade, we will proceed on the same assumption."

---

49 *Irish Nat. Ins. Co., Ltd.* v. *Aer Lingus Teoranta, Irish Nat. Ins. Co., Ltd.* v. *Aer Lingus Teoranta,* 1984 U.S. Dist. LEXIS (E.D.N.Y. 6 January 1984) at note 5.

50 *Irish Nat. Ins. Co., Ltd.* v. *Aer Lingus Teoranta*, 739 F.2d 90, 91 (2nd Cir. 1984).

The circuit court first decided that the district court had committed a reversible error because the Warsaw Convention, which was the basis of the plaintiff's claim, permits a plaintiff to bring suit at the "place of destination", which was New York. The Second Circuit then assigned error to the district court because it failed to accord to the plaintiff the same deference as it would have accorded to a United States plaintiff. The Second Circuit held that the plaintiff was due such deference under the terms of the Treaty of Friendship, Commerce and Navigation between the United States and Ireland. Finally, the Second Circuit found that the district court had committed an error in its weighing of the conveniences. Finding that the damage most likely occurred while the package was in the defendant's control, and finding that the defendant's planes fly regularly to New York, the court held that there was no reason that the case could not proceed in New York. This decision is obviously influenced by the Second Circuit's apparent belief that dismissing the action under *forum non conveniens* would represent a windfall to the defendant. Recognizing that the action simply would not be brought if it did not proceed in the United States, the court was unwilling to allow the defendant to escape liability for its wrongdoing.

The opinion of the Second Circuit in *Irish Nat. Ins. Co.*, a commercial case, must be contrasted with the recent opinion issued by the Fifth Circuit in *Gonzalez* v. *Chrysler Corp.*,[51] a wrongful death case. In *Gonzalez*, the plaintiffs, parents of a three-year-old child killed by the force of an airbag deployment in an automobile accident, brought suit against the car and airbag manufacturers claiming product liability, breach of warranty and negligence. The accident took place in Mexico, involved Mexican citizens and only Mexican citizens witnessed the accident. Moreover, the car was purchased in Mexico. However, if the suit were brought in Mexico, recovery would have been limited to US $2,500. In an attempt to tie the litigation to the Texas forum, the plaintiffs claimed that they had visited Texas, seen the car advertised in Texas and shopped for the car in Texas. Because of these facts, the district court found the litigation's connection to the forum to be tenuous and granted the defendants' motion to dismiss on the ground of *forum non conveniens*. The plaintiffs appealed to the Fifth Circuit and argued that the limit on wrongful death damages essentially deprived them of an alternative forum to seek redress.

---

51 *Gonzalez* v. *Chrysler Corp.*, 301 F.3d 377 (5th Cir. 2002).

The Fifth Circuit recognized that the cap on damages would nullify the lawsuit if the action was not allowed to proceed in the United States courts. Quickly disposing of the plaintiffs' first contention that Mexico was inadequate because it did not allow for strict product liability, the Fifth Circuit termed the plaintiffs' "second contention — that the damage cap renders the remedy available in a Mexican forum 'clearly unsatisfactory' — slightly more problematic". The plaintiffs advanced two compelling arguments regarding why the damage cap rendered the alternative forum inadequate. First, the plaintiffs argued that if they brought suit in Mexico, the most they could hope to achieve would be a *de minimis* recovery of US $2,500, which could not begin to compensate the parents for the loss of their child. Second, the plaintiffs argued that the plain economics of the situation meant that if the case was to proceed in Mexico, it was not feasible to bring suit there as the cost of litigating the case would outstrip any recovery.

The Fifth Circuit's response to the plaintiffs' arguments ignored justice and made a mockery out of the doctrine of *forum non conveniens*. Despite the pronouncement by the Supreme Court that "if the remedy provided by the alternative forum is so clearly inadequate or unsatisfactory that it is no remedy at all, the unfavorable change in law may be given substantial weight; the district court may conclude that dismissal would not be in the interests of justice",[52] the Fifth Circuit hid behind principles of comity and refused to admit that the US $2,500 recovery available made a mockery out of the value of human life. Arguing that Mexico, as a sovereign nation, made a deliberate choice in providing a specific remedy for this tort cause of action, the Fifth Circuit asserted that:

> ". . . the Mexican people, through their duly-elected lawmakers, have decided to limit tort damages with respect to a child's death. It would be inappropriate — even patronizing — for us to denounce this legitimate policy choice by holding that Mexico provides an inadequate forum for Mexican tort victims . . . In short, we see no warrant for us, a United States court, to replace the policy preference of the Mexican Government with our own view of what is a good policy for the citizens of Mexico".[53]

---

52 *Piper Aircraft Co.* v. *Reyno*, 454 U.S. 235, 254 (1981).
53 *Piper Aircraft Co.* v. *Reyno*, 454 U.S. 235, 381–82 (1981).

In reaching its conclusion, the Fifth Circuit relied on Judge Keenan's decision in *In re Union Carbide Corp. Gas Plant Disaster at Bhopal, India in December 1984*,[54] to support its opinion that finding the damages available in Mexico to be inadequate would be the equivalent of "imperialism". This reliance is misplaced. The plaintiffs in *Bhopal* never argued that India was an inadequate forum because of any cap on liability. The plaintiffs asserted that the delay and overcrowding of Indian courts, lack of contingency fee agreements and procedural devices such as class actions, the existence of filing fees (which had been waived for victims of the disaster) and potential inability to enforce the judgment in the United States rendered the forum inadequate.

The Fifth Circuit then met the plaintiffs' primary argument with a response that put the fault on the plaintiffs if they chose not to seek redress in the Mexican courts:

> "We nevertheless are unwilling to hold as a legal principle that Mexico offers an inadequate forum simply because it does not make economic sense for Gonzalez to file this lawsuit in Mexico. Our reluctance arises out of two practical considerations.
>
> "First, the plaintiff's willingness to maintain suit in the alternative (foreign) forum will usually depend on, *inter alia*, (1) whether the plaintiff's particular injuries are compensable (and to what extent) in that forum; (2) not whether the forum recognizes some cause of action among those applicable to the plaintiff's case, but whether it recognizes his most provable and compensable action; (3) similarly, whether the alternative forum recognizes defenses that might bar or diminish recovery; and (4) the litigation costs (i.e., the number of experts, the amount of discovery, geographic distances, attorney's fees, etc.) associated with bringing that particular case to trial. These factors will vary from plaintiff to plaintiff, from case to case. Thus, the forum of a foreign country might be deemed inadequate in one case but not another, even though the only difference between the two cases might be the cost of litigation or the recovery for

54 *In re Union Carbide Corp. Gas Plant Disaster at Bhopal, India in December 1984*, 634 F.Supp. 842, 867 (S.D.N.Y. 1986), aff'd as modified, 809 F.2d 195 (2nd Cir. 1987).

the plaintiff's particular type of injuries. In sum, we find troublesome and lacking in guiding principle the fact that the adequacy determination could hinge on constantly varying and arbitrary differences underlying the "economic viability" of a lawsuit.

"Second, if we allow the economic viability of a lawsuit to decide the adequacy of an alternative forum, we are further forced to engage in a rudderless exercise of line drawing with respect to a cap on damages: At what point does a cap on damages transform a forum from adequate to inadequate? Is it, as here, $ 2,500? Is it $ 50,000? Or is it $ 100,000? Any recovery cap may, in a given case, make the lawsuit economically unviable. We therefore hold that the adequacy inquiry under *Piper Aircraft* does not include an evaluation of whether it makes economic sense for Gonzalez to file this lawsuit in Mexico."[55]

The Fifth Circuit's refusal to reach this issue, and its position that economic viability of a lawsuit in the alternative forum is not a factor to be considered in the *forum non conveniens* inquiry, is in direct conflict with the Supreme Court's pronouncement in *Piper* that the interests of justice must be taken into account as well as opinions of other Circuit courts.[56] The choice between litigating in the United States or not litigating at all is not unique to the circumstances of *Gonzalez*. A survey found that between 1945 and 1985, of eighty-five transnational cases dismissed on the ground of *forum non conveniens*, only four per cent ever reached trial in a foreign court.[57]

---

55 *Gonzalez* v. *Chrysler Corp.*, 301 F.3d 377, 383 (5th Cir. 2002).

56 *Reid-Walen* v. *Hansen*, 933 F.2d 1390, 1398 (8th Cir. 1990) ("as part of the *Gilbert* private interest analysis, courts must be sensitive to the practical problems likely to be encountered by plaintiffs in litigating their claim, especially when the alternative forum is in a foreign country"); *Lehman* v. *Humphrey Cayman, Ltd.*, 713 F.2d 339, 346 (8th Cir. 1983), cent. denied, 464 U.S. 1042 (1984) (the district court "must be alert to the realities of the plaintiff's position, financial and otherwise, and his or her ability as a practical matter to bring suit in the alternative forum"); *Wilson* v. *Humphreys* (*Cayman*) *Ltd.*, 916 F.2d 1239, 1246–47 (7th Cir. 1990); *Rudetsky* v. *O'Dowd*, 660 F.Supp. 341, 346 (E.D.N.Y. 1987).

57 David Robertson, "*Forum non conveniens* in America and England: "A Rather Fantastic Fiction", 103 L. Q. Rev. 398, 418–19 (1987).

Impact of Pending Multi-District Litigation

When multiple suits are filed against a defendant alleging essentially the same cause of action or claims based on similar facts, the defendant will typically seek to have the multiple litigations consolidated into a coordinated proceeding. When the litigations have been filed in different district courts, the application is heard by the Panel on Multi-District Litigation, which decides whether the actions should be coordinated, as well as where the coordinated action will be heard. The coordinated litigation, typically referred to as the MDL proceeding, allows judicial economy by concentrating all of the discovery and prosecution of the multiple actions in one district, before one judge. Both plaintiffs and defendants benefit from the economies found in an MDL proceeding, and it reduces the risk of inconsistent judgments.

When a mass tort or product liability case has been consolidated for pre-trial purposes by the MDL Panel, the additional strains and burdens of adding claims of international plaintiffs to the overall proceeding should not unduly burden the MDL court or harass or oppress the defendant who is already responding to discovery requests and defending the action in that jurisdiction. Despite the seeming efficiency of hearing a handful of additional claims in a proceeding that may well encompass thousands of lawsuits, the courts have reached different conclusions when asked by defendants to apply the doctrine of *forum non conveniens* to dismiss actions brought by foreign plaintiffs.

In the MDL proceeding that concerned the product defects relating to roll-over accidents due to defectively designed automobile tires, *In re Bridgestone/Firestone Inc. ATX ATX ll and Wilderness Tires Product Liability Litigation*[58] (hereafter referred to as the *Bridgestone MDL*), the district court was handling thousands of individual product liability suits claiming that the defective products had resulted in personal injury, wrongful death or economic damage. A number of actions involving suits filed by foreign nationals were sent to the district court by the MDL Panel. The defendants moved to dismiss these actions on the basis of *forum non conveniens*. Using the suits filed by citizens of Columbia and Venezuela as test cases, the defendants

58 *In re Bridgestone/Firestone Inc. ATX ATX ll and Wilderness Tires Product Liability Litigation*, MDL-13 73, 190 F.Supp. 2d 1125 (S.D. Ind. 2002).

asserted that because the accidents caused by the defective tires occurred in those countries, the witnesses and access to proof strongly favored dismissing the claims in favor of those alternative fora. The defendants also asserted that the language differences would impose a burden on the district court and the parties, as many documents relevant to proving or disproving liability and damage were in Spanish.

The district court, in reviewing the motions to dismiss, found that Venezuela was not an alternative forum based on statements of the plaintiffs that they would not file their actions in that court, thus preventing the Venezuelan court from exercising jurisdiction over them. Arguably, this point of the *forum non conveniens* was wrongly decided and placed too much power in the party's ability to select forums in contravention of the doctrine. As the defendants aptly argued:

> "Of course, no one can force plaintiffs to refile these actions in Venezuela after they are dismissed in the United States. If plaintiffs willfully elect not to pursue their claims in Venezuela, that is their choice . . . But the critical point is that if these actions are dismissed, plaintiffs can file their claims in Venezuela. And if they do, defendants have agreed not to challenge the Venezuelan court's jurisdiction, thus satisfying Article 40 (subparagraph 3) — by the court finding that plaintiffs' decision not to file there would render the forum unavailable, the court set a dangerous precedent that would allow a plaintiff to avoid being sent to a more appropriate alternative forum based on the party's choice rather than the considerations of judicial economy."

Indeed, if the precedent set by the district court in the *Bridgestone MDL* was followed, it would render the doctrine of *forum non conveniens* hostage to the whims of the parties. To date, it appears that no other court has followed or adopted this reasoning. Moreover, it was not necessary for the district court to make such a finding in light of its determination when it balanced the public and private interest factors. The court found that because the defendants and the court were already engaged in the litigation process, there was no practical reason to split off the cases of the foreign plaintiffs to be heard by another forum. Dismissing the cases did not alleviate the burden on the court system, and litigating the cases could not be said to be oppressive or harassing when the defendants were already in the district defending against suits that had legitimate ties to the forum and would necessarily proceed. The district court recognized these practicalities when it held:

> "Millions of documents in English concerning liability have been produced by Ford and Firestone into the document depositories for this MDL. As Defendants correctly contend, at the time of the briefing on *forum non conveniens*, only about 2,000 of these documents had been marked as deposition exhibits, and at a trial, it is likely that even fewer documents would be introduced into evidence. Even with this discounted number of English-language liability documents, we find, nevertheless, that the translation burden of trying these cases in the Southern District of Florida is less than if the cases were tried in Colombia. First, translating even "several hundred" liability documents, as Defendants estimate, would be no small task. Second, most liability documents from Ford Motor de Venezuela and Bridgestone/Firestone Venezolana were originally authored in English or have already been translated from Spanish to English, and liability witnesses were deposed in English, via translation. For those cases in which Ford and Firestone plan to defend by pointing to poor driving of other parties, the accident report has already been translated into English. While Plaintiffs' prior medical histories probably are primarily in Spanish, records of subsequent treatment are in both English and Spanish. Of course, depending on Defendants' strategy, the testimony of accident witnesses and maintenance records must be translated into English for a U.S. trial, but, for each case, the amount of such evidence will be considerably less than the amount of evidence needed to prove defect and damage, the vast majority of which is in English."[59]

There existed no compelling reason to disturb the foreign plaintiffs' choice of jurisdiction, and the defendants' motions were denied.

---

59 *In re Bridgestone/Firestone Inc. ATX ATX ll and Wilderness Tires Product Liability Litigation*, MDL-13 73, 190 F.Supp. 2d 1125, 1142–43 (S.D. Ind. 2002) (internal citations omitted).

The presence of the *Bridgestone MDL* proceeding presented such judicial economies that the district court also retained jurisdiction over German plaintiffs injured in accidents in Venezuela. With respect to these plaintiffs, whose evidence regarding damages was likely to be in Germany, the court found:

> ". . . it is clear that while the United States may not be a particularly convenient forum for hearing these cases, the balancing of these factors certainly does not 'point towards' trial in Venezuela. Another reason to retain jurisdiction over these cases is that they arise from the same accident at issue in [other cases pending in the MDL]. Trying the cases in the same forum likely will be more efficient and will lessen the risk of inconsistent results. For these reasons, we find that the balancing of factors favors retaining jurisdiction over these cases also."[60]

The results reached by the district court in the *Bridgestone MDL* stand in stark contrast to cases filed by individual foreign plaintiffs that were subjected to a *forum non conveniens* dismissal motion before they were transferred to the MDL proceeding.[61] *Vasquez* was affirmed on appeal by the Fifth Circuit after the *Bridgestone MDL* opinion denying the defendants' *forum non conveniens* motions had been issued. The Fifth Circuit declined to follow the reasoning of the MDL court.[62]

Although courts handling other mass tort MDLs have not been as generous as the *Bridgestone MDL* court, its decision is not a lone voice crying in the wilderness. The district court for the Southern District of New York recently retained jurisdiction over the claims of foreign plaintiffs in a similar situation. In *In re Assicurazioni Generali S.p.A. Holocaust Insurance Litigation*[63] (referred to herein as the "Holocaust Insurance MDL"), the court was faced with the defendants' motions to dismiss the claims in favor of European

---

60 *In re Bridgestone/Firestone Inc. ATX ATX ll and Wilderness Tires Product Liability Litigation*, MDL-13 73, 190 F.Supp. 2d 1125, 1155–56 (S.D. Ind. 2002).

61 *Taylor* v. *Daimler Chrysler Corp., Bridgestone/Firestone, Inc.*, 196 F.Supp. 2d 428 (E.D. Tex. 2001); *Vasquez* v. *Bridgestone/Firestone*, 192 F.Supp. 2d 715 (E.D. Tex. 2001).

62 *Vasquez* v. *Bridgestone/Firestone*, 325 F.3d 665 (5th Cir. 2003).

63 *In re Assicurazioni Generali S.p.A. Holocaust Insurance Litigation*, 228 F.Supp. 2d 348 (S.D.N.Y. 2002).

courts. The district court used the position statement that the defendants had submitted to the MDL Panel against the defendants in determining the motion:

> "Generali itself concedes as much, stating in its motion before the MDL panel to consolidate the present actions in this district: 'New York is the most convenient forum to litigate the issues in the United States, as it is the home of Generali's United States Branch, Generali's counsel, and several of the firms representing plaintiffs'. (Swift Decl. Ex. E (Generali Mot. for Transfer of 8/11/00 at 6)) The fact that defendants currently do extensive business in New York and in this country belies any argument that defendants would be litigating in an unduly hostile or unfamiliar environment. Given plaintiffs' legitimate reasons for bringing suit in this forum, and given defendants' representations to the MDL panel, plaintiffs' choice of forum is entitled to strong deference under the Circuit's sliding scale approach in *Iragorri*. See *DiRienzo II*, 294 F. 3d at 28-29. Such deference is due notwithstanding the fact that plaintiffs are acting in a representative capacity."[64]

Also in *DiRienzo* v. *Philip Services Corporation*,[65] it was stated:

> "With respect to the complaint being filed in the Southern District of New York, plaintiffs have another reason that the law recognizes as valid: the transfer order of the Judicial Panel on Multi-district Litigation placed their cases there. Although the consolidated and amended class action complaint was filed after the transfer order — and the transfer order, standing alone, is not dispositive or outcome-determinative — nothing in the record suggests the filing was motivated by anything other than this order."

Indeed, like the German plaintiffs in the *Bridgestone MDL*, the presence of the multiple cases relating to Holocaust era insurance claims provided

---

64 *In re Assicurazioni Generali S.p.A. Holocaust Insurance Litigation*, 228 F.Supp. 2d 348, 352 (S.D.N.Y. 2002).

65 *DiRienzo* v. *Philip Services Corporation*, 294 F.3d 21, 28–29 (2nd Cir. 2002).

a British plaintiff with no connection to the forum to pursue his claims there despite the defendants' objections:

> "Plaintiff Tabaksman is entitled to considerably less deference in his choice of forum than the other plaintiffs in theirs because he is a British citizen. However, even given the low level of deference due his choice of forum, the fact that 11 other related Holocaust insurance cases are to be litigated in the district is a convenience factor that tilts sufficiently in his favor to preclude dismissal . . . Because of the convenience of trying Tabaksman's claims in conjunction with the other related cases in this consolidated proceeding, and because of the slight burden associated with such an action, defendants' motions to dismiss are denied with respect to plaintiff Tabaksman."[66]

Both the *Bridgestone MDL* and the *Holocaust Insurance MDL* attached importance to what they viewed as an expression of interest of their forums in keeping the litigation, thus finding that the public interest factors weighed in favor of retaining jurisdiction. In the *Holocaust Insurance MDL*, the court found that the enactment of certain legislation by the New York state courts (which the court admitted was not binding on the federal court) evidenced a public policy interest in providing a forum for such claims that outweighed the European countries' interests:

> "As far as the local interest in these cases, all potential forums in this case have some interest in the subject matter. The seven European forums under consideration all have an interest because the material events that gave rise to plaintiffs' claims occurred in those countries. Those forums also have an interest in redressing the harms inflicted by the Holocaust, which occurred on European soil . . . However, the interest of this forum in plaintiffs' claims is stronger because New York State has expressed a public policy interest in those claims through the New York Holocaust Victims Insurance Act of 1998 ('HVIA'), N.Y. Ins. L. § 2701 *et seq.* (McKinney 2000), whereas the connection between those claims and the relevant European forums relates primarily to

66 *In re Assicurazioni Generali S.p.A. Holocaust Insurance Litigation*, 228 F.Supp. 2d 348, 369–70 (S.D.N.Y. 2002).

> 70-year old insurance transactions between deceased emigrants and a multinational insurance conglomerate. The New York HVIA explicitly states that no action concerning Holocaust-era insurance claims arising between 1929 and 1945 shall be dismissed from the New York State courts on the ground of *forum non conveniens* (under N.Y. C.P.L.R. § 327), N.Y. Ins. L. § 2704(b), and it extends the state's statute of limitations on Holocaust-era insurance claims, N.Y. Ins. Law § 2704(a). The statute also imposes reporting requirements on New York-licensed insurance companies regarding their payment of Holocaust-era insurance claims. N.Y. Ins. Law § 2705. Although the *forum non conveniens* provision of the HVIA is not binding on this court, most directly because the N.Y. C.P.L.R. does not govern *forum non conveniens* dismissal in federal court, the provision does expressly indicate the state's desire to commit judicial resources to the litigation of plaintiffs' claims. It is hard to imagine a more clear indication that this forum has a strong public interest in the litigation of plaintiffs' claims than a piece of legislation explicitly stating that interest."[67]

Similarly, the *Bridgestone MDL* used the evidence of government interest through congressional hearings as a reason to retain jurisdiction:

> "Contrary to Defendants' assertions, however, the United States has some interest in the resolution of these cases . . . Plaintiffs present evidence that Ford and Firestone's early warning of alleged serious problems with their products stemmed from reports of unusually high accident rates in South America and other foreign markets. American interest in Ford and Firestone's investigations of these accidents has been high, on the theory that had the public and the relevant government agencies known of the problems sooner, fewer deaths and serious injuries would have occurred on U.S. highways. In fact, this topic was the subject of congressional committee hearings in the fall of 2000.
>
> "On the whole, the balance of public factors does not compel the dismissal of these cases on the ground of *forum non*

67 *In re Assicurazioni Generali S.p.A. Holocaust Insurance Litigation*, 228 F.Supp. 2d 348, 370 (S.D.N.Y. 2002).

conveniens. While we cannot ignore Colombia's interest in the safety of its citizens, neither can we ignore the U.S. interest in these cases as evidenced by Congressional testimony about the notice Ford and Firestone received on the alleged defects through the accidents in South America.[68]

Seeking Remedies Available under United States Statutory Law

As discussed at the beginning of this chapter, one of the defenses to a charge of forum shopping is the response that the plaintiff seeks to enforce a conduct regulating law that will further the public interest of the forum (the United States), particularly where public policy favors the enforcement of the law for the social good. While it is fairly well established that the United States has a strong public policy interest in enforcing its securities laws and ensuring the integrity of the securities markets, other laws have not faired as well.[69] The statute currently at issue is the Alien Tort Claims Act. Two recent district court cases have held that the existence of claims under the Alien Tort Claims Act does not prevent the court from conducting a *forum non conveniens* analysis and does not preclude the dismissal of such action.[70]

68 *In re Bridgestone/Firestone Inc. ATX ATX II and Wilderness Tires Product Liability Litigation*, MDL-13 73, 190 F.Supp. 2d 1125, 1146–48 (S.D. Ind. 2002) (internal citations omitted).

69 *Transunion Corp.* v. *Pepsico, Inc.*, 811 F.2d 127, 130 (2nd Cir. 1987) (*forum non conveniens* applicable in RICO cases notwithstanding special venue provision); *In re Aircrash Disaster Near New Orleans*, 821 F.2d 1147, 1163-64 (5th Cir. 1987) (*forum non conveniens* available under Jones Act notwithstanding special venue provision); *Cruz* v. *Maritime Co. of Philippines*, 702 F.2d 47, 47–48 (2nd Cir. 1983) (same); *Wells Fargo & Co.* v. *Wells Fargo Express Co.*, 556 F.2d 406, 431 (9th Cir. 1977) (*forum non conveniens* applicable to Lanham Act notwithstanding special venue provision); *Kempe* v. *Ocean Drilling & Exploration Co.*, 876 F.2d 1138, 1145 (5th Cir. 1989) (absence of equivalent of RICO in foreign jurisdiction does not bar dismissal on grounds of *forum non conveniens* where foreign law permits recovery for fraud, negligence, breach of fiduciary duty, etc.).

70 *Robert* v. *Bell Helicopter Textron Inc.*, 2002 U.S. Dist. LEXIS 7232 (N.D. Texas 24 April 2002); *Abdullahi* v. *Pfizer, Inc.*, 2002 U.S. Dist. LEXIS 17436 (S.D.N.Y. 17 September 2002).

The results reached by both of these district courts, which dismissed the actions in favor of the alternative jurisdictions, stand in seeming conflict with the Second Circuit's opinion in *Wiwa* v. *Royal Dutch Petroleum Company.*[71] In *Wiwa*, the Second Circuit reversed the district court's dismissal of the plaintiff's claims under *forum non conveniens* holding that the district court failed to, *inter alia*, give due weight to "the interests of the United States in furnishing a forum to litigate claims of violations of the international standards of the law of human rights".[72]

The Second Circuit found that:

> ". . . the TVPA [Torture Victim Prevention Act, 28 U.S. C. § 1350 App.] . . . recognizes explicitly what was perhaps implicit in the Act of 1789 — that the law of nations is incorporated into the law of the United States and that a violation of the international law of human rights is (at least with regard to torture) *ipso facto* a violation of U.S. domestic law".[73]

Based on this finding, the Second Circuit held:

> "The new formulations of the Torture Victim Protection Act convey the message that torture committed under color of law of a foreign nation in violation of international law is 'our business', as such conduct not only violates the standards of international law but also as a consequence violates our domestic law. In the legislative history of the TVPA, Congress noted that universal condemnation of human rights abuses "provides scant comfort" to the numerous victims of gross violations if they are without a forum to remedy the wrong. House Report at 3, 1992 U.S.C.C.A.N. at 85. This passage supports plaintiffs' contention that in passing the Torture Victim Prevention Act, Congress has expressed a policy of U.S. law favoring the adjudication of such suits in U.S. courts. If in cases of torture in violation of international law our courts exercise their jurisdiction conferred by the 1789 Act only for as long as it takes to dismiss the case

71 *Wiwa* v. *Royal Dutch Petroleum Company*, 226 F.3d 88 (2nd Cir. 2000).

72 *Wiwa* v. *Royal Dutch Petroleum Company*, 226 F.3d 88, 101 (2nd Cir. 2000).

73 *Wiwa* v. *Royal Dutch Petroleum Company*, 226 F.3d 88, 104–05 (2nd Cir. 2000).

> for *forum non conveniens*, we will have done little to enforce the standards of the law of nations.
>
> "This is not to suggest that the TVPA has nullified, or even significantly diminished, the doctrine of *forum non conveniens*. The statute has, however, communicated a policy that such suits should not be facilely dismissed on the assumption that the ostensibly foreign controversy is not our business. The TVPA in our view expresses a policy favoring our courts' exercise of the jurisdiction conferred by the ATCA in cases of torture unless the defendant has fully met the burden of showing that the *Gilbert* factors "tilt[] strongly in favor of trial in the foreign forum."[74]

Although the district court cases are seemingly in conflict with the Second Circuit's opinion, the different results can be explained due to the legal and factual differences in the three cases. With regard to the legal differences, neither Robert nor Abdullahi asserted claims under the Torture Victims Protection Act, which was at the heart of the Second Circuit's decision that the district court should have retained jurisdiction in *Wiwa*. Factually, there are important distinctions between the cases as well. In *Wiwa*, the plaintiffs filing the suit were United States residents who had established residency in the country for reasons independent of bringing suit in a United States forum. In *Abdullahi*, not one plaintiff was a United States resident. Indeed, none of the plaintiffs had ever even visited the country. In *Robert*, the plaintiff was a Canadian resident injured in a helicopter crash in Canada. Thus, as non-residents, their choice of forum was entitled to little or no deference by the court as compared to the residents in *Wiwa*.

Most important, however, are the underlying allegations of the three lawsuits. The plaintiffs in *Wiwa* alleged explicitly that the defendants had used Nigerian governmental entities to perpetrate the torts that were committed against them (or their decedents). Indeed, they alleged that the government entities took certain actions at the urging of the defendants and were active participants in the wrongdoing. In *Abdullahi*, the plaintiffs alleged that Pfizer only had the "blessing" of the government authorities in the form of permission to dispense the untested drugs to Nigerian citizens and use a hospital in the area where the epidemic was occurring. In *Robert*, the plaintiff

74 *Wiwa* v. *Royal Dutch Petroleum Company*, 226 F.3d 88, 106 (2nd Cir. 2000).

attempted to bootstrap jurisdiction by claiming that the defective product (the helicopter) had been sold in violation of "an agreement" between the United States and Canada governing the importing and exporting of aircraft parts. Both *Abdullahi* and *Robert* attempt to bring Common Law tort claims within the ambit of the Alien Tort Claims Act in order to confer jurisdiction on the United States court.

As noted by one commentator, the Alien Tort Claims Act does not confer federal jurisdiction over individual defendants acting independently of a foreign government. Rather, "jurisdiction has been granted over foreign states and individuals acting under the authority of a foreign state".[75] These cases stand in stark contrast to the allegations in *Wiwa*, which sought compensation for the types of wrongs the Alien Tort Claims Act and Torture Victims Protection Act were enacted to redress.

As all three cases recognized, the existence of claims under the Alien Tort Claims Act do not prevent a court from conducting a *forum non conveniens* analysis. In the course of such analysis, the nature and extent of the action's connection to the forum will be tested. Thus, attempts to create connections to the jurisdiction will likely not succeed. The district court's opinion in *Abdullahi* is currently on appeal. When the district court dismissed the action, it noted that a class action seeking compensation for precisely the same wrongs alleged by plaintiffs was pending in Nigeria and had been pending for several months. Defendant Pfizer was cooperating with discovery in that case, and it appeared that the class action would be resolved at some point in the future. Believing that the plaintiffs could obtain adequate compensation in the Nigerian forum, which had a greater public policy interest in hearing the dispute, the district court dismissed the action.

Shortly after the dismissal of the action in the United States, the class action proceeding in Nigeria self-destructed. First, the judge who was assigned to hear the case was arrested for corruption, essentially stopping all forward progress in the action. Thereafter, a second judge in Nigeria declined to take jurisdiction of the case. Eventually, the case was dismissed, presumably upon motion by the defendant. Should the plaintiffs be successful on appeal, it is more likely the result of the defendants' impatience in foreclosing the Nigerian court

75 14A Wright, Miller & Cooper, *Federal Practice & Procedure* (3rd edition, 1998) Section 3661.1, at 156 (citing cases).

action before the United States action was final and all appeals had been exhausted than the result of error in the district court's opinion. However, it bears noting that, even though the class action in Nigeria has been dismissed, the individual plaintiffs in the *Abdullahi* action can still file their claims in Nigeria as the dismissal was conditioned upon Pfizer waiving any statute of limitations defenses and consenting to jurisdiction.

Defense Strategies to Eliminate United States Interest in Litigation

Although it is difficult for a foreign plaintiff to persuade a district court to retain jurisdiction in the face of a *forum non conveniens* motion, defendants have employed many successful strategies in convincing the district courts to decline to exercise jurisdiction. Some of the more creative strategies have involved substantial risk to the defendant that it will have to pay some measure of damages at some point in the future. Most recently, Pfizer took a very large gamble in the actions which arose out of its use of the drug Trovan(r) in Nigeria during a meningitis epidemic before it was approved for use in humans. Pfizer had been sued in a class action pending in Nigeria. Soon thereafter, a group of Nigerian plaintiffs filed suit in the Southern District of New York seeking redress for injuries they allege were caused by the drug. An important factor in Pfizer's motion to dismiss based on *forum non conveniens* was the existence of the pending class action in Nigeria.

Rather than fight that action, Pfizer cooperated with the Nigerian court and actively engaged in moving the Nigerian case forward. Judge Pauley was persuaded by Pfizer's arguments that the Nigerian court was an adequate alternative forum, and found that the balance of public and private interest factors weighed heavily in favor of having the action in Nigeria proceed. The court noted:

> "Pfizer contends that not only is it subject to service of process in Nigeria, but it is also currently defending a lawsuit in Kano's Federal High Court filed five months prior to the instant complaint that arises from the Trovan treatment. In addition, Pfizer consents to jurisdiction in Kano's Federal High Court. Thus, Pfizer is subject to service of process in Nigeria . . . Pfizer further argues that Nigerian law provides

an adequate remedy for plaintiffs' claims because it recognizes negligence, medical malpractice, and personal injury claims. Plaintiffs do not dispute that Nigerian law prescribes those causes of action sounding in negligence with money damages as a potential remedy. Thus, Nigerian law provides an alternative basis for recovery even if it does not recognize the specific claims plaintiffs allege in this action".[76] In response to the plaintiffs' assertions that the legal system in Nigeria was corrupt (which would render it inadequate), the court cautioned:

> "This Court has a duty to exercise restraint when assessing the sufficiency of other nations, courts and legal systems. The Second Circuit has 'repeatedly emphasized that it is not the business of our courts to assume the responsibility for supervising the integrity of the judicial system of another sovereign nation'."[77]

Moreover, the court found that the plaintiffs' assertions of corruption were insufficient, especially as the plaintiffs had not alleged that Pfizer had attempted to exert any undue influence over the Nigerian court. With regard to the public interest factors, the court stated:

> "[i]t is undeniable that Nigeria has a very strong interest in this litigation. The Trovan test occurred in Nigeria, and all the alleged victims are Nigerian. Further, plaintiffs' allegations rely on the premise that Pfizer's alleged experiment was made possible with the aid of several of Nigeria's own government officials."[78]

However, what really tipped the scale in favor of dismissal was the on-going litigation in Nigeria combined with Pfizer's representations to the court of its cooperation with those proceedings:

> "Further, as plaintiffs concede, most of the documents and witnesses located in the United States are within Pfizer's

---

76 *Abdullahi* v. *Pfizer, Inc.*, 2002 U.S. Dist. LEXIS 17436 at *21–22 (S.D.N.Y. 17 September 2002).

77 *Abdullahi* v. *Pfizer, Inc.*, 2002 U.S. Dist. LEXIS 17436 at *26–27 (S.D.N.Y. 17 September 2002).

78 *Abdullahi* v. *Pfizer, Inc.*, 2002 U.S. Dist. LEXIS 17436 at *33–34 (S.D.N.Y. 17 September 2002).

> control. In addition, Pfizer has stipulated that it will facilitate any Nigerian action by providing plaintiffs with any relevant records; making past or present Pfizer employees available for depositions pursuant to 28 U.S.C. § 1782 n. 3; and using its "best efforts" to make any past and present employees of Pfizer who would be subject to subpoena in the Southern District of New York available to testify at trial in Kano at Pfizer's cost . . . Thus, the balance of the *Gilbert* private interest factors clearly weighs in favor of granting Pfizer's motion to dismiss for *forum non conveniens* because the vexation that it would incur in pursuing the relevant Nigerian discovery while litigating in this forum is grossly disproportionate to any convenience that plaintiffs may experience."[79]

The strategy employed by Pfizer successfully eliminated any public or private interest in having the action proceed in the United States forum. Due to the uncertain nature of the scale of damages that could be imposed by the Nigerian court, Pfizer was unable to employ a similar defense strategy that has been very successful. The Boeing Company has successfully had litigations dismissed by stating that it was willing to concede liability for the accident that was the subject of the suit, usually conditioned upon the suit proceeding in the foreign forum. If the suit was to proceed in the United States, Boeing would have contested liability. The end result of this concession was that the only issue remaining in the lawsuit was the measure of damages. As so many courts have found, the measure of damages is highly dependent upon where the tort occurred and the community reference for preventing such behavior in the future. Thus, upon Boeing's concession of liability, the balance of *Gilbert* factors tipped heavily in favor of dismissing the action.[80]

Conclusion

Although the application of the *forum non conveniens* doctrine tends to favor multinational corporate defendants over the rights of injured

79 *Abdullahi* v. *Pfizer, Inc.*, 2002 U.S. Dist. LEXIS 17436 at *36–37 (S.D.N.Y. 17 September 2002) (internal citations omitted).

80 *Myers* v. *The Boeing Company*, 794 P.2d 1272 (Wa. 1990); *Jennings* v. *The Boeing Company*, 660 F.Supp. 796 (E.D. Pa. 1987).

plaintiffs, the actual outcome of the test is highly dependent upon the individual judge making the initial determination. If the judge believes that the plaintiff has come to the United States to litigate for no other reason than the likelihood of a higher damages award, the case is unlikely to survive the dismissal motion.

However, if the plaintiff can provide a *bona fide* legitimate reason for seeking redress in the United States, the courts will likely retain jurisdiction, particularly where the litigation does not burden the court's docket. Even though the doctrine occasionally results in dismissals that seem contrary to the principles of justice, the overwhelming majority of cases show that judges conduct a thoughtful and thorough analysis before dismissing any action, thus ensuring that the doctrine fulfills its primary role of preventing the court system from being overwhelmed by cases that should rightfully be heard in other fora.

Product Liability under French Law

Vonnick le Guillou and Marie Bresson
Clyde & Co.
Paris, France

Introduction

Product liability in France is quite a complex matter. Directive 85/374/EEC of 25 July 1985 "on the approximation of the laws, regulations and administrative provisions of the Member States concerning liability for defective products" was implemented under French law more than ten years after the time limit for transposition by introducing into the Civil Code Articles 1386–1 to 1386–18. The intent of the Directive was to harmonize the laws of the European countries as regards consumers' rights but, in fact, it just added a new cause of action to the ones that already existed.

Indeed, where damage is caused by a product, the victim can opt between several causes of action to recover damages from the seller or the producer:

(1) The traditional existing causes of actions based on tortious or contractual liability, depending on whether or not the victim was contractually linked to the seller; and

(2) The specific cause of action against the producer (or importer) of a defective product, the defect being exclusively defined as a lack of safety — this cause of action is neither contractual nor based on tort, but it is a statutory cause of action based on strict liability and is available to consumers as well as to professional users.

The time limitation applying to the contractual causes of action is longer than the one applying to strict liability, but the burden of proof to demonstrate the negligence of the seller is on the victim. On the other hand, the specific cause of action for a defective product is subject to a shorter time limitation, but as this is a strict liability system, there is no need for the victim of damage to prove negligence or fault on the part of the producer. Another advantage for the buyer in taking action against the seller or the producer for contractual liability is that he can claim for damages when damage was solely caused to the defective product itself, which is not possible under the product liability rules.

It should be noted that causes of action in tort will not be studied here, as they are not specific to product liability. It is enough to remember that the producer or the seller of a product incurs liability towards the user of the product where it is shown that the negligence of the producer or the seller has caused damage.

Contractual Liability

The purchaser of a product is entitled to sue the seller based on the basis of the contract of sale. Different rules apply simultaneously in this area: French law, European Community Directives and international conventions. As France is a member of the Vienna Convention on the International Sale of Goods (CISG), French law only applies to domestic sale contracts, except if the parties to an international sale of goods agree not to apply the CISG to their contract.

French Law

It is important to note that French law distinguishes between mere sale of goods contracts (*contrats de vente*) and job contracts (*contrats d'entreprise*). The latter involve products that are made according to the client's specifications or instructions, that is, "tailor-made" production. The following rules only apply to basic sale of goods contracts, which means that the manufacturer offers a range of products for the buyer to choose from.

Where a purchased product is found to be defective, the buyer may take an action against the seller based on the product's lack of conformity or on the legal guarantee of the seller, depending on the circumstances. One criterion that enables a distinction between these two causes of action is the chronology. Prior to performance of the contract, the seller's main obligation is to deliver the product subject to the contractual terms. He may, therefore, incur liability for lack of conformity. Once the product is delivered, however, the seller guarantees the purchaser against hidden defects in the product that could appear. Another criterion, which is usually applied by case law, is rather subtle: the product lacks conformity if it is inappropriate for the specific use expected by the buyer as normally revealed by the contractual terms; whereas the seller's warranty for hidden defects will be involved if the product is inappropriate for normal use, with reference to an objective definition of such use. In any case, contractual liability of the manufacturer is also incurred towards a sub-buyer of the product, even though there is no formal contract between them.

Lack of Conformity

The seller's liability for lack of conformity of the delivered product is governed by Articles 1604 *et seq.* of the French Civil Code.

Definition The main duty of the seller resulting from a sale of goods contract is to deliver the exact product as agreed with the purchaser. If the product lacks conformity with the contractual terms or is of a lesser quality than what was agreed, the buyer may take an action against the seller based on contractual liability. Such lack of conformity is considered to be a breach of the seller's obligation to deliver the product. There is no statutory definition of conformity. Judges, therefore, refer to the contract terms or, if the contract terms are not sufficient, to an average quality.

Procedure Once the buyer notices a lack of conformity in the product, he shall refuse delivery of the product or, where the product has already been delivered, make complaints within a reasonable time. If he fails to do so, then the buyer's receipt of the product shall be deemed to be acceptance of the product despite its lack of conformity.

Lack of conformity may be claimed by the purchaser:

(1) As a justification for not paying the seller where an action is taken against him; or
(2) As a cause of action against the seller for performance or rescission of the contract.

The burden to prove the lack of conformity of the product is on the buyer. However, where the seller has placed a specific obligation upon himself (*obligation de résultat*), there is a presumption against the seller, and the burden is, therefore, on the seller to prove that he supplied a product in conformity with the contractual requirements.

Defenses The seller is not responsible if he proves that the breach was caused by:

(1) *Force majeure* or act of God, that is, an irresistible, unforeseeable and external event;
(2) Contributory negligence of the plaintiff; or
(3) Negligence of a third party.

Seller's Legal Guarantee

If a defect appears after delivery rendering the product unsuitable for normal use, the buyer may take an action for such hidden defect, provided that the defect could not have been discovered at the time of delivery and that it was inherent to the product.[1]

The seller's warranty is owed under three conditions. Firstly, the product is defective and has not been repaired, reference being made *in abstracto* to the normal use that is expected from the product rather than to the actual expectations of the buyer as regards the lack of conformity. Unlike liability for lack of conformity, minor defects are not covered by the seller's warranty. Secondly, the defect existed and was hidden to the buyer at the date of transfer of risk from the seller to the buyer. Once the buyer proves the existence of a hidden defect, French courts assume that professional sellers were aware of that defect when they sold the product. Thus, sellers cannot use their ignorance of the defect as a defense.

Thirdly, the buyer must bring an action against the seller on the ground of a hidden defect within a short period of time after discovery of the defect. This "short period of time" is rather severe and must be combined with the general time limitation, that is, ten years after the contract date for commercial contracts. If the general time limitation has expired, the action for a hidden defect is time-barred even though the claim was made within a short period of time after the discovery of the product's defect.

The seller's liability for a hidden defect is strengthened by its obligation to inform the buyer. The seller may be held liable if he did not provide the buyer with appropriate and sufficient information concerning the use of the product.

1 Civil Code, Article 1641.

Remedies

Contracting parties may agree to reduce or extend the seller's liability and/or remedies. Such contractual provisions may, however, be considered unlawful and, as such, not implemented. French case law is usually suspicious towards exculpatory clauses provided by purchase contracts and tends to limit their scope. Generally speaking, such clauses are valid only if they apply between professionals. Regarding a seller's guarantee for hidden defects, French courts rule them out systematically even between professionals, except between professionals with the same specialty.

Where damage is caused to the product itself, remedies provided by statutory law are different depending on the cause of action. Concerning damage caused by a hidden defect in the product, Article 1644 of the French Civil Code provides that the buyer may choose either to return the product to the seller and obtain a total refund of the purchase price, or to keep the product and get a partial refund.

If damage is caused by lack of conformity of the product, either remedies provided by the contract are applied or remedies considered as most suitable by the judge:

(1) Replacement or repair of the product;
(2) Unless otherwise provided by the parties, whether expressly or not, French judges may order a price reduction only in the case of a minor lack of conformity.

Where damage is caused to other property or to persons, French contract law provides that if a party does not perform its contractual obligations, it shall repair the damage caused to the co-contracting party by such breach.[2] This rule applies to damage caused by lack of conformity, that is, breach of the obligation to deliver the product.

Damages that may be awarded include:

(1) Economic loss and loss of profits; and
(2) Damage that was foreseeable at the time the contract was entered into by the parties, except if the party willfully breached the contract, in which case only indirect damage would not be recoverable.

2 Civil Code, Article 1147.

As for hidden defects, if a seller's guarantee is owed, the buyer is not entitled to damages unless the seller knew of the defect.[3] However, as mentioned above, under applicable case law, professional sellers are deemed to know the existence of the defect.

European Directive on Sale of Consumer Goods

Directive 1999/44/EC of 25 May 1999 on certain aspects of the sale of consumer goods and associated guarantees has not yet been transposed in France in spite of the expiration of the transposition period (no later than 1 January 2002). Considering that Directive 1999/44/EC does not distinguish between lack of conformity and hidden defect, French law would need radical changes in order to comply with it.

Directive 1999/44/EC indeed defines conformity with the contract by referring not only to the parties' specifications, but also to what can normally be expected from such goods.[4] This definition of conformity with the contract is similar to that of the CISG. The French rule on a seller's guarantee for hidden defects is, therefore, included within the European duty to deliver goods in conformity with the contract terms.

Pursuant to Directive 1999/44/EC, liability of the producer may be sought if the lack of conformity appears within two years following the delivery of the goods and if the buyer informs the seller within two months after he discovered the lack of conformity. If such lack of conformity appears within six months after delivery of the goods, it is presumed to have existed at the time of delivery. As for remedies, the Directive favors repair or replacement of the goods rather than a price refund.[5] It is important to note that the Directive addresses only consumers and does not apply to professional users. It furthermore sets minimum protection standards for consumers, allowing the Member States to make more stringent provisions.

Product Liability

This issue is dealt with by Directive 85/374/EEC on liability for defective products, as amended by Directive 1999/34/EC of 10 May

3 Civil Code, Articles 1645 and 1646.
4 Directive 1999/44/EC, Article 2.
5 Directive 1999/44/EC, Article 3 contains the applicable remedies.

1999, and transposed into French law by Act Number 98–389 of 19 May 1998 (French Transposition Act), itself introduced into the French Civil Code by the creation of Articles 1386–1 to 1386–18.

French Transposition Act

Generally speaking, the scope of liability for defective products resulting from the French Transposition Act is wider than under Directive 85/374/EEC, which means it grants better protection for consumers. Unlike Directive 1999/44/EC, which sets minimum requirements allowing the Member States to adopt better consumer protection, the rules set down by Directive 85/374/EEC are compulsory, unless otherwise expressly provided. Member States must comply with the Directive, and France was condemned by the European Court of Justice (ECJ) for its infringement.

Scope of Producer's Liability

Under the French Transposition Act, a producer is liable for damage caused by a defect in his product, whether the victim is a private consumer or a professional user, whereas Directive 85/374/EEC addresses only consumers.

Services are not considered as "products" for the purposes of producers' liability, but such liability applies whether the victim was a user of the product or not. As a result, in a case where a defective product used in the course of providing a service causes damage to the client, even without being delivered to that person, the product shall nevertheless be deemed to have been put into circulation by the producer.[6]

Product liability is incurred for any movable product, even though it is incorporated into an immovable. If the defective product is incorporated into another movable, the producer of the defective product and the person who incorporated the defective product are jointly and severally liable.

Whereas French statutory law does not define what product "conformity" is, nor what the product should conform to, Directive

6 European Court of Justice Case C-203/99 of 10 May 2001.

85/374/EEC, via the French Transposition Act, defines a defective product as follows:

> ". . . a product is defective when it does not provide the safety which a person is entitled to expect, taking all circumstances into account, including the presentation of the product, the use to which it could reasonably be expected that it would be put, and the time when the product was put into circulation".

Reference is not made to the quality of the product itself and its ability to perform what it is designed for, but to its degree of safety in reasonably foreseeable circumstances.

Conditions for Producer's Liability

The plaintiff is required to prove the damage, the defect and the causal relationship between the defect and the damage.[7] French courts and doctrine have been tempted to apply the same evidence rules as for guardian liability, where evidence of a fault or defect and of a causal relationship is not required from the victim. In a recent decision, the French Supreme Court, however, quashed a judgment that had admitted a producer's liability even although the victim had not proved that the product was defective and its relationship to the damage. The Supreme Court based its decision on the terms of Article 1386–9, mentioned above.[8] Subject to evidence by the plaintiff of a causal connection, a producer is also responsible for consequential damage.

Producer's Defenses

The French Transposition Act provides specific defenses.[9] The producer shall not be liable if he proves:

(1) That he did not put the product into circulation;

(2) That, given the circumstances, it is probable that the defect that caused the damage did not exist at the time when the product was put into circulation by him or that the defect appeared afterwards;

---

7 Civil Code, Article 1386-9.

8 Cassation Civ. 1e, 23 September 2003, Case Number 1191.

9 French Transposition Act, Article 1386-11.

(3) That the product was neither manufactured by the producer for sale or any form of distribution for economic purposes, nor manufactured or distributed in the course of his business;

(4) That the state of scientific and technical knowledge at the time when he put the product into circulation was not such as to enable the existence of a defect to be discovered, though the producer cannot prevail himself of development risk:
   (a) if damage was caused by an element of the human body or by products thereof; and
   (b) if, faced with a defect that has revealed itself within a period of ten years after the product was put into circulation, he did not take the appropriate steps to avoid its damaging consequences (although the ECJ has ruled that this limitation of the development risk defense infringes the EU Directive, as explained below);

(5) That the defect was due to compliance of the product with mandatory regulations issued by the public authorities — a producer may, however, be liable for a defect although the product was manufactured in accordance with good engineering practice or with existing standards or although it was granted an administrative authorization; or

(6) In the case of a manufacturer of a component, that the defect was due to the design of the product in which the component was fitted or to the instructions given by the manufacturer of the product.

Other defenses arc inspired from other causes of action, for example, the defense of contributory negligence. The liability of a producer may be reduced or disallowed where the damage is caused both by a defect in the product and by the fault of the victim or of a person for whom the victim is responsible. However, the liability of a producer towards a victim shall not be reduced where the act or omission of a third party contributed to the production of the damage.

Even though the French Transposition Act does not provide for cases of *force majeure*, the producer shall not be liable if the damage is caused by *force majeure*, as there is no causal connection between the defect and the damage.

Time Limitation

A double time limitation applies to an action for the recovery of damages based on a producer's liability for a defective product, whereby:

(1) Such an action shall be commenced within ten years after the actual product was put into circulation, except where there is fault on the part of the producer; and
(2) Such an action is time-barred after three years from the moment the plaintiff knew or ought to have known of the damage, the defect and the identity of the producer.

European Court Decision of 25 April 2002

After France complied with the Directive by implementing the Transposition Act of 19 May 1998, the ECJ ruled on 25 April 2002 that some provisions of the Transposition Act infringed the Directive. French law does not provide any deductibles regarding the amount of damages claimed by the victim. The ECJ decided that this rule infringed Directive 85/374/EEC, which provides for a lower threshold of Euro 500 in the case of damage done to property (there is no threshold in the case of personal injuries). The Government, therefore, intends to amend the French Transposition Act by adding a €500 threshold, under which a victim would not be allowed to take action against the producer.

The ECJ further decided that the obligation of follow-up included in the Transposition Act, which limits the development risk defense where the producer did not take the appropriate steps to avoid the damaging consequences of a defect that revealed itself within a period of ten years after the product had been put into circulation, was contradictory to Directive 85/374/EEC, which did not allow such limitation, although the development risk defense itself was optional.

When passed, an amendment to the French Transposition Act currently in preparation should withdraw this provision, but it should be noted that such an obligation of follow-up of the product is included in Directive 2001/95/CE of 3 December 2001 on general product safety (GPSD), the transposition of which in France is currently in preparation. In any case, in such circumstances, the producer's liability could alternatively be sought pursuant to tort or to contract liability based on the fault or negligence of the producer if he did not take the appropriate action to avoid any damage when a defect in his product was revealed.

Pursuant to Directive 85/374/EEC, the distributor is liable if he presents himself as the producer by putting his name, trademark or other distinguishing feature on the product and if he imports the product into the Community during the course of his business. However, in the terms of the Directive, such liability of the distributor shall be subsidiary and shall only apply where the producer cannot be identified. If the supplier informs the injured person, within a reasonable time, of the identity of the producer or of the person who supplied him with the product, he shall not be liable as the producer.

There is no such distinction under the French Transposition Act: a seller or any professional supplier is jointly and severally liable for the lack of safety of a product under the same conditions as the producer. The ECJ thus ruled that this provision of the French Transposition Act infringed Directive 85/374/EEC. Consequently, the French Government intends to amend it, so that sub-suppliers will be liable only if the producer remains unidentified.

In any case, according to the French Transposition Act, the remedy of a supplier against a producer is subject to the same rules as a claim brought by a direct victim of a defect. However, the supplier must take action within a year following the date of his being summoned.

As a result of these two condemnations by the ECJ, France will amend its applicable law to comply with Directive 85/374/EEC. In the meantime, French courts shall not apply the infringing provisions. As for products put into circulation before the implementation of the Directive, national laws shall be interpreted "as far as possible, in the light of the wording and the purpose of the Directive so as to achieve the result it has in view".[10]

Conclusion

The above rules are intended to state the legal rights of victims who suffer damage caused by defective products. In addition to these rules, national and European authorities are working to minimize the risks to consumers caused by defective products. In particular, several Directives apply to special products, as well as "new approach" (or "global approach") Directives, such as Directive 2001/95/CE of

10 European Court of Justice, 19 January 1982, Ursula Becker, rec. p. 53; European Court of Justice, 26 February 1986, Marshall, rec. p. 749.

3 December 2001 on general product safety, the transposition of which in France is currently in preparation.

The GPSD strengthens the duties of producers or of people who have placed products on the market with regard to safety and follow-up of the products. They must trace the origin of products, inform consumers of the risks that these products may present and adopt measures commensurate with the characteristics of the products enabling them to assess and prevent risks, which may involve withdrawing the products from the market or recalling them if necessary.

Pursuant to the GPSD, producers also have an obligation to inform national authorities where their products present risks with regard to consumer safety. Cooperation and the sharing of information between the European Member States is assured by the Community Rapid Information System (RAPEX).

Suppliers' Vicarious Liability for Defective Products in Danish and European Law

Georg Lett and Kristine Lilholt Nilsson
Lett & Co.
Copenhagen, Denmark

Introduction

Before the Product Liability Directive was adopted, Danish law on product liability was based on case law. It was considered as tort law, even if in contract. The condition for liability was negligence but, in reality, it was virtually strict liability in relation to causation. After the adoption of the Directive, it was difficult to tell any practical difference. Nonetheless, the legislator chose to maintain the case law based rules on product liability alongside the Act implementing the Directive.[1]

In the case law, suppliers were held liable not only for their own negligence, but also for any liability of the producer, but giving the supplier full right of indemnity against the producer. When implementing the Directive, it was decided to introduce a similar rule for product liability falling within the Directive.

Product Liability Legislation and Case Law

Danish Act on Product Liability

Section 10 of the Danish Act on Product Liability determines that the supplier of a product shall be immediately liable to the claimant and to subsequent resellers. Section 10 allows a claim against the supplier even if the supplier has shown no negligence. In such instances, the supplier will be left with a claim for indemnification against the producer and previous links in the line of distribution.

1 Act Number 371 of 7 June 1989.

The Commission has not contested this implementation but, inspired by a judgment of the European Court of Justice (ECJ), the question was raised whether the Danish implementation was in compliance with the Directive. In Case C-52/00, *Commission* v. *France*, the ECJ found that provisions in Article 1386–7 of the French Code Civil were not in compliance with the Product Liability Directive. Article 1386–7 provided that the supplier of a defective product was to be liable in all cases and on the same basis as the producer. This was, of course, interesting from a Danish point of view.

Danish Case Law

In one of the many pending cases before the courts in Denmark where suppliers are held liable for defective products, it was decided to try the issue before the ECJ. The facts of the case involved two consumers who allegedly fell ill from a salmonella infection after having consumed eggs bought at a supermarket. The consumers brought a claim for damages against the supermarket that supplied the eggs, and the supermarket brought a claim for indemnification against the plant that packed the eggs. The High Court of Western Denmark requested a preliminary ruling from the ECJ regarding Section 10 of the Danish Act on Product Liability.[2]

The questions to the Court aim at clarifying:

(1) Is it against the Directive to hold the supplier vicariously liable for defective products according to the rules of the Directive? and

(2) Is it against the Directive to maintain a set of rules laid down in case law within the area of the Directive according to which the supplier has a vicarious liability for the negligence of the producer?

Since the consumers in the salmonella case only raised a claim against the supplier, the answers will be decisive because a possible claim from the consumer against the producer is time barred. Much of the debate concerning the first issue will focus on interpretation of the French case.

2 Case C-402/03.

Commission* v. *France

In Case C-52/00, the ECJ found that Article 1386–7 of the Civil Code, providing liability for the supplier within the area of product liability, was not in compliance with the Directive. The wording of the French provision stated that "The vendor, hirer, except a lessor under a hire purchase agreement or a hirer assimilable thereto, or any other supplier in the course of business shall be liable for safety defects in their products on the same basis as the producer".

Article 3(3) of the Product Liability Directive determines that each supplier of a product shall be treated as its producer unless he informs the injured person, within a reasonable time, of the identity of the producer or of the person who supplied him with the product. The French provision extended the group of persons to also include other types of suppliers than the ones mentioned in the Directive.

In Paragraph 16 of the case judgment, the ECJ states that the margin of discretion available to the Member States in order to make provisions for product liability is entirely determined by the Directive itself and must be inferred from its wording, purpose and structure. In Paragraph 18 of the judgment, the Court points out that the Directive contains no provision expressly authorizing the Member States to adopt or maintain more stringent provisions in matters covered by the Directive in order to secure a higher level of consumer protection. In Paragraph 22, the Court rules that the Directive seeks to achieve, in the matters regulated by it, complete harmonization of the laws, regulations and administrative provisions of the Member States.[3]

The French Government did not deny that the Civil Code went beyond Article 3(3) of the Directive by equating the supplier and the producer,[4] but claimed that Article 1386-7 achieved the result sought by the Directive, since the supplier sued by the injured party may join the producer as a party. However, the ECJ held that the possibility of joining the producer had the effect of multiplying proceedings, a result that a direct action against the producer is intended to avoid.[5] The Court, therefore, declared that the French Government had failed to implement the Directive correctly.

---

3 Advocate General's opinion, Paragraphs 44, 45 and 47.

4 Paragraphs 36 and 37.

5 Paragraph 40.

Danish Implementation

Section 10 of the Danish Act on Product Liability provides that the supplier of a product shall be immediately liable to the claimant and to subsequent resellers. The French Article 1386–7(1) provided that the supplier was liable "on the same basis" as the producer. Article 1386–7(2) provided that the rules governing the claim of the injured party were applicable to the claim for indemnification from the supplier.

It has been argued that there is a difference between the French provision and the Danish provision, as the French rule provides liability while the Danish rule provides vicarious liability. If there is a difference, this difference cannot be relevant. The same result follows from the French Article 1386–7(2) as from Section 10 of the Danish Act on Product Liability. The unconditional right of recourse against the supplier creates a kind of liability that is similar to vicarious liability. It is only a reflection of the fact that the liability of the supplier does not exceed the liability of the producer. What both provisions have in common is that the supplier in both instances is held liable on the basis of the provisions of the Directive.

The possibility of a claim for indemnification leads to the same result as the Directive but, as the ECJ stated in Paragraph 40 of the ruling in Case C-52/00, this does not make the provisions in compliance with the Directive. The opinion of the Court was substantiated by the fact that the Directive was intended to avoid needless lawsuits.

The Explanatory Memorandum for the Directive, which was published along with the proposal for the Directive, stated:[6]

> "Liability based on Article 1 is that of the producer of the defective product. Dealers have not been included among those persons against whom claims may be brought insofar as they do not come under the exceptions specified in Article 2. Liability on the part of dealers in defective products, of the type provided for in the Directive, would indeed make it easier for the injured consumer to claim his rights. This would, however, be achieved at a high cost, since every dealer would have to insure himself against claims even in respect of products which are almost completely free of risk. This would lead to a sharp increase in the price of products,

6 *Bulletin for the European Community*, Supplement 11/76, at p. 14, Section 6.

without the protection of the consumer being increased otherwise than by facilitating proceedings. Moreover, the liability of the dealer would be in any event only an intermediate liability, since he in turn would claim against his suppliers and back to the producer. Finally, there is no reason to make the dealer liable since in the overwhelming majority of cases he passes on the purchased product in unchanged form, and therefore has no opportunity to affect the quality of the goods. Only the producer is capable of this. The Directive proceeds from the presumption (Article 5) that the defect must have arisen in the producer's production process. Merely to protect the good name of the product the producer will do everything to prevent defects by carefully organizing his production. None of these considerations apply to the dealer. It was, therefore, considered advisable to concentrate liability for defective products on the producer."

The Commission's Green Paper[7] posed a question as to whether the Directive should make other links in the line of distribution liable for defective products. In the Commission's Report,[8] the Commission found no reason to change the Directive in such a way that the supplier is made liable for defective products other than what already follows from Article 3(3) of the Directive. In this way, the Commission maintains that it finds it reasonable that the producer and not the supplier, as a general rule, is liable for defective products.

In the case before the Danish courts, the injured party argues that a declaration recorded in the Council minutes at the time of the adoption of the Directive leads to another result. The argument is based on a quote from the Council minutes stating that the Council and the Commission agree upon the fact that the Member States are free to adopt rules on the liability of suppliers, as these are not provided for in the Directive.

This can hardly be correct, as it is obvious that the Member States cannot adopt rules that do not comply with the Directive. The Member States can, of course, adopt rules on the supplier's own liability in instances where the supplier has the opportunity to affect the goods, for example, he inadequately stores them by not keeping them

7 COM (1999) 386 Final, at p. 27.
8 COM (2000) 893 Final, at p. 24.

refrigerated, labels them incorrectly or makes a mistake in delivery, delivering a laxative as toothpaste.

The French provision, as well as the Danish provision, is entirely different from this, as both provisions make the supplier vicariously liable for the producer's liability under the Directive. These arguments all point in the same direction, that is, that the Danish provision on liability of the supplier is not in compliance with the Product Liability Directive. This part of the case seems obvious.

Liability Based on Case Law

The other issue before the ECJ is whether it is in conflict with the Directive to maintain a set of rules on product liability established in case law. According to Danish case law, there are two main conditions for imposing product liability: the product must be defective or dangerous and must have caused damage to a person or a thing. The basic criterion is that the product is dangerous or defective in the sense that it has qualities that, during the course of normal use, could cause damage to persons or things. Secondly, the defective or dangerous condition of the product must be caused by negligence.

The liability for negligence is very stringent, as any defective or dangerous quality of the product implies negligence. Any individual excuses are not considered to be relevant. As previously stated, it is difficult to identify situations where these conditions will lead to other results than the Directive. Even outside the area of the Directive, the courts have sometimes used the terminology of the Directive.[9]

The injured party will have a free choice to hold either the producer or the supplier or both liable for a defective product, no matter who has acted negligently. Further links in the line of distribution are held responsible for the negligence of any previous party in the line – solely based on the fact of being part of the line of distribution.

Product liability based on case law implies, in the same way as the Danish Act on Product Liability, that the supplier is held liable for damage caused by the fact that the producer has delivered a defective product. Therefore, the supplier is held responsible for damage that he has had no possibility of predicting or avoiding. This situation is exactly the same as the situation created by Section 10 of the Danish Act on Product Liability, which holds the supplier liable for the

9 UfR 1997 p. 203V.

producer's liability under the Act and the Directive. There seems to be no relevant differences between the liability of the supplier based on tort law and the liability based on the Act.

One can ask whether the Directive can allow rules for liability of the supplier that are based on other provisions than the provisions laid down by the Directive if the rules are really identical when it comes to damage covered by the Directive. The main provision in the Directive covering this aspect of the discussion is Article 13, which provides that the Directive "shall not affect any rights, which an injured person may have according to the rules of the law of contractual or non-contractual liability or a special liability system existing at the moment when this Directive is notified".

According to Paragraph 21 of the ruling in Case C-52/00, the ECJ does not find that this provision can be interpreted as giving the Member States the possibility of maintaining a general system of product liability different from that provided for in the Directive. This is elaborated on in Paragraph 22, where the Court states that:

> "The reference in Article 13 of the Directive to the rights which an injured person may rely on under the rules of the law of contractual or non-contractual liability must be interpreted as meaning that the system of rules put in place by the Directive, which in Article 4 enables the victim to seek compensation where he proves damage, the defect in the product and the causal link between that defect and the damage, does not prelude the application of other systems of contractual or non-contractual liability based on other grounds, such as fault or warranty in respect of latent defects."

The intention behind these two paragraphs must be that the Directive allows a system of rules that apply along with the rules of the Directive as to liability for defective products resting on traditional rules of contractual or non-contractual liability. What is not allowed is a general set of rules specifically aimed at product liability, which regulate the area in a way that is different from the Directive in areas that are covered by the Directive. General non-statutory rules that deviate from the provisions of the Directive regarding personal injury or consumer property damage will open up for circumvention. According to the wording, the Product Liability Directive deals with "the acts, regulations and administrative provisions of the Member States". The heading does not mention rules that are laid down in the case law of the Member States.

In the Preamble to the Directive, as well as in the Explanatory Memorandum for the Directive,[10] it is stated that uniform rules on product liability are introduced due to divergences in the legislation of the Member States. Divergences in laws were found to affect the establishment and functioning of the Common Market directly in three different ways. First, divergences may distort competition in the Common Market as different rules with varying strictness lead to differences in costs for producers in the various Member States who are in competition with each other. Second, the differences in laws can affect the free movement of goods within the Community as different rules on liability can affect the decision on where to produce and/or sell products. Third, a differing degree of protection for consumers as a result of the differences in laws is not found to be compatible with a Common Market for all consumers. These three arguments must be valid in relation to rules of liability developed in case law, as well as rules provided in acts, regulations and administrative provisions.

Case C-183/00, *Commission* v. *Spain*, was about the validity of a general provision on tort from the time before the adoption of the Directive. The provision involved extra protection than that contained in the Directive, and the Court set aside the rule. Consequently, it is not important whether or not the provision on the supplier's liability existed in national law before the implementation of the Directive. The decisive factor is not whether the rule follows from legislation or case law. What matters is whether the provision is a result of the general law on torts or not.

Evidently, the rule concerning vicarious liability of the supplier is not a result of the law on torts. There is no general rule stating that one link in the chain of distribution is liable for the fault of previous links. Also, there is no general principle of liability for the negligence of others. The rule of vicarious liability based on Danish case law is not a rule of contractual guarantee either, as it governs both contractual and non-contractual relationships. Therefore, it seems difficult to uphold the vicarious liability of the supplier with reference to Article 13.

However, this part of case law may lead to surprises. The ECJ may decide that the Directive does not affect what is considered general tort law established in case law. If so, the supplier may still be held

10 *Bulletin for the European Community*, Supplement 11/76, at p. 11.

liable for any defect in the product, even if such a rule is abolished in the Act implementing the Directive. Although the two rules on vicarious liability are formally different, it will be difficult, if not impossible, to tell the difference. In practical terms, the legal situation will then be unchanged.

Product Liability in Brazil

Sérgio Pinheiro Marçal and Viviana de Castilho Barbosa
Pinheiro Neto Advogados
São Paulo, Brazil

Introduction

First of all, it should be mentioned that legal consumer relations in Brazil are regulated by Law Number 8078 of 11 September 1990, known as the Consumer Protection Code. According to Article 3 of the Consumer Protection Code, consumer relations encompass relationships relating to the production, transformation, assembly, creation, construction, import, export, distribution or marketing of goods, as well as the rendering of services, including banking, financial, credit and security services (labor relations excepted) conducted by private or public entities. In other words, consumer relations are all relations in connection with the production and placement on the market of goods and services, and the subsequent acquisition and use of them by the public at large.

Liability Systems

The relations governed by the Consumer Protection Code are necessarily composed of purchasers and end users (individuals, a group of individuals and legal entities), on one side, and suppliers of consumer goods or services, on the other. Article 2 of the Consumer Protection Code defines a consumer as "any individual or legal entity that acquires or uses products or services as an end user". It should be noted that, under Article 3 of the Consumer Protection Code:

> ". . . supplier means any individual or legal entity, whether public or private, Brazilian or foreign, as well as any unincorporated entities, engaged in production, assembly, creation, construction, transformation, import, export distribution or marketing activities or in the provision of services".

The Consumer Protection Code distinguishes two types of liability to which the product supplier may be subject, namely, liability as regards the product itself and liability for a flaw in the product.

Liability as regards the product itself, contained in Articles 12 to 17 of the Code, is related to the concept of a consumption accident and assigns the obligation to indemnify to the supplier of the product. Article 12 of the Code covers:

> ". . . the damage caused to consumers by defects stemming from design, manufacturing, construction, assembly, formulae, manipulation, presentation or conditioning of its products, as well as from insufficient or inadequate information on the use and risks thereof".

Liability for the product itself is strict, that is, it does not depend on the fault of the supplier. The consumer does not have the burden of proving negligence, imprudence or lack of skill on the part of the supplier. The existence of damage is sufficient, which must be remedied by the party connected thereto by the chain of causation.

Suppliers are also liable, in the civil sphere, for damages incurred by third parties, who American case law currently refers to as bystanders, that is, those who are not purchasers or owners of the products, but who suffer any type of damage the moment that the defect in the product manifests itself. This is the prevailing position in Brazilian case law, backed by Article 17 of the Code.

A supplier is only held not liable to indemnify a consumer for losses resulting from an accident caused by a product defect if it is proven that:

(1) The supplier did not put the product on the market;
(2) Although the supplier put the product on the market, there is no defect; and/or
(3) The accident occurred as a consequence of the exclusive fault of the consumer.[1]

One must further always bear in mind the risk that is reasonably expected in relation to the product or service and the adequacy of information concerning such risk that should be given to the consumer. The consumer or third party may file suit against all involved in the chain of production. Those who are not directly responsible

---

1 Consumer Protection Code, Article 12, Paragraph 3, clauses I, II and III.

will have a right of recourse against the party responsible. Only in express circumstances set forth under the law is there exemption from liability.

As for liability arising from a faulty product, this does not arise from any damage caused to the consumer, as in the case of product liability. In this case, liability arises from a fault that renders the product useless or inadequate for consumption, or reduces its value or quantity.[2] In this case, the ground for liability differs from that related to product liability. Liability for fault in quality or quantity involves supplier responsibility and is linked to contract default, given that the supplier must warrant adequate performance of the contract, placing the product or service on the consumer market in perfect condition for use.

Outside the consumer protection system, that is, in such cases in which a consumer relationship does not exist, the recently enacted new Civil Code shall apply. The Civil Code provides for indemnity against illicit acts and also for contract liability. The novelty introduced by this system is indemnity for damages irrespective of guilt, when the activity normally carried out by the author of the damage implies, by its very nature, a risk to the rights of third parties.[3]

As a rule, the State has no ancillary liability in relation to any kind of product, unless it is proven that the State is directly responsible for the event which caused the damage.

Ascertaining Person Responsible for Fault or Defect

The responsibility as regards the product itself is borne by the manufacturer, producer or builder, as the case may be, whether domestic or foreign, and by the importer. The importer, in fact, is answerable in its capacity as presumed supplier, while the remaining are answerable in their capacity of effective supplier. The merchant (also a presumed supplier) has been excluded from the general rule and is only answerable in a supplementary manner, as provided under Article 13 of the Consumer Protection Code, when the manufacturer cannot be identified or the product does not contain clear identification of the manufacturer, or when the merchant does not adequately store perishable products.

2 Consumer Protection Code, Article 18.
3 Civil Code, Article 927, sole paragraph.

The sole paragraph of Article 13 of the Consumer Protection Code provides for the right of the person who has paid compensation to claim reimbursement from all other joint holders of responsibility. Notwithstanding the fact that this provision is inserted in an Article dealing with the liability of a merchant, it is generally understood that the right of reimbursement must exist in relation to all other suppliers in the supply chain of the product, given the solidarity which exists among such suppliers.

The liability for a product fault or defect is jointly held by all suppliers and, unlike in the case of a consumer accident, the merchant receives no privileged treatment. Should the consumer sue the merchant, the latter will have a right of reimbursement against the party responsible for the fault or defect, and the same right is ensured to all other suppliers.

Obligation to Recall Products

According to Article 10 of the Consumer Protection Code, products that are very harmful or hazardous cannot be placed on the consumer market. However, both law and jurisprudence fail to clearly conceptualize the meaning of "very harmful or hazardous", so that the interpretation and scope of this phrase are subject to a case-by-case evaluation.

If a supplier acknowledges the harmful and hazardous nature of the product only after it has been placed on the consumer market, it is responsible for immediately informing both consumers and the proper authorities of the danger or hazard by means of media advertisements. The Code does not establish or make exceptions with regard to the means of communication, assuming that the media would be the only proper means to reach the mass of affected consumers.[4]

Article 10, Paragraph 1 of the Consumer Protection Code is regulated by Ordinance 789/2001, enacted by the Department for Consumer Protection (*Departamento de Proteção e Defesa do Consumidor* — DPDC), which is a branch of the Ministry of Justice. Ordinance 789/2001 establishes the obligation to communicate to the DPDC and the State and/or City Consumer Protection Offices the harmful or hazardous nature of a product when it is acknowledged by the supplier only after the product has been placed on the market.

4 Consumer Protection Code, Article 10, Paragraphs 1 and 2.

Failure to comply with Article 10, Paragraph 1 of the Consumer Protection Code and Ordinance 789/2001 theoretically subject the supplier to the administrative penalties set forth in Articles 56 and 57 of the Code. If the DPDC either acknowledges a lack of communication on the part of the supplier or decides that the supplier's communication was insufficient, it shall initiate administrative proceedings to find out whether the supplier has violated Article 10, Paragraph 1. If so, the penalties in Articles 56 and 57 shall apply, including a fine of not less than approximately US $80 or more than US $1,200,000, product seizure and destruction of the product.

On the other hand, police authorities, by order of the Public Prosecutor's Office or at the request of the DPDC, shall initiate a criminal investigation to ascertain criminal liability for the lack of mandatory communication, for late communication or for insufficient communication. A criminal investigation may or may not evolve into a criminal action if the author and material facts of the crime are ascertained.[5] Criminal liability affects anyone who contributed to the crime.[6] The supplier may also be sued in a civil court, whether jointly or severally, providing indemnity for any damage caused to consumers.

Causation

Burden of Proving Fault or Defect and Damage

The burden of proof may be shifted to the supplier, at the court's discretion, when certain elements are present. Whenever technical aspects are involved, the courts may order suppliers to submit proper evidence. The shift in the burden of proof is provided for under Article 6 (VIII) of the Consumer Protection Code, which stipulates as one of the fundamental rights of consumers:

> ". . . the facilitation of the defense of his rights, including shift in the burden of proof, in favor of the consumer, under civil law proceedings, whenever the ordinary rules of experience indicate that the claim is verisimilar or if the consumer is found to be the weaker party in the relationship, at the discretion of the Magistrate".

5 Consumer Protection Code, Article 64.
6 Consumer Protection Code, Article 75.

Thus, the provision transcribed above defines two situations under which a shift in the burden of proof may be ordered:

(1) When the claim brought by the consumer is found to be most probably true; or
(2) Where the supplier is found to be in a stronger position in its relationship with the consumer.

Ascertaining Liability among Producers of a Defective Product

Although liability for product defects is strict, the Brazilian legal system determines that proof of the cause and effect relationship will at all times be required. Thus, it is highly improbable that a given producer will be held to be answerable in the absence of proof that the damage was caused by a product of such producer. Although the Consumer Protection Code allows for the reversal of the burden of proof, such reversal is inadmissible in the case where proof is impossible. It should also be noted that, under Brazilian law, solidarity cannot be presumed, only insofar as it expressly arises from the law or from contract. It is, therefore, inconceivable to determine joint liability among producers based on market share or similar criteria.

Defenses

A supplier is only released from liability if it is successfully proven that:

(1) He did not place the product on the market or otherwise render the service;
(2) The defect does not exist; or
(3) The accident is exclusively attributable to the consumer.

The risks reasonably inherent in a certain product or service, as well as proper disclosure to consumers, must always be taken into account for liability purposes.

State of the Art or Development Risk Defense

There is no statutory definition concerning this matter, and it will be dependent upon the interpretation of legal doctrine and case law. With regard to liability, some jurists understand that the supplier's good faith and initial unawareness of the hazard shall not exempt it from liability for any damage that may arise, given that civil liability in consumer relation matters is objective.[7]

However, there are jurists who believe that the risk of development defense, exempting suppliers from liability, was adopted by the Code following a suggestion of the European Community. Pursuant to this trend, development risks may be qualified as legally irrelevant, meaning that they are not likely to hold the supplier liable for a fault in the product. It should, however, be mentioned that Article 12(2) of the Consumer Protection Code determines that a product shall not be deemed defective merely because another product of better quality has been placed on the market.

Compliance with Regulatory and/or Statutory Requirements

In the event of product liability, a common defense strategy is to claim compliance with legal requirements related to production. If a given company complies with all of the rules and regulations determined by the State for the manufacture of a given product, it can argue that it cannot be held liable for damage caused by such product. There is, however, the opinion that, as liability for the product itself is strict, it is not dependent on any actual fault of the supplier.

Possibility to Re-Litigate Issues

In Brazil, awards issued in similar suits or precedents are not binding on the magistrate, who must review each specific case based on its own merits. Allegations of fact related to the damage and to the defect shall be analyzed on a case-by-case basis, and may or may not be influenced by precedents or pending cases.

Procedure

The Federal Constitution has reserved for trial by jury all crimes willfully committed against life, therein including homicide, infanticide, assistance or instigation to suicide and abortion. In all other cases, whether civil or criminal, the award shall be issued by the magistrate alone. Given that the magistrate might not have the capacity to

7 Consumer Protection Code, Article 23.

directly verify and assess certain facts, their causes or their consequences, the work involved in pursuing these purposes shall be carried out by technical specialists. Expert witnesses act as assistants to the magistrate, and it is the magistrate who appoints them for the purpose of conducting a *bona fide* review of the evidence and facts and to submit, in the form of an expert opinion, a report on their observations or conclusions which can be derived therefrom. Expert witness evidence is provided for under Articles 420 *et seq.* of the Brazilian Code of Civil Procedure.

Preliminary Issues

The magistrate must assess the correctness of the suit from the moment he receives the initial petition, and may dismiss it if it does not meet legal requirements. After the initial reply has been submitted, the magistrate will review issues relating to:

(1) Defects in the process, that is, whether or not the procedural presuppositions related to competence, the parties and the conditions for suing are met;
(2) Non-suit; and
(3) Joint litigants, choice of defendant, denouncing of the suit or summons to the proceedings.

Once the proceedings have been cleared and put in due form, the magistrate can issue his award based on the contents of the papers or order the collection of evidence.[8] Preliminary issues are related to matters of law, not to matters of fact.

Testimonies

The judge has the power to interrogate the parties and their witnesses. The judge may take a deposition from any party at any stage of the proceedings, but ordinarily parties and witnesses testify only at the final public hearing. Testimonial evidence is generally presented in the following order: expert testimony, depositions of the parties and, finally, factual witnesses. The court may order any person referred to in testimonial or documentary evidence to appear and testify. When witnesses differ in their testimony, the court may order a confrontation to try to resolve the conflict.

8 Code of Civil Procedure, Article 328.

Expert testimony is presented during the period between the opening of the proceedings (*despacho saneador*) and the public hearing, generally in the form of written findings submitted to the clerk of the court. When expert testimony is needed, the judge will normally designate his own expert, and each party will also designate his own expert. The topics addressed by the experts depend on the questions devised by the parties and the judge. Once the fact-finding stage is concluded, the experts present their written conclusions. The experts may be called later to appear at the public hearing to answer any questions concerning their findings.

Documentary Evidence

Ordinarily, documentary evidence is introduced only in the initial stage of ordinary proceedings by attachment to the pleadings. The judge will also admit documentary evidence at a later stage to support unforeseen facts or to refute evidence presented by opposing counsel. The Brazilian procedural system does not impose any obligation on the parties concerning prior submission of the documents each party is in possession of. Nevertheless, in cases involving the State Prosecuting Authority or investigation proceedings conducted by competent authorities, there is a possibility to demand that certain documents be submitted at a stage preceding the actual court proceedings.

Civil Class Actions

Civil class actions are special proceedings established by Law Number 7347 of 24 September 1985 (Law Number 7347/85), which governs lawsuits involving liability for damage caused to:

(1) The environment;
(2) Consumers (not represented by individuals, but by the general public);
(3) Assets and rights of artistic, historical, tourist or scenic value;
(4) Any and all general public interests; and
(5) The economic order.

Civil class actions may seek pecuniary indemnity for damage or a specific court order determining that the party cease activities that may be negatively affecting the interests protected by Law Number 7437/85, or take specific measures to repair any damage caused. The Consumer Code has expanded the scope of Law 7347/85 by creating a new category of collective rights or interests. According to Article 82 of the Consumer Protection Code, the following parties are entitled to bring collective suits for the protection of consumer rights:

(1) The State Prosecuting Authority;
(2) The Federal, State and Municipal Administrations, including the Administration of the Federal District;
(3) Entities and bodies involved in direct or indirect public administration, even if they are not organized as specific legal entities, specifically dedicated to the protection of the interests and rights protected by the Consumer Protection Code; and
(4) Associations legally organized at least one year prior to bringing a suit, and which include in their purposes the protection of the interests and rights protected by the Consumer Protection Code, without the need for special authorization from the general meeting of its members.

Class actions are very frequently resorted to in Brazil. In fact, during the 1990s, one witnessed an outburst of class actions, many of which were brought by entities that had no legitimate right to do so, and special actions for homogeneous individual rights. Given the facilities ensured by this procedure, the entities referred to under Article 82 of the Consumer Protection Code often resort in error to class actions for the purpose of vindicating rights that do not arise from a common cause, and which should be dealt with in individual actions. There is currently a vast amount of case law in terms of class suits, covering a wide area of subject matter. It is, beyond doubt, a common procedure which is routinely brought before the courts.

Appeal Options

Brazilian procedure establishes a single judge at first instance and a collegial tribunal of three judges at second instance. A final first instance decision can be appealed, the second instance court affording the litigants a new trial. In some cases, review by a court of third, or even fourth, instance will be permitted. The Code of Civil Procedure sets forth the following types of appeals:[9]

(1) Appeal;
(2) Bill of review, seeking a review of interlocutory decisions;
(3) Request for a rehearing *en banc*;

9 Code of Civil Procedure, Article 496.

(4) Request for clarification;
(5) Ordinary appeal, which may be brought before the Supreme Federal Court or Superior Court of Justice as a last instance in the case of writs of *mandamus*, *habeas corpus*, *habeas data* and injunctions that are awarded by the higher courts;
(6) Special appeal, which may be brought before the Supreme Court of Justice as a last instance against an award that is contrary to a Treaty or a Federal Law;
(7) Extraordinary appeal, which may be brought before the Supreme Federal Court if the decision challenged contravenes provisions of the Federal Constitution; and
(8) Special appeal for the resolution of a conflict in previous jurisprudence or extraordinary appeal.

Time Limits

For the purpose of submitting complaints related to defects found in products or services by the end consumer within the appropriate time limits, two kinds of defects must be considered:

(1) Apparent defects — an action must be brought within thirty days for a non-durable product or service and ninety days for a durable product or service, the term being calculated, in both cases, from the delivery of the product (irrespective of shelf time) or from the completion of the performance of the service;[10] and
(2) Hidden defects — the same term of thirty or ninety days applies, as in the case of apparent defects, but the term is to be calculated from the time the hidden defect becomes apparent.[11]

Article 27 of the Consumer Protection Code regulates the extinction of the right to demand indemnity for damage caused by a product or service (liability for damage). There is a time limit, as in the case of the aforesaid terms, for exercising the right to complain about apparent or hidden defects that render a product or service unfit or inadequate for consumption (liability for defect). According to Article 27, the right to demand indemnity for damage caused by a product or service ends after a term of five years, to be calculated from the time the damage and the person causing it become known.

10 Consumer Protection Code, Article 26(1) and (2).
11 Consumer Protection Code, Article 26(3).

The magistrate in charge of the case does not have the power to interfere in the time limits defined by the Consumer Protection Code, whether to increase, reduce or refrain from enforcing the relevant provisions. By the same token, the age and character of the consumer may not interfere with the calculation of the terms.

Damages

In general terms, regardless of the type of civil liability, whether strict or fault-based, loss and damage encompass:

(1) Actual damage, which corresponds to all losses effectively incurred by the victim by virtue of the harmful event; and

(2) Loss of profits, which represents the legitimate and expected gains which the same failed to receive due to the accident.

Actual damages may be claimed for damage of a material nature and pain and suffering, that is, moral damages. In order to provide reparation for property damage, the courts set an amount deemed necessary for the injured party to resume his prior economic *status quo*. The actual number of claims arising from the same incident is irrelevant, since the main purpose of the Brazilian legal system is to ensure full recovery for all victims of an incident or accident. Therefore, there is no maximum limit on the damages recoverable from one manufacturer for a series of claims arising from one incident or accident.

Specifically in terms of consumer rights, the Consumer Protection Code defines the following general indemnity obligations:

(1) Indemnity for damage caused to consumers due to defects arising from the design, manufacture, construction, assembly, formulae, handling, presentation or packaging of a product, as well as for insufficient or inadequate information concerning its use and risks;[12]

(2) Indemnity for damage caused to consumers due to defects related to the rendering of services, as well as for insufficient or inadequate information concerning the enjoyment and risks thereof;[13]

(3) Indemnity for defects in quality or quantity that render a product useless or inadequate for the consumption for which it is intended, or which reduce its value, as well as defects arising

12 Consumer Protection Code, Article 12.

13 Consumer Protection Code, Article 14.

from inconsistency of information contained on the container, packaging, labels or advertisement, subject to variations inherent in the nature of the product, the consumer being entitled to demand the replacement of defective parts;[14] and

(4) Indemnity for defects in product quantity whenever, subject to variations inherent in the nature of the product, its net contents are less than that indicated on the container, packaging, label or advertisement, the consumer being entitled to demand, at his option:
   (a) a pro rata reduction in the price;
   (b) replacement of the product by another of the same kind, brand or model free from such defects; or
   (c) immediate reimbursement of the amount paid, subject to monetary indexation, at no detriment to the obligation to provide indemnity for any loss or damage caused.[15]

As to the provision of services for the purpose of repairing a given product, the supplier will be implicitly bound to use original, adequate and new spare parts or components, or those that conform to the technical specifications of the manufacturer, save, as to the latter, on the express authorization of the consumer to proceed otherwise.[16]

Punitive Damages

The Brazilian legal system does not recognize the concept of punitive or exemplary damages. What has been accepted recently, by one trend in case law, is the theory of discouragement, according to which the amount of thc award for pain and suffering is set at a level so as to discourage repetition of the illicit practice. However, indemnity for pain and suffering, leaving aside rare questionable exceptions, has not generally been set at an exorbitant amount by the Brazilian courts.

Costs and Funding

Recovery of Legal Fees and Other Expenses

Brazil operates under the principle that the losing party pays all court costs, as well as the other side's attorneys' fees, according to requirements

14 Consumer Protection Code, Article 18.
15 Consumer Protection Code, Article 19.
16 Consumer Protection Code, Article 21.

established by law. Brazilian judges normally fix attorneys' fees at ten to twenty per cent of the amount of the award. Recovery of the party's own costs does not automatically follow from the award and will, at all times, be subject to the criterion of reasonableness and to effective proof that it represents material damage.

Public Funding

Pursuant to the Federal Constitution, "judicial assistance will be granted to those who need it in the manner established by law".[17] Law Number 1060, enacted on 5 February 1950, establishes the basic principles for legal aid. To secure legal aid, a person without sufficient means must file a petition with the judge declaring that he does not have sufficient assets to bear the expenses of the lawsuit. If the petition for legal aid designates a lawyer who expressly declares that he is willing to accept the appointment, the judge must have fair cause to refuse to appoint the lawyer indicated. If a judge decides to grant a legal aid petition that does not specifically designate counsel, he will request that a public legal aid agency (if one exists in his area) name a lawyer to represent the applicant. If there is no such legal aid service, the judge will ask the bar association to appoint a lawyer. In a municipality where there is no representative of the bar association with powers to make such appointments, the judge himself will appoint a lawyer to take the case. The lawyer cannot refuse to take the assignment without a reasonable excuse. A person receiving legal aid is excused from payment of all judicial costs.

Lawyers' fees, expert witness fees, the costs of the proceedings and other charges are to be paid by the losing party whenever the beneficiary of legal aid prevails. If an attorney representing a person without sufficient means prevails, the attorney's fee cannot exceed fifteen per cent of the recovery. Prevailing case law is deemed to have revoked the provision concerning the percentage of such fees. Article 22 of the Minors and Juveniles Statute, which regulates the issue, has assigned to the magistrate conducting the case the power to set fees according to a pre-set schedule.

17 Federal Constitution, Article 5, LXXIV.

In the event that the beneficiary of legal aid is the losing party in the suit, such party shall bear the legal costs and attorney fees, provided that he is able to do so without damage to his own support or to that of his family, within a period of up to five years from the final award.

Civil Liability for Defective Products in Spain

Miguel Torres Mingot
L.C. Rodrigo Abogados
Madrid, Spain

Introduction

The civil liability of manufacturers, importers and suppliers is currently ruled in Spain by the provisions of Act 22/1994 of 6 July 1994 on Civil Liability for the Damage Caused by Defective Products (Defective Products Act — DFA).[1] The DFA was enacted in Spain as a consequence of Directive 85/374/EEC,[2] which sought to unify the different systems of the Member States of the European Community and improve protection for consumers. The DFA was amended by Act 14/2000, which implemented for Spain Directive 1999/34.[3]

Prior to the enactment of the DFA, product liability was basically governed by the General Act for the Defense and Protection of Users and Consumers (Consumers Act 1984).[4] The basic features of these provisions were the allocation of the burden of the proof to the manufacturer or provider of services, strict liability, joint and several liability if there are several parties and compensation for damage arising in contract or tort. As a consequence of the enactment of the DFA and its First Final Provision, these rules no longer apply in connection with products defined as such in the DFA, although the Consumers Act 1984 remains in force regarding liability arising from other sources, such as services.

It should be noted that, to date, there has only been one reported decision issued by the Supreme Court applying the DFA to a personal

1 In force since 8 July 1994, although it should have been implemented by the latest on 30 July 1988.

2 Council Directive of 25 July 1985 on the approximation of the laws, regulations and administrative provisions of the Member States concerning liability for defective products, 85/374/EEC, OJ 1985 L 210/29.

3 Council and European Parliament Directive of 10 May 1999, 1999/34/EEC, OJ 1999 L 141/20.

4 Act 26/1984 of 26 July 1984, Articles 25–28.

injury case, while there are a wide range of decisions issued by the Courts of Appeal (*Audiencias Provinciales*), courts with territorial jurisdiction in each Spanish province. The latter are not strictly and technically considered case law, although they are commonly used as support, especially in those circumstances in which the Supreme Court has not had the chance to render a decision.

Overview of Defective Products Act

In general terms, the DFA follows the provisions of Directive 85/374, although there are some differences. The DFA has fifteen Articles, one interim provision and four final provisions. The DFA starts with the declaration of the general principle, in Article 1, according to which producers and importers should be liable for the damage caused by the products they respectively manufacture or import. In accordance with Article 4, the legal definition of a producer is:

(1) The manufacturer of a finished product;
(2) The manufacturer of a component part;
(3) The manufacturer of a raw material; and
(4) Any person who, by putting his name, company name, trademark or other distinguishing feature on the product, presents himself as a producer (an apparent producer).

An importer is defined in the same Article as he who, within the course of business, brings a product into the European Union for sale, hire, lease or any other form of distribution.

Suppliers have a different regime. Following Article 3 of Directive 85/374, Article 4.3 of the DFA makes suppliers liable if they do not inform the injured party within three months (a "reasonable time" in Directive 85/374) of the identity of the producer or of his own supplier. Suppliers are also obliged to provide the name of the importer within the same term to avoid their own liability even if the producer is identified since, as mentioned above, the importer is be domiciled outside the European Union.[5] In addition and further to the regime stated in Directive 85/374, the Single Additional Provision in the DFA sets forth that suppliers shall be held liable under the same

5 Decision of the Court of Appeal of Tenerife of 23 September 2000 (JUR 2001/18469) stated that a supplier's liability is subsidiary to a producer's or importer's liability, as he does not take part in the manufacturing process.

conditions as producers or importers if they have supplied the product knowing the existence of the defect.[6] This notwithstanding, a supplier is entitled to claim for recovery of any compensation paid from the manufacturer or importer.

A product is considered, in accordance with the current DFA wording,[7] to be any movable property, even that forming part of another, including gas[8] and electricity. Before the amendment of the DFA by Act 14/2000, the DFA excluded from the definition of product raw materials and agricultural, fishing and hunting products, provided that they had not been processed in any way. These are currently included. Although there appear to be no reported cases concerning such products between the enactment of the DFA and its amendment in December 2000 (effective from 1 January 2001), the fact was that the exclusion led these products to fall within the more restrictive strict liability regime for the protection of users and consumers. Therefore, the initial idea of the legislator proved not to be effective.

Pursuant to Article 3 of the DFA, a product shall be considered defective when it does not provide the safety that could be legitimately expected by the user, considering all the circumstances, and especially the presentation of the product, the reasonable use thereof and the time at which it is introduced onto the market. The claimant seeking compensation should prove the damage, the defect and the causality relationship between both,[9] taking all circumstances into account while, in accordance with Article 6 of the DFA, the manufacturer or importer may be released from liability if he is able to prove that:

(1) He did not put the product into circulation;
(2) Under the circumstances, it is possible to presume that the defect did not exist when the product was put into circulation;
(3) The product was neither manufactured for sale or any form of distribution for economic purposes, nor manufactured or distributed by him in the course of a professional or business activity; or

6 Decision of the Court of Appeal of Barcelona of 17 June 2002 (JUR 2002/278204) allocated liability to a supplier, as it sold the product even knowing that the purchaser was going to use it in a certain way, which did not correspond with the features of the supplied product.

7 Defective Products Act, Article 2.

8 It should be noted that gas is not included as a "product" in the definition of product in Article 2 of Directive 85/374.

9 Defective Products Act, Article 5.

(4) The product was manufactured in accordance with mandatory provisions.

Finally, the manufacturer may be released from liability if he proves that the existing technical or scientific knowledge was not such as to enable the existence of the defect to be discovered, provided that the product is not a medicine, food or product for human consumption. In addition, a producer or importer of a given component of a final product shall not be held liable if he is able to prove that the defect resulted from the design of the product in which it was fitted or included or if the product was manufactured in accordance with the instructions of the manufacturer of such final product.

In accordance with Article 7 of the DFA, all persons regarded as liable under the DFA shall be liable on a joint and several basis. Liability shall not be reduced if the damage occurs as a consequence of the defect and any third party action, without prejudice to the right of claiming against such third party for his corresponding share in the damages.[10] However, a manufacturer's liability would disappear or be reduced if the damage arises from the defect and an action of the injured party (contributory negligence).[11] Although the DFA does not state anything in this regard, the burden of proving such negligence of the injured party rests on the manufacturer in accordance with the general evidence rules.[12]

Pursuant to Article 10.1 of the DFA, the liability of producers and importers is limited to personal injury and, on a limited basis, to property other than the product, provided that the said goods are used privately, that is, not business assets, consistent with the consumer protection framework. There is a legal deductible of €390.66.[13] Article 10.2 of the DFA states that any other damage, including pain and suffering, may be compensated in accordance with the general civil legislation (contract or tort liability), while Article 15 of the DFA completes this provision setting forth that the actions stated in the DFA do not affect any other rights of the injured party arising from contract or tort against the manufacturer, importer or any other party.

---

10 Defective Products Act, Article 8.

11 Defective Products Act, Article 9.

12 Civil Proceedings Act, Article 217, according to which the burden of proof rests on the party that raises the facts to the proceeding.

13 In compliance with Article 9(b) of Directive 85/374, which states that such deductible should be lower than 500 ECU.

Damage arising from nuclear accidents does not fall within the scope of the DFA in the event that such damage would be covered by international treaties to which the European Union Member States may be a party.[14]

Article 11 of the DFA sets forth a total liability limit amounting to €63,106,270.96,[15] provided that the injuries have been caused by identical items with the same defect.[16] Actions based on the DFA shall be time-barred after three years starting from the moment at which the injured party suffered the damage.[17] The Spanish wording prefers to state a certain date instead of the concept of "becoming aware" stated in Directive 85/374. Actions of manufacturers or distributors against third parties have a shorter limitation period: one year starting from the date of payment.[18] However, as a general limit pursuant to Article 13 of the DFA, rights and recovery actions for damages stated in the DFA shall be extinguished after ten years from the time the product was introduced onto the market.

Aiming at ensuring consumer protection as much as possible, Article 14 of the DFA declares that contractual exclusions or limitations of liability shall not be considered valid. For the purposes of this chapter, the only relevant final provision is Number 1, which, as already mentioned, declares the inapplicability to products under the legal regime established in the Consumers Act 1984.

The Defective Product

The first step in analyzing the possible existence of a relevant defect for the purposes provided for by the DFA is given in its Article 2. If the product does not provide the safety that any person is entitled to

14 Defective Products Act, Article 10.3.

15 Pursuant to Article 16 of Directive 85/374, not less than ECU 70-million.

16 Commission Report of 31 January 2001 COM (2000) 893 final states that only three Member States have adopted financial limits, and the little information available seems to show that such limits are high enough to cover any claim.

17 Defective Products Act, Article 12.1. Article 10 of Directive 85/374 states that "the limitation period shall begin to run from the day on which the plaintiff became aware, or should reasonably have become aware, of the damage, the defect and the identity of the producer".

18 The statute of limitations may be interrupted by any judicial or out-of-court claim and the acknowledgement of the debtor (Civil Code, Article 1973), and the count begins to run again from that moment.

expect, it may be regarded as defective. Therefore, the core issue is the lack of safety. In the words of the Supreme Court,[19] "the definition of defect stated in the law, following Directive 85/374/EEC, is flexible and wide and in the absence of subjective items, safety is considered as a mandatory requirement of the product". If the product is not safe, it should be regarded as defective. This seems to lead to strict liability, considering that the breach of the duty of safety implies per se a defective product and that the level of diligence of the manufacturer is not essential in considering a product defective. This is consistent with the releasing of the injured party from the burden to prove negligence on the part of the manufacturer in order to be awarded compensation for damage. However, it should be noted that, in accordance with Article 10.1 of the DFA, compensation is limited to personal injury and, under certain circumstances, to products other than the defective one. Thus, if the claimant seeks additional compensation for other headings, such as loss of profits, he should prove negligence.

This notwithstanding, since 15 January 2004 and following the enactment of Royal Decree 1801/2003 of 26 December 2003,[20] which implements for Spain Directive 2001/95 on general safety of products,[21] the foregoing has a more objective framework. The main objectives of the new requirements are:

(1) To clarify and extend the scope of the Directive in order to ensure that all products relevant to consumer health and safety are adequately covered;
(2) To complete and reinforce the obligations on producers, in particular, in order to ensure that they provide the appropriate information to the authorities on product risks and recall dangerous products when necessary;
(3) To make a more effective use of standards in order to apply consistently the concept of a safe product;
(4) To reinforce the powers and tasks of the competent authorities for market surveillance and the enforcement of the Directive's requirements;

19 Supreme Court Decision of 21 February 2003, RJ 2003/2133.

20 Derogating Royal Decree 44/1996 of 19 January 1996, which implemented Council Directive 92/59/EEC.

21 Directive 2001/95 of the European Parliament and of the Council of 3 December 2001 on general product safety, OJ 2002 L 11/4.

(5) To promote a more systematic and structured approach to market surveillance and enforcement activities;
(6) To establish a framework for collaboration between the authorities of the various Member States on risk assessment, testing of products and market surveillance;
(7) To improve the Rapid Alert System for circulating and following up information on measures and action related to products posing serious risks;
(8) To enable exchange of Rapid Alert notifications with third countries and, in particular, with candidate countries;
(9) To streamline the concepts, conditions and procedures applicable to Community-wide rapid intervention measures; and
(10) To ensure that products withdrawn following Community rapid intervention measures are not exported to third countries.[22]

Both the rules under the Royal Decree and under the Directive state that their aim is to ensure that only safe products are put on the market. In the first place, the Royal Decree covers all kinds of new, used or repaired products offered to consumers or offered for consumption within the framework of a service relationship. In the second place, Article 2(a) of Royal Decree 1801/2003 takes basically the same definition of "safe product" as Directive 2001/95:

> "Any product which, under normal or reasonably foreseeable conditions of use including duration and, where applicable, putting into service, installation and maintenance requirements, does not present any risks or only the minimum risks compatible with the product's use, considered to be acceptable[23] with a high level of protection for the safety and health of persons, taking into account the following points in particular:
>
> "1. The characteristics of the product, among them its composition and packaging.[24]

22 www.europa.eu.int/comm/consumers/cons_safe/prod_safe/gpsd/revisedGPSD_en.htm.

23 "and consistent" in the wording of Directive 2001/95.

24 "Instructions for assembly and, where applicable, for installation and maintenance", continues the text of Directive 2001/95, which has not been included in the same point of the Spanish wording but in point number 3.

"2. The effect on other products, where the use of the former with the latter is reasonably foreseeable.

"3. The information included in the product, in particular, the labeling; any warnings and instructions of use and disposal; assembly instructions, and where applicable, installation and maintenance and any other indication or information regarding the product.

"4. The categories of consumers at risk when using the product, in particular, children and the elderly."

On the other hand, a dangerous product should be that which does not meet the definition of a safe product.

The expression "safety that should be legitimately expected", under Article 3 of the DFA, should be construed in accordance with Rogel,[25] excluding the mere compliance with legal rules as a cause of release, as the law does not state "legally expected", but "legitimately expected". This legal scholar understands that legal rules cannot be considered a safety standard as, normally, they provide minimum requirements or can become obsolete as a consequence of technical developments.

However, it should be noted that, in accordance with Article 3 of Royal Decree 1801/2003 (also Article 3 of Directive 2001/95), a product shall be deemed safe when it accommodates mandatory provisions in Spain concerning health and safety requirements for the marketing of the product. If such provisions for the reasonable guarantee of safety do not exist, safety shall be assessed taking into account other elements, such as national provisions, standard rules, Commission recommendations, good practice codes or state of the art and technology. In any event, as the general duty of producers in accordance with Article 4 of Royal Decree 1801/2003 is to put on the market only safe products, it should be concluded that the opinion of Rogel should still be regarded as valid for those products not manufactured or presented in accordance with mandatory rules.

---

25 Rogel Vide, "Tort Aspects Arising from Damage Caused by Defective Products with and without Considering Case Law" (*Aspectos de la responsabilidad civil extracontractual resultante de daños causados por productos defectuosos sin y con la Jurisprudencia en la mano*), RGLJ Number 5, September–October 1999.

For instance, a Decision of the Court of Appeal of Vizcaya[26] held that a cleaning product was defective "from a technical legal point of view" as a consequence of the lack of information on the label as it did not warn what action should be taken if the product made contact with the skin, even if the label complied with the mandatory provisions for production and sale of detergents.[27]

Pursuant to the DFA rules, following Directive 85/374, the safety that the product should offer is not considered only on an objective basis, but in view of "all the circumstances" that should be taken into account, particularly the product's presentation, its reasonable use and the time at which it is put into circulation. Decisions of the Courts of Appeal of Cáceres and Córdoba[28] consider that a product is defective when it simply does not offer the legitimately expected safety. It is not relevant that the defect may have arisen within the manufacturing process, as the result of a defective design or as a consequence of lack of information given to the consumer. The failure to meet the safety standard is the core issue in regarding the product as defective. Therefore, safety should be measured in accordance with general standards and not those particular ones of the parties involved.[29]

Presentation

A product could be dangerous from an objective point of view, for instance, fireworks or guns, thus the safety that a user is entitled to expect should be measured accordingly, but also considering that the user should be aware that such products should be carefully used. Presentation includes not only adverts, but also the duty to provide information to possible purchasers in leaflets or on the product's packaging.[30]

---

26 Decision of the Court of Appeal of Vizcaya of 16 December 2002 (AC 2003/822).

27 Royal Decree 770/1999.

28 Decision of the Court of Appeal of Cáceres of 18 April 2002 (AC 2002/1330); Decision of the Court of Appeal of Córdoba of 20 March 2000 (AC 2000/910).

29 The Sixth Whereas of Directive 85/374/EEC states: "To protect the physical well-being and property of the consumer, the defectiveness of the product shall be determined by reference not to its fitness for use but to the lack of safety which the public at large is entitled to expect; whereas the safety is assessed by excluding any misuse of the product not reasonable under the circumstances."

30 Further to the provisions of Royal Decree 1801/2003, information rights are expressly set forth in several provisions of the Consumers Act 1984, such as Articles 2.1°d, 3.2°, 4.2° and 5.2.k, and specifically Article 13.1.f, which requires that products should bear instructions and indications for their correct use or consumption, warnings and foreseeable risks, which should be true, efficient and enough in relation to their essential features.

Additionally, the concept of presentation includes the specific section of the public to which the product is addressed. Consequently, the information given should be clear enough for this section of the public, informing them of, *inter alia*, the use, danger, technical issues and maintenance of the product. Therefore, presentation should be complete, clear, correct and accurate to ensure safety.[31]

A Decision of the Court of Appeal of Baleares[32] considered that although the labeling of the product complied with mandatory regulations, it was not sufficient as the label did not warn users sufficiently about the dangers of the product. In this case, the product, a pesticide manufactured for agricultural purposes, was sold to a consumer for private use. Among other necessary warnings, the labeling did not indicate that it should be used only by professionals, especially because the product was inflammable and could explode in certain circumstances. Another Decision of the same Court of Appeal[33] considered the existence of a breach of the duty to inform as the information available to consumers did not warn about a slight possibility of adverse effects of a medicine, which had already been notified to the health authorities, but not considered relevant for consumers by the medicine's producer.

Other circumstances to bear in mind should be any specific labeling or presentation requirements, such as those stated in Council Directive 79/112/EEC, provided, of course, that damage is caused. In addition, a Decision of the Court of Appeal of Caceres[34] considered a yo-yo to be defective as the instructions for use of the product were in a foreign language.

Solé[35] believes, however, that consumers are expected to have a minimal knowledge of basic functioning requirements and minimum safety requirements. In such circumstances, the manufacturer has an obligation to inform and warn above such level of standard knowledge that is supposed that a normal user has.

---

31 José Luis Rodríguez Carrión, *Civil Liability for Damage Caused by Defective Products* (*La responsabilidad civil por los daños causados por productos defectuosos*) (Revista General de Derecho, Valencia, 2000) at pp. 94 *et seq*.

32 Decision of the Court of Appeal of Baleares of 30 March 2001 (JUR 2001/179396).

33 Decision of the Court of Appeal of Baleares of 19 July 2000 (JUR 2000/296591).

34 Decision of the Court of Appeal of Caceres of 18 April 2002 (AC 2002/1330).

35 Solé I Feliú, *The Concept of Defect of the Product in the Civil Liability of the Producer: Act 22/1994 of 6 July 1994 on Civil Liability for the Damage Caused by Defective Products* (*El concepto del defecto del producto en la responsabilidad civil del fabricante: Ley 22/1994 de six de julio de Responsabilidad Civil por los daños causados por productos defectuosos*) (Tirant lo Blanch, Valencia, 1999) at p. 190.

In the traditional words of the Spanish Civil Code, the standard duty of care is compared to that of a "good father". While this could be true in some cases, certainly the trend of Directive 85/374 and the DFA would lead to a different end. For instance, although even the Supreme Court applied in this case the Consumers Act 1984, its Decision of 10 June 2002[36] stated that children's products, such as sweets, should contain proper information for correct use and consumption as they may imply risks when they are consumed by children of up to three years of age. A Decision of the Court of Appeal of Navarra,[37] also under the Consumers Act 1984, considered that there was a lack of information as the purchaser was a consumer. The information provided would have been sufficient for a person with technical knowledge of the product, but not for a normal consumer with standard knowledge.

Reasonable Use

The Sixth Recital of Directive 85/374 states that "safety is assessed by excluding any misuse of the product not reasonable under the circumstances". It is expected that consumers use the product according to its natural features. Obviously, when the product is used in contravention of the instructions or in a different way than that which it is rational to expect, the product cannot be regarded as defective, even if damage results. The injured party will only be entitled to compensation when he has used the product in a normal and ordinary way, considering all the different forms in which the product could be utilized. Consequently, misuse leads to contributory negligence or total fault on the part of the injured party,[38] in which case the compensation for damage will be reduced accordingly or even denied. Needless to say, the burden of proving misuse or contributory negligence rests on the producer as defendant.

In any event, the presentation of the product is closely connected with the concept of reasonable use, as the information and warnings that the producer gives to the public may be essential in ensuring the correct and safe use of the product.

36 RJ 2002/6198.

37 Decision of the Court of Appeal of Navarra of 18 September 2002 (AC 2002/481).

38 Defective Products Act, Article 9.

Time When Product Is Put into Circulation

It should be noted that such time is very relevant for the DFA, which refers to it in several Articles, including Articles 3.1, 6.1(a), (b) and (e) and 13, and defines the application of the DFA to products in the single interim provision. As for legal doctrine,[39] "to put into circulation" means to introduce the product onto the market, sell it or put it at the disposal of consumers. Neither Directive 85/374 nor the DFA contain a definition of this very basic phrase. Professor Vela[40] considers this moment to be when the final product of a given economic activity is normally supplied or marketed, not necessarily purchased, by a consumer. This involves proactive conduct on the part of the manufacturer or importer.

It should be noted that the abovementioned Decision of the Court of Appeal of Baleares[41] considered that the product was put into circulation when the consumer purchased it. This was very relevant, as the product was acquired on 16 July 1994, while the DFA came into force on 8 July 1994. Thus, if the court had considered that the product had been put into circulation earlier, it would not have applied the DFA, but the Consumers Act 1984 because the interim provision of the DFA states that it does not apply to products put into circulation before the moment it came into force.

It has been discussed whether the moment at which a product is put into circulation refers to the first time it is generally introduced onto the market or to the time of the sale of the particular product that has caused damage and is considered defective. In this regard, Professor Vela[42] cites a Decision of the Court of Appeal of Baleares[43] which, contrary to his opinion, states that the date a product is put into circulation is not the day upon which it is manufactured, but the date upon which the product and its design, materials and any other relevant

39 Jose Luis Rodríguez Carrión, *Civil Liability for Damage Caused by Defective Products* (*La responsabilidad civil por los daños causados por productos defectuosos*) (Revista General de Derecho, Valencia, 2000) at p. 208.

40 Vela, *Application Criteria for the Regime of Civil Liability Derived from Defective Products* (*Criterios de Aplicación del régimen de responsabilidad civil por productos defectuosos*) (Comares, 2004) at pp. 75 *et seq.*

41 Decision of the Court of Appeal of Baleares of 30 March 2001 (JUR 2001/179396).

42 Vela, *Application Criteria for the Regime of Civil Liability Derived from Defective Products* (*Criterios de Aplicación del régimen de responsabilidad civil por productos defectuosos*) (Comares, 2004) at p. 77.

43 Decision of the Court of Appeal of Baleares of 28 March 2000.

issues are considered finished and are ready to be made available to users and consumers. This judicial opinion could be very relevant for the purposes of the extinction of liability in accordance with Article 13 of the DFA, which is also consistent with Directive 85/374. Such liability disappears upon the expiry of a period of ten years from the date on which the producer put into circulation the actual product that caused the damage.

Meaning of "Actual Product" for Limitation Purposes

Generally speaking, as Professor Vela considers, the manufacturing date of a specific product is a more certain day for the calculation of the moment at which it was put into circulation. As the cited Decision of 28 March of 2000 of the Court of Appeal of Baleares would imply, if the product was acquired at the end of the ten-year term but the defect arose after that term, the consumer would not enjoy the protection of the DFA rules, which seems to be a solution rather contrary to equity and the consumer protection that the DFA seeks to ensure.

In this regard, the Decision of the European Court of Justice of 10 May 2001 has stated that:

> "Article 7(a) of Directive 85/374/EEC of the Council of 25 July 1985 on the approximation of the laws, regulations and administrative provisions of Member States concerning liability for defective products is to be interpreted as meaning that a defective product is put into circulation when it is used during the provision of a specific medical service, consisting of preparing a human organ for transplantation, and the damage caused to the organ results from that preparatory treatment."

Therefore, it seems that the European Court of Justice understands that a product is put into circulation when it is "delivered" to the final user.

Considering that the aim of the DFA and Directive 85/374 is the protection of injured parties, the "actual product" should be considered that which effectively causes the damage. For the same reasons, the date upon which it is put into circulation should be that upon which it is marketed, so it seems logical to consider that the statute of limitations for the "actual product" — ten years — should refer not to the moment at which such product is designed, but the moment it is marketed. Regarding the statute of limitations, Professor Gutiérrez[44] considers, in accordance with Professor Bercovitz, that such term could be correct in general terms, but it may not be enough in relation to products with a longer life than ten years.[45]

Article 2 of the DFA states that "in any case, a product shall be deemed to be defective if it does not offer the same safety as other products of the same range". It is important to note that this provision does not appear in Directive 85/374. The expression "in any case" should be construed independently from all the foregoing circumstances, meaning that the parameters for the determination of the defectiveness of a product shall not be the expected safety in general, but the comparison between the safety (or lack of safety) offered by a certain product and other products manufactured within the same range, which may provide the safety that a person is entitled to expect. This gives the injured party an easier way of proving the defect, as instead of assessing presentation and reasonable use, he need only compare the product with another. For instance, in an air bag failure, the car shall be defective if all the other air bags installed in other cars of the same brand and model work or have worked properly.

To finish with the defectiveness of the product, it should be noted that a given product could not be considered defective only because the product is subsequently put into circulation in a more developed form. These are the "development risks". As Professor Bercovitz stated,[46] it could happen that a safe product, when it is put into circulation, may be considered subsequently defective (not safe) as a consequence of improvements, developments or even amendments to the law or regulations. Therefore, Article 3.3 of the DFA is essential to avoid the liability of producers in connection with those products that

44 Pilar Gutiérrez Santiago, *Civil Liability for Defective Products: Practical Issues* (*Responsabilidad civil por productos defectuosos. Cuestiones prácticas*) (Comares, Granada, 2004) at p. 427.

45 The Eleventh Recital of Directive 85/374 states that products age in the course of time, higher safety standards are developed and the state of science and technology progresses; whereas, therefore, it would not be reasonable to make the producer liable for an unlimited period for the defectiveness of the product; whereas, therefore, liability should expire after a reasonable length of time, without prejudice to claims pending at law.

46 Rodrigo Bercovitz, "Liability Regime for Defective Products and Services in Force in Our Legal System" (*El régimen de responsabilidad por productos y servicios defectuosos vigente en nuestro ordenamiento*), EC, Number 34 (1995) at p. 126.

were initially correct, but could be considered defective after a certain number of years. However, Article 3.3 only applies if the defectiveness of the product is "for this sole fact", that is, it does not cover other safety failures that may render the product defective. The aim is to avoid the application of current safety standards to products manufactured in the past. For instance, cars must now have safety belts in the rear seats. However, those cars manufactured and put into circulation before such rules came into force should not be considered defective products even if, in the event of an accident, it could be proved that those passengers wearing rear safety belts would not have been injured.

It may be concluded that the abovementioned legal requirements, in accordance with the Recitals of Directive 85/374 and the DFA, lead to a strict liability regime under which the basic circumstances are the features of the product that has caused damage, without considering at all the possible fault or negligence of the producer, but only the existence of a defect, bearing in mind, however, that once the existence of such defect has been established, the producer or importer may be exempt from liability under certain circumstances.[47]

Proof of the Defect

Article 5 of the DFA, following Directive 85/374, requires the injured party to prove the defect in a product, the damage and the causality between both, while the existing regime before the enactment of the DFA (under the Consumers Act 1984) simply required the damage to be proved and the causality relationship between the use of the product and the damage. For other damage, the general civil liability regime requires proof of the existence of fault or willful misconduct.[48] However, it should be noted that the "theory of risk" developed by the Supreme Court imposes a certain strict liability regime when damage arises from a risky activity, bringing profit to the party that performs it. Such party is obliged to strengthen its duty of care and is considered liable if damage results. Therefore, the burden of proof is reversed, imposing upon the defendant the burden to prove that he did not act negligently, and releasing the claimant from proving fault or negligence on the part of the defendant.

47 Defective Products Act, Article 6.

48 Civil Code, Article 1.101 (contract) and Articles 1902 *et seq.* (tort).

Therefore, the strict liability regime stated in the Consumers Act 1984 for products would have been replaced by an intermediate system under which the proof of the fault of the defendant required under the usual civil liability regime is substituted by the evidence of a defect in the product.[49] The position of claimants seems now to be more difficult as they have the burden of proving the defect, while formerly they did not. However, whether this is a real additional burden or not depends on how the courts understand such a duty of claimants.

Many decisions of the courts of appeal have ruled that, provided that the damage arose within the normal use of the product, without a reasonable explanation for the cause of the accident, it should be presumed that the product was defective.[50] However, Article 3.1 of the DFA requires the taking "into account of all the circumstances of the case". For these courts, a strict requirement of proof of the defect by claimants would imply the imposition of an excessive burden on the injured party. Some decisions even referred to such request as *probatio diabolica*,[51] which would lead to huge difficulties for proving the defect, weakening the rights of consumers in relation to compensation due.

Professor Lois Caballe,[52] deems that proof of the defect implies showing evidence of a certain level of negligence or fault on the part of the producer. Therefore, the liability regime of the DFA would not really be strict, as "fault" is included within defect, thus there is the need to prove the fault indirectly through the defect. In a similar way, Professor Rodríguez Carrión[53] defines the regime as a strict liability regime, but incomplete or attenuated, as even contrary evidence is

---

49 Decision of the Court of Appeal de Caceres of 18 April 2002 (AC 2002/1330).

50 Decision of the Court of Appeal of Cantabria of 7 November 2000 (JUR 2001/47513); Decision of the Court of Appeal of Orense of 10 November 1999 (AC 1999/2092); Decision of the Court of Appeal of Cadiz of 16 March 2002 (JUR 2002/140327); Decision of the Court of Appeal of Córdoba of 21 February 2003 (AC 2003/808).

51 Decision of the Court of Appeal of Granada of 25 January 2000 (AC 2000/266); Decision of the Court of Appeal of Caceres of 18 April 2002 (AC 2002/1330).

52 Lois Caballe, *Liability of Manufacturers for the Defects in Its Products* (*La responsabilidad del fabricante por los defectos de sus productos*) (Tecnos, 1996) at pp. 222 *et seq.*

53 Rodríguez Carrión, *Civil Liability for Damage Caused by Defective Products* (*La responsabilidad civil por los daños causados por productos defectuosos*) (Revista General de Derecho, Valencia, 2000) at p. 161.

admitted, which did not happen under the Consumers Act 1984,[54] which only allowed the proving of misuse by the consumer. Furthermore, this legal scholar considers that the burden of proving the defect implies that there is no presumption of liability of the manufacturer, thus avoiding all kinds of unjustified claims, considering that the claim should be mainly based on an expert report.

However, it should be noted that the Report of the European Commission on the application of Directive 85/374[55] considers in connection with the burden of proof that "in practice, due to technical complexities, high expenses for expert reports or the disappearance of the product (aliments or medicaments), it could be difficult to prove that a product was defective and the causality link". The conclusion of the Report about Spain[56] is that, in those cases in which the product has disappeared or it is difficult to establish the origin of the defect, the courts have based their decisions on presumptions. Article 386 of the Civil Proceedings Act sets forth:

> "From an admitted or proved fact, the court may within the process presume the certainty of another fact, if between that admitted or proved and the presumptive one there is a direct and precise link, in accordance with human criteria. The judgment should include the reasoning taken by virtue of which the court has established the presumption."

Even applying the pre-existing regime to the DFA,[57] the Supreme Court declared that the exclusion of the presumption would hinder very much the protection that it aims to offer to injured parties.[58] It should be noted that the trend is to release the injured consumer from costly experts' reports that may hinder his rights under Directive 85/374 and the respective national provisions.

The Report considers, in general, that the matter of proof of a defect is deeply influenced by the national procedural rules, describing the Spanish system as being very formal. The presumption trend in favor of claimants has proven this to be very true, as sometimes the presumption system is applied in such a rigorous way that it actually

---

54 Consumers Act 1984, Articles 25–28.

55 Brussels, 31 January 2001, COM (2000) 893 final, at p. 14.

56 Brussels, 31 January 2001, COM (2000) 893 final, at p. 15.

57 Consumers Act 1984, Articles 25-28.

58 Decisions of 26 June 1993 (RJ 1993/5380) and 4 October 1996 (RJ 1996/7034).

leaves the producer without a possible defense, as the direct and precise link required by Article 386 of the Civil Proceedings Act is not always met, and thus the presumption does not appear directly connected with the fact from which it should be inferred. This notwithstanding, a Decision of the Court of Appeal of Tarragona[59] considered that the existence of a defect cannot simply be inferred from the breakage of the product. Professor Gómez Calero[60] considers that the existence of a defect should be proved, being contrary to presumptions of defects as a consequence of apparently reasonable explanations for the failure of a product.

Therefore, two different circumstances may be distinguished:

(1) When the alleged defective product has disappeared (broken, lost or eaten); and
(2) When the product can be preserved, where the consumer, therefore, is or should be required to provide more clear evidence of the existence of the defect, usually through experts' reports and allowing the defendant to examine the product, if possible.

Those defects arising from a lack of or insufficient information may be included within the second category.

A Decision of the Court of Appeal of Burgos[61] found that "it is not always necessary to prove the specific defect which has caused the damage but to prove the existence of the defect", which leads to a simple consideration of the possible breach of the safety standards and not the defect itself. Such an option may be inconsistent with other decisions that effectively require from claimants precise evidence of the defect. However, under certain circumstances, if it is proved that a product caused damage, the exact defect may not be relevant, for instance, why an airbag failed, if it is proved that it did actually fail.[62]

---

59 Decision of the Court of Appeal of Tarragona of 18 July 1998 (AC 1998/1546).

60 Gómez Calero, *Civil Liability for Defective Products*, (*Responsabilidad Civil por productos defectuosos*) (Dykinson, 1996) at p. 78.

61 Decision of the Court of Appeal of Burgos of 13 February 2003 (JUR 2003/122404).

62 Court of Appeal of Cantabria of 7 November 2000 (JUR 2001/47513), which considers that the decisive element is to consider the safety of the product (a broken soda pack), as it is expected that the pack should allow safe transport; Court of Appeal of Orense of 29 November 2001 (JUR 2002/23035), which considered a car that caught fire as defective irrespective of the cause of the fire; Decision of the Court of Appeal of Sevilla of 11 July 2003 (JUR 2003/219316); Decision of the Court of Appeal of Orense of 5 February 2001 (JUR 2001/123517).

In connection with the presumptions and the current DFA, it should be noted that, under the prior specific regime for product liability,[63] it was rather usual for the courts to presume a defect in a product,[64] as such regime reversed the burden of proof on the defendant. Thus, the only way for a producer to obtain dismissal of a claim would be to prove misuse or contributory negligence of the claimant.

A review of judicial decisions rendered in connection with the DFA provisions should begin with a decision of the Supreme Court[65] which, after explaining that the only fact proved was that the consumer took a bottle from the shelf and the bottle exploded, considered that the product was defective. The product was put onto the market, as it was bought by the consumer from a retailer. However, the Supreme Court did not clearly explain why it decided upon the existence of the defect. It stated that:

> ". . . the notorious lack of safety of the bottle which caused the injuries of the claimant has been sufficiently proved and, therefore, as the product is not safe, obviously it is a defective product since it was put into circulation".

The Supreme Court considers safety to be a requirement of the product, as any consumer is entitled to use the product without personal or financial risks. In addition:

> "The existence of the defect arises from the definition thereof stated in Act 22/1994 and it should be necessarily related to the safety that the product should offer and, should this not happen, it is mandatory to consider the product as defective, with the reversal of the burden of proof, corresponding to the producer proving its correctness or any of the causes of release legally stated."

As the Supreme Court considered the explosion of the bottle to have been correctly proved, such product did not offer the safety that the

---

63 Consumers Act 1984, Articles 25–28.

64 Supreme Court Decision of 23 June 1993 (RJ 1993/5380); Supreme Court Decision of 4 October 1996 (RJ 1996/7034); Supreme Court Decision of 11 October 2001 (RJ 2001/8735); Decision of the Court of Appeal of Asturias of 4 June 2001 (AC 2001/1371); Decision of the Court of Appeal of Palencia of 31 December 1999 (AC 1999/2453).

65 Decision of the Supreme Court of 21 February 2003 (RJ 2003/2133).

consumer was entitled to, although the Decision neither analyzed the conditions of Article 3.1 of the DFA (circumstances), nor did it apply Article 3.2 of the DFA, which is not stated in Directive 85/374, and according to which a product shall be deemed defective if it does not offer the same safety as other products of the same range. Finally, the Decision does not give enough information about the possible reasons for the explosion that the producer may have provided to the court. Therefore, this Decision does not help very much in unifying the case law in this area.

Other decisions give a much more clear view of the construction of proof of a defect, even if these decisions are not technically considered case law, as this is only reserved to the Supreme Court, provided that it renders at least two decisions in the same way based on similar circumstances.

A Decision of the Court of Appeal of Barcelona[66] presumed the existence of a defect based on witness evidence and mere reasoning to establish the causality between the defect and the damage. In this case, the injured party passed away some days after drinking beer of a certain brand and his brother was injured after tasting the beer. The owner of the place where the beer was served threw it away, so the product was not available for testing, but a wide range of unusual consequences were inferred from the hospital reports. The court stated that "it should be presumed in accordance with Article 386 of the Civil Proceedings Act that the beer was defective", not only on the basis of the testimonies, but also due to the lack of evidence of the producer, which did not produce any evidence about the bottle cleaning process before the date of the accident, even though it recognized that, in the past, certain dangerous elements were used.

The court also took into account other items, such as the consequences of the meal eaten by other people present, who were not injured and did not drink from the bottle in question. Finally, it ruled that the product was defective because of the disinfecting elements used or for new products used in the manufacturing process. The legal grounds for the decision of the court are very sound, accurate and complete, as the decision applies a presumption in a logical way. Even if the court did not have direct proof, it established the basis for the presumption from other evidentiary elements available in the case and deducted the reasons for the lack of safety. In addition, the court

66 Decision of the Court of Appeal of Barcelona of 25 April 2003 (AC 2003/1762).

considered the incomplete evidence produced by the manufacturer. Other decisions with similar reasoning have been rendered by the Court of Appeal of Valladolid[67] and the Court of Appeal of Toledo.[68]

A Decision of the Court of Appeal of Córdoba[69] presumed the existence of a defect from a necropsies report based not on the analysis of the product itself but on animals found dead after being fed with the product. As the expert found an excess of certain chemicals in the animals, the court deduced that the product caused the deaths. However, a Decision of the Court of Appeal of Cadiz[70] ruled that the existence of a defect in a bottle should be deduced from the mere circumstance of the explosion of the bottle.

In connection with damage caused by fireworks, Decisions of the Court of Appeal of Valencia[71] and Barcelona[72] show that it is possible to prove a defect without the product, stating that a decision in favor of a strict requirement of the injured party in this regard be regarded as *probatio diabolica* because of the difficulties that direct proof would imply for the claimant.

A Decision of the Court of Appeal of Granada[73] considered that the fact that the cap of a soda bottle was violently expelled when the injured party, a girl of twelve years old, tried to open it was enough proof of the existence of a defect, as there could not be any other explanation. Finally, a Decision of the Court of Appeal of Cantabria[74] states that "it is the injured party who should prove the defect in the product; but this does not mean that such evidence should be direct and that presumptions should be excluded".

The trend of the courts is to release injured parties from proving damage through the examination of the relevant manufacturing process, establishing the existence of a defect from the consequences of the use of the product. Contrary to the arguments used by other courts, a Decision of the Court of Appeal of Zaragoza[75] dismissed a claim because, "from the analysis of the evidence produced at the hearing, it

67 Decision of the Court of Appeal of Valladolid of 19 January 2001 (AC 2001/916).
68 Decision of the Court of Appeal of Toledo of 26 October 2001 (JUR 2002/17661).
69 Decision of the Court of Appeal of Córdoba of 24 November 2003 (AC 2003/1774).
70 Decision of the Court of Appeal of Cadiz of 16 March 2002 (JUR 2002/140327).
71 Decision of the Court of Appeal of Valencia of 12 July 2001 (JUR 2001/279709).
72 Decision of the Court of Appeal of Barcelona of 9 May 2000 (JUR 2000/210970).
73 Decision of the Court of Appeal of Granada of 12 February 2000 (AC 2000/851).
74 Decision of the Court of Appeal of Cantabria of 7 November 2000 (JUR 2001/47513).
75 Decision of the Court of Appeal of Zaragoza of 18 March 2002 (JUR 2002/119167).

cannot be inferred, with total certainty and without doubt, what was the cause of the breakage of the bottle". The only available evidence was the declaration of the claimant, which had some contradictions. This was, however, not the only reason for reversing the first instance decision, as the court deemed that the existence of the defect could not arise from mere guesswork or hypothetical reasoning. Finally, it was not admitted that the explosion proved the defect. In addition, the defendant produced an expert report that concluded the technical impossibility of such an explosion.

It is clear, therefore, that courts usually apply the presumption rules in those cases where the product is not available, although occasionally the failure is not considered to be sufficient evidence of the existence of a defect. In connection with defects of products that are available for the examination of experts, the Court of Appeal of Córdoba[76] dismissed a claim in a case of damage to a computer device arising from the electricity supply, as the claimant did not provide the testimony of the person who repaired the computer.

A Decision of the Court of Appeal of Vizcaya[77] dismissed a claim, considering that the defect in an airbag was not proved, as the expert had inspected the car, but could not check the airbag system because it had already been repaired and the repair documents did not show any action on the airbag system. In addition, the court considered that the claimant could have produced other documents, such as insurance reports.

A Decision of the Court of Appeal of Sevilla[78] considered electricity to be a defective product for causing damage to the computer of the claimant. It considered that the defect was proved as the after-sales and technical service informed the claimant that the failure of the computer was a consequence of a malfunction in the electrical system; thus, the supply was defective. In addition, the claimant, an insurance company bringing the action by way of subrogation, produced an expert report, which concluded that the computer of the insured had been in good order.

A Decision of the Court of Appeal of Castellón[79] considered a ladder defective in view of photographs produced by the claimant, deducing that the lack of resistance of the ladder because of a

76 Decision of the Court of Appeal of Córdoba of 21 February 2003 (AC 2003/808).
77 Decision of the Court of Appeal of Vizcaya of 1 September 2003 (AC 2003/1607).
78 Decision of the Court of Appeal of Sevilla of 24 September 2003 (AC 2003/1698).
79 Decision of the Court of Appeal of Castellón of 21 February 2001 (JUR 2001/176295).

deformity was not logical. A Decision of the Court of Appeal of Navarra[80] considered that a device was defective as the expert reported that the damage did not arise as a consequence of misuse by the consumer. The expert also concluded that such device was not manufactured in accordance with the producer's instructions.

A Decision of the First Instance Court of Zamora[81] rendered that an airbag was defective, relying not only on the expert report but also on the car itself. Therefore, if the airbag did not work properly, while all the other circumstances for that were met, this could only happen as a consequence of defective installation or manufacture, concluded the court. This decision also states that, in accordance with the condition of the car, the airbag should have worked, otherwise a similar incident would have happened with other cars of the same brand, which shows that this decision also considered the product to be defective under Article 3.2 of the DFA because it did not offer the same safety as other products in the same range.

When the product is or could be available, the foregoing decisions show that the trend of the courts is not to presume a defect based on the sole circumstance of the breakage or defective performance of the product, but clear evidence is required to consider the product defective. Finally, it should be noted that when determining the existence of a defect, hospital reports are often considered to be good evidence, as generally a person arriving at hospital gives as much true and correct information as possible about the accident, seeking the best possible assistance.

The next step in obtaining compensation is to prove the causality between the damage and the defect. In this regard, a Decision of the Court of Appeal of Córdoba[82] stated that the claim should be dismissed. The Decision states that "the defect should be relevant enough to give rise to a causality relationship with the damage". In this case, relating to the failure of a fire extinguisher, the claimant had the duty to maintain the device. Thus, the court ruled that the claimant had been negligent, following the fact that it was not clear whether the extinguisher had been used and not replaced, which also shows that no presumption of existence of a defect was applied.

---

80 Decision of the Court of Appeal of Navarra of 13 May 1999 (AC 1999/5869).

81 Decision of the First Instance Court of Zamora of 1 September 2000 (AC 2000/1534).

82 Decision of the Court of Appeal of Córdoba of 24 March 2003 (AC 2003/360).

Release from Liability for Producers and Importers

Article 6.1 of the DFA allows producers or importers[83] to be released from liability under certain circumstances:

(1) If they are able to prove that they did not put the product into circulation;
(2) If, under the circumstances, it is possible to presume that the defect did not exist when the product was put into circulation;
(3) If the product was neither manufactured for sale or any form of distribution for economic purposes, nor manufactured or distributed by them in the course of a professional or business activity;
(4) If the product was manufactured in accordance with mandatory provisions; or
(5) If it is proved that technical or scientific knowledge was not such as to enable the existence of the defect to be discovered.

This is limited, however, by Article 6.3 of the DFA, as producers shall be fully liable in cases in which products are medicines, food or alimentary products for human consumption.[84]

A specific cause of release is stated in Article 6.2 of the DFA for producers or importers of products that are incorporated into a final product, who may be released from liability if they prove that the defect arises as a consequence of the design of the final product or if the final producer's instructions for manufacturing the component were followed.

In the first place, it would only be necessary to discuss the existence and evidence of these causes once the claimant has duly proved the defect, the damage and the causality between both. If any of them is not proved, then it would not be necessary for the producer

83 The Decision of the Court of Appeal of Tenerife of 23 September 2000 (JUR 2001/18469) understood that even if the word "supplier" is not mentioned in the wording of Article 6 of the DFA, the supplier should have the same rights as producers and importers.

84 The Spanish legislator made use of the possibility granted by Article 15.1(b) of Directive 85/374.

to have recourse to the protection of Article 6 of the DFA.[85] The existence of causes of release implies that the DFA liability regime shall be considered strict but not absolute,[86] as proof to the contrary may be admitted. In this regard, the Commission Report of 1 March 2001 refers to liability as "objective", but also "relative".[87] It should be noted that the causes of release must be proved by the producer following proof of the defect by the claimant. In addition, pursuant to Article 14 of the DFA, exclusion or limitation of liability clauses shall be considered null and void.

Causes under Article 6.1(a) and (c) of the DFA basically require proof that the product did not enter onto the market, either because it was not put into circulation or because it was not intended to be sold or distributed. This is because liability is triggered when the product is put into circulation.[88] In the second place, pursuant to the provisions of Article 6.1(d) of the DFA, compliance with mandatory provisions excludes liability, which rests on government bodies. This means that compliance with non-mandatory uniform or standard rules (UNE or ISO), even if they are generally accepted, would not be enough to release the producer from liability if a defect arises as a consequence.

Therefore, the two basic cases in which a producer or importer may claim release from liability, defending his manufacturing process, are:

(1) Under Article 6.1(b) of the DFA, if it can be presumed that the defect did not exist at the time when the product was put into circulation; and

---

85 Decision of the Court of Appeal of Madrid of 18 December 2000 (JUR 2001/90238); Decision of the Court of Appeal of Santa Cruz de Tenerife of 19 April 2002 (AC 2002/898); Decision of the Court of Appeal of Malaga of 23 June 2003 (AC 2003/1426), which all consider that once the three requirements of Article 5 of the DFA are met, a fourth circumstance is presumed: the defect was caused by the producer. However, this presumption is considered *iuris tantum*, that is, evidence to the contrary may be admitted, so the producer could be released from liability if he can prove any of the circumstances provided for in Article 6 of the DFA.

86 Decision of the Supreme Court of 19 April 2000 (RJ 2000/2979).

87 Commission Report of 1 March 2001, at p. 14.

88 José Luis Rodríguez Carrión, *Civil Liability for Damage Caused by Defective Products* (*La responsabilidad civil por los daños causados por productos defectuosos*) (Revista General de Derecho, Valencia, 2000) at p. 205. This author also considers that the product may be put into circulation once it is delivered for transport: at p. 208.

(2) Under Article 6.1(e) in connection with development risks, provided that the product is not included within Article 6.3 of the DFA.

Release from Liability under Article 6.1(b)

The producer shall only be liable if the defect has arisen within the manufacturing process of the product, as he loses control of the product once it is put into circulation. Considering that third parties, distributors or retailers may damage the product during transport, storage and sale, the producer cannot be held liable for such third parties' actions, in a similar way to the exclusion of liability provided for in Article 9 of the DFA when damage arises from misuse or contributory negligence on the part of the consumer. Direct evidence is, however, required. This cause of release enables the producer to break the causality relationship between the defect and the damage, which the claimant must prove.

Both Directive 85/374 and the DFA do not require full evidence of the non-existence of a defect because this burden would be excessive for the producer or importer,[89] as they do not have the product for review. It should be noted that, while Directive 85/374 states the word "probable", the DFA contains the words "it is possible to presume". The DFA states that this should be assessed "in accordance with the circumstances of the case", which may be several. Professor Vela[90] suggests that these may be:

(1) Manufacturing process features;
(2) Nature of the product or existence of non-defective products in the same range;
(3) Time since the product was put into circulation;
(4) Conditions for use; and
(5) Circumstances related to transport and distribution.

Professor Rodríguez Carrión also includes quality control and the time elapsed from the moment at which the product was put into

89 This difficulty is also acknowledged by Professor Pilar Gutiérrez, Santiago, *Civil Liability for Defective Products: Practical Issues* (*Responsabilidad civil por productos defectuosos. Cuestiones prácticas*) (Comares, Granada, 2004) at p. 298.

90 Vela, *Application Criteria for the Regime of Civil Liability Derived from Defective Products* (*Criterios de Aplicación del régimen de responsabilidad civil por productos defectuosos*) (Comares, 2004) at pp. 102 and 103.

circulation to the time when the defect arose.[91] Another additional element could be the installation of the product. It is clear that expert reports shall be of the essence for the success of this cause of release.

Transport and distribution give rise to interesting issues. Firstly, it should be accepted that the producer puts the product into circulation when he delivers the product to the carrier (Ex works, FOB) or to the distributor or retailer. In such cases, certain circumstances occurring after the product is delivered cannot be considered the liability of the producer, although there are contradictory opinions.[92] This notwithstanding, if the defect arises from a manufacturing defect and the intervention of a third party, for instance, the carrier or a supplier of a component, the producer shall not be released from liability, although he is entitled to claim from such third party its corresponding share of the damages.[93]

The Supreme Court ,[94] referring in general to Article 6 of the DFA, rejected the cause of release alleged by the producer, who alleged that he was the producer of the soda and not the producer of the bottle which blew up and caused the damage. The Supreme Court considered that, as this party had manufactured the final product, the fact that he was not the producer of the bottle was not relevant. Furthermore, the Supreme Court simply stated that it found no element for considering a cause of release, which leads one to think that the evidence of the producer was not adequate. In this vein, several Court of Appeal decisions have simply ruled that the producer did not show sufficient proof that would allow a presumption that the defect did not exist when the product was put into circulation, and thereby awarded damages.[95]

---

91 José Luis Rodríguez Carrión, *Civil Liability for Damage Caused by Defective Products* (*La responsabilidad civil por los daños causados por productos defectuosos*) (Revista General de Derecho, Valencia, 2000) at p. 211.

92 José Luis Rodríguez Carrión, *Civil Liability for Damage Caused by Defective Products* (*La responsabilidad civil por los daños causados por productos defectuosos*) (Revista General de Derecho, Valencia, 2000) at p. 212 defends this interpretation, while Professor Vela, *Application Criteria for the Regime of Civil Liability Derived from Defective Products* (*Criterios de Aplicación del régimen de responsabilidad civil por productos defectuosos*) (Comares, 2004) at p. 77, deems that delivery to the carrier does not mean that the product is put into circulation.

93 Defective Products Act, Article 8.

94 Supreme Court Decision of 21 February 2003 (RJ 2003/2133).

95 Decision of the Court of Appeal of Malaga of 18 January 2000 (AC 2000/342); Decision of the Court of Appeal of Navarra of 13 May 1999 (AC 1999/5869); Decision of the Court of Appeal of Cadiz 16 March 2002 (JUR 2002/140327); Decision of the Court of Appeal of Pontevedra of 11 October 2002 (JUR 2003/29035); Decision of the Court of Appeal of Zaragoza of 3 July 2000 (JUR 2000/270942).

A Decision of the Court of Appeal of Córdoba[96] concerned the malfunction of a taxi car, which was still within the commercial guarantee period and duly maintained. The court stated that the arguments of the manufacturer as to the presumption of non-existence of the defect should be dismissed as it did not produce objective and reasonable evidence. The producer tried to prove the probability of the absence of a defect through declarations from the maintenance service, who only pointed out mere hypothetical reasoning, while the court found that it is not normal for a car to suffer such defects within one year after its purchase. This Decision shows that the presumption required for producers should be consistently proved and that mere suggestions are not enough.

A Decision of the Court of Appeal of Tenerife[97] dealt with the quality control process of a beer manufacturer. The expert report showed that while there were controls to avoid the presence of solid elements during the bottling process, the producer had no further control devices for such purposes once the bottles were full and closed. It was further determined that the piece of glass that caused the damage was of the same type as the bottles. The court considered, however, that, as a consequence, the piece of glass could have been dropped inside the bottle "by any circumstance".

A Decision of the Court of Appeal of Vizcaya[98] dismissed the argument of an electricity company, which claimed that the electricity was not defective when it was put into circulation, as the company was not only responsible for the production but also for the supply of electricity and it had not complied with its duties to ensure that the consumer receive electricity in a proper condition for use.

Release from Liability under Article 6.1(e)

The circumstance that technical or scientific knowledge would not be such as to enable the existence of a defect to be discovered is a controversial matter. In this regard, risks of development include the possible danger of putting into circulation a certain product while the producer is not absolutely certain about its safety, taking into account the state of the art (technical or scientific knowledge). This implies that producers are required to be diligent, that is, as a consequence of

96 Decision of the Court of Appeal of Córdoba of 30 July 2003 (AC 2003/1142).

97 Decision of the Court of Appeal of Tenerife of 19 April 2002 (AC 2002/898).

98 Decision of the Court of Appeal of Vizcaya of 20 November 2001 (JUR 2001/92787).

technical or scientific knowledge at a given moment, they could not foresee the risk and the damage.

Professor Vela[99] considers that this cause of release is contrary to the strict liability regime that the DFA intended to implement to ensure the protection of consumers, and could even be contrary to the legitimate expectation of safety of the product. Rogel[100] considers that as long as the existence of a defect is recognized, irrespective of the difficulties in discovering it, the injured party should be compensated, as such party should not bear the risks that give benefits to those who put the product on the market, while Rodriguez Carrión defends the opposite position.[101] In any event, the Preamble to Royal Decree 1801/2003 states that even if there is compliance with mandatory rules or standard codes, this does not exclude in full the possibility of considering that a product would not be safe. Therefore, Spanish law requires adequate preventive measures.

Professor Gutiérrez[102] suggests that once a given producer discovers a defect in a product, in order to preserve and ensure the safety of consumers, he should be legally obliged to expressly warn the public about these circumstances and even to recall the product. Following the implementation in Spain of Directive 2001/95 by means of Royal Decree 1801/2003 of 26 December 2003, such obligation now exists, and even the regulatory authorities can take measures to recall a product. In addition, other legal scholars discuss whether this cause of

---

99 Vela, *Application Criteria for the Regime of Civil Liability Derived from Defective Products* (*Criterios de Aplicación del régimen de responsabilidad civil por productos defectuosos*) (Comares, 2004) at p. 106. Also, Sonia Rodríguez Llamas, *Civil Liability Regime for Defective Products* (*Régimen de la responsabilidad civil por productos defectuosos*) (Aranzadi, Pamplona, 2002) at p. 131.

100 Rogel Vide, "Tort Aspects Arising from Damage Caused by Defective Products with and without Considering Case Law" (*Aspectos de la responsabilidad civil extracontractual resultante de daños causados por productos defectuosos sin y con la Jurisprudencia en la mano*), RGLJ Number 5, September–October 1999, at p. 605. In the same way, Sonia Rodríguez Llamas, *Civil Liability Regime for Defective Products* (*Régimen de la responsabilidad civil por productos defectuosos*) (Aranzadi, Pamplona, 2002) at pp. 132–133.

101 José Luis Rodríguez Carrión, *Civil Liability for Damage Caused by Defective Products* (*La responsabilidad civil por los daños causados por productos defectuosos*) (Revista General de Derecho, Valencia, 2000) at p. 218.

102 Pilar Gutiérrez Santiago, *Civil Liability for Defective Products: Practical Issues* (*Responsabilidad civil por productos defectuosos. Cuestiones prácticas*) (Comares, Granada, 2004) at p. 308.

release should apply solely to producers or also to distributors,[103] as the latter do not manufacture the product. However, the *Green Book*[104] considers that this provision has been included for the benefit of investigation and development and even for the insurance sector. Indeed, the Report of the Commission of 31 January 2001 understands that it is not necessary to amend the existing regime, although it should be noted that it was decided to appoint an experts' committee for these purposes.

The issue is to determine what the state of technical or scientific knowledge was when the product was put into circulation. In this regard, and although several legal scholars defend different options, a Decision of the European Court of Justice[105] ruled in connection with Article 7(e) of Directive 85/374 that it is technical and scientific knowledge at the most advanced level that should be taken into account, provided that this was available to the producer when the product was put into circulation.

Finally, in connection with food, medicines and other products for human consumption, while it is clear that the cause of release stated in Article 6.1(e) of the DFA cannot be used by the producer or importer, nothing prevents them from claiming that the product is not defective pursuant to any of the other causes of release provided for in Article 6.1. Pursuant to Article 6.3 of the DFA, no development risks are allowed as a cause of release of liability in connection with these products.

While there appear to be no reported cases in which the cause of release stated in Article 6.1(e) of the DFA and prohibition in Article 6.3 have been applied, it should be noted that Spanish courts have dealt with cases involving medicines and have applied strict liability

---

103 Professor Rodrigo Bercovitz, "Implementation into Spanish Law of Directive on Civil Liability for Damage Caused by Defective Products" (*La adaptación del Derecho español de la Directiva comunitaria sobre responsabilidad por los daños causados por productos defectuosos*), EC, Number 12 (1987) at p. 116. Also, for importers, Sonia Rodríguez Llamas, *Civil Liability Regime for Defective Products* (*Régimen de la responsabilidad civil por productos defectuosos*) (Aranzadi, Pamplona, 2002) at pp. 135–136 or Tobajas, "Fault in Act 22/1994 Concerning Civil Liability for Damage Caused for Defective Products" (*La culpa en la Ley 22/1994 sobre responsabilidad civil por daños causados por productos defectuosos*), *Actualidad Civil* (2002–2) at p. 788.

104 *Green Book*, at p. 22.

105 Decision of the European Court of Justice of 29 May 1997, C-300/95, Rec. 1997, I-2649.

against the producer of such medicines under the former regime of the Consumers Act 1984.[106]

Compensation for Damage Arising from Personal Injury

There is no obligation on Spanish courts to take any objective reference to compensate for death or personal injury, except for traffic accidents, for which an objective Schedule for assessment of personal injuries is applied. As the Schedule provides objective rules for such assessment, it is usual for the parties to refer to it generally in personal injury cases and the courts mostly accept it. The problem when applying such rules, which contain compensation for pain and suffering and certain percentage increases for loss of profits, is that, in several cases, the courts have applied the Schedule in full.

Such award breaches Article 10.2 of the DFA, which obliges the claimant who seeks compensation for damage other than that covered by the DFA (personal injury, death or damage to property other than the defective product itself) to comply in full with the general civil liability rules. Specifically, this means that the fault or negligence of the producer should be fully proved, irrespective of the proof of a defect in the product,[107] evidence of which is not sufficient to compensate damage such as pain and suffering or loss of profits.

For instance, a Decision of the Court of Appeal of Granada[108] compensated expenses incurred for medical care and stated that the compensation for personal injury included pain and suffering. Curiously, this Decision recognizes that other civil actions are available and can be jointly brought, but it does not refer at all to the possible fault or negligence of the producer, which are basic requirements for the existence of civil liability under the general regime. In the absence of these issues, a claimant proving the existence of a defect, the damage and the causal link between both should only be entitled to receive compensation for personal injury, death or damage to

106 Supreme Court Decision of 5 October 1999 (RJ 1999/7853). In this case, the medicine was in its experimental phase, so if the DFA had been in force for this case, it would have not applied because the product was not put into circulation.

107 Defective Products Act, Article 5.

108 Decision of the Court of Appeal of Granada of 12 February 2000 (AC 2000/851).

property other than the defective product itself, and not for other items if fault does not appear to have been clearly proved.

Other decisions that have granted compensation for pain and suffering in breach of Article 10.2 of the DFA are those rendered by the Courts of Appeal of Madrid, Badajoz and Vizcaya.[109] In other cases, the claimant brought joint actions based on the DFA and tort and obtained compensation for pain and suffering, although the decisions[110] do not mention anything in connection with the proof of fault or negligence on the part of the producer, which is still a clear breach of Article 10.2 of the DFA for the same reasons.

Conclusion

The DFA follows fairly consistently the provisions of Directive 85/374. Spanish courts consider that the definition of a defect should be construed with flexibility, seeking due protection of consumers, although the implementation of Directive 2001/95 through Royal Decree 1801/2003 on the general safety of products may have an impact upon future case law. Spanish courts accept, on a general basis, presumptions to establish the existence of a defect, although the facts from which the defect may be presumed depend on the evidence available. Evidence requirements are stricter when the product is or was available for expert review.

The legitimate expectation of safety is normally the standard used to determine whether a product is safe or defective. Generally speaking, causes for release from liability stated in Article 6 of the DFA require strong evidence. Regarding compensation, damages are mostly awarded in accordance with the Schedule for assessment of personal injuries in traffic cases, although this is not mandatory. Pain and suffering, and sometimes other damages, have occasionally been granted under the DFA, although legally it is required that the claimant also bring an action based on tort or contract.

109 Decision of the Court of Appeal of Madrid of 26 April 2001 (JUR 2001/189566); Decision of the Court of Appeal of Badajoz of 8 April 1999 (AC 1999/674); Decision of the Court of Appeal of Vizcaya of 16 December 2002 (AC 2003/822).

110 Decision of the Court of Appeal of Santa Cruz de Tenerife of 19 April 2002 (AC 2002/898); Decision of the Court of Appeal of Madrid of 31 July 2001 (JUR 2001/283132).

Comparative Analysis of Key Aspects of Product Liability Law in China and the United States

Will W. Shen
Lovells
Hong Kong
and
Iris H.Y. Chiu
University of Leicester
United Kingdom

Introduction

Product liability law, which imposes liability on manufacturers and suppliers for harm caused by defective products, may be the fastest growing area in modern tort law. At the turn of the 21st century, scholars remarked, "product liability occupies a central role in . . . law".[1] This is partly due to the fact that consumers across the world file millions of product liability suits each year,[2] which promotes the development of product liability law and practice, and partly due to the need to meet social demands in consumer protection, product standards and trade convergence in the post-industrialization of the 20th century.

Legal theories and principles adopted in pre and post-industrialization periods are obviously fundamentally different. For example,

1 Owen, Montgomery and Keeton, *Product Liability and Safety Cases and Materials*, 3rd ed., University Casebook Series, June 1996, at p. 1.

2 In addition to its direct influence upon the legal system and principles, product liability litigation has tremendous impacts on the whole of society. For instance, the Chinese Government treats product liability and quality cases as a major problem, which brings instability to the nation. This might be true, especially considering that product liability cases involve an extremely high level of damages (in response to rising medical costs) and physical and psychological pain to the victims.

negligence or the doctrine of "no fault, no liability" was widely adopted and implemented in the pre-industrialization period to encourage the development of industries. However, in the post-industrialization period, strict liability became the dominant system. The difference demonstrates a changing attitude or policy concern toward product liability, defective products and responsible manufacturers. Different systems of law also treat product liability in different ways and at different levels of sophistication and detail. This chapter deals in a comparative manner with the development of product liability law in the United States and China and, from there, some inferences are drawn as to the larger ideas of legal tradition and methodology in the two jurisdictions.

China is undergoing both a phase of rapid industrialization and a phase of trade liberalization. Where industrialization is concerned, much foreign investment in China lies in manufacturing and the United States has a significant stake in investment in the manufacturing sectors. Product explosion in the domestic market gave rise to issues of product safety, product standards and the protection of consumers. On a more practical level, due to the high volume of trade between the United States and China and the enormous amount of American foreign investment in China, United States manufacturers in China, as well as investors from other developed countries, would have an interest in understanding and perhaps being involved in the development of Chinese product liability law, as they are immediately concerned. With China's accession to the World Trade Organization (WTO), and an increasing embracing of free market and free trade principles, it is estimated that investment and trade will further increase between China and the United States. Trade is often a platform upon which other forms of convergence take place, and it may also be anticipated that increased trade in products may result in a convergence in product standards and liability regimes.

On an academic level, this study hopes to highlight the key substantive issues in product liability in the United States and China, and through this examine how the law is developed in the relatively mysterious and unique legal system in China, as well as how the legal system in China is being fashioned in transition in this era of demand for law reform following China's modernization, urbanization and, most importantly, economic development, largely due to trade with foreign parties and foreign investment.

In a larger context, China's legal reform begun with its implementation of its "reform and open door" policy since the early 1980s. The Government launched the movement of re-establishing the legal system in both substantive and procedural aspects. Recent legislative changes in China have introduced greater fairness, transparency and predictability. China, however, is still encountering difficulties. Some serious problems remain enshrined in legal reform. For example, the role of law emphasizes its instrumental use to accomplish policy goals and heavily favors the interests of the State over the individual. There are uncertainties of interpretation and implementation and the lack of public comment on law-making that challenge the legitimacy of legislation and its application. The separation of powers and advocating of judicial independence also sensitively and critically affect the entire legal system.

The Civil Law influences on Chinese law will be elaborated upon later, but for now it is sufficient to say that the recognition of pandectist roots in Chinese law led to the promulgation of the General Principles of Civil Law in 1985. The Civil Law tradition in China, coupled with specific promulgations in recent years to meet social needs, have changed the Chinese legal landscape dramatically, although the Chinese legal framework can hardly be said to be very similar to Western models. Western legal forms and concepts associated with the establishment of a fully functional legal system are no longer treated as bourgeois liberalism and have been partially transplanted into Chinese legal system. For instance, the concept of natural justice has, to a certain extent, been introduced into some newly promulgated regulations, that is, the Administrative Penalty Law. However, the concept is rather new in China, plagued as it is by a tradition of arbitrary and unfettered administrative action. Thus, chances are high that it will meet much resistance from local governments at all levels. A nascent concept of separation of powers, therefore, appears more elusive than ever.

Comparing the substantive law aspects of product liability law provides the ability to understand the legal frameworks that have been adopted in the United States and China, and to ascertain both the roots of product liability law and its future direction, especially in China. As China is a legal system in transition, its legal framework is at a more adaptable stage than that of the United States. Thus, there is room to see if there are areas that Chinese product liability law may address in the future and, more broadly, whether the legal framework of product liability law may be further changed and adapted following an understanding of the relatively more sophisticated legal framework in the United States, as well as the forces of trade and possible convergence.

Legal Framework of Product Liability in the United States and China

The birth of modern product liability law in the United States was largely due to the rise of the industrial revolution and the frequent appearance of product liability cases in the early 1900s.[3] Nevertheless, most of its early beginnings were found in the tort-contract hybrid warranties of quality, both express and implied.[4]

The early Common Law dealt with defective products by finding whether or not the producer or seller had made an express or implied warranty as to the quality of the product, and liability was premised on the breach of such warranty. As the functions of manufacturing and retailing separated during the course of industrialization, the law had to cope with an existing obstacle to consumer recovery.[5] The law was reluctant to allow end users of products who had no contractual privity with the manufacturer to sue in contract. Hallmarks of the modern law of product liability are the elimination of the privity requirements in an action against the seller of a defective product in the 20th century[6] and the emergence of the doctrine of strict liability.[7]

Overall, United States product liability law consists of three important parts:

(1) Strict liability, which assumes that a manufacturer or supplier shall be liable for damage to consumers resulting from defective products regardless of fault;

3 James A. Henderson Jr. and Aaron Twerski, "Closing the American Product Liability Frontier: The Rejection of Liability without Defect", 66 N.Y.U. Law Rev. 1263 (November 1991). Strict liability was upheld in the seminal case of *Henningsen* v. *Bloomfield*, 32 N.J. 358, 161 A.2d 69 (1960).

4 Toward the end of the 19th century, some courts finally began imposing an implied warranty of quality on manufacturers.

5 *Winterbottom* v. *Wright*, 10 M.& W. 109, 152 Eng. Rep. 402 (Ex. 1842).

6 *MacPherson* v. *Buick Motor Co.* 217 N.Y. 382, 111 N.E. 1050 (1916).

7 *Greenman* v. *Yuba Power Products, Inc.* 59 Cal. 2d 57, 377 P.2d 897, 27 Cal. Rptr. 697 (1962).

(2) Warranty law, which remains an appropriate vehicle to redress a consumer's frustrated expectation and is an effective vehicle for determining how to compensate pure economic losses caused by defective products; and
(3) The doctrine of negligence, which has become less important in product liability cases, but is still often cited in the context of design defects.

The nature of the United States legal system is based on Common Law and, therefore, both contractual actions and tortious actions in strict liability or negligence have been developed in case law.[8]

Strict liability in tort for defective products was largely developed by Section 402A of the Restatement (Second) of Torts after the landmark case of *Greenman* v. *Yyuba Power Products*.[9] The Restatements of various laws, although not having the force of law, acted as codifications of vast areas of Common Law, and helped to promote the convergence of the Common Law in many areas throughout the states in America. The Restatement pertaining to product liability was quickly applied in case law.[10] State legislation also filled in the gaps that precedents did not cover. For instance, a large number of statutes unify and affect such matters as statutes of repose, joint liability, damages and statutory compliance. In addition to product liability cases, lawyers to both victims and defendant companies should consult any statutory enactments. The codification of legal terms, principles and terminology is also an effective and efficient method of clearing up ambiguity in applying rules.

A successful, if not the most successful, effort at codification of American law is the Uniform Commercial Code, the underlying purposes of which are to simplify, clarify and modernize the law governing commercial transactions. So far, however, codification in the area of product liability is still at state level. The American Law Institute (ALI) in 1992 committed itself to helping to reduce the confusion and

---

8 Zweigert & Kotz, *Introduction to Comparative Law* (Oxford Clarendon, 1998, 3rd ed.) Chapters 14–18.

9 *Greenman* v. *Yuba Power Products, Inc.*, 59 Cal. 2d 57, 377 P.2d 897, 27 Cal. Rptr. 697 (1962).

10 *Kaneko* v. *Hilo Coast Processing*, 654 P.2d 343, 347 (Haw. 1982); *Carey* v. *Hy-Temp Mfg., Inc.*, 702 F. Supp. 666, 671 (N.D. Ill. 1988).

ambiguity surrounding product liability by undertaking to prepare a Restatement (Third) of Torts: Product Liability.[11]

Since there has been such disparity in the case law and specific legislation dealing with product liability in all the fifty states of the United States, the quest for a uniform codification of the product liability rules has turned to Congress. Since 1979, bills have been presented each year, in either the House or the Senate, to "federalize", if not centralize, and thus to render a uniform system of product liability law. Some of these proposals have been modest and directed toward a limited number of issues; others have attempted to regulate many, but not all, aspects of product litigation. Both houses of the Congress passed the Common Sense Product Liability Legal Reform Act of 1996, which was, however, vetoed by President Clinton. In 1998, a further effort at reform, the Product Liability and Reform Act, which capped punitive damages for small businesses at the greater of US $250,000 or twice the amount of compensatory damages, failed to receive enough votes to be passed.

In summary, a codification of product liability law at a federal level has not taken place. Although repeated efforts have failed to lead to a federal product liability statute, the features of product liability law in the United States allow one to distill a similarity in the features as well as approaches to the substantive law. Thus, this chapter does not make a distinction between different state laws explicitly, but discusses the general product liability landscape and system in the United States as a whole.

Although there is yet some way to go before a federal approach to product liability may be found, the Restatement has harmonized state approaches and state legislation has largely adopted the general approach of the three-fold types of liability outlined earlier. It is worth noting that, in the general legal landscape of consumer protection, there is a plethora of federal legislation allowing aggrieved consumers to seek redress through private litigation, including the Deceptive Trade Practices Consumer Protection Act, the Telephone Consumer Protection Act and the Anti-Cybersquatting Consumer Protection Act, which protect various aspects of consumer grievances. These federal developments illustrate that there is a degree of consensus as to the extent of consumer protection viewed to be desirable

---

11 The new Restatement was published in 1998, and the courts have begun to apply it.

across the United States. Thus, it may be a matter of time before another attempt to pass a federal product liability bill may be made.

As for contractual liability in warranty for product quality, consumers with disappointed expectations who are not necessarily injured by a product may be able to claim for the loss in economic value of the product. This action is wider in scope than the tortious product liability action, which is based on a minimum form of protection of consumer safety and not on helping consumers get what they bargained for. The development of law in this area is also through case law, but the Uniform Commercial Code has provided some consistency in the interpretation and application of the law.[12]

Design defects in a product that result in disappointed expectations for an end user may not be actionable under the law of contractual warranty if there is no privity of contract. This grievance may not be redressed if a consumer cannot proceed under tort law. However, it is arguable that tort is an appropriate forum for such claims. This, as will be discussed later, is an area which is still a work in progress.

As far as China is concerned, the birth of product liability law came with the beginning of industrialization, which started a quarter of a century ago. The reform towards a modern legal system also exploded into adolescence, and the development of strict liability in tort started in the early 1990s. Product quality and liability in China became an issue due to social dissatisfaction with the defects found in both legitimate and counterfeit goods. Despite official consternation publicized in the Chinese media and considerable efforts since the early 1980s at launching a consumer rights protection drive, many industry players, both domestic and foreign, continue to manufacture products far short of expected quality standards. China had to have a legal solution. However, by examining the Civil Law roots in China,[13] a brief set of general Civil Law principles drawn heavily on

12 In product liability law, statutes are important. For instance, the Uniform Commercial Code provides many operative sections with regard to express and implied warranties. For example, Section 2–318 of the Uniform Commercial Code offers possible approaches to the scope of the warranty. Another example is the statute of limitations. Under Section 2–725 of the Uniform Commercial Code, claims for breach of warranty run four years from the date of sale.

13 An old Chinese Civil Code was enacted by the nationalist government between 1929 and 1931 and was based on the German Civil Code. However, with the entrenchment of the socialist government in 1949, the earlier code was kept in obsolescence and no new Civil Code was drafted until the early 1980s.

the pandectist influences in the old-fashioned Civil Codes were enacted as the General Principles of Civil Law 1986.

The Civil Law was the main legal source in China governing product liability before the promulgation of the Product Quality Law.[14] In general, the Civil Law and the Legal Interpretation of the Civil Law issued by the Supreme People's Court have provisions stipulating the system of obligations, elements of tortious liability and procedural issues.[15] It should be noted that courts have no power to interpret laws and rules in China. Article 126 of the current Constitution mandates that courts "exercise judicial power independently, in accordance with the provisions of the law". As a general rule, the power to interpret laws is delegated to the National People's Congress Standing Committee under Article 67(4) of the Constitution.

The system of obligations under the Civil Law comprises contract, tort, quasi-contract and quasi-delict, for example, unjust enrichment and liability for invalid contracts. Article 84 states:

> ". . . [an] obligation is a relationship of specific rights and duties between parties, arising either from terms of a contract or from a provision of law. The one that enjoys a right is the obligee and the one that bears the duty is the obligor. The obligee has the right to demand that the obligor perform his duty according to the terms of the contract or the provisions of the law".

The Civil Law adopts the general principle of "no liability without fault" and makes it clear that "fault" is the general standard of liability for tortious conduct.[16] Obviously, manufacturers' and/or suppliers' liability were confined to a limited extent. More importantly, the motivation behind adopting this limited principle of liability was to promote the development of China's infant industries and commerce.

As China became increasingly industrialized and manufacturing boomed, product quality and liability have become the primary targets of consumer complaints and civil judgments. The Chinese press is replete with examples of dissatisfied customers who have

---

14 Product Quality Law, promulgated on 22 February 1993 and effective as of 1 September 1993 and amended on 8 July 2000.

15 The Legal Interpretation of the Civil Law, adopted by the Judicial Committee of the Supreme People's Court on 26 January 1988.

16 General Principles of Civil Law, Article 106(2).

purchased faulty manufactured goods, especially consumer durables, such as refrigerators and television sets. There have also been numerous reported cases of injury, and even death, linked to certain goods, such as pharmaceutical, food and drink products. Thus, the general regime of fault-based law of civil obligations was increasingly unable to meet genuine consumer grievances as it was not easy to prove "fault".

The social demands of a newly industrialized economy appear to be similar whether they are in the United States or China. The domestic need for consumer protection and safety was the main impetus for more law reform in product liability law in both the United States and China. However, in the United States, although private litigation and case law took the lead in developing strict liability for product defects in tort, consumer demands have also resulted in complimentary legislation. However, as characteristic of both a Common Law legal tradition, where the law was developed in a piecemeal way to meet actual needs at ground level, and of the social culture in America, where the enforcement of private rights took the lead in shaping legal development, the rights granted to persons to enjoy products free from injurious defects remain private rights, enforceable by private individuals. State regulation, if any, is complimentary and did not take the lead.

The Chinese legal framework was first premised on the General Principles of Civil Law and has largely developed because of a major piece of legislation, the Product Quality Law. As such, the legal framework for product liability in China has mainly been dependent upon statutory provisions. The other significant feature of the Product Quality Law is that it is both a regulatory piece of legislation, complete with administrative and criminal penalties, and a piece of legislation that confers civil rights to litigate. The Product Quality Law contains both private law enforcement and criminal and administrative measures to punish errant manufacturers. Thus, there is a strange duality in the product liability regime in China. Furthermore, new administrative measures for standardization, supervision and licensing of a wide range of industrial products were introduced.[17] The measures covered imported goods, as well as those designed for

17 The Government has finally become aware that it cannot be in the interests of the whole community to encourage carelessness and disregard for human life and property and that there must be substantial changes to the existing legal framework.

export.[18] Some measures were typical of a centrally planned socialist economy and sought to set forth and maintain product standards by administrative means. A notable distinction between the American and Chinese systems is the role and function the government is supposed to assume and play. In the United States, administrative agencies do not often set forth and enforce standards for products except in certain cases, when the product in question has been procured for government use.[19] Some Chinese laws also offered rewards for success and threatened punishment for non-compliance.

The Product Quality Law, which was specifically enacted to deal with product liability, largely supercedes many of the general requirements found in the General Principles of Civil Law in terms of substantive law. The legal framework for product liability is further supported by the existence of consumer protection rights legislation specifically catering to consumers' rights to be warned, instructed and to pay a fair price for products. Although consumers' rights deal with more issues than product liability, the existence of the Consumer Protection Law, Advertising Law, which protects consumers from

18 Regulations for the Safety Control of Dangerous Chemical Items, issued by the State Council on 17 February 1987; Provisions for "Three Warranties" of Certain Domestic Electrical Appliances, issued on 30 July 1986; Regulations for the Administration of Veterinary Pharmaceuticals, promulgated on 21 May 1987; Provisional Regulations for the Administration of Quality Licensing of Exported Electrical Products, promulgated by the State Council on 20 February 1986; Regulations for the Administration of Military Industrial Product Quality, promulgated on 5 June 1987; Regulations for the Appraisal of Superior Quality Products, promulgated on 10 April 1987; Measures for the Supervision and Control of the Quality of Import Commodities, jointly formulated by the State Administration for Import and Export Commodities Inspection, the State Economic Commission, the MOFTEC and the General Administration of Customs, promulgated on 3 September 1987; Law on the Protection of the Rights and Interests of Consumers, adopted on 31 October 1993 by the National People's Congress and promulgated on 31 October 1993; Advertising Law, adopted on 27 October 1994 by the National People's Congress and effective from 1 February 1995; Food Hygiene Law, adopted on 30 October 1995 by the National People's Congress and promulgated on 30 October 1995; General Standards for the Labeling of Foods, promulgated on 4 February 1994 by the State Bureau for Technical Supervision and effective from 1 February 1995; Regulations for the Investigation and Punishment of Food Labeling Violations, issued on 20 June 1995 by the State Bureau of Technical Supervision; Shanghai Municipality Provisions for Anti-Unfair Competition, adopted on 28 September 1995; and numerous local regulations in this regard. This list is not intended to be exhaustive, but to indicate the depth and breadth of recent relevant legislation in China.

19 *Boyle* v. *United Technologies Corp.* 487 U.S. 500, 512 (1988).

misleading advertisements, and local legislation in state provinces to similar effect, all serve to highlight the supporting climate for the growth and development of coherent product liability law in China led by State regulation.

Before the passage of the Product Quality Law, the Regulations Concerning Liability for the Quality of Industrial Products, issued on 5 April 1986, were the only systematic regulations in this field. The Product Quality Law, a unique Chinese amalgam of Civil Law and administrative provisions, defines product quality and prescribes the means by which it is to be maintained. The term "product quality" is close to the phrase "product safety" in United States law, which is used to describe regulatory law and the systems of rules, for example, the Federal Aviation Act and the Toxic Substances Control Act, established by legislatures and administrative agencies of federal, state and occasionally even municipal governments to regulate the safety of products sold to the public. The Chinese legislature obviously intended to combine product safety (or quality) standards with product liability. In fact, the Product Quality Law does operate *ex ante* by seeking to prevent product-caused accidents and diseases before they occur. In addition, some administrative and criminal measures were adopted in the Product Quality Law. It also sets out the consequences for breach of quality control requirements, including both administrative and criminal penalties, as well as civil liability in contract or tort.

Under the Product Quality Law, manufacturers are required to satisfy certain minimum quality requirements. Specifically, a manufacturer is required to:

(1) Comply with State or industrial standards for the protection of health, personal safety and the safety of property and not create "unreasonable danger" to persons or property;[20]
(2) Produce products that "possess the properties for use that should be possessed by the product" unless any flaws in the product are clearly identified;[21] and
(3) Produce products that conform to standards carried on the product or its packaging, and quality standards indicated in product descriptions or samples.[22]

20 Product Quality Law, Article 14(1).
21 Product Quality Law, Article 14(2).
22 Product Quality Law, Article 14(1).

Sellers may be implicated in product liability cases in China for their own misconduct. In practice, the seller might be sued together with the manufacturer. Under the Product Quality Law, the seller may be held liable for:

(1) Products which do not possess properties for use which such products should possess, unless prior clear indication of the deficiency is provided;
(2) Products which do not conform to standards stated on the product or their packaging; and
(3) Products which do not conform to the quality indicated by product descriptions or samples.

There are differences between the Civil Law, which is premised on a "no fault, no liability" system, and the Product Quality Law, which instead builds up a strict liability system, as there is no requirement for proof of the subjective element of fault. Specific legislation should usually prevail over general legislation, but some courts may fail to cite correct laws and still apply negligent or fault liability in product liability cases. However, such an "infant" mistake does not take place and appear too often.

The Product Quality Law of 1993 was further amended on 8 July 2000 to cover a wider range of product issues.[23] The new Product Quality Law of 2000 refines the liability of manufacturers and sellers of products of unmerchantable quality, the smuggling of counterfeit or substandard goods, authoritative excesses, inept officials and graft.

As explained earlier, the Chinese product liability regime is young, but has grown very rapidly in tandem with the economic development of the country. It thus did not have the benefit of the decades of incremental fashioning and judicial interpretation that has shaped the product liability regime in the United States. Statutory intervention by the central government in enacting a new liability regime was perhaps the most efficient way of putting a legal framework into place.

As the Product Quality Law, unlike other legislation such as the Economic Contract Law, which was enacted chiefly to meet the needs of foreign trade and investment, was enacted mainly to deal with social concerns, the character of the legislation reflected the government's perception of what may be the necessary legal tools to combat

23 As the economy diversifies and economic reform develops further, some provisions of the previous Product Quality Law are no longer relevant.

manufacturing evils. Thus, the law employed an amalgam of measures, both in private administrative and criminal law. This perhaps underlies the Chinese perception of the law as a social tool rather than an institution on its own.

The scope of product evils was widened significantly under the Product Quality Law but, unlike in the United States, the Product Quality Law does not differentiate sufficiently between different types of product complaints. Compared to the United States system, where the Common Law reasoning has refined more clearly different types of product issues and has thus pigeonholed the available actions for different product issues, China has adopted the approach of considering diverse product ills together, an approach which can be further refined in due course. The imposition of State intervention is a feature of both a centrally run economy and a less legalized society, but this political and social backdrop may allow statutory intervention to take a "broader brush" approach in dealing with diverse product ills.

What Is a "Product"?

Definition of "Product" in the United States and China

The first critical issue to be examined in product liability law is the definition of a "product". The definition of a "product" is also discussed in relation to who is liable for product defects.[24] Under American law, the definition of a "product" is not that straightforward and is determined on a case-by-case basis. A definition may be found in Section 402A of the Restatement or case law. Generally speaking, a product is usually thought of as tangible personal property.[25]

American courts usually examine whether the goods involved in the cases are "provided, sold or otherwise placed in the stream of commerce products manufactured [by the producer]".[26] If a product "is not

24 Sometimes the questions of "who is liable" and "what is a product" merge, but sometimes they are quite different and merit separate treatment.

25 A product can be a good or chattel, which is more or less synonymous with "goods" as adopted in Section 2–105(1) of the Uniform Commercial Code. Nevertheless, some litigation has involved transactions other than the typical sale of tangible goods.

26 *Cafazzo* v. *Central Medical Health Services, Inc.*, Supp Court of Penn., 1995, Pa. 668 A.2d 521.

manufactured and then introduced into the stream of commerce for sale", the court is then reluctant to characterize it as a product for the purposes of strict liability in tort.[27] On the other hand, some courts have construed the concept of a "product" broadly so that product liability has extended the definition of "product" beyond tangible goods. For example, electricity,[28] natural products,[29] real estate construction[30] and services can fall within the definition of a "product".

A "product", as defined in Article 2 of the Product Quality Law, refers to a commodity sold following processing or manufacturing. According to this definition, the commodity becomes a "product" once it meets two main criteria. First, the commodity must be manufactured for sale.[31] The manufacturer may be exempted from liability where the product has not been circulated for public consumption. The manufacturer is, therefore, not responsible for any damage sustained in relation to the product if it does not sell the product or only produces it for other reasons, such as testing or scientific experiments. This criterion may cause confusion since, in some cases, the transaction may not involve a sale. The product may have been leased or merely loaned by the owner. The injury-causing "product" may also not be a typical, mass-produced chattel, but instead a house, a toxic substance, a recipe, electricity or a poisonous spider in a pair of pants. It should be noted that "sale" here only refers to being put into commercial consumption from the very beginning instead of a transaction between the plaintiff and the defendant.

Second, the commodity must be processed or manufactured. In this case, naturally occurring resources such as gas, coal and oil do not fall within the definition. However, even if such resources are nominally processed, they may constitute a product. Chinese judicial

---

27 *Menendez* v. *Paddock Pool Construction Co.*, Court of Appeals of Arizona, 172 Ariz. 258, 836 P.2d 968.

28 *Houston Lighting & Power Co.* v. *Reynolds* (Tex. 1988). The court defined electricity as a tangible "product" in *Lewis* v. *Big Powderhorn Mountain Ski Corp.*, Court of Appeals of Michigan, 1976 (69 Mich.App. 437, 245 N.W.2d 81).

29 *Sease* v. *Taylor's Pets* (Or. App. 1985). In this case, the court held that a pet shop was strictly liable for injuries resulting from the sale of a rabid skunk.

30 *Blagg* v. *Fred Hunt Co., Inc.* (Ark. 1981). This case was about real estate fixtures such as a house. In this sense, the real estate fixtures here are different from the case of a construction project discussed below.

31 Article 2 of the Consumer Protection Law further defines the term "consumption", which refers to a product or service purchased for use in "daily life".

opinion on this point[32] can be understood by reference to a case in Shanxi Province where a peasant, Mr. Zhang, purchased four tons of coal from a small coal mine. When he put the coal into the stove in winter, the stove exploded and the explosion damaged Mr. Zhang's right hand. During the investigation, it was found that detonating caps were mixed into the coal. The court held that the coal was exploited and sold by the coal mine. Therefore, the coal should be a product and governed by the Product Quality Law.

If, for example, a Chinese pet shop sells a rabid skunk, would the shop be liable for injuries caused by "defective" skunks on the ground that a skunk is a natural product? The answer might be no, since such damage caused by the skunk are not subject to the Product Quality Law. According to the definition provided, it is hard to fit a pet into the definition of "product", which refers to goods that are sold following processing or manufacture.

The United States approach in allowing case law to refine the definition of a "product" has allowed product liability to adapt to changing times and different conceptions of what may be sold in the stream of commerce. However, as the Chinese approach is purely statutory, judicial interpretation could be limited, to a certain extent, and thus many objects found commercially available may not be subject to the legislation.

Furthermore, in the United States, sales of defective products may give rise to strict liability in tort, while other injurious acts arising out of the same transaction may give rise to liability for negligence or breach of contract. A plaintiff can bring a number of claims in one action that arise out of the same facts. This is not allowed in Chinese law because an action in relation to a defective product would be brought under the Product Quality Law as one action, even for different injurious aspects or "claims". This difference between the United States and China is a procedural one, but its history may be traced back to the Common Law system of writs, where plaintiffs formulate actions using claims that are based on infringement of private rights. Thus, different infringements of different rights arising out of the same facts may give rise to multiple causes of action. In China, however, where there may be a number of grievances attributed to the same set of facts, the operative cause is the same and, thus, there is

32 Yang Li and Liu Yanlin (ed.), *Analysis on Cases of Protecting Consumers' Legal Rights* (Chinese Law and Politics University Publishing House, 1994) at p. 24.

only one cause of action or complaint. This is because the Chinese perception of law is that law deals with "wrongs" and not the "enforcement of rights".

The Chinese have a developed cultural perception of "wrongs" as a legacy of the imperial culture of emperors and the predominance of social order by command. Therefore, as far as product liability is concerned, if the operative cause is a defective product, then there is one "wrong", that is, one action against the product defect. This action is not further characterized as "contractual" or "tortious". This may partly be due to the Civil Law perception of a wider law of civil obligations, but may also be due to a lack in Chinese cultural perceptions of "rights", and thus refined ideas of different types of rights do not feature prominently in Chinese law. The characterization of a claim in China would also depend on whether a defective product within the meaning of the Product Quality Law is found, and not based on what the product has done.

Thus, if a potential plaintiff has been injured by an object that may not fall within the definition of a "product", Chinese law may not be able to provide efficient protection to a victim unless there is another cause of action under another piece of legislation or under the General Principles of Civil Law.

Who Is liable?

As mentioned above, the definition of a "product" also involves the question of who assumes the liability. As a general rule in the United States, manufacturers and suppliers are strictly liable for defective products, and some courts are inclined to adopt a more objective standard to expand the scope of the responsible party in product liability cases.

In the case of *Cafazzo* v. *Central Medical Health Services, Inc.*,[33] in order to determine a "supplier", the court applied a four-part test, which focuses on:

(1) Which members of the marketing chain are available for redress;
(2) Whether imposition of liability would serve as an incentive to safety;

---

33 *Cafazzo* v. *Central Medical Health Services, Inc.*, Supreme Court of Penn., 1995, Pa. 668 A.2d 521.

(3) Whether the supplier is in a better position than the consumer to prevent the circulation of defective products; and
(4) Whether the supplier can distribute the cost of compensation for injuries by charging for it in his business.

In principle, this four-part test mainly premises its reasonableness on the key issue of who is in the best position to reduce the risks.

In practice, American courts expand the scope of "manufacturer and supplier" to any party who is in the best position to reduce the risk, and adopt this standard to determine whether strict liability in tort is applicable (also known as the "risk reduction test"). For instance, a laundromat is held strictly liable in tort as a "lessor" of defective washers and dryers that injure its patrons. Although the laundromat is not engaged in the distribution of the product, in the court's opinion, it, in the same manner as a manufacturer, retailer or lessor, provides the product (perhaps more precisely, services) to the public for use by the public and, consequently, plays more than a random and accidental role in the overall marketing enterprise of the product in question.[34] With regard to the definition of "supplier", Section 402A of the Restatement (Second) of Torts provides a clearer view in relevant part as follows:

"(1) One who sells any product in a defective condition unreasonably dangerous to the user or consumer or to his property is subject to liability for physical harm thereby caused to the ultimate user or consumer, or to his property; if

"(a) the seller is engaged in the business of selling such a product; and

"(b) it is expected to and does reach the consumer without substantial change in the condition in which it is sold."

The United States law thus examines the relationship between the parties to find out if the defendant is in the chain of distribution of the product. According to this principle, a used goods dealer is not held liable for defective products, since it is entirely outside the original chain of distribution of the product.[35] This distribution chain test is

34 *Garcia* v. *Halsett*, 82 Cal.Rptr. 420, 423 (Ct.App.1970).
35 *Tillman* v. *Vance Equipment Co.*, 596 P.2d 1299, 1303–1304 (Or. 1979).

also adopted in the Restatement (Second) of Torts. For example, Section 402A-2, Comment (b) provides that "in addition, as long as the plaintiff establishes that the product was defective when it left the hands of a given seller in the distributive chain, liability will attach to that seller". This test strengthens the risk-reduction test, where there is no direct relationship with either a manufacturer or a seller, that is, where the party has no channel of communication by which it can exchange information as to possible dangerous defects in particular products and correct or warn of pre-existing defects in the products, and thus such a party should not be asked to bear the risk of product liability.

Chinese law and courts do not adopt the approach of making liable the "party-in-a-better-position" to bear the risk. Instead, the Chinese courts adhere strictly to the parameters of the Product Quality Law and apply liability to the manufacturer, supplier or any party in the chain of distribution of a commodity. However, the irony is that Chinese legislation does not have a clear definition of "manufacturer" or "supplier". Elements of general application of fault liability thus come in when the courts determine the persons liable. Chinese courts have legally defined as "manufacturer" or "supplier" a person in the distribution chain who may be at fault for causing the risk. It has been held by Chinese courts that a tortious duty with respect to defective products is not merely owed by the manufacturer,[36] but also the seller,[37] persons who have stored or transported the goods and even administrative departments.

Departments in charge of quality control and supervision in China are many and varied. They include administrative departments for standards and measurements, commodity inspection, quality supervision, industry and commerce and the enterprise's own quality control departments, as well as the local standards bureaus, testing centers, labor bureaus and the Certification Office of the State

36 Neither the Civil Law, the Product Quality Law nor the Consumer Protection Law provide definitions on certain important terms such as "manufacturer". Therefore, it is not clear whether the term only includes manufacturers of finished products or if it also includes the producer of any raw material or component that goes into the product.

37 The General Principles of Civil Law, the Product Quality Law and the Consumer Protection Law all fail to define the term "seller". It is likely that the "seller" can be broadly interpreted. Generally speaking, the term "seller" can cover legal persons who sell products to consumers under sales agreements or any companies in the chain of distribution of products.

Economic and Trade Commission. The various liabilities of State governmental bodies in respect of the torts of their subordinate workers are expressly provided for in the Civil Law, and precedents for liability exist even though it is a relatively recent development in Chinese legal practice.[38]

Liability arises only where control and supervision are lax, thus suggesting that the primary basis is fault. According to the Product Quality Law, product quality supervision departments or other State authorities and product quality inspection institutions may not recommend products to the public; and they may not participate in the business of dealing in products through such means as supervising the manufacture or sale of products. In breach of this rule, the authority at a higher level or the procuratorial authority shall order it to rectify the situation and to eliminate the effects of its violation. Any illegal revenue shall be confiscated. The leading personnel directly in charge and the other directly responsible personnel shall be subject to disciplinary sanctions according to law if the case is serious. The duty of administrative departments, however, was never contemplated in the drafting of the Civil Law. This duty arises instead by virtue of the Product Quality Law, which provides that those administrative departments "whose control and supervision [of quality] are lax shall bear joint and several liability".[39]

Transporters and agents, however, are merely obliged not to mishandle the goods in their care so as to render them substandard in quality. This idea hails from the 1986 Product Quality Liability Regulations, which provide that "when damage [to goods] is caused by reasons clearly attributable to storage, transport, or loading and unloading, the storage or loading and unloading enterprise shall bear liability".[40] This provision was to allow the manufacturer or seller to claim a contribution from the transporter or agent whose fault served as the real cause of the goods' substandard quality. Opinions about the scope of the responsibility vary. One view is that the manufacturer, distributor or retailer and the administrative departments responsible for

38 Dicks, "Legal Opinion", *China Trade Report*, November 1981, at p. 11, citing a case of environmental pollution where the public health department and environmental protection department paid compensation to a fish farm. In a mediated agreement, the departments admitted fault for allowing a hospital to discharge water with dangerous chemicals, thus killing the fish.

39 Product Quality Law, Article 4.

40 Product Quality Liability Regulations, Article 13.

quality control and supervision each have the responsibility not to allow goods of substandard quality to enter the market. For manufacturers and sellers, this is clear from the Civil Law itself. The Chinese courts have effectively extended the statutory ambit of liable persons, and this shows the struggle faced by courts used to fault-based principles in civil law and the new notion of strict liability.

While it is noteworthy that both the United States and China have not limited the scope of liable persons, the United States has determined liability on an approach more akin to policy than in China. In China, the Civil Law roots and the Chinese legal culture of finding out "who was wrong" still predominate in determining who ought to bear the consumers' loss. Although this may arguably be a more purely legal approach, China has yet to come to grips with the erstwhile tangoing relationship between tort and compensation.[41]

Product liability is both a matter of compensation and legal liability. In fact, the adoption of strict liability in the United States signifies the predominance of the compensation concern over doctrinal precepts in product defects. China's adoption of strict liability in the Product Quality Law also indicates that compensation is a more pressing concern than doctrine. However, if doctrinal analysis based on fault is to be used to determine the persons to bear the loss, one may lose sight of the larger objective of compensation. For example, if the product is rather volatile and becomes dangerous due to a carrier's haphazard handling, the carrier may be at fault in Chinese law, but the carrier may not be in a position to bear the loss. There is perhaps room for the development of statutory clarification of the objective of compensation, given that judicial interpretation is an uncertain and perhaps under-developed phenomenon in China.

What Is a "Defect"?

Liability under the Chinese Civil Law and Product Quality Law

Liability under the Chinese Civil Law applies to any damage caused to property or persons "due to the substandard quality of goods".[42]

41 For a more general discussion of the relationship between tort and the issue of compensation for social accidents and hazards, *see* Peter Cane, *P.S. Atiyah's Accidents, Compensation and the Law* (London, Butterworths, 1999) (6th ed).

42 General Principles of Civil Law, Article 122.

The duty not to cause damage is thus defined in terms of "substandard quality" rather than the more familiar American concept of "defect". Under Chinese law, the meaning of "substandard quality" is defined by reference to administrative and technical specifications, but may sometimes be defined by general notions of safety, as seen below. As mentioned above, Chinese law authorizes governmental bodies to adopt, regulate and enforce standards. For example, Article 6 of the Product Quality Law provides that "the State encourages the practice of scientific quality control methods and the adoption of advanced and scientific technologies, and encourages enterprises to cause the quality of their products to achieve and surpass industry, national and international standards". Article 7 further requests "governments at every level to . . . guide and supervise producers and sellers in strengthening product quality management and raising product quality".

In one case, the plaintiff, Ms. Gao Pingping, asked her friend to buy a bedding mat from Shanghai Guang Hua Daily Handiwork Business Department. The Ming Zhi Mat Manufacturing Company produced the mat in Anji County, Zhejiang Province. After the plaintiff used it for one week, her ears began to itch and hives developed on her legs. Soon thereafter, the condition became more serious. In its medical examination, Shanghai Ruijin Hospital confirmed that the rash was caused by lacquer used to paint the mat. Because Gao was three months pregnant, however, the doctor only prescribed a medicinal ointment for the patient. After several months, however, the disease became more serious and the doctor had no choice but to prescribe Gao a certain medicine that was forbidden during pregnancy. The medicine caused Gao to have a miscarriage in June 1991. In its ruling, the Shanghai Huangpu District People's Court concluded that the defendant was responsible for the plaintiff's loss, including medical costs and lost wages, because the defendant could not provide the court with a quality appraisal or examination report proving that the mat would not cause skin allergies. Therefore, the product was deemed "substandard".[43]

The definition of substandard is thus unclear and may mean the lack of any independent appraisal of the product. It is noted that the parts of a product that may fall short of substandard may include not

---

43 *China Trials and Cases Collection* (China People's Public Security University Press, 1992) at pp. 615–618.

only inherent defects in the product itself,[44] but also its packaging,[45] labeling[46] and instructions,[47] such requirements also extending to matters having no relevance to product safety, such as product licensing.

Article 27 of the Product Quality Law provides a full set of rules as to the labeling of products. The labeling of a product must conform to the following requirements:

(1) It must have a product quality inspection certificate;
(2) The product name and the producing factory's name and address shall be displayed in Chinese;
(3) Should the product's characteristics and usage requirements necessitate the display of the product's specifications, grade and the names and quantities of its major constituents, such information shall be displayed in Chinese — if consumers require prior information of the product's specifications, grade and the names and quantities of its major constituents, such information shall be displayed on the outer packaging or relevant information shall be provided to consumers beforehand;
(4) Products to be used within a certain period of time shall clearly carry their production date, period of safe use or date of expiry in a prominent place; and
(5) Products the improper use of which is likely to cause the products themselves to be damaged or to endanger personal safety and/or the safety of property shall carry a warning mark or a warning in Chinese.

The responsibility created in Article 122 of the Civil Law for substandard products is owed to anyone who sustains personal injury or property damage resulting from a substandard product. As liability is tortious, no contract is necessary between the parties. Potential plaintiffs include purchasers, consumers and certain third parties. For example, one case is discussed in a textbook where a child was scalded by a thermos flask that burst while being carried by a passerby. The flask

44 Product Quality Law, Articles 14 and 34. Quality requirements also include factors such as the design and manufacturing of the given product.
45 Product Quality Law, Article 27.
46 Food Labeling Regulations.
47 Product Quality Liability Regulations, Article 9(4).

burst because of a defect and, therefore, the author concluded that the manufacturer was liable to compensate the child for injuries sustained.[48]

Non-compliance with government or industry health and safety standards[49] used to be the deciding factor when determining if a product was substandard. Under Chinese law, most products when sold in China must include some form of examination certification,[50] and certain products, such as firecrackers, food and drugs, must be examined and approved by the designated departments.[51] Chinese law also distinguishes between "compulsory" and "recommended" standards. Compulsory standards relate to guarantees of personal safety and property, and are implemented through laws and administrative legislation.[52] It is less clear whether falling short of "recommended standards" would render a product to be held substandard.

The presence of a State certification system for various products also helps aggrieved consumers to pursue a remedy against the State should it certify as safe a questionable product. This illustrates the presence of a centrally controlled or even "nanny" State in overseeing product liability for a young consumer public, and it remains to be seen if the legal landscape will change to one that is predominantly private law based, as in the United States.

The Product Quality Law initially set out three factors for determining product quality, that is, standards may be specified in legislation, State standards or standards specified in individual contracts.

---

48 *Civil Liability of Tort* (Zhang Peilin ed., 1987) at p. 39.

49 The "standards" referred to in the Product Quality Law are those set out in the National Standardization Law, adopted by the State Council on 29 December 1988 and its Implementing Rules of the National Standards Law, adopted by the State Technology Supervision Bureau on 6 April 1990.

50 The new certification mark, the China Compulsory Certification, was created by the Administrative Rules on Compulsory Product Certification, promulgated by the State Administration for Quality Supervision, Inspection and Quarantine on 1 December 2001 and effective as of 1 May 2002. The Certification and Accreditation Administration issued the Compulsory Product Certification Catalogue in December 2001. In total, 132 products in nineteen categories are subject to China Compulsory Certification: Will Shen *et al.*, *International Consumer Protection Law*, "China" chapter (Kluwer, 2002).

51 Food Hygiene Law, Article 27; Law on the Administration of Drugs, Article 4.

52 It is easy for consumers to tell whether products are of good quality and comply with State standards because China adopts a quality certificate system, which requests manufacturers to attach a quality certificate issued by the Government to products: Product Quality Law, Articles 5 and 27(1).

According to Article 13 of the Product Quality Law, "industrial products . . . must conform to national and industry standards for the safeguarding of health, personal safety and the safety of property". In China, under the National Standardization Law, "standards" are classified as "State", "industry" and "local" standards. "State standards" are formulated by the State Bureau of Standards of the State Council for the "technical requirements that need to be unified nationwide". Overall, a "standard" is not treated as a source of law in China. Therefore, it is impossible for governments (except the State or local Bureau of Standards) to promulgate standards through a "law" or a "rule".

The Chinese Government has not laid down standards for all products. However, there are standards for most, if not all, products. In particular, the State strictly enforces standards for hazardous goods that are fragile, flammable, explosive, toxic, corrosive or radioactive. In practice, it is easy for manufacturers to find applicable standards in their own industries. In the United States, some kinds of products are more thoroughly regulated than others, and the courts have held that state product liability law is pre-empted by some federal product regulatory schemes, for example, rules requiring airbags in cars or specifying the warnings on cigarette packages. However, few products are so thoroughly regulated as to displace tort law.

The Product standards relate to the "application" to which the product is put, the safety of the product and any other special requirements specific to a particular product or service.[53] Therefore, liability for a defective product is not based on some inherent objective defect in the product, such as a flaw in its design or production, but on its failure to meet any of the quality requirements stated or legislatively provided for within the scope of application, safety and specificity. Strict liability only arises when the end user's losses or injuries are caused by the failure of the product to meet the above-stated requirements, and not where injury has resulted *per se*. If the injury cannot be attributed to the failure of the specific standards applicable, the victim may be bereft of a remedy under the Product Quality Law and would have to try and start a cause of action under the general civil law, in which case the plaintiff would have to prove that the product was generally "substandard".

53 Where there are no national or industry standards, the products must conform to the requirements for the safeguarding of health, personal safety and the safety of property: Products Quality Law, Article 13.

Recently, however, the Product Quality Law has introduced a broader concept of "defect" into the law. A "defect" can be:

(1) Anything "unreasonably dangerous" in the product that may cause personal injury or property damage to the consumer;[54] or

(2) Non-conformity of the product to prescribed standards for the protection of personal safety or property, which reflects the earlier formulation as described.[55]

Product liability for non-compliance with standards or a "defect" and product liability for "substandardness" under the General Principles of the Civil Law may be argued to be equivalent. In practice, the specific nature of the Product Quality Law would prevail over the general civil law, so that the latter may give rise to a more general cause of action akin to the underlying rubric of tort in the United States when the cause of action cannot specifically be founded on product liability. On a conceptual level, however, this is a unique problem, as China has imported Common Law statute-type specificity into its general Civil Law framework. Thus, where there may be a conflict or contradiction, it is uncertain how legal development will take place. This is related to a broader perception in Chinese culture of law as a social instrument and not a tradition.

Thus, in the piecemeal introduction of laws, the Chinese were not concerned about the essential differences in the legal tradition and methodology underlying the Civil and Common Law traditions, but more about whether the particular legal formula would work to solve social problems. Such an instrumentalist approach would prove to bring about more conceptual difficulties in the future, as trade interaction with foreign counterparts would bring into question the incompatibility of Western understandings of what a legal tradition entails and the Chinese way of using law. Academics already have myriad problems trying to understand the character of the Chinese legal system.[56]

---

54 This is the same principle as the one adopted in Section 402A of the Restatement (Second) of Torts. The rules stated in this Section apply only where the defective condition of the product makes it unreasonably dangerous to the user or consumer. The article sold must be dangerous to an extent beyond that which would be contemplated by the ordinary consumer who purchases it, with the ordinary knowledge common to the community as to its characteristics.

55 Product Quality Law, Article 34.

56 Randall Peerenboom, "The X-Files: Past and Present Portrayals of China's Alien Legal System" (Winter 2003), *Washington University Global Studies Law Review*, at p. 37.

On the issue of a "defect" as defined in the Product Quality Law, "unreasonably dangerous" is a vague concept and it can be expected that the courts will continue to decide whether a defect exists by reference to objective standards, such as quality standards issued by relevant Chinese authorities, which can be illustrated by the *Xu Yan* v. *Wu'an Fireworks Factory and Sima Fireworks Factory*, adjudicated by Jiang Du County People's Court in Yangzhou, Jiangsu province.

An eight-year old boy was injured when playing with firecrackers sold by the two defendants in 1988. The boy's father sued the defendants for the loss of use of his right arm. The defendant admitted the quality problem, but argued that the child's parents should also assume partial responsibility for failing to provide adequate supervision of their son. The court, however, rejected this argument and ordered the defendants to accept full liability because the firecrackers were, in fact, produced without the approval of their department in charge.[57]

Chinese law does not distinguish between defects in manufacture, design and warning, as United States law does. However, in practice, reference to this three-fold classification of defects is made in case law, which is illustrated by a number of cases.

In one case,[58] a factory bought a refrigerator from the defendant in 1995. Later, the plaintiff, an employee of the factory, was electrocuted as he was holding the handle of the refrigerator. Examination of the refrigerator by the standardization bureau found that one phase of the return circuit of the magnetic starter of the refrigerator was not properly wired, which had caused a break in the circuit and, consequently, resulted in an increase in the current. The power to the refrigerator should have been automatically cut off under such a situation. However, because there was no cut-off and relay in the starter, the motor continued to operate, which caused the body of the refrigerator to be electrified. To make things worse, no ground wire was installed, resulting in the electrocution of the plaintiff.

The defendant argued that this brand of refrigerator had been classified as a quality product by the provincial authority and was put into use after trial operations conducted by its technicians. The defendant further argued that, before this accident, the refrigerator had worked

57 *China Trials and Cases Collection* (China People's Public Security University Press, 1992) at pp. 637–641.

58 *Collection and Analysis on Cases Concerning Consumer Protection Law and Product Quality Law* (Law Press, 1999) at pp. 119–120.

properly for thirty days. Based on these reasons, the defendant attributed the accident to the employer's failure to install an earth. The court found that the plaintiff's death was caused by the electrified body of the refrigerator, which was the result of the improper wiring of the magnetic starter, which is a manufacturing defect.

In determining a manufacturing defect, Chinese courts also seek technical advice from specific organizations.[59] In another case, the plaintiff bought a television in 1990. Some months later it exploded as the plaintiff was watching it with his family members, which resulted in the injury of his son and damage to his video recorder. The television manufacturer drew the conclusion that the incident was caused by a sudden rise in voltage of electrical current.

The court requested the Household Appliances Examination Centre to conduct an investigation into the explosion. The Centre found that the explosion was caused by the picture tube, which was not of good quality and would explode if there was a sudden fluctuation in the current or if the tube was operating continuously for more than five hours. In a test conducted by the Centre, four of the five television sets produced by the manufacturer showed certain problems when working continuously for about five hours or when there was some fluctuation in the current. The court held that it was a manufacturing defect and ordered the manufacturer to compensate the plaintiff for his losses.

The commentary on the following case also examines the influence of State quality certifications on Chinese courts when determining product liability:

> "Villager Zhu was building a house and to this end purchased four concrete beams from a concrete factory. Villager Shen engaged a construction team to build Zhu's house. During construction, the four concrete beams fractured causing Zhu's death and serious injuries to other laborers. Zhu's mother and wife sued the concrete factory for medical expenses and lost earnings as compensation. The defendant argued that the beams were of good quality and the accident was caused by Zhu's fault in building the house because Zhu did not use the beams after the required curing period. Based on the report of the Shanghai Construction

59 *Collection and Analysis on Cases Concerning Consumer Protection Law and Product Quality Law* (Law Press, 1999) at pp. 79–80.

Quality Examination Centre, the court drew the conclusion that the concrete beams were substandard. The court held that Zhu's mother and wife were properly first and second plaintiffs, respectively, and that the concrete factory was liable to compensate the plaintiffs for their losses.[60]

In light of the cases discussed above, the decisions may be read as making clear that the court's finding of a defect is not due to an objective inference or understanding of how the product should be or work but, rather, due to evidence of certification of quality or otherwise for the product in question. There may be an over-reliance upon the administrative systems of certification by the courts such that the finding of fact is no longer an independent judicious exercise calling for evidence from independent sources. However, the prevailing commercial reality is that most manufacturers must obtain approvals from the Government prior to manufacturing. Moreover, before circulating products on the market, manufacturers must obtain quality certificates from the Government indicating the quality of the products. Furthermore, practically speaking, the courts will treat quality certificates or governmental approvals as *prima facie* evidence in determining whether the products in question satisfy State standards and are in good condition. There is, however, the possibility that liability may shift from manufacturers to regulators for lapses in regulatory compliance. Thus, the further growth and refinement of the product liability regime may require much more relinquishment of State intervention and strengthening of the civil liability regime.

"Defects" in American and Chinese Product Liability Laws

The ALI's new Restatement (Third) of Torts: Product Liability set forth three different types of defects[61] for which product liability is imposed: manufacturing defects (sometimes referred to as construction defects or production defects), design defects and marketing defects. The new Restatement defines manufacturing defects as

---

60 *Shen Feng-ying* v. *Jiang Shan County Concrete Factory*; *China Trials and Cases Collection* (China People's Public Security University Press, 1994) at pp. 809–814.

61 David W. Leebron, "An Introduction to Product Liability — Origins, Issues and Trends" (December 1991), *Annual Survey of American Law*, at p. 395, where the three-fold classification of types of defects is accepted as prevalent in United States law.

departures from intended product designs,[62] that is, imperfections that cause products to fail to perform their intended functions.

Courts have interpreted "manufacturing defects" by inquiring objectively into how a product ought to work and what the defect in the complaint pertains to. Product defects in terms of manufacturing defects also include failure to warn of certain dangers in using the product, or failure to provide sufficient information about the construction of the product, as part of a product defect. Design defects, however, are regarded separately.

Under United States law, in marketing products, a commercial manufacturer or seller is required to provide necessary instructions regarding proper use and warn of hidden risks in using the products. In failing to do so, the seller may be liable for supplying a defective product even if the product in question is free from manufacturing defects and even if the product design is not unreasonably dangerous. Comment (j) to Section 402A of the Restatement (Third) of Torts: Product Liability regards a seller's failure to give directions or a warning as "unreasonably dangerous". It seems that the Restatement adopts a negligent standard whereby a seller might be exempted from giving a warning about the product if the product is only dangerous or potentially so. As a general rule, the Restatement does not subject a product seller to liability for failing to warn or instruct regarding obvious and generally known risks.

This was, however, not certain in Chinese law, but the case of *Zhang Jieting* v. *Toyota Automobile Co. Ltd.* seems to illustrate that Chinese law would regard as a manufacturing defect a failure in instructions or description of the product to alert end users of risks.[63]

While driving home, the plaintiff, Zhang Jieting, crashed his Celica convertible into the south wall of Qinghua University. Zhang's car was designed and sold for the American market and was equipped in accordance with the United States Vehicle Safety Standards, including a driver's side air bag. The air bag did not open upon impact and Zhang sustained serious head injuries and subsequent memory loss. The plaintiff initiated a lawsuit in the Beijing Haidian District People's Court in 1996, demanding compensation from the Japanese automobile company for his injuries. Toyota argued that the car sold to the plaintiff was built in line with China's Vehicle Safety

62 Restatement (Third) of Torts: Product Liability, Section 2(a).

63 *China Trials and Cases Collection* (China People's Public Security University Press, 1996) at pp. 224–228.

Technology Requirements, which do not require the manufacturer to install a driver's side air bag. Therefore, there was no defect. The defendant also pointed out that the car's manual clearly stated that any warranty on the car was only applicable to the United States and Canada and, therefore, the company would not be liable to the victim.[64] The court ultimately ordered Toyota to compensate the plaintiff for medical and hospital fees of RMB 13,685.75 and to pay the lawyer's fee for the plaintiff in the amount of RMB 410. The plaintiff's RMB 0.99-million claim for psychological losses was rejected.

Under United States law, this is a straightforward product defect — the airbag did not do what it was supposed to do and no warning was attached. However, as the defendant argued, the Chinese law concerned did not require the installment of an airbag in the car. Therefore, the issue must turn on a different basis, that is, whether the lack of information that the airbag is not installed constituted a product defect. The court held that the instructions accompanying the car did not include certain vital information or sufficient warnings regarding malfunctioning of the car (or its parts) and that constituted a "defect" in the car. The case may, therefore, support the principle that the manufacturer must provide adequate instructions and other product information to ensure that the consumer can use a product safely.

Under Chinese law, however, it is not clear how much information provided by the manufacturer would be regarded as adequate. Can a manufacturer escape liability if it places a catch-all warning on the products? For example, a drug manufacturer includes a warning in or with the pill dispenser: "Do Not Take This Drug Without Your Doctor's Continued Supervision". In China, such a warning may be sufficient but, in the United States, this is unlikely to be allowed by the courts.[65] An overly broad but practically useless warning should not automatically preclude the manufacturer or distributor's liability.

Failure to warn resulting in strict liability under American law has evolved from negligence liability to a greater extent than strict liability for "pure" manufacturing or design-defects-type liability. Unlike a manufacturing or design defect, which can be evaluated without

64 It seems that the two parties mainly focused on the disclaimer clauses in the consumer manual rather than the inherent manufacturing defect in the product.

65 However, in America, such a warning does not give a manufacturer any leeway: *MacDonald* v. *Ortho Pharmaceutical Corp.* 394 Mass. 131, 475 N.E.2d 65 cert. denied, 794 U.S. 920 (1985).

reference to the conduct of the manufacturer, the determination of a warning defect must refer to a manufacturer's conduct and intent. The manufacturer's knowledge or the fact that he should have known of the risk is a prerequisite for strict liability. However, as distinct from negligence, plaintiffs do not need to prove carelessness but, rather, that the knowledge could have been accessible to the manufacturer or supplier and it was not conveyed. These basic rules could be useful in clarifying Chinese legal ambiguity in understanding manufacturing defects as a result of failure to warn or convey necessary information pertaining to risks in construction or use.

As regards design defects, product liability law in the United States draws a line so that aggrieved users of defective designs may not seek a remedy under product liability law. A design defect may be a flawed design, which causes the product to fail to perform its intended function. A design defect may also be the failure of an expressly warranted design, where it is warranted by the seller that the product will perform safely and not cause injuries.[66] Sometimes, a defective design may be regarded as a manufacturing defect in the context of product malfunction.[67] However, the majority of design defects involve disappointed expectations or breach of warranty, and an action would only lie in contract for the recovery of such expectation losses. An action in tort may only be brought for a design defect in limited circumstances.

The United States courts have framed a test to see if the type of design defect involved would preclude the plaintiff from proceeding or allow him to proceed with a tortious action after all. This tortious action is different from a strict product liability action, but does justice to the individual injured plaintiff in some cases. The "open and

66 *Baxter* v. *Ford Motor Co.*, 168 Wash. 456, 12 P.2d 409 (1932).

67 Section 3(b) of the Restatement (Third) of Torts: Product Liability recognizes this point by stating that a product design occasionally causes the product to malfunction in a manner identical to that which would ordinarily be caused by a manufacturing defect. To most laymen, as well as most legal professionals, manufacturing and design defects might not be easy to distinguish. Some scholars may think that if a product is defective in design, the entire product line is flawed in the same way, not just the individual product. A particular product may be made as the designer intended it to be made, but the product was poorly (that is, negligently) designed with too much risk, which could have been avoided through use of a superior design. However, technically speaking, it is not that important to make a clear distinction since, in whatever category, the defendant shall be liable for defects.

obvious" test is often used.[68] This test is drawn from the roots of negligence law and ascertains whether a manufacturer has exercised a certain degree of care in his design so as to avoid any unreasonable risk of harm to anyone who it is reasonably foreseeable would be, or is likely to be, exposed to the danger. If the defect is obvious, the manufacturer fails to adhere to its "duty of care".

Some courts also allow a tortious action for design defects if the defect is "unreasonably dangerous". This standard is somewhat analogous to the Uniform Commercial Code's warranty of fitness and merchantability. This test is consistent with the legislative purpose in drafting Section 402A of the Restatement (Second) of Torts, which regards "unreasonably dangerous" as a means of confining the application of strict tort liability to an article that is "dangerous to an extent beyond that which would be contemplated by the ordinary consumer who purchases it, with the ordinary knowledge common to the community as to its characteristics". Major factors in determining "unreasonably dangerous design" include:

> ". . . the gravity of the danger posed by the challenged design, the likelihood that such danger would occur, the mechanical feasibility of a safer alternative design, the financial cost of an improved design, and the adverse consequences to the product and to the consumer that would result from an alternative design . . .".[69]

In comparison, in China, there is hardly any developed jurisprudence with regard to design defects and other defects actionable under a general regime of tort instead of strict liability in product liability. This is surprising considering that the understanding of "substandard" in the Civil Law may allow greater judicial discretion in compensating aggrieved consumers, and the scope of "defect" in the Product Quality Law also allows for wide judicial interpretation and development. Instead, one can see the over-reliance of courts upon the lack or otherwise of State certification of quality in determining the presence of a "defect", which would further impede the development of the courts' interpretation of "defect". The level of sophistication in Chinese jurisprudence in defining the scope of product

---

68 *Dreisonstock* v. *Volkswagenwerk, A.G.*, 489 F.2d 1066 (4th Cir. 1974); *Height* v. *Kawasaki Heavy Industries*, 461 A.2d 757 (N.J. Super. 1983).

69 *Barker* v. *Lull Engineering Co.* 573 P.2d 443 (Cal. 1978).

liability is still rather basic, and this may be viewed in a wider context. The courts' cautious approach may be due to their position in the legal system, that is, that a constitutional understanding of the role of the courts is not yet fully developed in China.

However, the relative superiority of legal sophistication in the United States in classifying the different types of product defects and determining the different causes of action available is due to the predominant need for private law enforcement of civil rights in relation to faulty products. Where private litigation is concerned, an adversarial system requires a refined ferreting out of what is a right and what is not. Thus, private litigants have provided the landscape, with relatively little State intervention, for judicial articulation of the scope of various rights and appropriate causes of action in the United States. The more protective framework in the Chinese legal system consisting of administrative and criminal elements of enforcement would perhaps mitigate the need for such development of sophisticated case law jurisprudence, as the social need for consumer protection could still be met by direct State enforcement. However, it remains to be seen if the growth of a maturing consumer public in China may also bring about growth in private litigation, and thus a need for judicial interpretation to be improved. Moreover, trade between the two jurisdictions may result in legal convergence, and the administrative mechanisms may be only a transitory way of combating product defects.

Damages

Compensation

Upon proof of causation of injury or disease by a product defect, the victim is entitled to compensation so that he can be restored to his pre-injury condition. Although the subject of compensation presents relatively few theoretical problems, it is always a contentious issue, both in China and the United States, where the plaintiffs complain of inadequacy of compensation, while manufacturers and suppliers are afraid of over-compensation. In the language of United States lawyers, compensatory damages include damages that are awarded to compensate for pain and suffering and other emotional harm, as well as damages that compensate for out-of-pocket expenses. Basically, this is the same as the term used in China. However, for convenience, "compensation" here is divided into four parts for a more detailed discussion. As a general rule, in order to be recompensable, the expense must be reasonably related to the defendant's conduct.

As to medical expenses, the United States courts support a wide range of items, such as doctor's bills, X-rays and hospital bills. In some cases, psychiatric care is also an allowable item of medical expense.[70] In addition, the plaintiff ordinarily must take reasonable steps to mitigate the injuries.[71] A limitation upon the recovery of medical expenses is that the expenses must be reasonably necessary for treatment and reasonable in amount. Usually, attorney fees are fixed by the party and the attorney prior to the suit on a certain percentage basis. In some cases, after negotiation, a certain amount of attorney fees can be decided.

The Chinese Product Quality Law reiterates basic principles on compensation originally found in the Civil Law. Losses recognized by the Civil Law include medical expenses, nursing costs during the treatment period, loss of income due to absence from work and disabled persons' living allowance where the product defect is deemed to have caused physical injury, for example, the victim is handicapped or suffers a loss of a certain physical function as a result of bodily injury. If the defective product causes death, additional losses, such as funeral expenses, death compensation (to the family of the deceased) and necessary living expenses for the dependents of the deceased, are also recoverable.[72] In the case of property damage caused by a defective product, the defendant must either restore the plaintiff's property to its original condition or pay compensation at the market rate for the damage, as well as compensation for other major losses, including indirect economic loss.

The Product Quality Law does not provide any specific guidance on the calculation of compensation other than the broad outlines found in the Civil Law, that is, the principles of reasonableness, legality and fairness. When reviewing a plaintiff's claim, Chinese courts must take these points into consideration. In certain circumstances, the courts will reject an unreasonable claim for indirect damage, as

70 *Browning* v. *United States*, 361 F. Supp. 17 (E.D. Pa. 1973).

71 *Aisole* v. *Dean*, 574 So. 2d 1248 (La. 1991).

72 Supreme People's Court's Legal Interpretation of the Civil Law, Part V; Product Quality Law 2000, Article 44.

the following case demonstrates.[73] The plaintiff, Ms. Hu, had her hair colored by the defendant, the Hua An Hairdresser Centre. The next day, she developed a rash on her face and head. Hu requested that the defendant compensate her medical fees, transportation costs, loss of income and nutrition expenses. The request for nutrition expenses was rejected because the court, relying on an opinion from the hospital, found that a skin allergy patient does not need special nutrition during the course of medical treatment.

The types of expenses recoverable under United States and Chinese law for physical injury and consequential losses due to product defects are generally similar. Both United States and Chinese law allow recovery for impairment of the ability to earn. United States courts have set out some specific factors for determining the size of the award for diminished earning capacity. Such factors include the plaintiff's basic earning capacity, the percentage by which the plaintiff's earning capacity has been diminished, the duration of the disability and the life expectancy of the plaintiff. However, it is difficult to ascertain the Chinese courts' method for calculating diminution. The courts often award an amount on a case-by-case basis. However, some rational analysis of the amount to be awarded was carried out in Ms. Hu's case above, and it remains to be seen if litigation would further help courts in clarifying their reasoning.

Emotional Distress

It may be reasonable to expect that, in addition to losses resulting from physical injury, compensation may be claimed for mental distress, that is, nervous shock. It has been estimated that, in American product liability cases, recovery for intangible harm accounts for nearly fifty per cent of the total recovery.[74] Recovery for mental suffering associated with bodily disfigurement may also be includable as an element of pain and suffering.[75] However, pain and suffering is the most difficult element of recovery to measure. From a purely monetary point of view, recovery for psychological injury (non-economic loss) has been of prime importance in product liability cases.

---

73 *Hu Huijun* v. *Hua An Hairdresser Centre*; *China Trials and Cases Collection* (China People's Public Security University Press, 1992) at pp. 619–622.

74 American Law Institute, *Reporters Study — Enterprise Responsibility for Personal Injury* (1991) at p. 201.

75 *Kravenas* v. *Algonquin Township*, 13 Ill. App. 3d 1000, 301 N.E.2d 490 (1973).

United States courts have long permitted recovery of damages for pain and suffering and do not call it emotional distress. Awards for purely mental anguish apart from the physical pain associated with personal injuries have been allowed, but they are more controversial. Chinese law only awards compensation for emotional distress which is caused by physical injuries. Purely mental anguish, without any physical pain or suffering, is not generally recoverable under Chinese law. In some cases, however, such as defamation, Chinese courts will consider and award some compensation to the victim even without physical pain or injury.

Neither the Civil Law nor the Product Quality Law addresses recovery of compensation for "psychological" injury. Chinese academics are also not agreed on the legal position in China. Some argue that there should be no compensation for psychological loss because Article 120 of the Civil Law restricts compensation for mental distress to injury to name, portraiture, fame and honor. Although Article 98 of the Civil Law states that the right to life and health should be protected, the definition of health is not clear. Others argue that there should be compensation for psychological loss because, in product liability cases, the victims always suffer from pain as well as property damage.[76]

It is within the discretion of Chinese courts whether to allow such a claim. The court has the right to determine how much the tortfeasor should compensate the victim's losses based on factors such as the degree of fault, details of the tort, consequence and effect.[77] Nevertheless, Chinese courts are loath to order compensation for distress or similar psychological injuries. In the *Gao Pingping* case above, the parties reached an agreement through mediation whereby the defendant would compensate the plaintiff in the amount of 2,350 yuan for her economic and "psychological" loss due to her pain and suffering. Thus, such losses may be recovered as part of a lump sum settlement, including settlement for physical injuries. The recognition of mental anguish as a separate head of loss is still fraught with obstacles.

Many product liability cases involve psychological reactions to deleterious substances in food and drink and long-term psychological or personality changes. Thus, courts will have to face the fact that

---

76 For a detailed discussion, refer to Liu Shiguo, *Study on Compensation for Damage in Modern Tort* (Law Press, February 1998) at pp. 161–177.

77 Opinions on Implementing the General Principles of Civil Law (Trial), Article 150; Explanation on the Issues of Judging Cases Concerning Fame, Article 10.

plaintiffs wish to claim for mental anguish. The difficulties faced by the courts are, firstly, the circumstances in which the courts will be able to recognize that there is mental distress; secondly, whether recovery for emotional distress alone is allowable in a case where there is no accompanying physical injury; and, thirdly, how losses arising from mental distress are to be computed.

Looking at the United States, where claims for mental distress have succeeded, the United States courts do not appear to adopt objective standards when deciding whether there is mental suffering caused by defective products. In the case of *Kroger Co.* v. *Beck*,[78] the defendant argued that there was no specific evidence of the damage. The court relied on certain facts provided by the plaintiff and the testimony provided by the plaintiff's husband that the plaintiff had suffered great anxiety because she strongly reacted to the incident by pulling everything off the table and having nightmares about the incident. The court then drew the conclusion that recovery is allowed where the physical effects that could be produced by the foreign object produced the emotional result as well. The court rejected the defendant's argument that there must be showing of fatal or deleterious consequence. It appears that the United States courts are sympathetic towards the victim and may or may not require objective medical diagnosis in order to award losses for mental anguish. Furthermore, the courts have universally allowed mental distress as a legitimate damage item where the distress is caused by or accompanied by illness or physical injury.[79]

In Missouri, plaintiffs no longer need to prove physical harm in order to recover for emotional distress, but the distress must be "medically diagnosable" or "medically significant". The latter may be looser than "medically diagnosable". The general trend of not barring emotional distress claims may also be seen in the wider context of tort law development in the United States. In the United States, one can claim for emotional distress caused by witnessing another's pain.[80]

---

78 Court of Appeals of Indiana, 1978, 176 Ind.App. 202, 375 N.E.2d 640. In this case, the plaintiff bought a prepackaged sirloin steak from Kroger grocery store. When she ate the steak, she felt a sharp pain in the back of her throat. She yanked the steak out and found an inch-long piece of metal which was the tip end of a large hypodermic needle used for injecting animals.

79 R. Dickerson, *Product Liability and the Food Consumer* (1951).

80 Michael K. Steenson, "The Anatomy of Emotional Distress Claims in Minnesota", 19 *William Mitchell Law Review* 1 (Winter 1993).

Chinese courts have not yet ventured greatly into developing a coherent body of law to determine the circumstances for recovery and ascertaining the amount of damages. Perhaps with the maturing of the consumer public, such claims cannot be avoided by the courts for long, and it is hoped that a coherent body of law will be developed to ascertain when and how recovery for mental anguish would be allowed in product liability, whether it be led by legislation or judicial refinement.

In the United States, amounts of awards are usually determined by juries and, in some states, the plaintiff's attorney is allowed to suggest a round figure in dollars for the plaintiff's pain for whatever time segment that attorney chooses.[81] This is then a starting point for the juries to work on. The mechanics of the amount allowed are not always articulated.

Pure Economic Loss

Pure economic loss refers to the loss of value of the product due to a product defect or financial loss caused to the plaintiff of a type unrelated to physical injury. As the strict liability in product liability law is premised on its tortious nature to protect the general public, redress for pure economic loss cannot fall within product liability.[82]

In China, civil liability is premised on damage to person or property. Civil rights include property rights, personal rights and economic interests. Can one, therefore, make an argument for recovery of pure economic loss? Unlike American[83] and British Common Law,[84] China's product liability regime applies more broadly and may include damage to a defective product itself. This is illustrated by the following case.[85]

Mr. Sun Yongxiang spent sixty yuan purchasing a piece of cloth from the Beijing Xuan Wu Men Nei Department Store and sent the cloth to a tailor to make two pairs of trousers. After wearing one of the pairs of trousers for only one week, the plaintiff discovered that the

81 *Duguay* v. *Gelinas*, 104 N.H. 182, 185–187, 182 A.2d 451, 453–454 (1962).

82 *Casa Clara Condominium Association, Inc.* v. *Charley Toppino & Sons, Inc.*, Supreme Court of Florida, 1993, 620 So.2d 1244.

83 *East River S.S. Corp.* v. *Transamerica Delaval, Inc.*, 106 S.Ct. 2295 (1986).

84 *D&F Estates Ltd.* v. *Church Commissioners for England* [1988] 2 All E.R. 992.

85 *China Trials and Cases Collection* (China People's Public Security University Press, 1994) at pp. 804–807.

trousers shrank. The plaintiff then sued the department store and demanded that the defendant bear civil liability. With the support of the local Consumers Association in Beijing, the defendant contended that it was only liable to refund the cost of the material and refused to compensate Mr. Sun for other losses, such as payment for the tailoring of the trousers and transportation costs incurred by the plaintiff between his home and the department store. However, the court upheld the plaintiff's claim based on the Product Quality Law.

This surprising phenomenon may be due to the fact that the concepts of "substandard" under the general civil law and that of "defect" under the Product Quality Law are yet insufficiently circumscribed by precedent interpretation and thus could include the situation where the product defect is a loss in value, being the product damage itself. Furthermore, as remedies under Chinese law are not pigeonholed into tortious or contractual, the absence of this Common Law framework has allowed a broader inquiry into whether a remedy is allowed under the law and, if so, there should be no further doctrinal impediment.

The recoverability of other types of pure economic loss, such as lost profits in tort, may also be possible. According to the Contract Law, compensation for breach of contract includes both losses actually caused by the breach of contract and profits that could have been obtained.[86] In the case below, an analogy with the Contract Law has been made to allow a tortious case to proceed towards recovery for lost profits, which is highly unusual.[87]

In November 1984, the defendant's Panamanian-registered vessel M.V. Agamemnon wrongfully dragged anchor while moored in the Huangpu River Shanghai Harbor, and thereby destroyed an underwater electricity cable. The power network was, therefore, cut off from a substation, a high voltage industrial zone and the seventh city south power generator station, which caused a power cut and damaged equipment at the substation, the high voltage industrial zone and the surrounding area. Fourteen factories stopped production, resulting in

86 Contract Law, Article 113, adopted by the Second Session of the Ninth National People's Congress on 15 March 1999 and effective from 1 October 1999. Article 113 also states that the profits that could have been obtained should not exceed the sum of the loss that the delinquent party had anticipated or should have anticipated when concluding the contract.

87 *Hangwu Company* v. *Shanghai Power Supply Bureau*, *Gazette of the Supreme People's Court of the People's Republic of China*, 20 March 1986, at p. 28.

a loss of profit to both the power generator station and the factories. The Shanghai Maritime Court held that, on the facts proven, the defendant's conduct was in breach of the Maritime Safety Law and awarded a total of 230,264 yuan damages for the cost of repairing the cable damaged by the anchor, for the damage to the equipment and for the loss of profits caused by the power cut. However, as the case is not a product quality case, it is uncertain if lost profits may be recovered under the Product Quality Law by analogy.

Punitive Damages

In the United States, an award of punitive damages for the victims of product liability is not unheard of. An award of punitive damages may serve as a deterrent to manufacturers who indulge in shoddy manufacturing and cause physical jeopardy to consumers. The rationale behind an award of punitive damages is essentially one of meeting the needs of social policy. Punitive damages awards were quite rare in product liability cases until the 1980s. However, they have been on the increase in both size and frequency. Usually, such awards are rendered in automotive litigation. Currently, they can be awarded in all product liability cases. Under United States law, the plaintiff, however, needs to prove aggravated wrongdoing, and not just the existence of a harmful defect or even simple negligence, in order to recover punitive damages. In short, there is no strict liability for punitive damages.

In the United States, punitive damages is a controversial issue. The commentators who support punitive damages hold the view that punitive damages are an appropriate remedy. Manufacturers have a powerful hold over the means of discovering and correcting product hazards. Therefore, manufacturers would, both from a desire to avoid liability and from a generalized sense of social responsibility, prudently use their resources to prevent excessively hazardous products from reaching or staying on the market.[88] In conclusion, the imposition of punitive damages is an effective legal tool to deter all manufacturers and suppliers from acting with disregard for the public interest and welfare. Overall, the major function of punitive damages is to punish manufacturers' gross misbehavior. Nonetheless, the use

88 Owen, "Punitive Damages in Product Liability Litigation", 74 Mich.L.Rev. 1258 (1976).

of punitive damages may not realize this purpose in the marketplace for a variety of complex reasons.

First, there is not a practicable and objective standard adopted in determining the application of punitive damages. Punitive damages should generally be awarded for outrageous conduct because of the defendant's evil motive or his recklessness. As a matter of law, it is important to have a finding of a guilty state of mind necessary for a punitive damages assessment. In assessing punitive damages, the trier of fact needs to consider a lot of factors, such as the character of the defendant's act, the nature and extent of the harm to the plaintiff that the defendant caused or intended to cause and the wealth of the defendant.[89] However, the determination of state of mind and "outrageous" behavior is technically difficult and subjective in practice.[90] The imposition of punitive damages may then be subject to judges' or juries' subjective judgment.

Second, a subjective judgment may cause an excessive punitive damages award and, therefore, result in over-punishment for the defendants and over-compensation for the plaintiffs. The courts may exert some control over the process of determining such awards, from discovery safeguards and pre-trial rulings to remittur or reversal on appeal. Courts are likely to be more cautious as to the threat of over-punishment from multiple awards for a single product mistake. One of the most perplexing problems for courts and juries has been the determination of appropriate amounts for punitive damages awards. Section 908(2) of the Restatement (Second) of Torts provides that punitive damages may be awarded for conduct that is outrageous because of the defendant's evil motive or his reckless indifference to the rights of others.

In assessing punitive damages, the trier of fact can properly consider the character of the defendant's act, the nature and extent of the harm to the plaintiff that the defendant caused or intended to cause and the wealth of the defendant. This widely accepted formulation is not very helpful in directing judges in calculating appropriate amounts for punitive damages awards. In addition, some courts and legislatures have taken other factors into account; for instance, the

89 Restatement (Second) of Torts, Section 908(2).

90 In the case of *Gryc* v. *Dayton-Hudson Corp.*, 1980, 297 N.W.2d 727, cert. denied, 449 US 921, 101 S.Ct. 320, 66 L.Ed.2d 149 (1980), the court pointed out that this test could not properly determine state of mind because of the manufacturer's compliance with the federal safety standard.

seriousness of the hazard to the public, the profitability of the marketing misconduct and the duration of both the improper marketing behavior and its cover-up.[91] Overall, these additional factors are only some perspectives relating to the three major factors stated in the Restatement (Second) of Torts.

In some cases, the ratio of punitive damages to compensatory damages has never exceeded 2:1 in California or 7:1 in any jurisdiction. However, in other cases, the ratio of the jury's award of punitive damages as against compensatory damages has been 20:1.[92] Excessive punitive damages can lead to undesirable economic and social consequences, particularly its negative effects upon the economy. Over-punishment may discourage product development, end the business life of a manufacturer and cause many innocent stockholders to suffer extinction of their investments for the sake of a single error.

Unlike the punitive damages award in the United States, Chinese law imposes the punitive element on errant manufacturers by means of regulatory or administrative penalties, or even criminal liability. This highlights the policy concern that there needs to be a public law element in enforcing product liability law, and building punitive damages into a largely private law type of enforcement in the United States is rather inconsistent with such a private law framework. The Chinese duality in product liability enforcement may acknowledge the public law element in utilizing administrative and criminal penalties, but may stifle the development of jurisprudence in the private law sphere, which may, arguably, from the United States experience, be seen as a more reliable social and legal force in translating social needs into legal enforcement. As regards this issue, there is probably no clear doctrinal or policy answer as to how product liability should be enforced.

Regulatory Penalties

The Product Quality Law provides an enforcement mechanism co-existent with private law enforcement in the form of regulatory penalties. Different monetary penalties are stipulated for different kinds of illegal behavior. Article 49 of the Product Quality Law

91 Owen, "Punitive Damages in Product Liability Litigation", 74 Mich.L.Rev. 1257, 1319 (1976).

92 *Vossler* v. *Richards Manufacturing Co.*, California Court of Appeal, 1983, 143 Cal.App.3d 952, 192 Cal.Rptr. 219.

provides that if anyone produces or sells products that do not comply with State or industry standards for the safeguarding of health, personal safety or the safety of property, a fine equivalent to not less than the value of the illegally produced or sold products and not more than three times such value shall be imposed. Article 50 provides that where products are adulterated, improper elements mixed with products, spurious products passed off as genuine products, products of poor quality passed off as quality products or substandard products passed off as products that are up to standard, a fine of not less than fifty per cent of the value of the products manufactured or sold and not more than three times such value will be imposed.

Monetary penalties can also be imposed on other parties, such as transporters in the distribution chain. For instance, a fine of not less than fifty per cent of the illegal revenue and not more than three times such revenue will be imposed if anyone makes facilitating arrangements in terms of transportation, custody or storage in relation to the production or sale of products that he knows or ought to know to be products the production and/or sale of which is prohibited.[93]

Under certain circumstances, a product quality inspection institution or certification institution might be fined not less than RMB 50,000 and not more than RMB 100,000 if it is found to falsify inspection results or issues a sham certificate.[94]

Administrative Penalties

Administrative penalties, such as revocation of business licenses, are also provided in the Product Quality Law. If the product does not comply with government or industry standards and, therefore, damages consumers' health, personal safety or the safety of property, the following penalties may be imposed on the manufacturer and/or seller:

(1) The manufacturer/seller may be required to cease production;
(2) Confiscation of income from the substandard products;
(3) Fines of two to five times the income derived from the defective products; and
(4) Revocation of business license.

93 Product Quality Law, Article 61.

94 Product Quality Law, Article 57, which also provides that the leading personnel directly in charge and the other directly responsible personnel will be fined not less than RMB 10,000 and not more than RMB 50,000.

Criminal Penalties

According to the Product Quality Law, all manufacturers and sellers found in serious breach of product liability provisions will bear criminal liability. The Criminal Law,[95] as amended in 1997, provides the legal basis for criminal liability for the manufacture and sale of "fake" or "inferior" products.[96] Criminal liability is borne by the offending enterprise itself, persons in direct control of the enterprise and other directly responsible persons. Imprisonment or fines may also be imposed, depending on the circumstances. More severe sanctions, such as capital punishment or life imprisonment, may also be imposed, for example, for the manufacture and sale of counterfeit pharmaceuticals causing death or serious bodily harm.

The goals of punitive damages are to expose manufacturers' gross misconduct, punish manufacturers guilty of flagrant misbehavior and deter all manufacturers from acting with similar disregard for the public welfare. Technically, punitive damages are decided by the jury in the United States. However, there is no such jury system under the Chinese legal system. Punishment may, however, be better levied by State imposed penalties than punitive damages. The former may be more efficient in enforcement and highlights the underlying need in tort to incorporate some punitive elements that may not be sufficiently addressed in private law. The coincidence of State enforcement and private law enforcement is not incredulous. In many jurisdictions, securities regulations for insider trading or breaches of disclosure in prospectuses attract both a civil law action by investors and administrative penalties levied by securities regulators.[97] Excessively high punitive damages not limited by statute may also bring financial ruin to relatively infant manufacturers and suppliers, and that may be seriously harmful to China's economy. In this sense, administrative and criminal penalties can better serve to maximize compliance with the rules of law in China.

---

95 Criminal Law, adopted by the National People's Congress on 1 July 1979, effective as of 1 January 1980, revised on 17 March 1996 and revised again on 14 March 1997, the latest revisions being effective as of 1 October 1997.

96 For example, the manufacture and sale of fake pharmaceuticals, toxic food or substandard fertilizer: Criminal Law, Articles 140 and 150.

97 For example, the Corporations Act in Australia, the Securities and Futures Act in Singapore and the Financial Services and Markets Act in the United Kingdom.

Some may question the appropriateness of a criminal penalty system in product liability. The Chinese criminal penalty system is largely based on the manufacturers' criminal intention. In fact, it may be superior to the vague concepts of "malice", "reckless" or "willful and wanton", which are articulated by United States courts to justify a punitive damages award. Of course, a criminal penalty system might be arguably too severe to manufacturers and suppliers. However, in China, almost all important economic laws incorporate criminal liability, which is an essential characteristic of not only a centrally planned economy, but also a legal system that is developed with the imposition of mainly State measures and regulatory muscle.

Defenses

Contributory Fault

It is estimated that over two-thirds of all injuries related to consumer products have nothing to do with the design or the performance of the product, but relate to the misuse or abuse of the product.[98] When the consumer knew or ought to have known about the product defect or misused the product, the manufacturer may raise contributory fault as a defense.

In the United States, many states have enacted product liability "reform" statutes providing various defenses based on a plaintiff's misconduct. The conduct is sometimes defined in terms of "reasonable care", which effectively allows contributory negligence to be raised as a defense. Arizona's statute, for example, states a defense for use of the product contrary to its instructions or warnings "if the injured person knew or with the exercise of reasonable or diligent care should have known of such instructions or warnings".[99] However, the test is not whether the plaintiff actually knew of the danger confronting him, but whether, in the exercise of reasonable care, he should have known that he was in a situation of peril.[100]

The Chinese Civil Law provides that the tortfeasor's civil liability may be reduced in part or in full if the victim's failure to exercise

98 Byington, "Consumer Product Safety Commission", *Trial Magazine* (February 1978) at p. 25.
99 *Product Liability Reports* (CCH) Paragraph 90, 312.
100 *Budzinski* v. *Harris*, 189 S.E.2d 372, 375 (Va. 1972).

reasonable care for his own safety was a contributing cause of his own injury.[101] In many of the published cases, the defendants argued that the loss was partially caused by the plaintiff's or a third party's fault or negligence. For instance, in the concrete beam case discussed above, the defendant attributed the accident to the plaintiff's misconduct in dealing with the concrete beams. In the *Xu Yan Fireworks* case above, the defendant argued that the child's parents should also assume partial responsibility for failing to provide adequate supervision of their son.[102] Contributory fault must be proved by the defendant, as is illustrated in the following case.[103]

The plaintiff bought five bottles of Shanghai Beer (a brand name), produced by the Shanghai Beer Co. Ltd. in August 1993. The next morning, a beer bottle suddenly exploded, causing serious injuries to the plaintiff's leg. The plaintiff brought a suit against the manufacturer for compensation in the total amount of 8,325.50 yuan, including 2,000 yuan for medical treatment.

The defendant argued that:

(1) The beer bottles were manufactured in compliance with the national standard (GB 4544–84) by another factory under sub-contract; and
(2) Saccharomycete in the beer was sterilized through pasteurization before the beer was put into the bottle, which showed that the quality was up to standard.

The defendant further argued that, since improper usage by the plaintiff could not be excluded from the possible causes of the explosion, the defendant should not assume civil liability. The trial court rejected the defendant's argument on the grounds that the defendant failed to provide either relevant evidence supporting its assertion or a written appraisal as to the product quality. The court, therefore, held that the defendant was liable.

In practice, however, Chinese courts generally reject the defense of contributory fault in product liability cases if raised by the defendant. It is uncertain why this defense is so sparingly allowed, but there are some cases which exempt the seller's or manufacturer's

101 General Principles of Civil Law, Article 131.

102 *China Trials and Cases Collection* (China People's Public Security University Press, 1992) at pp. 637–641.

103 *Chinese Trials and Cases Collection* (China People's Public Security University Press, 1994) at pp. 807–809.

liability. For example, a manufacturer producing canned food was not required to bear civil liability when a consumer realized that food had passed its use-by date, but nonetheless ate it and suffered food poisoning.[104] Chinese courts also do not place emphasis upon the plaintiff's knowledge, experience, background, age[105] and behavior in determining whether the plaintiff is at fault. More theoretically, the courts need to look into foreseeability, which means that a man ought to have foreseen in a general way consequences of a certain kind. It will not avail him to say that he could not foresee the precise course or the full extent of the consequences, being of that kind, which in fact happened.[106]

The United States law, however, utilizes an approach of comparative negligence in strict product liability, which has never been seriously discussed in Chinese law. Under the strict liability theory, the importance of "comparative negligence" or "comparative fault" should have waned somewhat since, ironically, strict product liability is no longer connected with manufacturers' or suppliers' negligence or fault. Rather, the rationale of modern strict liability is based on public interest or public policy, which demands that responsibility be fixed whenever it will most effectively reduce the hazards to life and health inherent in defective products in the marketplace. This understanding is consistent with Section 402A and its comments, which are the basic text for modern product liability. Section 402A deals with liability that is not based on the negligence of the manufacturer or seller, but on strict liability. Contributory negligence might not be an applicable defense when such negligence consists only of failing to discover the defect in the product. Partly because of this interpretation, some courts have refused to allow any defense of contributory negligence.[107]

The United States courts may also hold that plaintiffs who misuse a product — use it for a purpose neither intended nor foreseeable by the defendant — may be barred from recovery. It is a difficult question as to whether "product misuse" should be treated as a damage-reducing factor rather than as a total bar. Some courts and

104 Wang Liming (ed.), *Civil Law — Torts* (People's University Press, 1996) at p. 434.

105 In *Porter* v. *United Steel & Wire Co.* 436 F.Supp. 1376 (N.D.Iowa 1977), the court ruled that a plaintiff was too young to be contributorily negligent and that the parents' negligence in failing to instruct or supervise the child would not be imputed to her.

106 Harper and James, *Torts 20.5(6)* (1956).

107 *Melia* v. *Ford Motor Co.*, 534 F.2d 795 (8th Cir. 1976).

legislatures have only reduced and not barred a plaintiff's recovery in the case of misuse. The plaintiff's damages are only recoverable when the plaintiff makes "normal and proper use" of the defendant's products.[108] Furthermore, the United States courts distinguish between "foreseeable" and "unforeseeable" misuses. As a general rule, injuries produced by unforeseeable misuse should remain outside the scope of recovery, since manufacturers would appear to have no duty to prevent them.[109] Nevertheless, in some cases, the courts have ruled to the contrary.[110]

The adoption of a pure form of comparative negligence reduces but does not prevent a plaintiff's recovery. In some cases, the doctrine of comparative negligence is labeled as "comparative causation", by which the parties' negligence is to be compared and the equitable apportionment or allocation of loss is ultimately decided.[111] However, a plaintiff who knows a product is in a dangerous condition and proceeds disregarding this known danger may not recover at all for resulting injuries based on his assumption of risk.[112] The key here is that a plaintiff must voluntarily expose himself to a known and appreciated danger.

Comment (n) to Section 402A of the Restatement (Second) of Torts 1965 sets forth three elements that must be shown before a plaintiff can be barred from recovery. The defendant must show that:

(1) The plaintiff himself actually knew and appreciated the particular risk or danger created by the defect;
(2) The plaintiff voluntarily encountered the risk while realizing the danger; and
(3) The plaintiff's decision to voluntarily encounter the known risk was unreasonable.

Usually, the third factor might be ignored in practice. While seemingly theoretical, the reasonableness of any decision to encounter a known danger is significant. Moreover, the court is more concerned with the apparent reasonableness or unreasonableness, rather than

---

108 *Daly* v. *General Motors Corp.* 575 P.2d 1162 (Cal. 1978).

109 *States* v. *R.D. Werner Co.*, 799 P.2d 427 (Colo.Ct.App.1990).

110 *Mauch* v. *Manufacturers Sales & Services, Inc.*, 345 N.W.2d 338, 348 (N.D. 1984).

111 In some cases, comparative fault is applicable: *Busch* v. *Busch Const., Inc.*, 262 N.W.2d 377 (Minn. 1977).

112 This doctrine was contained in Comment (n) to Section 402A of the Restatement (Second) of Torts 1965.

the actual reasonableness of the decision to do so. Whether a user has assumed the risk of using a product known to be dangerously defective is fundamentally a subjective test, in the sense that it is his knowledge, understanding and appreciation of the danger that must be assessed, rather than that of the reasonably prudent person.[113]

The factors of the user's age, experience, intelligence, actual or conscious knowledge and understanding, as well as the obviousness of the defect and the danger it poses, will all be relevant to the determination of the issue. For instance, an intelligent adult familiar with the product is more likely to be found to have assumed a risk than an inexperienced adult or child.[114] Knowledge of the general hazard involved in operating a product will not support the assumption of risk defense.[115]

Chinese law does not expressly adopt the defenses of assumption of risk and misuse. As discussed below, assumption of risk, closely allied with an open and obvious defect, might be linked with and reflected in some Chinese statutory defenses. To a certain extent, the defense of "misuse" is linked with the doctrine of "comparative negligence", whereby the consumer is at fault or is negligent in misusing the product while, on the other hand, the manufacturer might be liable for defects or failure to warn. These defenses may, however, be raised as evidence towards proof of the defense of contributory fault in China.

Thus, although the defense of contributory fault is accepted both in the United States and China, the defense in China is less developed in jurisprudence and is also not commonly allowed. This may perhaps be due to the Chinese courts' unwillingness to apply a defense to strict liability, as their understanding of strict liability would be very much a Chinese understanding of compulsory and serious that has remained in the Chinese psyche through eras of imperial rule and decades of centralized authority. The lack of a sophisticated understanding of "strict liability" as it would be understood in Common Law as only going to not inquiring into the mental state of the defendant, is instrumental in the flawed application of law by Chinese courts. Furthermore, some Chinese judges forget to consider the applicability of the general defense of contributory fault when dealing with the Product Quality Law, as the defense is found in the

113 Restatement (Second) of Torts, Section 496D, Comment (c).

114 *Mackowick* v. *Westinghouse Elec. Corp.*, 541 A.2d 749 (Pa. Super. Ct. 1988).

115 *Heil Co.* v. *Grant*, Court of Civil Appeals of Texas, 1976, 534 S.W.2d 916.

General Principles of Civil Law. This may be a problem with training and expertise, but it may also be a problem highlighting the piecemeal fabric of the Chinese legal system at present, incorporating the Civil Law tradition, which should be premised on comprehensive general principles, but is undermined by a gradual piecemeal Common Law approach that introduces specific laws to deal with specific issues.

Statutory Defenses

In addition to contributory fault, the Product Quality Law also provides three statutory defenses. The first defense is that the product has not been put into commercial circulation.[116] This defense is consistent with the legal definition of "product" in the Product Quality Law. This was clearly illustrated in a case[117] where the plaintiff used a cosmetic which was stolen by her boyfriend from the research center of the defendant manufacturer. The cosmetic caused serious injury to the plaintiff's skin. The plaintiff brought the lawsuit to the court and asked for compensation. The defendant argued that the cosmetic used by the plaintiff was under trial and not in circulation. The court upheld the defendant's argument and rejected the plaintiff's claim on the ground that the product was "not put into circulation".

However, even samples circulated by a university may constitute commercial circulation. This is illustrated by a case[118] in which the plaintiffs, comprising 2,004 peasants in Hubei province, bought a total of 5,675 kilograms of GER-1 seeds from the defendant, the Hunan Agricultural University, in early 1994. In October of the same year, the peasants only harvested 200 kg of rice per mu, much lower than the average production capacity of 450 kg per mu. The defendant denied liability and argued that the seeds were samples only and that the provision of the seeds was just for promotional purposes and not for sale. Moreover, when the peasants used the seeds, the University sent students to teach the peasants the appropriate method. The University also argued that the main reason for the low production was that the climate in the relevant area was unsuitable for the seeds.

116 Product Quality Law, Article 29(1).

117 Liu Wenqi, *Comparative Study on Legal System of Product Liability* (Law Publishing House, 1997) at p.168.

118 *Chinese Trials and Cases Collection* (China People's Public Security University Press, 1996) at pp. 265–270.

In its ruling, the trial court rejected the defendant's argument because the University's sales office had signed a sales contract for the seeds with the peasants' representative. Further, the seed was developed by a professor at the same university without passing the necessary approval and examination as stipulated by the Regulations on the Administration of Seeds.[119] The sales contract constituted sufficient evidence to prove the commercial relationship between the parties.

Functionally, the defense of "not in commercial circulation" may be justified as an "assumption of risk". Since the manufacturer or seller has not placed the products in the marketplace, the user should be aware of possible or foreseeable defects therein, and to consume or use such products anyway may indicate that the user has decided to assume the risks involved.

The second defense is that the defect causing the damage did not exist at the time the product was put into circulation,[120] which is similar to "not defective when supplied" under the European Product Liability Directive.[121] This defense exempts the manufacturer from liability if he can show that when the product was supplied, there was no defect. The consumer should not be allowed to raise an issue of product liability for subsequently developed imperfections that may be due to wear and tear, as is illustrated by a case where the plaintiff bought a bicycle pump. One year later, when the plaintiff used the pump, the spring in the pump shot out and injured the plaintiff's eye. The court refused the plaintiff's claim against the manufacturer of the pump because the plaintiff ignored the fact that a nut had become loose. The court issued the ruling on the ground that there was no defect in the product when it was put into circulation.[122] In order to use this defense, the manufacturer should be able to prove that warnings, use-by dates and instructions were issued to the end users at the relevant time.

---

119 Regulations on the Administration of Seeds, promulgated on 13 March 1989 by the State Council.

120 Product Quality Law, Article 29(2).

121 Council Directive 85/374/EEC of 25 July 1985, OJ L 210/29, Article 3(3). The reason China transplanted some legal terms from Europe rather than the United States may be that the European Union is using codes and statutes that are easy to "copy". American statutes seem different from those of Civil Law countries in the sense of the use of not particularly user-friendly cross-references and "exceptions".

122 Yang Lixin (ed.) *Compensation in Torts* (Law Press, 1997) at p. 116.

The third defense, similar to undiscoverable latent danger or the development risk defense in the European Directive, is that the level of science and technology at the time the product or technology was put into use was not sufficient to detect the existence of the defect.[123] The manufacturer may escape liability if the defect existed when the product was put into circulation, but could not be detected at that time.

Under United States law, manufacturers might be exempted from liability for unavoidably unsafe products. Some products, with the present state of human knowledge, are quite incapable of being made safe for their intended and ordinary use. This is very common in the field of drugs. Also, the courts have accepted the defense of "undiscovered danger".[124] The rationale for this defense is the recognition of the limitations on human skill and knowledge in the scientific community existing during the specified period and the encouragement of the development of the state of the art.

It should be noted that Chinese statute law has not adopted the component defense under the European Product Liability Directive, whereby component manufacturers can escape liability for defects in a final product that are not attributable to a defect in a component part. In practice, however, Chinese courts may analyze this issue as a matter of causation. If a claim is made for damages, the loss must have been caused by the violation of an enumerated right. In the case of breach of contract or tort, the plaintiff generally has the burden to prove that the defect has specifically caused his loss or injury. In product liability cases, however, the burden of proof shifts to the defendant, who must provide compelling evidence that the product is not defective.

General Defenses and Contractual Exclusion of Liability

It is a feature of the Civil Law tradition that general defenses against civil liability are codified. Thus, it appears that the six general defenses under the General Principles of Civil Law may apply to a product liability action under the strict liability regime of the Product Quality Law. These are:

(1) The performance of a duty, such as a doctor performing emergency surgery, or where a fireman destroys property in order to save other property from destruction by fire;

123 Product Quality Law, Article 29(3).

124 *Beshada* v. *Johns-Manville Products Corp.*, 90 N.J. 191, 447 A.2d 539 (1982).

(2) The exercise of a right, such as the right to evict an unlawful tenant;
(3) Legitimate self-defense;[125]
(4) The avoidance of difficulty in an emergency;
(5) The consent of the victim that is, *volenti non fit injuria*; and
(6) The relevant time limit for bringing a claim has lapsed.[126]

As discussed earlier in relation to contributory fault, it is yet uncertain whether the Chinese courts understand strict liability as akin to "absolute liability", such that defenses are seldom allowed. However, if Chinese courts accept the applicability of the general defenses to product liability actions, then it may be said that a similar understanding of strict liability exists in both the Chinese and American contexts, except that the source of law relating to defenses is different. Being a Common Law jurisdiction, defenses against product liability actions in the United States have been created in a piecemeal manner by statute or case law. However, as China has also adopted the Common Law style of specific defenses under the Product Quality Law, it is envisaged that the general defenses would be relied upon only in the most arguable cases, where a defense cannot be framed under the specific law.

Conclusion

This chapter has dealt with several substantive aspects of product liability in the United States and China.[127] In both jurisdictions, a major similarity is in the use of strict liability to pin down manufacturers and suppliers in product liability. The use of specific legislation also reflects that the need for product liability arose out of similar contexts, in a growing industrialized State with an explosion of production and consumption, and, thus, the social need to protect consumer

125 The Product Quality Law provides the defendant with three major defenses, which are similar to those in the European Communities Product Liability Directive of 1985.

126 The statute of limitations is four years from the delivery of the goods: Uniform Commercial Code, Section 2–725. The tort limitation may be shorter, but is likely to run only from the time of the plaintiff's injury or perhaps discovery of that injury.

127 Some procedural aspects, such as the availability of contingency fee arrangements in the United States, and thus the proliferation of class actions, may have been crucial to the development of United States jurisprudence in this area as they facilitate litigation.

safety in a maturing consumer society. It may yet be seen if trade increases between the United States and China after China's accession to the WTO, which may result in legal convergence in this area.

As strict liability is the exception rather than the norm in establishing legal liability, the scope of product liability would have to be clearly defined so that manufacturers and suppliers are aware of their potential liabilities. The area of defining the scope of "product" or "product defect" is relatively more developed in the judicial interpretation in United States courts than the judicial interpretation in Chinese courts. This may be due to the longer history of development of product liability litigation in the United States, and it remains to be seen if Chinese jurisprudence in this area may be further defined. However, as mentioned earlier, Chinese courts have been cautious in developing interpretive jurisprudence as they rely excessively upon State certifications. Also, in the wider context of the constitutional evolvement of the understanding of the role of courts, the value of precedent may yet be uncertain.

In summary, the chief differences between substantive product liability law in the United States and China are due to two main ideological factors. One is that the Chinese cultural understanding of the law is as an instrument rather than a tradition, and that the Chinese perception of legal claims is based on "wrongs", not on rights.

The Chinese cultural and philosophical perception of law as a social instrument and not a legal tradition explains the presence of the dual system in Chinese product liability consisting of both private law and administrative or criminal public law. It also explains the courts' broad-brush approach to economic loss recovery in product defect cases, and its application of remedies available under the Contract Law as a "remedies law" in the tortious *M.V. Agammemnon* case. The approach to remedies and the lack of a private/public distinction in Chinese law show a pragmatic approach that treats remedies and enforcement as a cure for the symptoms of grievance and, therefore, to be dispensed if appropriate, if such dispensation treats the grievance.

This is fundamentally different from the doctrinal approach taken in Common Law, where the type of remedies doctrinally follows from the legal causes of action. From the perspective of any academic who is used to thinking in terms of legal traditions, the lack of a coherent doctrinal basis in many Chinese legal frameworks would be disturbing. It is also disturbing in the sense that the lack of a legal tradition would result in a heavy reliance upon the lawmakers, that is, the

Government, to promulgate, frame, interpret and even implement the laws. This is because there is no independent legal tradition of providing an independent judicial infrastructure for legal development. This perpetuates and reinforces central control and development of the law, which may be gradually questioned as China faces pressures of convergence from Western trading parties who seek to operate in legal systems that they are more assured of.

This leads to the other point that the Chinese enactments that bear a resemblance to the West, such as the Contract Law and even some elements of the Product Quality Law, including the incorporation of the concept of "defect", may not be sufficient to assure Western trading partners, especially if such piecemeal resemblances are not based on the same assumptions underlying Western legal traditions. The Chinese concept of law has always been a predominantly public law one, based on enforcement against what is "wrong", defined by command in the imperial eras, and now by instruction and law promulgated by local and central government. The promulgation of the Civil Law in 1985 opened up the possibility that there may be a growth in the understanding of private law. However, private law growth must be matched by a social and political acceptance of private rights. Although the Chinese Civil Law is based on the German Civil Law tradition, the same underlying philosophical perspectives of "rights" are not entrenched in society. The social communitarian philosophies of Confucius, a legacy of command in imperial China and the structure of a centrally planned economy and social system today under the Chinese Communist Government are not familiar with "rights". They are familiar with "wrongs" and accept a product defect as a "product wrong".

The refinement of United States product liability law is based on a legal system strongly entrenched in a philosophy that embraces individual rights. Private law is about determining the circumstances of infringement of an individual's rights and making the infringer bear responsibility for the infringing act. Thus, United States law has developed an articulation of contractual, as well as tortious, rights in the area of product liability. In China, the lack of definition of various rights attached to expectations of product use and performance highlight this key ideological difference, and more Chinese emphasis is placed upon various forms of enforcement against "product wrongs".

With this background in mind, it would be too simplistic to say that Chinese law is younger and thus less sophisticated and that its centrally run characteristic is only transitional, as the economy is still maturing and managed development would be less chaotic. Convergence may take place because of trade pressures and pressures from foreign investors, but the quality of the convergence ultimately must be ascertained as to whether such convergence entails a reform in the Chinese legal system in terms of forging a tradition, and introducing underlying philosophies upon which to base the coherent development of law, or whether such convergence is merely piecemeal and symptomatic in nature, and would sit uneasily in the underlying fabric of Chinese law, which is based on social instrumentalism and is heavily reliant upon the force of authority. Overall, it is predicted that China's genetic approach to law may not be easily and quickly "transformed", since it has been heavily path-dependent and coherently inherited.

However, a noteworthy feature in the Chinese product liability regime is its creation of a civil liability regime beside the administrative one. The fact that consumers themselves are allowed to seek redress for the harm caused by defective products is a significant change from China's traditional, vertically integrated economic system. There is no doubt that the Chinese consumer public is gradually learning how to redress their private rights in the private sphere, which may be the next wave in Chinese legal reform.

Understanding the product liability regime of various countries requires more than a descriptive analysis of substantive law; it requires an appreciation of the ideological perspectives reflected in those provisions. Perhaps all that can reasonably be concluded is that the free market ideology and the individual creation of wealth in freedom of contract and business have played a prominent role in the growth and success of the Chinese economy and in the formulation of Chinese product liability laws.[128] However, there is still an uneasy balance between allowing free market principles to shape legal reasoning in the development of laws or legal infrastructure, and reliance on administrative structure as an enforcement option, and the imposition of criminal liability representing a need for government regulation of the market.

This may reflect a belief in the inability of the market to adjust the interests of producers and consumers and an acceptance of arguments

128 The roles and influence of interest groups are hard to evaluate in China, and the nuances of legislative deliberation are difficult to capture even in one's own culture.

for regulation relying on examples of market failure. The adherence of the Chinese laws to the twin ideologies set out earlier rests on a theoretical view that the perfect market is highly unrealistic in a developing country and that central management is perhaps required to meet imperfections and correct externalities. Adequate and accurate consumer information empowers consumer choice and efficient market decisions. By contrast, inadequate or inaccurate information undermines the market and can harm and endanger consumers.

On a more immediate level, recognition of the superior bargaining power of many producers inclines towards State intervention to aid consumers.[129] However, whether aiding consumers may be better done by strengthening private law frameworks, such as in the United States, or adopting a dual approach, such as in China, would entail a query not only of a legal, but also social nature.

Note: The authors wish to thank Professor Rebecca Eisenberg of the University of Michigan Law School for her invaluable comments on an early draft.

129 Indeed, product liability law and, in a wider sense, consumer protection law are seen as supporting free market economies. Consumer information provisions support efficient markets and restrictions on abusive practices and, along with minimum standards, increase confidence in the market, thereby bolstering rather than weakening it.

Product Liability Law and Shareholder Value Creation

George J. Siedel
University of Michigan Business School
Ann Arbor, Michigan, United States

Introduction

This chapter has two themes. First, in recent years there has been a convergence of the law across Common Law and Civil Law countries that has changed traditional notions of comparative legal advantage. Second, in the new era of legal convergence, company managers and their legal advisors need to think more systematically about how the law can be used to create value for their shareholders. Product liability is used to illustrate a plan for creating shareholder value.

Convergence of Legal Systems

Managers who are burdened by onerous legal requirements might be tempted to move their companies to countries with friendlier legal environments. In the language of international economics, certain countries have a comparative advantage because they provide cost advantages over other countries. At onc time, one element of that cost advantage was a company-friendly legal environment.

A company's ability to achieve comparative legal advantage has declined in recent years as a result of convergence of the law. While this convergence might take a variety of forms, the most powerful is the migration of law across political borders. An article in the *Economist*, describing a new California law, noted a common migration pattern: "California today, America tomorrow — and the rest of the world the day after".[1] However, laws also migrate from other countries to the United States. For instance, certain elements of United States employment law, such as workers' compensation, are based on a European model.

1 "No California, There is No Santa", *Economist*, 13 May 1989, at p. 33.

Substantive Law Convergence

Both substantive and procedural law are affected by convergence. Substantive law convergence that impacts businesses includes the following examples.

Contract Law

The Convention on Contracts for the International Sale of Goods (CISG) is a leading example of contract law convergence. Adopted by over sixty-two countries, the goal of the CISG (as stated in the Preamble) is to promote international trade by removing legal barriers that arise when contract rules are not uniform.

Environmental Law

At one time, executives might have been tempted to move operations to countries with lax environmental regulation. Today, however, environmental law has become more uniform throughout the world, with stiff penalties for violation of the law. For example, a large United States company decided to close operations in Jiangsu Province in China when it could no longer operate a plant at a profit because of new environmental legislation.[2]

Securities Regulation

In recent years, securities regulation has become a high priority as countries have attempted to encourage investor confidence in the market. For example, major industrial countries around the world have adopted legislation that calls for stiff penalties for individuals convicted of insider trading.

Sexual Harassment

Here, again, major industrial countries around the world have enacted laws that include harsh penalties for individuals convicted of sexual harassment. The penalty in France, for instance, for a manager

2 Jingzhou Tao, "Environmental Liability of Foreign Invested Enterprises in the People's Republic of China", *International Business Lawyer*, July/August 2000, at p. 314.

who abuses authority to obtain sexual favors can include a one-year prison term.[3] In addition to legislation, courts also create uniformity in the law. Courts outside the United States, including at least one conservative, mainly Muslim country (Malaysia), have cited United States decisions in sexual harassment cases.[4]

Product Liability

The theory of strict liability for defective products originated in the United States, then spread throughout Europe, and has now been adopted by a number of countries in the Pacific Rim region, including Japan, China, Australia and the Philippines. Product liability law will be discussed in greater detail later.

Procedural Law Convergence

Historically, the legal process in the United States could be distinguished from the legal process in other countries in at least five areas. Today, because of a combination of changes in the United States system (the first three areas described below) and the adoption of certain elements of United States legal process by other countries (the last two elements below), even the legal process is moving toward uniformity.

Jury Trials

While juries are not uncommon in criminal trials outside the United States, the United States is the only country in the world to use jury trials extensively in civil cases. However, the use of juries in civil cases is diminishing for a variety of reasons. For example, businesses increasingly require arbitration clauses in business contracts with their employees and customers, certain types of cases are not heard by juries, and judges freely exercise their right to dismiss cases before they reach a jury. As one bar leader lamented, "For the first time in our country's history, the future of the jury system is in serious jeopardy".[5]

---

3 "Sexual Harassment at the Workplace — Part Two", EIRR, January 1998, at p. 28.

4 "Ruling in Malaysia on Sexual Harassment is First of Its Kind", *Asian Wall Street Journal*, 9 January 1997, at p. 2.

5 Mark Curriden, "Putting the Squeeze on Juries", *American Bar Association Journal*, August 2000, at p. 53.

Punitive Damages

Unlike the United States, most countries do not allow plaintiffs to recover punitive damages. However, punitive damages have been under attack recently on two fronts in the United States. First, states have enacted laws that place a cap on punitive damages. Second, the United States Supreme Court has adopted guidelines in two recent cases that place limitations on the award of punitive damages in lower courts.[6]

Legal Expenses

In the United States, in contrast to other countries, the traditional rule was that the loser in litigation does not pay the winner's legal costs. It is now common for new legislation to provide that, in litigation related to the legislation, the loser must pay the winner's legal costs.

Contingency Fees

Plaintiffs' attorneys in the United States can enter into a contingency fee agreement with their clients whereby payment of attorneys' fees is contingent upon a successful outcome of the litigation. The contingency fee model, which enables middle class citizens (who do not qualify for free legal aid) to access the court system, has been exported recently to several countries in Europe and Asia.

Class Actions

Class actions, long a staple of the United States legal system, have been adopted by other legal systems as well, including Australia, Canada, the United Kingdom, China and Japan.

Cross-Border Movement of Products and Services

Even when a company is based in a home country the law of which is not subject to convergence, laws of other countries are important because of the cross-border movement of products and services,

---

6 *State Farm Mut. Aut. Ins. Co.* v. *Campbell*, 71 U.S.L.W. 4282 (2003); *BMW of North America, Inc.* v. *Gore*, 517 U.S. 559 (1996).

which further minimizes opportunities for notions of traditional comparative legal advantage. In other words, in a global economy, it is difficult for companies to isolate their activities to countries that provide a friendly legal environment. For example, a manufacturer based outside the United States that sells its products in the United States becomes subject to liability under United States product liability law to consumers injured by the products. This means that even when the company is manufacturing in a low-cost legal environment, it will incur the higher costs of the United States legal system because of its activities there.

An underlying rationale that courts in one country might use to accept jurisdiction over parties from other countries was noted in *Judas Priest* v. *Second Judicial District*.[7] In 1985, a few days before Christmas, two men visited a lonely churchyard in Nevada with a sawed-off shotgun. One of the men used the gun to commit suicide; the other attempted suicide, but survived. The survivor and the mother of the deceased man then brought suit against the band Judas Priest (residents of the United Kingdom) and their British corporations in Nevada, claiming that the band's album *Stained Class* caused both the suicide and the attempted suicide.

Before it could decide the case, the court first had to determine whether it had the right to hear the case. In other words, does a court in Nevada have the right to determine the liability of British citizens and their corporations? The court decided that it did have the right to hear the case, noting that:

> ". . . the only alternative forum available to the plaintiffs would be the courts of England. An overseas lawsuit is admittedly expensive and burdensome. While it is true that the members of Judas Priest will now be forced to defend a lawsuit in a country distant from their own, it is more equitable to place such a burden on them, and not the plaintiffs, because the band members *consciously and deliberately chose to develop a worldwide market*". [Emphasis added.]

In a global economy, many more companies than in the past are likely to choose "consciously and deliberately . . . to develop a worldwide market", with the result that, like the members of Judas Priest, they face potential legal liability and regulation in countries other than the

7 *Judas Priest* v. *Second Judicial District*, 760 P.2d 137 (1988).

low-cost country in which they are based. This risk, of course, also extends to companies based in the United States that market their goods and services abroad, as there is a trend for foreign courts to exercise jurisdiction over United States companies.[8]

Beyond selling products and services abroad, two factors that have recently gained prominence make it difficult for companies to increase shareholder value by taking advantage of relatively low legal costs in their home countries. First, company operations increasingly cross jurisdictional lines as business process outsourcing becomes more popular:

> "[C]orporations also see great promise in shifting work such as call-center operations, data entry and accounting duties overseas. Lower costs, operations redundancy and better service in many cases are among the reasons so-called business process outsourcing (BPO) is starting to take off — especially in India".[9]

The spread of operations across country lines forces companies to take into account legal requirements in the countries where the outsourcing is based.

The second recent factor that alters traditional notions of comparative advantage is the Internet. In a widely publicized 2002 case, for instance, an entrepreneur in Australia sued Dow Jones for defamation based on an article that the company made available on servers in New Jersey. The High Court of Australia decided that the company had to defend the lawsuit in Australia.[10] As noted in the *Wall Street Journal*, the company issued a statement indicating its disappointment that it must defend the "proceedings in a jurisdiction which is far removed from the country in which the article was prepared".[11] The same article notes that the uncertainty created by such decisions has led some online businesses "to give up customers in some countries rather than leave themselves open to possible libel, product liability and other kinds of lawsuits in these countries".

8 "All the World's a Forum", *National Law Journal*, 11 February 2002, at p. B13.

9 "What Works, What Doesn't: Lessons from Two Companies that Outsource Back-office Tasks", 19 December 2002, available at http://knowledge.wharton.upenn.edu/.

10 *Dow Jones* v. *Gutnick* [2002] HCA 56.

11 Matthew Newman, "So Many Countries, So Many Laws", *Wall Street Journal*, 28 April 2003, at p. R8.

A Plan for Creating Shareholder Value

A major concern of managers is the creation of value for their owners — the shareholders who have invested in their companies. In order to create value, a company must achieve competitive advantage over other companies. In essence:

> "Competitive advantage grows fundamentally out of value a firm is able to create for its buyers [through products and services that are offered at lower prices or that are unique] that exceeds the firm's cost of creating it."[12]

Law is problematic for managers concerned with the creation of shareholder value because of the expenses generated by litigation and regulation. As noted previously, in a world increasingly moving toward convergence, there is little opportunity to find safe havens that offer the opportunity to reduce legal expenses. As a result, a new plan is needed — one that will enable companies not only to reduce legal costs, but also to create value for their customers. A four-step plan — called the Manager's Legal Plan — is designed to encourage managers to develop new forms of competitive advantage for their companies.[13]

The plan is described below and will later be applied to product liability. Attorneys who work with managers to develop and implement the plan add value to their clients that goes beyond traditional legal advice. The first two steps in the plan are fairly conventional, the third step is built on best practices already used by leading companies and law firms, and the fourth step encourages companies and firms to move beyond existing practice.

Understand the Law

As a starting point in the Manager's Legal Plan, managers must gain an understanding of the law. Some managers are already grounded in legal frameworks, concepts and tools through undergraduate or graduate study in a business school, while others may have no formal legal education. In either event, corporate lawyers play a key educational

12 Michael Porter, *Competitive Advantage* (New York, Free Press, 1985) at p. 3.

13 George Siedel, *Using the Law for Competitive Advantage* (San Francisco, Jossey-Bass, 2002).

role in translating the complexities of the law into understandable and useful concepts that enable their manager-clients to make sound business decisions. In fact, a recent survey of chief executive officers (CEOs) concluded that the most important role of a corporate attorney is that of an educator about legal issues.[14]

Make a Business/Legal Decision

Once the manager is thoroughly grounded in the law and a legal analysis has been completed, it is time for a decision. Although beyond the scope of this chapter, some useful tools are available to assist managers in their decision-making. One of these tools is decision tree analysis,[15] a process that involves:

(1) Drawing a diagram of the decision that looks somewhat like a tree on its side;
(2) Assigning probabilities to the uncertain events depicted in the decision tree, along with values for the end points on each branch of the tree; and
(3) Calculating an expected value of, say, a decision to continue with litigation rather than accepting a settlement offer.

Commercial software is available that simplifies the use of decision-tree analysis for making legal decisions.

Another tool — actually a set of tools and processes — is collectively known as alternative dispute resolution (ADR). The tools include the adoption of an ADR policy statement by senior management, the use of suitability screens to select the most appropriate ADR process and contract clauses that encourage or require the contracting parties to use ADR to resolve business disputes.

Develop Business Strategies and Solutions to Prevent Legal Problems

The first two steps in the Manager's Legal Plan are conventional because managers are often forced to use them when they make business decisions that have legal implications. The last two steps are more difficult to implement because they call for a proactive

---

14 American Corporate Counsel Association, "In-House Counsel for the 21st Century", 7 September 2001, available at http://www.acca.com/Surveys/CEO.control.html.

15 George J. Siedel, "The Decision Tree: A Method to Figure Litigation Risks", *Bar Leader*, January–February 1986, at p. 18.

management role. Given limited time availability, managers understandably want to move on to other matters once a decision has been made, especially when they fail to understand that the law can be a vehicle for creating competitive advantage. Even when they have good intentions, and want to learn from their legal experience, the reality is that managers spend almost eighty-seven per cent of their time coming to conclusions and only thirteen per cent in learning from their experience.[16] To successfully implement the third step, managers — with the encouragement of their legal advisors — must develop the discipline to set aside time after a decision has been reached to brainstorm with corporate counsel about strategies and solutions that will prevent or minimize the problem in the future.

Reframe Legal Concerns as Business Concerns

For certain legal issues, the third step might be the end of the story. However, for other issues, managers and their attorneys might find it productive to attempt to reframe legal concerns as business concerns. Reframing is a challenging task because mental frames that enable simplification of a complex world are an important element of rational decision making. Viewing a problem as a legal concern brings into play legal frameworks, concepts and tools that enable the development of a rational solution. However, mental frames also limit the mental horizon in that, by looking at the problem through a narrow lens, one might miss better solutions that would be obvious if the problem had been examined from a broader perspective.[17]

Applying the Plan to Product Liability Concerns

Although crisis is an overused word, company liability for defective products is approaching a crisis stage, triggered in recent years by asbestos liability. According to a 2002 RAND report,[18] over ninety per cent of United States industries have been affected by asbestos

16 J. Edward Russo and Paul J. H. Schoemaker, *Winning Decisions: Getting It Right the First Time* (New York, Doubleday, 2002) at p. 9.

17 J. Edward Russo and Paul J. H. Schoemaker, *Decision Traps* (New York, Fireside, 1990) Chapters 3 and 4.

18 Stephen J. Carroll, *et al.*, *Asbestos Litigation Costs and Compensation* (Santa Monica, RAND, 2002).

litigation, resulting in twenty-two corporate bankruptcies between 2000 and 2002 alone. However, asbestos litigation is not only a United States problem. In Europe, for example:

> "... the deadly mineral was used for longer and to more devastating effect than almost anywhere in the world. [It is] estimated that 250,000 people will die of asbestos-related cancer in western Europe during the next 35 years".[19]

In addition to asbestos, the use of other products, such as automobiles, drugs and tobacco, has resulted in consumer injury and large product liability awards. Clearly, companies that can minimize product liability costs have the opportunity to create value for their shareholders. The Manager's Legal Plan offers a framework for product liability cost reduction.

Understand Product Liability Law

In order to develop appropriate strategies and solutions, managers must first be grounded in the three basic theories that are commonly asserted in product liability cases — contract theory based breach of warranty and two tort theories: strict liability and negligence. Warranty liability is based on express warranties, such as statements in promotional literature distributed by the seller, and implied warranties that pass to the buyer automatically unless disclaimed by the seller. For instance, in the United States, Section 2–314 of the Uniform Commercial Code provides that sellers give an implied warranty of merchantability that goods sold by merchants are of fair, average and ordinary quality and fit for ordinary purposes. Section 2–315 provides that, in certain circumstances, sellers also give an implied warranty of fitness for a particular purpose.

Under the tort theory of strict liability, as formulated in Section 402A of the Restatement (Second) of Torts, sellers who sell products that are unreasonably dangerous are liable for physical harm even though "the seller has exercised all possible care in the preparation and sale of his product". In other words, sellers can no longer defend product liability cases by arguing that they exercised all possible care

19 "UK and Europe About to Follow American Course", *Financial Times*, 8 September 2002, available at http://0-global.factiva.com.lib.bus.umich.edu/en/arch/display.asp (6 November 2002).

in manufacturing a product. This theory of product liability represents a classic example of convergence of the law described previously, as it first spread on a state-by-state basis across the United States, then was adopted by countries in the European Union, and is currently spreading through countries in the Pacific Rim region, such as Japan, China, Australia and the Philippines. In China, for example, more than half a million product liability lawsuits were filed annually in the years following the adoption of a new product liability law. According to an article in the *Wall Street Journal*:

> "Product liability, a concept practically unheard of here 20 years ago, has caught the attention of China's consumers — and they're applying it with a vengeance. For decades, the Chinese had little recourse when they were shocked, burned or dismembered by shoddy State-produced goods. Now, they can sue."[20]

For reasons to be discussed below, managers should understand not only the principle of strict liability, but also the underlying theory that has led countries around the world to adopt the principle. While managers might easily conclude that their companies have been targeted because they have "deep pockets", in fact, judges and legal scholars view strict liability as a doctrine that shifts the costs of injury from the victim to society at large through price increases by companies. As noted in a legal treatise: "[Strict liability] is not a 'deep pocket' theory but rather a 'risk-bearing economic' theory. The assumption is that the manufacturer can shift the costs of accidents to purchasers for use by charging higher prices for the costs of products."[21]

The second tort theory, negligence, was dominant in product liability cases before the emergence of strict liability. Although it might appear that strict liability supercedes negligence, the latter theory still plays an important role in product liability cases. For example, in determining whether the design of a product is reasonable, most United States courts use a balancing test, which compares a product's risks and benefits.

---

20 Craig S. Smith, "Chinese Discover Product Liability Suits", *Wall Street Journal*, 13 November 1997, at p. B1.

21 W. Page Keeton, Dan B. Dobbs, Robert E. Keeton and David G. Owen, *Prosser and Keeton on the Law of Torts* (St. Paul, MN, West, 1984) at p. 693.

Decide to Continue Product Liability Litigation or Settle

As discussed previously, there are tools available for managers, working with corporate counsel, to decide whether to continue product liability litigation or settle. Decision tree analysis is a powerful tool for analyzing the substantive issues in the case. This analysis will produce an expected value of the litigation that can be compared with a settlement offer. Complementing the substantive analysis are a wide variety of alternative dispute resolution processes and tools that facilitate settlement discussions.

Beyond decisions relating to a specific product liability case, a company might decide to invest resources in product liability reform. At first blush, law reform would seem to create an opportunity for competitive advantage in that it might lower legal costs. However, the advantage is often illusory because law reform also benefits the company's competitors — even "free riders" who do not invest their own resources in reform initiatives. In the words of Northwestern University professor Leigh Thompson: "Those who fail to contribute are known as defectors or free riders. Those who pay while others free ride are affectionately known as suckers".[22]

Develop Strategies and Solutions Addressing Product Liability

Working with corporate counsel, managers can develop a variety of solutions to minimize their companies' product liability exposure. These approaches might include strategic, structural and operational approaches.

Strategic Approach

The ultimate strategic issue is whether a company should begin (or continue) to manufacture products that carry a significant product liability risk. In making this strategic decision, managers might be tempted to focus on this question: "What is our exposure to damages if customers are injured by our product?" However, this question overlooks the theory that underlies strict liability in tort. As discussed previously, strict liability is based on the assumption that

---

22 Leigh Thompson, *The Mind and Heart of the Negotiator* (Upper Saddle River, NJ, Prentice Hall, 1998) at p. 227.

companies are able to shift the cost of accidents to customers by raising prices. As a result, the strategic question should be reframed as: "If we are held liable for damages, are we able to cover this liability through price increases?"

For example, in recent years, the tobacco industry has been hit with billions of dollars of liability through judgments and settlements. However, in large part, tobacco companies have been able to pass their losses on to customers by raising prices. A US $206-billion settlement with forty-six states was covered by a US $0.76 increase in the price of a pack of cigarettes, prompting this commentary in a *Wall Street Journal* article: "Where does the [state settlement] money come from? Generally speaking, not the bottom line . . .. Viewed from the consumer perspective, the settlements effectively transfer vast wealth from smokers to states and lawyers on both sides."[23]

Organizational Approach

A well-known (at least to corporate attorneys) organizational approach to minimizing product liability exposure is the use of subsidiaries to manufacture products that create high product liability exposure. While attorneys can create subsidiaries that, in theory, should protect parent corporations from liability, managers often take actions that cause courts to pierce the protective corporate veil represented by the subsidiary. For example, if the parent corporation is involved in development of the product or if the parent exercises a great amount of control over the subsidiary so that it is not treated as an independent corporation, a court might pierce the corporate veil and hold the parent liable.

Operational Approach

Operational approaches that might minimize product liability exposure relate especially to two of the three theories discussed previously: contract theory and negligence. As noted above, contract theory is based on breach of express and implied warranties. Express warranty liability can be avoided simply by not giving express

23 Milo Geyelin, "Yes, $145 Billion Deals Tobacco a Huge Blow, However, Not a Killing One", *Wall Street Journal*, 17 July 2000, at p. A8.

warranties, an approach that might lead to a skirmish between the legal and marketing departments, as the latter might consider express warranties to be important in marketing strategies. Implied warranties can be excluded through the use of appropriate language in the contract. For instance, in the United States, Section 2–316 of the Uniform Commercial Code provides that both the implied warranty of merchantability and the implied warranty of fitness for a particular purpose can be excluded by the use of expressions such as "as is" or "with all faults".

Negligence is often asserted in cases where a plaintiff claims that the design of a product was defective. In defense, companies should be prepared to argue that they exercised reasonable care in their design process. Key elements of the process include:

(1) Identification of foreseeable uses of the product;
(2) Identification of risks associated with those uses;
(3) Redesign to eliminate those risks; and
(4) The development of warnings in cases where the risk cannot be eliminated by redesign.

The redesign step (3) is especially important. As noted above, courts might use a balancing test that compares a product's risks with its benefits. Products should be redesigned to reduce or eliminate risks when this can be done in a manner that does not substantially affect the cost, desirability or performance of the product. The sequencing of the third and fourth steps — product redesign and the development of warnings — is also important as it is unlikely that a company will be protected from liability in cases where it warned customers of a danger that could have been eliminated through design changes.[24]

Reframe Product Liability Legal Concerns as Business Concerns

Reframing legal concerns as business concerns is perhaps the most difficult step in the Manager's Legal Plan because it is more of an art than a science and might not be useful in every legal situation. However, when it does work, this step can be valuable in creating shareholder value. For example, managers are often upset by the notion that they must take into account the foreseeable uses of a product

24 *Uniroyal* v. *Martinez*, 977 S.W.2d 328 (1998).

during the design process. Often trained as engineers, they feel that their products are designed for a particular use and that anyone of minimal intelligence will use the product for that purpose. They become especially agitated by cases in which a plaintiff wins substantial damages for injuries incurred after using a product for a purpose other than its intended use.

In their anger at plaintiffs and their attorneys, the law of product liability and the legal system in general, they often overlook a fundamental truth. Their customers often use products for unintended purposes for a reason — there are no products available that serve their needs. For instance, how might customers use hairdryers for purposes other than drying their hair? There is a long list of uses, including starting barbecues, drying glue and paint, defrosting refrigerators and drying pets. Why do individuals use hairdryers for these purposes? Because they need a variety of products that will provide warm air. Because these products are not available on the market, individuals must use hairdryers for a number of unintended uses. Managers who are customer-oriented and market-driven should be able to move beyond their frustration with the law and use information gathered in determining foreseeable uses for new product development purposes. The introduction of new products on the market, in turn, is an important element in gaining competitive advantage.

Conclusion

The role of the corporate lawyer is gradually evolving from that of a gatekeeper to a gateway to business opportunity.[25] Attorneys at some companies, such as the McDonald's Corporation, focus their attention on the company's customers.[26] At other companies, like DuPont, attorneys have borrowed creative business models from other business functions to reduce legal costs.[27] At still other companies, law departments strive to become profit centers or, in the

25 Stephen E. Nowlan, "Gatekeeper to Gateway", *LD21*, Spring 2001, at p. 3.

26 "Ask the General Counsel", *ACCA DOCKET*, January–February 1996, at p. 39.

27 Daniel B. Mahoney, "When Pruning Is in Order", *Business Law Today*, July–August 1997, at p. 13.

words of General Electric's general counsel, attempt to "creatively enhance revenue and profit for the business unit"[28] they work with.

This chapter has described a plan, called the Manager's Legal Plan, that accentuates the importance of corporate lawyers in serving as key gateways that will enable companies to achieve their strategic objectives. A product liability application has been used to illustrate the plan. As illustrated by this application, one of the key elements of the plan is the ability to reframe legal concerns as business concerns. A side benefit of the reframing process is that it can be useful in developing ethical standards for a business. One ethical standard that emerges from the product liability scenario, for example, is "develop safe products that meet customer needs". This standard is more meaningful to managers than many ethical principles because it is grounded in the realities of shareholder value creation.[29]

---

28 "GE and the Art of Systematic Common Sense", *Corporate Counsel*, August 2000, at p. 51.

29 George Siedel, *Using the Law for Competitive Advantage* (San Francisco, Jossey-Bass, 2002) at p. 167.

Overview of Product Liability in Argentina

Luis E. Sprovieri
Baker & McKenzie
Buenos Aires, Argentina

Introduction

In Argentina, the area of product liability is beginning to gain attention from the business community. The lack of specific provisions addressing the multiple aspects of this field of the law, coupled with local litigation practices and procedures, seem not to favor a dramatic rise in the filing of lawsuits. However, some features of Argentina's current political, financial and social situation could be fostering substantial changes. This chapter briefly discusses this scenario. In doing so, it addresses topics such as consumer protection law, product liability under the Argentine Civil Code, judicial procedure and the organization or Argentina's judicial system as regards courts that entertain product liability cases.

Legal Framework

In Argentina, there is no specific body of provisions governing the law on product liability. Consequently, the courts that have decided on alleged damage caused by products have had to resort to general provisions on torts, breach of contract and implied warranties. Notwithstanding the enactment of Section 40 of Law 24240, the Consumer Protection Law (CPL), its scope does not extend to every possible factual scenario.

Following these general provisions and a wealth of scholarly opinions on the subject, it is widely accepted that no privity is required for a manufacturer to be held liable for injury suffered by the final user or consumer. Usually, when a manufacturer has not acted as the immediate vendor of a defective product, principles of strict liability apply.

For that purpose, the original intent of existing regulations has been broadened. For instance, Section 1113 of Argentina's Civil Code provides for liability of the owner and/or guardian of objects causing damage, as well as that of the owner and/or guardian of defective or dangerous objects. Argentine courts have extended the interpretation of this provision so as to include individuals and corporations who benefit from an object without respect to its ownership or custody.

It is understood that a manufacturer who introduces a defective or dangerous product onto the market benefits from that product. By this means, the manufacturer is usually held liable without regard to how many people have handed the product down the market chain since it left the manufacturer's custody and reached the final user or consumer. This solution departs from an earlier doctrine laid down in a case in the Buenos Aires Commercial Court of Appeals decided in 1985. In *Rincon de Avila*, the court did not apply tort law, but broadened contract law principles so as to deem that each player in the market chain "acts on behalf of" the manufacturer and passes down the warranties originally included in the first contractual relationship. This doctrine, generally rejected by other courts and scholars, has not been generally applied since then.[1] Some courts have also found the manufacturer liable, but on grounds of negligence, as opposed to strict liability. When a lawsuit is decided on negligence principles, judges often apply the *res ipsa loquitur* doctrine, finding the manufacturer negligent just by determining that the product was defective.

When the manufacturer is in privity with the final user or consumer, cases are usually decided on grounds of breach of contract. The same applies to immediate vendors, such as distributors or retailers, who are subject to the law of contract, their conduct being adjudged on these grounds. Courts and commentators agree that selling products entails an implied "warranty of safety", according to which the products are expected not to cause harm to their buyers.

Some paradoxical consequences result from the lack of specific provisions governing damage caused by products. For instance, the statute of limitations is influenced by the role that the manufacturer played in introducing the product onto the market. When the manufacturer is the immediate vendor of the product, the statute of limitations is ten years. When there is somebody else in between, for

1 C.N.Com., Sala B, 25 September 1985, *Rincón de Avila, Soc. en Com. por Accs.* v. *Cooper Argentina, S.A. et al.*", La Ley 1986-C-6.

example, a distributor or retailer, the statute of limitations for filing an action against the manufacturer drops to two years. Under the CPL, the statute of limitations is three years.

The CPL became effective on 15 October 1993. There was no prior regulation concerning the protection of consumers. Regulatory Decree 1798/94 implemented the CPL. As statutorily provided and commonly construed by its commentators, the CPL is a public policy law, meaning that the parties to any consumer relationship, that is, the vendor and final consumer, cannot agree to carry on their relationship on terms departing from those provided by the law.

Definition of Consumer and Scope of Protection

The CPL defines a consumer as an individual or legal entity that purchases a product or obtains a service for a price and for its final consumption, own benefit or that of its family or social group. An individual or legal entity that purchases, stores, uses or consumes goods or services or uses them in a production, transformation or marketing process, or to render services to third parties, is not deemed to be a consumer. Thus, the purpose of the CPL is to protect end users, that is, consumers, including business end users.

The CPL marked a major change in the way that the Argentine legal community deals with consumers, their rights and the enforceability of those rights. Before the enactment of the CPL, no specific body of law addressed these topics. The provisions of the CPL are not restricted to product liability, but were drafted to govern several aspects of consumer protection, such as a consumer's right to adequate information, his protection against hazards and provisions that should be deemed void when part of a consumer contract. Likewise, the CPL established sanctions for those violating consumers' rights, and organized an arbitral system specially designed to resolve small claims of consumers against manufacturers, distributors and vendors. This chapter will concentrate on the aspects of the CPL that influence product liability.

Territorial Application of Law 24240

The CPL establishes that the obligations set forth in the statute apply to every person or entity that produces, imports, distributes or commercializes products or provides services to consumers in a professional manner, even occasionally. It is not necessary for a producer and/or vendor to be based in Argentina in order to be reached by the provisions of the CPL. Any producer and/or distributor may be deemed subject to the CPL as long as his products are introduced onto the Argentine market. An issue of enforceability of the sanctions contained in Section 47 of the CPL may arise, but at least in theory each step in the production and distribution chain will be subject to the CPL and will have to comply with its provisions, without regard to the place of incorporation, nationality or domicile of its headquarters. At the same time, in terms of tort liability, each step in the chain may be deemed liable for damage caused to an Argentine consumer. The La Hague Convention on Product Liability of 2 October 1973 may also apply.

Liability for Damage

The producer, manufacturer, importer, provider, seller or whoever puts its brand on the goods provided or services rendered shall be held jointly and severally liable for any damage caused to the consumer as a consequence of any defect in or risk associated with the goods or services. In addition to the general provisions of tort law, Section 40 of the CPL provides for the tortious liability of each company or individual involved in the manufacturing, distribution and/or marketing process. It may be said that Section 40 defined the scope of tort liability, which, before its enactment, was subject to sometimes conflicting judicial decisions. However, the broad rule of Section 40 does not apply to every possible product liability case.

Statute of Limitations

Pursuant to Section 50 of the CPL, the limitation period that applies to the actions and sanctions set forth by the CPL is three years.

Product Liability under the Civil Code

Shortcomings of the Consumer Protection Law

When the CPL became effective in October 1993, it was passed into law without the product liability provisions it contains today, as amended. At the time of promulgating the bill that Congress approved as Law 24240, President Menem vetoed some of the sections of the original draft. Among those provisions was Section 40, the rule dealing with liability. It was not until 1998 that Congress obtained the majority needed to "insist" upon passing some of the provisions of the CPL that the Executive Branch had vetoed. By means of a new bill, ultimately passed as Law 24999, Congress re-introduced Section 40 into the CPL.

Partly as a consequence of the foregoing, the liability proviso of Section 40 does not apply to every possible product liability case. In the first place, as legal provisions are not, in principle, retroactive, Section 40 does not apply to damage inflicted before 7 August 1998, when Law 24999 became effective. On the other hand, the CPL applies only to "consumers" as defined by its Section 1. Thus, by-standers and commercial users (those that cannot be characterized as "end users") are not subject to the protection of the CPL. These limits in the scope of protection of the CPL mean that tort law provisions and other general principles of the Civil Code still apply to many product liability cases.

Apart from the CPL and the Civil Code, the National Constitution also contains a specific provision dealing with consumer protection. Article 42 of the Argentine Constitution reads as follows:

> "In the consumer relationship, consumers and users of goods and services have the right to protection of their health, safety and economic interests, true and adequate information, freedom of choice and conditions of equal and respectful treatment.
>
> "Thc Authorities shall provide for the protection of those rights, education of consumers, defense of competition against every manner of distortion of the market, control of natural and legal monopolies, quality and efficiency of public services and the establishment of associations of consumers and users.
>
> "Legislation shall establish efficient procedures to prevent and resolve disputes, as well as the regulatory framework for public services under national jurisdiction, providing for the necessary participation of associations of consumers and users and interested Provinces in the controlling agencies."

It is apparent from the foregoing that there is no single body of law regulating the complex field of product liability in Argentina. This absence of specific and comprehensive rules results in some differences in the way product liability cases are treated, depending on the application of the CPL or the Civil Code. These differences are somewhat apparent in terms of duties, standing, liability and the applicable statute of limitations.

Role of Scholarly Opinions

Another aspect that cannot be undermined is the influence that scholarly opinions have had on shaping product liability law in Argentina. Until quite recently, product liability cases were somewhat scarce in Argentina. There were few reported judicial decisions, and they showed no consistency in their rulings. Besides, the absence of specific provisions and the subsequent need to resort to general tort principles made product liability a fertile field for scholarly discussion. It can be said that, in the 1970s and 1980s, product liability was more a theoretical exercise among law professors than a topic present in judicial decisions.

With such a scenario, it is safe to say that the boundaries of product liability in Argentina were first drawn in textbooks and scholarly articles and only then accepted by the judiciary. In fact, when the first identifiable wave of product liability cases reached the courts, the bench had little to do but choose among the already developed legal theories, as scholars had elaborated on them. In discussing the law of product liability under the Civil Code, therefore, one must take into account the influence that early scholarly opinions had in the development of certain landmark judicial decisions reported since 1995.

Liability under the Civil Code

Pursuant to the Argentine Civil Code, two systems of liability co-exist: contractual liability and extra-contractual liability. As some differences between these two systems may influence how cases are decided, for example, the extent of liability and the statute of limitations, it is important to determine whether certain harmful conduct falls within one set of provisions or the other. Once the applicable set of rules has been determined (contractual or extra-contractual), the next question to address is whether the harmful conduct should be adjudged under negligence or strict liability principles. Obviously, choosing one source of liability or the other can deeply influence a product liability case and somewhat compromise its result. The differences as to the burden of proof between these two possible systems might be decisive as to the success of a case.

As per Argentine legal doctrine, the principles of strict liability and negligence apply either to contractual or extra-contractual liability. To a great extent, the discussion engaged in by local scholars during the 1970s and 1980s revolved around whether to apply strict liability or negligence principles to product liability cases. This was not a futile discussion, the success or failure of possible product liability cases being at stake. It was somewhat clear from the outset of this scholarly discussion that when a manufacturer or retailer has acted as immediate vendor of a product, his harmful conduct should be adjudged following the principles of contractual liability. In fact, a sales contract exists between the manufacturer and the victim when the former has acted as direct or immediate vendor and the latter as buyer.

Likewise, scholars agreed that the principles of extra-contractual liability apply to a manufacturer who is not the immediate vendor of a product. The legal basis for such extra-contractual liability, however, remained contested. By some accounts, extra-contractual cases should be decided under the rules of strict liability. For others, extra-contractual cases were not beyond the scope of the negligence principles that generally apply in many tort cases.

The discussion centered around three different possible scenarios:

(1) The liability of the manufacturer who was the direct vendor of the harmful product;
(2) The liability of the manufacturer who was not the direct vendor of the harmful product (distributors and/or retailers intervening in the commercial chain); and
(3) The liability of the distributor or retailer selling a harmful product manufactured by another.

Manufacturer as Direct Vendor of Product As per Section 1198, first paragraph, of the Argentine Civil Code, "contracts shall be executed, construed, and fulfilled in good faith, pursuant to which the parties are understood or could have been understood to be acting with due care". From this generic principle, scholars and courts have derived an implied warranty of safety. For instance, a court had the opportunity to hold that the course of action against the direct vendor is contractual in nature and its basis is the warranty of safety ancillary to the sale contract.[2] Sellers assume a "duty to deliver a result" consisting of the provision of safe goods that adequately fulfill the function they were designed for according to their nature and predictable use.

Further, this legal theory states that contractual obligations or duties to deliver a result are based on strict liability. In other words, in order to obtain redress, the claimant need not prove negligence on the part of the vendor; it is sufficient to prove the defective condition of the product and a causal link between that defect and the alleged damage. The mere existence of a defect leads to an assumption of negligence *res ipsa loquitur.*[3]

Manufacturer Who Is Not Direct Seller of Product In the majority of the decisions rendered on product liability, manufacturers often confine their role to the manufacturing process, leaving the distribution of the products to a sometimes complex commercial chain. By this means, importers, distributors, wholesalers and retailers pass the product down from the manufacturer to the final user or consumer.

To date, where the manufacturer has not sold the product directly to the consumer, Argentine courts have concurred on applying Section 1113 of the Civil Code.[4] Pursuant to Section 1113, the duty of the tortfeasor extends to damage caused by the things he serves from and to the things he has under his care. Scholars and courts have construed this rule as justifying the "economic utility" doctrine and have attributed liability to a manufacturer, importer or intermediary who does not sell the product directly to the consumer. Under this doctrine, the manufacturer and all of the participants in the commercial chain benefit from the product and should, therefore, be responsible for any resulting damage.

Section 1113 also provides for the liability of the owner and/or guardian of objects causing damage, as well as that of the owner and/or guardian of defective or dangerous objects. Argentine courts

2 C.N.Com., Sala B, 31 August 2001, *L., M.A.* v. *Ortopedia Alemana S.A.*

3 C. 1ª Civ. y Com., Sala II, Lomas de Zamora, 16 July 2002, *Aldecoa, Oscar* v. *Firestone de Argentina*; C 5ª Civ. y Com., Córdoba, 11 November 1996, *César, Inés M.* v. *Supermercado Corner et al.*, La Ley Córdoba 1998–1127; C.N. Com., Sala B, 28 June 2002, *Manessi, Alberto V.* v. *General Motors de Argentina S.A.*, La Ley 2002-F-324.

4 C. Civ. Com. Trab. y Familia Bell Ville, 20 November 1992, *Bisutti, Luis* v. *Cooperativa Agropecuaria San Mart¡n de Camilo Aldao Ltda. et al.*, Jurisprudencia Argentina 1994-II-186.

have extended the interpretation of this provision to include manufacturers without regard to their ownership or custody of the product. Understandably, products often cause harm well after they have left the manufacturer's plant. Nevertheless, Argentine scholars and courts have agreed that the manufacturer remains a "guardian of the structure" of the product and is responsible even after its initial sale.

This is the typical strict liability scenario. Section 1113 of the Civil Code is generally understood as the basis for the majority of extra-contractual strict liability cases in Argentine law. Pursuant to this rule, the claimant need not prove negligence on the part of the defendant. In order to be freed from responsibility, the manufacturer must prove an interruption in the causal link between the defect and the damage, such as the victim's negligence or the harmful behavior of a third party outside the relationship between the manufacturer and the injured consumer.

Distributor or Retailer Selling Product Manufactured by Another
In this scenario, the contractual liability principles deriving from Section 1198 of the Civil Code apply. Hence, an implied warranty of safety makes the direct vendor of a product manufactured by another responsible for any damage the product may have caused.

The Argentine concept of defective product matches its American counterpart. In general, a product is deemed to be defective if it has a design defect, a manufacturing failure or lack of adequate warnings. In addition, Argentine product liability rules also apply to dangerous products. Dangerous products are those that, even in absence of an identifiable defect, entail a risk that has not been assumed by the consumer. The characterization of certain products as dangerous and the possibility of the consumer's assuming that risk are still subject to discussion in Argentine legal doctrine. Often, such characterization derives from a case-by-case analysis.

Judicial System

Argentina is organized as a republic with a federal structure. The Constitution vests the powers of the judiciary in a Supreme Court and other lower courts as Congress may establish. The organization of the federal judicial system also applies to the courts sitting in Buenos Aires. The organizing statutes divide courts by subject matter into two levels, first and second instance, with the Supreme Court as the court of last and extraordinary resort.

In addition, the Constitution provides that each province is to organize its own judiciary. Hence, there are federal and local courts co-existing in each province. The structure of the judiciary of each province is similar to the federal judiciary, with a Supreme Court, courts of appeal and lower courts. The jurisdiction of the provincial courts includes all matters that do not fall within federal jurisdiction, such as the application of provincial law and civil, commercial, criminal, mining, labor and social security statutes enacted by the national legislature.

Under Argentina's federal system, substantive law is reserved to the National Congress, while each provincial legislature enacts its own procedural rules. By this means, different procedural codes for civil, commercial, labor, criminal and administrative proceedings apply in each province. The proceedings followed before the federal and provincial courts are, in general, very similar. With the exception of a few provinces, the procedural codes provide that most judicial actions must be carried out in writing.

Within the City of Buenos Aires, both civil and commercial courts have jurisdiction over product liability cases, depending on the ground for complaint. Generally, when direct vendors are named as defendants, national commercial courts accept jurisdiction without significant objection. Conversely, when the direct vendor is not involved in the lawsuit, but the defendant is just the manufacturer or any other player in the commercial chain (apart from the final retailer), the case is generally heard by ordinary (non-federal) civil courts.

In the provinces, as civil and commercial jurisdictions are not split, local courts having both types of jurisdiction often hear product liability cases. Federal jurisdiction very seldom applies.

Trends in Product Liability in the Argentine Market

Product Liability Litigation over the Last Three Decades

Although reported product liability cases can be found that were decided in the late 1950s and 1960s, they are rare. The 1970s witnessed the filing of several cases against bottling companies for soda bottle explosions. In the 1980s and 1990s, several cases were decided against manufacturers of cars, food and home appliances. In the late 1990s, some causes of action were "imported" from the United States. Cases were filed alleging damage arising out of silicon gel breast implants and HIV infection from blood derivatives (mainly clotting products, such as Factor VIII and Factor IX). Similarly, less than a hundred cases were filed against cigarette manufacturers for the purported harmful nature of tobacco products. Remarkably, asbestos-related diseases, which were the basis of thousands of filings in the United States, have not been alleged in Argentina.

To date, no final decisions have been reached on breast implant and Factor VIII/IX cases, but some influential judicial decisions have been reported in favor of the tobacco industry, deeming that the claims were barred by the statute of limitations or that the plaintiff had assumed the risk of smoking.

Current Trends

The lawsuits related to breast implants, HIV and tobacco were the result of an initiative of a handful of entrepreneurial attorneys. This entrepreneurial approach seems not to be common in Argentina's legal practice. In Argentina, there are no incentives in place for huge lawsuits or widespread litigation in the field of product liability. For instance, class actions are not allowed, discovery is limited and ethical standards strictly prevent lawyers from being involved in advertising practices.

At the same time, the plaintiff bar consists of small law firms or solo practitioners; medium-sized law firms are rare. Plaintiffs' lawyers customarily work on a contingency fee basis. Product liability litigation, especially when it relates to drugs or medical devices, encompasses extensive research, expertise and expense, which solo practitioners and small law firms are not in a position to cope with. In addition, such cases often imply innovative approaches that Argentine courts have not yet had the opportunity to decide upon. As a result, even when a defective product is involved, allegedly injured individuals tend to sue physicians, retailers or car drivers instead of manufacturers. There are well-developed sets of rules for that purpose, and defendants are usually well covered by insurance. Finally, the concept of mass torts is not present in Argentina's legal theory, and aggregation mechanisms are poorly developed and seldom used.

Movement Towards a More Active Approach

Notwithstanding the foregoing, some voices — mainly from the academic community — are advocating the adoption of group litigation. Since early 2000, several law review articles have examined the American class action and the Brazilian group litigation device. American scholars have been invited to lecture in Buenos Aires. Likewise, a landmark judicial decision,[5] entered on 16 March 2000, for the first time ever granted standing to the ombudsman in seeking redress for damage inflicted on thousands of individuals. The court also acknowledged the possibility of splitting the issues at stake. It entered a group decision concerning liability and enabled individuals to file ancillary petitions solely aimed at determining individual damages.

Along the same lines, the legislature of the Province of Buenos Aires recently passed a statute that may prove to be influential in product liability cases. The Province of Buenos Aires is the largest province in Argentina, with 13,827,000 people out of the 36,260,000 inhabitants of the country.[6] Further, it contains a good deal of Argentina's industries and some of its wealthiest consumers. Its legislature recently enacted Law 13133, the Code on the Implementation of the Rights of Consumers and Users. Law 13133 specifies that the principles that the CPL establishes at federal level should be applied in the Province. This objective seems to have been accomplished. Exercising its constitutional prerogatives, the legislature of the Province of Buenos Aires has gone further, enacting procedural rules denoting a major change in the way that consumer protection and product liability cases are dealt with. Due to its influence in Argentina's economy, the Province of Buenos Aires usually serves as the testing ground for legal reform. Thus, how this reform works in practice may very well inspire comparable changes in other provinces and at the federal level.

Among the changes that Law 13133 introduced, the most remarkable is the enactment of a type of group or class action. Pursuant to Section 24 of Law 13133, when a lawsuit has been initiated in furtherance of rights common to a group of consumers, any settlement will benefit all of the consumers affected by the same facts that justified the complaint. Those consumers shall be entitled to prove their

---

5 *Defensoría del Pueblo* v. *EDESUR*.

6 As per the 2001 census.

standing, actual harm and collect damages through an ancillary and simple proceeding with the sole purpose of enforcing settlement in each particular case. In order to facilitate adequate information regarding settlement in a consumer protection case, the court shall order its publication. By this means, a rather straightforward lawsuit may end up giving rise to thousands of ancillary or derivative actions involving consumers who, although having been affected, did not participate in the original lawsuit.

As per Section 28 of Law 13133, in consumer cases, a judicial decision on the merits shall have the following effects:

(1) If it favors the complainant, it shall benefit all affected consumers notwithstanding their not participating in the lawsuit;
(2) If it favors consumers' rights, other consumers may file an ancillary petition aimed at proving their standing and actual harm, and collecting damages;
(3) If it rejects the complaint, it does not prevent other consumers from initiating their own lawsuits; and
(4) If it rejects the complaint for lack of evidence, other consumers shall be entitled to initiate judicial actions with the objective of producing new evidence.

To facilitate consumers in exercising these rights, the court shall make public decisions entered in consumer protection cases.

Other rules also facilitate instituting judicial actions with consumer protection roots. Consumers and consumer associations are exempt from litigation costs and expenses, such as court fees. Should one or more consumers decide to withdraw a claim, this abandonment of the case shall not be binding upon others, who will be entitled to continue the lawsuit. Last, but not least, when a first instance decision favors a consumer, as a prerequisite to filing a challenge on appeal, the other party must deposit the amount of the award, accrued interest and litigation costs and expenses.

In Argentina, there is sometimes a gap between law and reality; legal rules do not always work as they appear to on paper. It remains to be seen what the effect of these recently enacted rules will be for local consumers, manufacturers, service providers and the community at large.

Apart from the enthusiasm some scholars show when discussing the adoption of group litigation, the consensus of opinion is that a widespread adoption of class actions in tort cases would be inadvisable.

Argentina's judiciary, with its flaws and conservative approach, may be ill prepared to handle huge cases, such as those filed in foreign countries.

Products Involved in Consumer Actions

Automobiles

Recently, a rise in reported judicial decisions involving car manufacturers has been taking place. Argentine courts have applied to car manufacturers and car retailers the product liability principles developed over the past decade. Most of the reported cases have dealt with manufacturing defects, such as steering system and wheel failures and radiator explosions. No cases have yet involved design defects.

A recent case stands as a landmark decision in this area. In *De Blasi de Musmeci*, decided on 5 October 2001, the Commercial Court of Appeals sitting in Buenos Aires ruled for the plaintiff, granting her an unprecedented award of US $800,000.[7] The court also ordered a mandatory general recall of a car model for inspection and replacement of its steering mechanism. This was the first time ever that the Argentine judiciary had issued such an order.

Tobacco

Around 100 tobacco cases are currently pending before the Argentine courts. To date, few final decisions on the merits of these cases have been published. In all the reported decisions, local courts have dismissed the claims, deciding in favor of the defendant.[8] In doing so, the courts have deemed smokers' claims as barred by the two-year statute of limitations or by the plaintiff's assumption of risk.

The claimants filed their complaints after several years of heavy smoking, a practice that is widely known as being dangerous to health. Thus, since information on the danger of engaging in such conduct is at the disposal of every consumer, no smoker can claim to

7 C.N.Com., Sala C, 5 October 2001, *De Blasi de Musmeci, Claudia* v. *Sevel Argentina Sociedad Anónima et al.*

8 C.N.Civ., Sala H, 26 February 2001, *Lodoli, Roberto* v. *Massalin Particulares S.A.*; C.N.Civ, Sala H, 18 October 2002, *Barone, Victor Renato* v. *Nobleza Piccardo SAICF*; C.N.Civ., Sala K, 1 December 2000, *Minisini Verdi, Luis* v. *Nobleza Piccardo S.A.*, Jurisprudencia Argentina 2001-II-630, La Ley 1 February 2001.

be ignorant of the consequences of his conduct and file a claim for redress after several years of smoking. Further, the warning printed on cigarette packages since the late 1980s acts as a means of obtaining actual and meaningful knowledge of the danger that smoking entails. On the other hand, in one of the cited cases, the court considered that reports on the addictive nature of cigarettes issued by the United States Food and Drug Administration do not prove by themselves that a given smoker cannot quit his habit if actually determined to do so.

Prospects

Some features of Argentina's current financial situation and social circumstances may lead to a rise in product liability filings. Albeit that there are obstacles, as briefly described above, four sets of conditions are in place for expansion in this field.

Firstly, some big players in Argentina's insurance market have recently suffered a remarkable crisis resulting in their insolvency, thus leaving alleged tortfeasors uninsured. This may move plaintiffs' lawyers to sue deep-pocket defendants, such as major corporations, instead of individuals. Secondly, as the Argentine financial crisis also reached the legal profession, practitioners might find themselves compelled to seek innovative causes of action and structure joint ventures with other small law firms. Thirdly, Argentine consumers are becoming more and more educated every day. There are several consumers' associations advocating the rights of their constituents and acting as watchdogs of manufacturers. Lastly, more than ever, global communications are putting local practitioners in touch with news of speculative litigation and huge recoveries being granted elsewhere, especially in the United States.

Conclusion

As discussed above, in Argentina, there is no specific body of provisions governing the law of product liability. Section 40 of the CPL provides for the liability of those involved in the manufacturing, distribution and marketing of products. However, Section 40 does not apply to every possible product liability case, for example, it does not apply to damages inflicted before 7 August 1998. On the other hand, by-standers and commercial users or consumers are not included within the CPL's protection. Due to these shortcomings in the CPL's protection of consumers, many product liability cases are decided resorting to general principles of tort, breach of contract and implied warranties.

In this way, principles of contractual strict liability apply to direct vendors of products (manufacturers or retailers), while extra-contractual strict liability applies to manufacturers who have not sold the harmful product directly to the consumer. Negligence principles are very seldom applied. When negligence is present in a judicial decision, it is often accompanied by the *res ipsa loquitur* principle, that is, the defective condition of the product proves by itself that the manufacturer acted carelessly.

As discussed above, some features of Argentina's current financial situation and social circumstances appear to be leading to a rise in product liability filings. In addition, a type of group or class action is slowly making its way into Argentine law. As this new device is so recent, however, its ultimate results remain to be seen.

Recall and Reimbursement of Related Costs in International Commerce

Christian Thomas Stempfle
Nörr Stiefenhofer Lutz
Munich, Germany

Introduction

The recall of mass products has been constantly on the increase in recent years. As can be seen almost daily in the media, not only the automotive industry but other industries, such as the pharmaceutical industry and the food industry, are affected. In relation to the Federal Republic of Germany, product recall was intensified by the implementation of the Product Safety Act (ProdSG), which came into force on 1 August 1997. The Product Safety Act, under certain circumstances, authorized the official ordering of product recalls. This Act has, however, now been replaced by the Appliance and Product Safety Act of 6 January 2004 (*Geräte- und Produktsicherheitsgesetz* — GPSG). In practice, difficulties often arise, firstly, as to the question of whether and to what extent a product recall must be ordered and implemented in order to avoid liability and criminal law consequences.

If a recall is decided on, the second question of who is ultimately responsible for the costs of the recall arises. While this may initially usually be the manufacturer of the recalled products or recalled batch, it may be, in the increasingly fragmented distribution of work, that it is not the manufacturer alone who is responsible for the design or manufacturing defect that has rendered the product recall necessary. Often, a supplier of a defective part may be at least jointly liable for the recall. It must, therefore, be clarified under what conditions in German law the manufacturer may have recourse against other participants in the chain of suppliers. Different approaches to this question are found in German legal literature and prevailing German case law.[1]

The subject is rendered more difficult if — as is often the case — the recall must be conducted on a cross-border basis. It is this situation that is the main issue dealt with in this chapter. The conditions under which a recall must be conducted and national recourse through the supply chain, however, will be dealt with first. Secondly, the international aspects of a product recall and the reimbursement of related costs will be referred to.

Illustrative Example of a Recall

The German electrical manufacturer X, operating both in Germany and internationally, includes very popular domestic appliances in its product spectrum. These include a kitchen hob known as "Famosa IV". In 1999, kitchen fires arose through the use of the "Famosa IV", in four cases causing considerable material damage and in one case slight injuries (smoke inhalation). Internal investigations at X at the end of 1999 showed that the kitchen fires were caused by a defective plate, which led to the heating of the kitchen hob without it being switched on. The plates were supplied by the Danish supplier D with which X cooperated until the end of 1998. The number of kitchen fires at first showed a reduction at the end of 1999, but increased out of proportion at the beginning of 2000. The management of X, therefore, decided in 2000 to conduct a wide-ranging recall and exchange of the "Famosa IV". The recall extended to all appliances supplied up to the end of 1998 that were fitted with plates from supplier D.

Principles and Extent of Recall Obligation

The obligation to recall dangerous products from circulation under certain conditions has derived from tort law.[2] The recall obligation is

1 Müller and Dörre, VersR 1999, 1333; *Krause*, NZVersR 1999, 153; OLG München, NJW-RR 1999, 1657, *Wohnmobile*; OLG Karlsruhe, NJW-RR 1995, 594, *Dunstabzugshaube*.

2 Civil Code, Sections 823 *et seq.*

thereby generally classified under the tort obligation of care.[3] According thereto, anyone who creates or maintains a source of danger to the public is obliged to take all reasonable measures to protect from damage persons who come into contact with the source of danger in an authorized manner.[4] As only specified legal interests (freedom, body, health, life and property) — as listed in Section 823(1) of the Civil Code — are protected thereby, the recall obligation extends only to the protection of these legal interests, not to the protection of property in general. Further, a duty to conduct a product recall may arise if ordered by a competent authority on the grounds that the product does not comply with the health and safety requirements of Section 4 of the Appliance and Product Safety Act.

If a manufacturer or supplier, in spite of the recall obligation under tort law, does not conduct a recall, this in itself does not involve legal consequences. However, if damaging events occur after a recall should have been instituted, which result in an infringement of the interests of third parties protected under Section 823(1) of the Civil Code, the party obliged must expect consequences under civil law, criminal law and possibly administrative law. Under civil law, compensation claims by injured parties, who would not have been injured if the manufacturer or supplier had instituted a recall of the defective product in good time, come into consideration. From the criminal law point of view, investigation of negligence causing bodily injury or death may be considered if damage to health or death has arisen from a defective product that should have been recalled. Finally, in administrative law, the competent authorities will not only consider the ordering of a recall, but the business license of the manufacturer may also be reviewed (and even revoked) from a trade law point of view.

The recall obligation applies, in principle, to all who are responsible for the defect in the product.[5] The responsible parties include not only the end manufacturer of a product, but also the supplier of defective parts, insofar as such defective parts make the recall necessary.[6] The recall obligation itself, therefore, does not constitute an independent duty of care with consequent liability upon which compensation claims against the end manufacturer or supplier may be directly based. The recall obligation results rather from the product

3 Palandt and Sprau, *Bürgerliches Gesetzbuch*, Section 823 BGB, marginal note 173.
4 Palandt and Sprau, *Bürgerliches Gesetzbuch*, Section 823 BGB, marginal note 46.
5 OLG Karlsruhe, NJW-RR 1995, 594, *Dunstabzugshaube*; Link, BB 1985, 1424.
6 Müller and Dörre, VersR 1999, 1333.

monitoring duty, according to which each manufacturer of a product and each supplier of parts of the product is obliged to monitor the behavior of the product on the market — including in relation to its use with other products — and, on becoming aware of a potential unknown risk, is obliged to take the necessary measures.[7]

A recall is, therefore, necessary as a precaution against damage if it serves to prevent an imminent or anticipated risk of damage to the legal interests of third parties.[8] However, not every product defect automatically triggers the obligation to recall. If a warning or new instructions to the consumers is adequate to remove the danger quickly and securely, no recall is necessary. If all possible consumers or users cannot be reached with instructions on the correct use of the product because they are not known, a warning through the mass media as to the manner in which the danger may be prevented may be appropriate.[9]

A recall is indicated, particularly in the case of mass products in daily use, if a product design or manufacturing defect appears and, as a result, damage to the legal interests referred to in Section 823(1) of the Civil Code may be anticipated, and such anticipated damage cannot be prevented by an instruction to the product users. Consideration of individual cases is necessary. The more important the legal interest threatened, the lower the requirements as to the probability of damage. However, the tendency of prevailing German case law is still that the recall remains the *ultima ratio*.[10]

The measures that must be taken by the manufacturer (or supplier) to remove the danger imposed by the product are to be assessed according to general principles, in particular, the principle of proportionality. Which measures are appropriate, necessary and reasonable for the prevention of the danger is, therefore, to be examined.[11] In the case of the above illustration, it is clear that, in 2000, as it must have been ascertained that a considerable number of kitchen hobs fitted with the defective plates and a disproportionate increase in the number of incidents was noted, the obligation of the end manufacturer and the supplier to conduct a recall (at least) was established.

---

7 BGHZ 80, 199; BGH NJW 1990, 906; BGHZ 99, 167.

8 OLG Düsseldorf, NJW-RR 1997, 1344.

9 Molitoris, "Der Produkthaftungsfall", *Beck'sches Rechtsanwaltshandbuch 2001/2002*.

10 BGH NJW 1990, 2650, *Lederspray*; OLG Karlsruhe, VersR 1986, 1125, *Milchkühlanlage*; Link, BB 1985, 1424.

11 Michalsky, BB 1998, 961.

This would not be the case if the kitchen hobs were subject only to a rather theoretical potential risk from the defective plates and no actual case of damage had occurred, despite observation over a long period. Nevertheless, in such a case, caution is required. If it cannot be stated with certainty that the product defect is only a theoretical danger, product recall should be seriously considered, particularly in the case of danger of injury or death of the user of the product or third parties.

Reimbursement Claims in the Case of National Recall

In the above example of the electrical manufacturer X, it conducted a recall with effective publicity though at considerable cost, and it now intends to demand reimbursement of this cost from the supplier D. Such a claim can, in German law, be based on the various legal grounds. The first ground to be considered is that of contract, as the recall was ultimately caused by the defective parts supplied.[12] Prevailing German case law, however, discusses a recourse claim under tort law.[13] Finally, the costs of the recall can be based on an agency of necessity (*Geschäftsführung ohne Auftrag*).[14]

Contractual Claims

Under the amended German law of obligations, such a claim can be based on a breach of obligation under Section 280 of the Civil Code, which reads:

> "If the obligor fails to comply with the duty arising under the obligation, the obligee may claim compensation for the loss resulting from this breach. This does not apply if the obligor is not liable for the failure."

Under the former law of obligations, compensation claims in the case of a sales contract against a supplier arose only if a warranty was given that the delivered goods were of a specified quality and the

12 Müller and Dörre, VersR 1999, 1333.

13 Civil Code, Sections 840 and 426; OLG Karlsruhe, NJW-RR 1995, 594, *Dunstabzugshaube*; LG Hamburg, VersR, 1994, 2999, *Rettungsinsel.*

14 Müller and Dörre, VersR 1999, 1333; Herrmann and Fingerhut, BB 1990, 725.

warranty referred[15] to the intention to be responsible for the actual damage — in this case the cost of a recall — or in the case of fraud.[16] These restrictions have been removed in the new law of obligations. The principal obligation of the seller now includes the supply of an article free of defects, and the supplier must, if this obligation is breached, provide full compensation, even in the case of simple negligence.[17] If, therefore, a supplier provides defective parts and if a recall of the end product becomes necessary because of these defective parts, the supplier is liable for all resulting costs. The additional requirement, however, is that the end manufacturer can present and prove that there was no alternative to the recall to remove existing risks from third parties. It is also necessary to establish to what extent these costs are actually caused by the product defect.

However, as regards a contractual reimbursement claim, it must be taken into account that, in a business relationship, the purchaser has an obligation to examine parts supplied and to complain in the case of defects.[18] The purchaser is obliged to examine the goods without delay after delivery and, if a defect is ascertained, to notify the seller of the same without delay. If the purchaser fails in this respect, the goods are deemed to have been accepted and contractual claims for these defects and any resulting damage are then excluded.[19] The period for complaint depends on the circumstances of each case, although a complaint later than two weeks after the defect has been ascertained is deemed to be late in all cases.[20]

This obligation of examination and complaint in business relationships has proved to be an effective defense in German law for the avoidance of claims regarding material defects and compensation. If the purchaser of the goods cannot establish that the goods were examined without delay after receipt and that defects ascertained were notified without delay to the seller, claims for compensation based on material defects are excluded. This is particularly problematic in cases in which, in the absence of a guarantee of quality, the obligation of examination and complaint can be dispensed with or reduced. The

---

15 BGB, VersR 1973, 523.

16 Civil Code (former version), Sections 463 and 480 BGB.

17 Palandt and Heinrichs, Civil Code, Section 280 BGB, marginal note 360.

18 Commercial Code, Section 377.

19 BGHZ 66, 212; BGHZ 101, 339; BGHZ 107, 337.

20 Baumbach and Hopt, Commercial Code, Section 377 HGB, marginal note 26; BGHZ, 93, 348.

obligation is, however, not exclusive to German law, but is also included in Articles 38 *et seq*. of the United Nations Convention on the International Sale of Goods (CISG).

Reimbursement under Section 823(1) of the Civil Code

The end manufacturer cannot claim the costs of a recall using a compensation claim under tort. This is because the recall results in only financial loss to the manufacturer, and this is not a subject for compensation under the general tort provision of Section 823(1) of the Civil Code. The recall is intended to prevent the infringement of the legal interests contained in this Section in relation to a third party, so a tort claim on the part of the manufacturer against the supplier for the recall costs does not arise.[21]

This applies even if a protected legal interest of the end manufacturer is infringed because of the delivery of a defective part by the supplier. This is shown by the judgment of the Federal Supreme Court of 31 March 1998.[22] In this case, defect-free parts of the manufacturer of a device were combined with defective transistors supplied for an electronic motor car central locking system and, therefore, inseparably attached from an economic point of view. Removal of the defective transistors would have involved destruction of the defect-free parts of the manufacturer as well as the steering plate. The Federal Supreme Court saw, in the complete loss of the parts, a destruction of the material substance, and thereby property damage to the manufacturer by the supplier. However, the court rejected the manufacturer's claim for reimbursement of recall costs because these arose under the contractual expectations of the manufacturer. The recall costs were, according to the court, not the result of the infringement of the protected legal interests of the manufacturer, and such a claim is not supported by a claim in tort.[23]

Claim under Sections 840 and 426 of the Civil Code

In German case law, the right of recourse of the manufacturer against the supplier is based mainly on recourse against joint and several

21 BGH VersR 1983, 346, *Hebebühne*; Link, BB 1985, 1424.

22 BGH NJW 1998, 1942, *PKW-Zentralverriegelung*.

23 Civil Code, NJW 1998, 1942, *PKW-Zentralverriegelung*.

debtors (*Gesamtschuldnerregress*) ordered by tort law.[24] Sections 840 and 426 of the Civil Code apply if a number of parties alongside each other are responsible for the damage caused by a tortious act. This means that each damaging party is liable to the party entitled to compensation for the entire damage. Such party may claim for the damage only once.[25] It is not necessary in this case for each of the damaging parties to be equally responsible. The degree of responsibility can vary.[26] While both the manufacturer and the supplier are responsible for placing a defective product onto the market, making them both, in principle, guilty of an act giving rise to liability, it is, however, a precondition for the direct application of Sections 840 and 426 that an infringement of the legal interests of a third party has arisen and that actual damage has been caused thereby.

As, however, the purpose of a recall is precisely to prevent infringement of the legal interests of, and damage to, a third party, the element of actual damage to a third party required by Sections 823, 840 and 426 of the Civil Code is absent.[27] According to German case law, damage resulting in a right to compensation does, as an exception, arise also if the injured party has taken measures to prevent an anticipated damaging event.[28] However, it is required that damage that is subject to compensation is only recoverable if the prevention measures are taken in the event of a concrete imminent damaging event.[29] Ultimately, it is crucial whether the preventative measures taken in the absence of infringement of legal interests are sufficiently causally connected to an act of the damaging party, namely, caused by the placing onto the market of a defective product, and thereby attributable to the end manufacturer (and to the supplier).

The recourse claim for recall costs under a joint and several liability claim in tort is also problematic because the costs usually incurred by a recall cannot be attributed to any concrete damaging event, but constitute preventative measures or expenses in order to avoid an

24 Civil Code, Sections 840 and 426; OLG Karlsruhe, NJW-RR 1995, 594, *Dunstabzugshaube*; LG Hamburg, VersR 1994, 299, *Rettungsinsel*.

25 Civil Code, Section 421; Palandt and Sprau, *Bürgerliches Gesetzbuch*, Section 840 BGB, marginal note 3.

26 Palandt and Sprau, *Bürgerliches Gesetzbuch*, Section 840 BGB, marginal note 3.

27 Müller and Dörre, VersR 1999, 1333.

28 OLG Karlsruhe, VersR 1986, 1125, *Milchkühlanlage*; OLG München, VersR 1992, 1135, *Druckluftbremsen*.

29 *MüKo BGB-Grunsky*, Civil Code, Section 249 BGB, marginal note 65.

imminent risk, and as such are not recognized in German tort and compensation law. This is clear from the position of Lange,[30] according to which only such costs that are incurred in the course of a recall with regard to an imminent and actual concrete event are subject to compensation. In accordance with this opinion, only those measures are subject to compensation under tort that are taken with regard to a concrete event, which would actually occur without such measures. According to this opinion, therefore, each case must be examined as to whether a defect in the product, which would have caused a certain damaging event if the recall had not been conducted, exists. In the case of a recall, which usually affects either a series or a batch of products, this would have to be proved with regard to thousands of individual cases, a task which, in practice, is impossible.[31]

In addition, in compensation law, a concrete causal connection must exist between the expenses incurred and the actual event causing the damage. Therefore, in relation to a recall, the question arises as to what damaging event has been prevented by what costs. This may be possible to demonstrate for costs involved in the removal of a defect that is a risk to third parties, as these costs will be attributable to a specific product. However, it is problematic as regards such costs that refer generally to the recall, such as handling costs in the case of distributors, notification of the recall through the media, personnel costs for the implementation of the recall and dealing with the recall. Such costs cannot be attributable to concrete causes.

Finally, compensation for re-manufacturing costs, which often arise in the case of a recall, is also problematic in German tort and compensation law. These costs are not necessarily incurred in the removal of an infringement of legal interests, but the repair of the defective product, and usually exceed what is necessary for the avoidance of the anticipated damage. The anticipated damage, however, can often be simply prevented either by non-use of the defective product,[32] by the removal of the defective part or the return of the defective product. A general obligation of the manufacturer or supplier to repair the defective product does not arise on the basis of tort law.[33]

---

30 Lange, *Schadenersatz*, 2nd ed., Section 6 VIII 4.

31 Müller and Dörre, VersR 1999, 1333.

32 Diederichsen, NJW 1978, 1281.

33 *Pieper*, BB 1991, 985; *Herrmann*, BB, 1985, 1801; Brügge and Meier, VersR 1983, 501.

Nevertheless, recourse under a joint and several liability claim in tort is excluded if it is established retrospectively that an assumed obligation to recall, in fact, did not exist. In principle, compensation law can provide only reimbursement of such precautionary expenses that were actually necessary to prevent damage. With reference to recalls, this means that reimbursement of recall related costs can be claimed only in those cases in which the recalled product was actually subject to a product defect that would have led to damage if the recall had not been conducted.

Agency of Necessity

Because of the existing tort law problems, German legal literature discusses whether the recourse claim of a manufacturer against a supplier can be based on an agency of necessity (*Geschäftsführung ohne Auftrag*).[34] This institution is provided for in Sections 677, 683, sentence 1, and 670 of the Civil Code and requires that an objective third party transaction be carried out by the agent on behalf of the principal without the authority of the principal. This claim is intended to include all cases in which a person, in the interests of a third party, but without being authorized by it, acts on behalf of that party and expenses are thereby incurred. For example, in the case of a rescue by a third party of a crew member in an emergency at sea, this is seen as an affair of the shipowner and of the rescued party, with the result that the rescuing party has a claim for expenses incurred.[35] The acting party has a claim to expenses even if the act is carried out contrary to the will of the principal, but in the public interest.[36] Examples are costs incurred in recovering a ship's equipment lost in a waterway,[37] the removal of a danger to traffic on the road caused by waste,[38] the righting of an overturned tanker[39] or the removal of contaminated milk powder.[40]

34 *Negotiorum gestio* — conducting another's affairs without having authority to do so; Müller and Dörre, VersR 1999, 1333; Herrmann and Fingerhut, BB 1990, 725; *Graf von Westphalen*, DB 1982, 1655.

35 BGHZ 67, 368.

36 Civil Code, Section 679.

37 BGHZ 65, 384.

38 BGHZ 65, 354.

39 BGHZ 63, 167.

40 BGHZ 110, 313.

A claim under Sections 677, 683, sentence 1, and 670 of the Civil Code requires an objective third party act carried out by the agent. Acts by a manufacturer in the interests of a supplier carried out in compliance with a recall obligation fulfil this requirement in principle. However, the recall is not only in the interests of the supplier, but also in those of the manufacturer. As stated above, both, in principle, are responsible to the product user and third parties for the placing of the defective product onto the market. A third party act (*auch fremdes Geschäft*) is sufficient for a reimbursement claim based on *Geschäftsführung ohne Auftrag.*[41] An act within the meaning of Section 677 of the Civil Code is thereby constituted if the supplier, either together with the manufacturer or exclusively, is responsible for the product defect that caused the recall.

A further requirement is the presence of the intention to perform a third party act. In this respect, it is not a problem if the manufacturer acts also by reference to his duty of care to perform a recall. However, the manufacturer may not act on the assumption that he is performing an act only on his own behalf, as then the intention to act for a third party would be absent and the provisions on *Geschäftsführung ohne Auftrag* would not be applicable, even if the supplier were jointly and severally responsible.[42] The latter, however, is seldom the case in practice because a recall, in general, is not conducted without at least preliminary clarification of the cause of the product defect ascertained and the damage anticipated. In practice, the manufacturer, when ordering a product recall, will act in the knowledge that he is protecting not only his own interests, but also the interests of the supplier.[43]

The application of the principles of *Geschäftsführung ohne Auftrag* is not prevented if the recall is ordered by the authorities. It is only crucial that the manufacturer was not authorized to conduct a recall by the supplier. Whether, in conducting the recall, the manufacturer acts on the basis of a tort or public law obligation (not a contractual obligation or undertaking) has no influence upon the principle of *Geschäftsführung ohne Auftrag.*[44]

Finally, the act (the product recall) must be in the interests of the principal (the supplier). This is the case if the act (the product recall)

41 Palandt and Sprau, *Bürgerliches Gesetzbuch*, Section 677 BGB, marginal note 6.
42 Müller and Dörre, VersR 1999, 1339.
43 Müller and Dörre, VersR 1999, 1339.
44 Müller and Dörre, VersR 1999, 1339.

is objectively useful and materially of benefit.[45] As the manufacturer usually has better facilities for the conduct of a recall, this criterion is usually fulfilled. The manufacturer knows the sales structure and is, therefore, more easily able to access the necessary customer data for the recall than the supplier, and also has recourse to the necessary sales structures. This again means that the manufacturer — compared to the supplier — can conduct a recall more efficiently and less expensively.

If the supplier expressly refuses his consent to the conduct of a recall, this will, in most cases, be irrelevant, according to Section 679 of the Civil Code. The conduct of a recall is, in most cases, in the public interest, as it concerns the prevention of danger to body, life, health or property.[46] The extent of the compensation claim of the manufacturer is measured, according to Sections 683, sentence 1, and 670 of the Civil Code, by the expenses of the manufacturer deemed necessary for the conduct of the recall.[47] Expenses that may be the subject of compensation are all voluntary contributions that are made for the purpose of the action and also those necessarily consequential upon the conduct of the recall.[48] This includes expenses incurred in the preparation and promotion of the action and which the principal would normally have had to bear if he acted in the place of the agent.[49]

It is a problem, however, in the case of a claim under *Geschäftsführung ohne Auftrag*, that considerable costs may arise by the involvement of the manufacturer's own employees in a product recall. This applies in particular in relation to the investigation of the cause and the organization and implementation of the recall. In principle, according to prevailing German case law, the expenses of employees and work that the agent involves in the action is not included in the expenses covered under Section 670 of the Civil Code.[50] This problem is, however, not yet resolved as the reimbursement claim of the agent under Section 670 relies on the law of agency, which does provide for remuneration for the act to be carried out.

---

45 RGZ 149, 205; BGH NJW-RR 1993, 200.

46 BGH VersR 1969, 562.

47 Palandt and Sprau, *Bürgerliches Gesetzbuch*, Section 683 BGB, marginal note 8.

48 BGHZ 8, 222; BGH NJW 2000, 3712.

49 *MüKo BGB-Seiler*, Section 670 BGB, marginal note 9.

50 Palandt and Sprau, *Bürgerliches Gesetzbuch*, Section 670 BGB, marginal note 3.

In order to prevent difficulties in establishing a reimbursement claim, it may be recommended that the recall be conducted, insofar as possible, by third parties, so that as little as possible is attributable to the manufacturer's own effort.

Cross-Border Recall

Choice of Law

If a cross-border recall is to be conducted, further problems are presented, both with regard to whether a recall is indicated and in relation to the problem of recourse through the supply chain for recall costs incurred. If, in the above example, the kitchen hob "Famosa IV" was sold not only in Germany but also in France, Italy and Holland, it would have to be examined in relation to all of the legal systems in question whether adequate grounds for a recall existed. However, if a German manufacturer is involved, it should be noted that if foreign consumers or third parties are injured by the defective product and the injured parties claim compensation in Germany, the German court concerned will apply the law which is indicated under the principles of German private international law.

Article 40 of the Introductory Law to the German Civil Code (EGBGB), in this context, provides an option for the injured party. According thereto, in the case of tort claims, the law of the State in which the damaging party acted applies. German law, in that case, decides whether an act is classified as a tort.[51] The place of the act is, therefore, the place in which the act giving rise to liability was committed, that is, the place where the cause of the infringement of legal interests arose.[52] In the case of product liability, this is either the manufacturer's principal place of business or the place where the product was placed on the market.[53] The injured party, however, has, in the case of cross-border torts in accordance with Article 40(1), sentence 2, of the EGBGB, the possibility of choosing the law of the place where the infringement of the legal interest occurred.[54] Article 40(2), sentence 1, of the EGBGB provides an exception to

51 BGH FamRZ 1996, 604.
52 Palandt and Heldrich, BGB, Article 40 EGBGB, marginal note 3.
53 Palandt and Heldrich, BGB, Article 40 EGBGB, marginal note 10.
54 Palandt and Heldrich, BGB, Article 40 EGBGB, marginal note 4.

this, according to which, if the liable party and the injured party, at the time of the act, had their usual places of residence in the same State, the law of that State applies.

These principles are deviated from if, for legal or factual reasons, a significantly closer connection exists with the law of a State other than the law which would be applicable on the above grounds.[55] Factual connections arise in particular when dealing with mass damage, for example, aircraft or railway accidents.[56] All the circumstances of the case are to be considered. Application of the law of the market may even be considered for product liability.[57]

If a German manufacturer or supplier were involved in the conducting of a recall, what are the implications for the option under Article 40 of the EGBGB? As, in principle, tort claims in accordance with Section 40(1), sentence 1, of the EGBGB are subject to the law of the place where the act causing the infringement of a legal interest is committed, the recall must be conducted if German law requires a recall. If, however, a recall is not indicated by German law, it remains to be examined under the other possible applicable legal systems, for example, the place of infringement of the legal interest or the market, as to whether a recall is required. Because, at the time of the discussion of the necessity of a recall, damage will not already have occurred, in order to determine the applicable law, there must be a hypothetical examination of where injury to a third party by the defective product may be anticipated.

Reimbursement of Recall Related Costs

Recourse for the costs of recall is also problematical in the case of a cross-border recall. Distinctions must be made between various possible situations. In the example given, if the recall is conducted by a German manufacturer, but the defective part that caused the recall is provided by a foreign supplier, a number of bases for a claim with regard to the recall costs can be considered.

---

55 Introductory Law to the German Civil Code, Article 41.

56 *Wagner*, IPRax 1999, 211.

57 Palandt and Heldrich, BGB, Article 41 EGBGB, marginal note 4.

Contractual Reimbursement Claim

A claim for recall costs could be based on contract because of a breach by the supplier, that is, the supplying of a defective part. If the case is brought before a German court, the question of the applicable law will be decided by reference to the law chosen by the parties. Such a choice of law is admissible, in principle, under German private international law.[58] Article 27(1) of the EGBGB reads:

> "The contract is subject to the law chosen by the parties. The choice of law must be made expressly, or must be adequately clear from the provisions of the contract or the circumstances of the case. The parties may make a choice of law either for the contract as a whole or parts thereof."

If the parties have chosen German law, the claim could be based on breach in accordance with Section 280(1) of the Civil Code, but only if the breach was the cause of the recall. This is the case if the recall because of the defective part was intended to avoid the threat of infringement of the legal interests of third parties. As explained above, a product recall is applicable where consumer goods are produced in such a way that their use in accordance with the instructions given provides a danger of damage to health or other legal interests of the consumer or a third party contrary to their justifiable expectations.[59]

Only if a recall is objectively justified and the measures taken for the removal of the danger are appropriate, necessary and reasonable does a contractual claim for compensation by the manufacturer against the relevant supplier come into question. The situation is more difficult if contractual claims are excluded, for example, because of the limitation period or failure to complain under Section 377 of the Commercial Code. In this case, recourse must be made to the abovementioned joint and several liability claims or the *Geschäftsführung ohne Auftrag*.

Joint and Several Liability

With regard to a claim under joint and several liability, the question of applicable law must first be clarified. If the parties have agreed upon

58 Introductory Law to the German Civil Code, Article 27.

59 BGH NJW 1990, 2560, *Lederspray*; LG Aachen, JZ 1971, 507, *Contergan*.

the application of German law, this then applies, according to German private international law, to the contract, its interpretation, the performance of the obligations thereunder, the consequences of non-performance of these obligations, the consequences of invalidity of the contract, the various methods of extinguishing the mutual obligations and the period of limitation.[60] According to German private international law, tort law, unjustified enrichment and the *Geschäftsführung ohne Auftrag* must be separately assessed with regard to the applicable law.

If a compensation claim is based on joint and several liability in tort, the question of the applicable law is to be decided in accordance with the law governing the tort,[61] because the law applicable to the tort governs not only the issue of liability (tortfeasor or joint tortfeasors), but also the nature of the liability of several tortfeasors (joint or partial liability) and any claims between the tortfeasors.[62] The question of whether the conditions for joint and several liability in tort under the applicable law are to be clarified independently, or whether the law applicable to the tort is applicable to them also, is not yet clarified. It would seem to be correct that the reimbursement claim in the case of joint and several liability in tort, including the conditions for joint and several liability, should be governed by the law applicable to the tort.

However, the problem remains that the law applicable to the tort under German private international law does not separately deal with the joint and several liability claim. As described above, Article 40 of the EGBGB provides, merely as a principle, that tort claims should be governed by the law of the State in which the damaging party acted. It is precisely in the case of joint and several liability in international commerce that the problem arises of various possible damaging parties having acted, leading to competition between several possible jurisdictions in which the damaging act could have been committed.

In order to resolve this conflict, recourse to Article 33 of the EGBGB may be an alternative as, thereunder, the applicable law in the case of an assignment of a debt and the statutory transfer of the debt is provided for. According to Article 33 of the EGBGB, where

60 Introductory Law to the German Civil Code, Article 32.

61 Introductory Law to the German Civil Code, Articles 38 *et seq.*

62 *MüKo BGB-Kreuzer*, Article 38 EGBGB, marginal note 283.

one of several jointly liable parties satisfies the creditor, the following applies:

> "If a third party has the obligation to satisfy a creditor, the law applicable to the obligation of the third party shall apply to the question of whether he is entitled to claim against the debtor in whole or in part according to the law applicable to the relationship. This applies also if several persons are liable for the debt and the creditor has been satisfied by one of them."

While this provision refers only to the assignment of a debt in the case of payment by one of several jointly liable debtors, it indicates nevertheless that it could be applied by analogy to the question of the law applicable to joint liability in tort. Thereby, the law to which the debt is subject would govern the question of the law applicable to the claim of the joint debtor who has paid the creditor in accordance with Article 33(3), sentence 2, of the EGBGB.[63] The conditions for the application of Article 33(3), sentence 2, of the EGBGB would be that:

(1) More than one debtor is involved;
(2) The various debtors are liable to the creditor for the same debt — it is not necessary that the debts are subject to the same law, and it is adequate, in accordance with the prevailing opinion, that the creditor can demand satisfaction only once and that the debtors are equal in rank among themselves;[64] and
(3) One of the debtors has satisfied the creditor.

Applied to the question of recourse for costs after the conduct of a recall, this means that if, for instance, foreign supplier D conducts the recall after the refusal of domestic manufacturer X, and if D then claims partial reimbursement of the recall costs because, besides the supplier's defective spare part, a construction defect made the recall inevitable, the

63 Staudinger and Hausmann, Article 33 EGBGB, marginal note 83; *MüKo BGB-Martiny*, Article 33 EGBGB, marginal note 29; Soergel and von Hoffmann, BGB Article 33 EGBGB, marginal note 27.

64 *von Bar*, IPR, 2. Band, 1991, marginal note 584; Staudinger and Hausmann, BGB, Article 33 EGBGB, marginal note 83; *MüKo BGB-Martiny*, BGB, Article 33 EGBGB, marginal note 29; Soergel and von Hoffmann, BGB, Article 33 EGBGB, marginal note 27.

following preconditions for the analogous application of Article 33(3), sentence 2, of the EGBGB would have to be examined:

(1) The foreign supplier and the domestic manufacturer must have been obliged to conduct the recall under the law applicable to each of them; and

(2) With regard to the law applicable to the joint and several liability between them, the law under which the recall obligation of the party who conducts the recall arises is decisive.

This shows how impracticable the solution is because, ultimately, this would lead to a race between those obliged to conduct a recall. The applicable law would then depend upon who actually conducted the recall at his expense. The solution is also problematic insofar as, in typical international recall situations, costs of the recall are often borne both by the supplier and the end manufacturer, with the resulting application of various legal systems to the relevant parts of the recall. Ultimately, it must be taken into account that this solution constitutes a system breach because Article 33 of the EGBGB does not apply to claims outside contract. In the case of joint liability in tort, however, this is a claim outside contract.

For these reasons, the applicable law should be decided by the law applicable to the tort and not by analogous application of Article 33(3), sentence 2, of the EGBGB. While this leads — as stated at the beginning — to problems, as several recall obligations at different locations of the act and, therefore, various legal systems compete, Article 41 of the EGBGB provides for the possibility of applying the law with which there is a special connection, whether this is on legal or factual grounds.[65] If, therefore, the recall is conducted by foreign supplier D, there is a significantly closer connection, within the meaning of Article 41 of the EGBGB, either to the law of the State in question in which the recall is conducted or the law of the State in which the relevant market of the recalled product is situated or in which the product was manufactured.

As both the first and the second alternative seem to fail in international business, as several possible points of connection exist, it might then be that the place of manufacture of the product is decisive as regards the applicable law.

65 Introductory Law to the German Civil Code, Article 41(2), Number 1.

Agency of Necessity

All of these difficulties can be avoided if the compensation claim of the party conducting the recall is not based on joint and several liability, but on a *Geschäftsführung ohne Auftrag*. Under German private international law, such claims are subject to the law of the State in which the act (the recall) is taken.[66] The law indicated by Article 39(1) of the EGBGB decides both on the conditions and content of all claims arising out of a *Geschäftsführung ohne Auftrag*, in particular, the extent of compensation that the agent can claim.[67] If the recall is carried out by a foreign supplier and, because the supplier's defective spare part, being a construction defect, made the recall inevitable, it is extended to various States, under Article 41(2) Number 1 of the EGBGB, the law of the State in which the party carried out the conduct leading to the recall is applicable. In the example given above, this would be the State in which the registered office of the supplier is located.

This solution avoids the practical difficulties that arise with the application of tort law to recourse between supplier and manufacturer, although this appears to be closer to the factual situation, in principle, if no contractual claim exists. However, it remains to be taken into account that prevailing German case law so far relies upon the claim under joint and several liability in tort, in spite of the considerable legal difficulties that arise, as described above.

Conclusion

Although it is not very satisfactory, the prerequisites under which a product recall must be conducted and the recall related costs must be reimbursed have not yet been clarified under German law. Prevailing German case law in this context is rare. One of the reasons for the absence of relevant judgments is that, in the area of product liability, decisions as to whether liability claims arise are made by the insurers involved. In the past, product liability matters were often settled by a decision of the insurer involved. This attitude, however, has been changing since September 11. In international commerce, the legal

66 Introductory Law to the German Civil Code, Article 39.

67 Palandt and Heldrich, BGB, Article 39 EGBGB, marginal note 1.

assessment of recall and reimbursement questions is even more complex. However, the following principles can be identified as applicable to international commerce:

(1) It has to be determined whether an obligation to recall exists — in a case involving a German manufacturer, according to German international law principles, German law is applicable if the defective product was manufactured in Germany (and the damaged party does not opt for the law of the State in which the infringement of its legal interests occurred);

(2) If German law is applicable, a recall is *ultima ratio*, but a recall must be conducted if it is the only method of removing the risk of damage to third parties caused by the defective product;

(3) If the defect is due to defective spare parts delivered by a supplier to the manufacturer and a recall becomes necessary, which is then conducted by the manufacturer, the supplier may have to reimburse the recall related costs either on the grounds of a contractual damage claim (breach of contract), reimbursement of joint and several debtors in tort or, in the absence of a contractual claim, under a *Geschäftsführung ohne Auftrag*;

(4) In the absence of a contractual claim, to avoid problems as regards applicable law, the *Geschäftsführung ohne Auftrag* is the preferable basis for a claim by the party conducting the recall; and

(5) These principles also apply the other way around, as regards reimbursement for recall costs, if the recall is not conducted by the manufacturer, but the supplier, if the supplier is not the only party responsible for the recall.

Aviation and Product Liability Cases in the United States

Gerald C. Sterns
Sterns & Walker
Oakland, California, United States

Warsaw Convention

"Accident" Defined

The essential basis for holding an airline liable under the Warsaw Convention[1] is a finding that an "accident" has occurred within the meaning of Article 17 of the Convention. Because the Convention does not specifically define what an "accident" is, courts have been presented with the difficult task of determining whether a particular aviation incident was or was not an Article 17 "accident".

The Supreme Court of the United States in *Air France* v. *Saks*[2] sets forth the seminal and working definition of "accident", a definition which is now also generally followed in other jurisdictions:

> "An unexpected or unusual event or happening that is external to the passenger, and not where the injury results from, the passenger's own internal reaction to the usual, normal and expected operation of the aircraft."

The Supreme Court stressed that the working definition of accident was not fixed or rigid and should be "flexibly" applied after assessment of all the circumstances surrounding a passenger's injuries. Though the Supreme Court has offered some guidance for courts to follow, defining an "accident" remains a daunting task for judges. There has been a great deal of litigation in the United States courts

---

1 Warsaw Convention for the Unification of Certain Rules Relating to International Transportation by Air, concluded at Warsaw, Poland on 12 October 1929, 49 Stat. 3000, T.S. Number 876, 137 LNTS 11 (1934), reprinted in note following 49 U.S.C. Section 40105 (1997).

2 *Air France* v. *Saks*, 470 U.S. 392 (1985).

over whether or not any given set of circumstances constitutes an "accident" under Article 17, for example:

(1) Crew failure to move passenger with high sensitivity to tobacco smoke away from smoking section of aircraft — Yes in *Husain* v. *Olympic Airways*;[3]
(2) In flight altercation with fellow passenger — No in *Price* v. *British Airways*;[4]
(3) Sexual assault on female by fellow passenger — Yes in *Wallace* v. *Korean Airlines* and *Tsevas* v. *Delta Airlines*;[5]
(4) Hijacking or terrorist act — Yes in *Pflug* v. *Egyptair Corp*;[6] *Evangelinos* v. *Trans World Airlines, Inc.*[7] and *Day* v. *Trans World Airlines*;[8]
(5) On board heart attack — No in *Krys* v. *Lufthansa German Airlines*;[9]
(6) Delay in responding to on board heart attack and failing to have proper medical equipment on board — Yes in *Fulop* v. *Malev Hungarian Airlines*;[10]
(7) Deep vein thrombosis — Maybe, discussed later;
(8) In-flight turbulence of a "severe" or "extreme" nature — Yes in *Magan* v. *Lufthansa*, but otherwise No;[11] and
(9) The presence of water on the staircase used to reach tarmac — Yes in *Gezzi* v. *British Airways*.[12]

Exclusivity

The Supreme Court of the United States has held that the Warsaw Convention provides the exclusive remedy for any injury or death alleged to have occurred during the course of international transportation, as defined by the Convention.[13] Therefore, a passenger is precluded from

---

3 *Husain* v. *Olympic Airways*, 316 F.3d 829 (9th Cir. 2002).

4 *Price* v. *British Airways*, 91 Civ. 4947, 1992 WL 170679 (S.D.N.Y. 7 July 1992).

5 *Wallace* v. *Korean Airlines*, 214 F.3d 293 (2d Cir. 2000); *Tsevas* v. *Delta Airlines*, Number 97 C0320 (N.D. Ill. 1997).

6 *Pflug* v. *Egyptair Corp.*, 961 F.2d 26 (2d Cir. 1992).

7 *Evangelinos* v. *Trans World Airlines, Inc.*, 550 F.2d 152 (3rd Cir. 1977).

8 *Day* v. *Trans World Airlines*, 528 F.2d 31 (2nd Cir. 1975).

9 *Krys* v. *Lufthansa German Airlines*, 119 F.3d 1515 (11th Cir. 1997).

10 *Fulop* v. *Malev Hungarian Airlines*, 00 Civ. 1965 (S.D.N.Y. 2003).

11 *Magan* v. *Lufthansa*, 181 F.Supp.2d 396 (S.D.N.Y. 2002).

12 *Gezzi* v. *British Airways*, 991 F.2d 603 (9th Cir. 1993).

13 *El Al Israel Airlines Ltd.* v. *Tseng*, 525 U.S. 155 (1999).

maintaining an action for personal injury under state or other law when the terms of the Convention do not apply.[14] The result is that the airline is no longer subject to liability for damage if the case is not covered by the Convention.

Before *Tseng*, if a judge determined a case to be outside the Warsaw Convention, it could still find Common Law negligence and award damages much higher than could have been recovered under the Convention. Of course, such a result can no longer happen under *Tseng*. Consequently, there has been a "role reversal" in the attempts of counsel to fit a case within or outside the Convention. Before *Tseng*, plaintiffs tried hard to stay out of Warsaw, since damages were limited. The combination of *Tseng* and almost all airlines waiving damage limitations under the International Air Transport Association (IATA) Accords now favor, if not require, plaintiffs to bring their claims under the Warsaw Convention.

Deep Vein Thrombosis

Deep vein thrombosis (DVT) cases present some very special problems, and the law of the United States is very much in flux. Currently, courts in England, Germany and Canada have ruled that DVT cannot constitute an "accident", apparently irrespective of the circumstances. Courts in Australia have held to the contrary. There is one federal court in the United States that has denied summary judgment in a DVT case, holding that the totality of the circumstances surrounding the onset, which can include not only the pitch of the seat, but other factors such as humidity, warnings or the lack thereof and oxygenation in the cabin, made the case one that had a triable issue to be determined by a jury. A case in the California Federal District Court, which was lost by a plaintiff who suffered DVT after twenty hours in a cramped seat, with no other factors, is being brought before the Ninth Circuit Court of Appeals.

14 *El Al Israel Airlines Ltd.* v. *Tseng*, 525 U.S. 155 (1999), at pp. 166–176.

Other Warsaw Convention Issues

Mental and Emotional Distress Unaccompanied by Physical Injury

In *Eastern Airlines, Inc.* v. *Floyd*, the Supreme Court held that Article 17 does not allow recovery for purely mental injuries unaccompanied by physical injury.[15]

The aftermath of Floyd, which left open the question of whether mental injuries accompanied by physical injuries were recoverable under the Convention, created a split of authority within the federal circuits on this issue. In *Carey* v. *United Airlines*,[16] a first class passenger aboard a United Airlines flight from Costa Rica to Los Angeles alleged that he suffered "physical manifestations of injury" in the form of nausea, cramps, perspiration, nervousness, tension and sleeplessness after a flight attendant humiliated him after he attempted to tend his ailing children seated in coach class. Relying on the Third Circuit's decision in *Terrafranca* v. *Virgin Atlantic Airways Ltd.*,[17] the Ninth Circuit Court of Appeals held that a passenger's physical manifestations of emotional distress do not satisfy the "bodily injury" requirement of Article 17. The plaintiff must demonstrate direct, concrete, bodily injury as opposed to mere manifestations of fear or anxiety.

---

15 *Eastern Airlines, Inc.* v. *Floyd*, 499 U.S. 530, 535 (1999). In May 1983, an Eastern Airlines flight from Miami bound for the Bahamas experienced a loss of engine pressure. The plane began losing altitude, and the passengers were informed that the plane would be ditched in the Atlantic Ocean. Fortunately, the crew managed to get the engines restarted and landed the plane safely in Miami. A group of passengers on the flight brought separate suits against the airline claiming damages solely for mental distress arising out of the incident. During the flight from Florida to the Bahamas, power was lost on all three engines. Eastern Airlines conceded that the planes' engine failures and subsequent preparations for ditching the plane amounted to an "accident" under Article 17, but argued that Article 17 requires physical injury as a condition for liability. The United States Supreme Court agreed. Focusing on the French words *lesion corporelle* in the French text of the Warsaw Convention, the court concluded that it should mean "bodily injury". Applying a narrow translation based on post-1929 conduct and interpretation by the signatories, the court also concluded that the drafters did not intend to allow recovery for purely mental injuries. Therefore, the "accident" must cause death, physical injury or a physical manifestation of injury.

16 *Carey* v. *United Airlines*, 255 F.3d 1044 (9th Cir. 2001).

17 *Terrafranca* v. *Virgin Atlantic Airways Ltd.*, 151 F.3d 108 (3rd Cir. 1998) — a passenger's weight loss was not a physical manifestation of injury under the Warsaw Convention.

More recently, in May 2002, the Eighth Circuit, in *In Re Air Crash at Little Rock, Arkansas*, was asked to decide whether an airline passenger suing under the Warsaw Convention could recover for mental injuries accompanied by physical injuries.[18] This case was the result of a 1999 American Airlines flight that crashed on the runway at Little Rock Airport in Little Rock, Arkansas. The pilot and ten passengers were killed. Ms. Lloyd, a passenger on the flight, was severely injured. She suffered numerous physical injuries, including a puncture to her leg, traumatic quadriceps tendonitis and smoke inhalation. Nine months after the accident, Ms. Lloyd was diagnosed with post traumatic stress disorder (PTSD). Her doctor testified at trial that this was likely to be a result of the crash. Her doctor also testified that Ms. Lloyd had a physical injury to her brain due to her chronic PTSD. The jury returned a US $6.5-million verdict in favor of Ms. Lloyd. American Airlines appealed the verdict arguing that the verdict was not only excessive, but that it bore no reasonable relationship to Ms. Lloyd's injuries. American Airlines made an unprecedented argument that emotional injuries are not recoverable at all under Warsaw. In the alternative, American Airlines argued that if recovery for mental injuries were allowed, they must flow directly from the passenger's physical injuries.

Relying on the Northern District of California ruling in *Jack* v. *Trans World Airlines, Inc.*,[19] the court decided to follow the "flow from" approach. The court disagreed with the district court that a showing of any physical injury was sufficient to trigger recovery for all emotional damage, regardless of its causal connection. The court concluded that damages for mental injury must proximately flow from the physical injuries caused by the accident. The court did find that some of Ms. Lloyd's mental injuries flowed from her physical injuries, but not all, and certainly not to the sum of US $6.5-million. Thus, the court held that emotional damages are recoverable under the Convention to the extent that they are caused by physical injuries suffered in the accident.

Ms. Lloyd filed a writ of certiorari with the United States Supreme Court. On 29 October 2002, the court denied her petition. Accordingly, the Court of Appeal's decision remains the prevailing rule in the Eighth Circuit regarding recovery for mental injuries under the

---

18 *In Re Air Crash at Little Rock Arkansas* (*Lloyd* v. *American Airlines*), 291 F.3d 503 (8th Cir. 2002).

19 *Jack* v. *Trans World Airlines, Inc.*, 854 F.Supp. 654, 665–668 (N.D.Cal. 1994).

Convention. Lower courts are still somewhat divided as to whether or not, once a physical injury is established, any and all emotional distress suffered may be recovered. Alaska Airlines Flight 261 is an example. In this case, during an international flight from Mexico to San Francisco, the MD-87 Aircraft suffered a severe malfunction of the horizontal stabilizer (top of the T-tail). The flight crew attempted to deal with the problem in flight, but the stabilizer failed in a full runaway down position. The plane then became inverted and flew in a negative 3G configuration for several minutes, then crashed into the ocean in California territorial waters.

Some plaintiffs sought survival damages under admiralty law, alleging that the doomed passengers suffered severe fright and fear of impending death. To circumvent Floyd, they submitted expert evidence that "physical injury" must have occurred to each, due to the impact of the 3G forces, which would produce seat belt bruises and injuries. The defense, however, countered that the mental anguish of the passengers was not caused by nor flowed from the seat belt lesion, but rather the fright and fear — a pure mental component. This case is presently still pending.

Jurisdiction and Venue in Warsaw Cases

Article 28 of the Warsaw Convention specifies four places where a claim may be brought against a carrier:

(1) The domicile of the carrier;
(2) The principal place of business of the carrier;
(3) The point at which the ticket was purchased; or
(4) The destination, which is the last line on a ticket — in a round trip situation, both the point of origin and destination are the same.

The United States courts have held that the provisions of Article 28 constitute subject matter jurisdiction and that the court cannot hear the case unless its requirements are met. In a recent decision from the Ninth Circuit Court of Appeals in California, *Hosaka* v. *United Airlines*,[20] the court held that Article 28(1) of the Warsaw Convention overrides the discretionary power of the federal courts to dismiss an action for *forum non conveniens*. In a non-Warsaw case, United

20 *Hosaka* v. *United Airlines*, 305 F.3d 989 (9th Cir. 2002).

States courts have inherent power to decline to hear a case even though there is jurisdiction. This doctrine is a very big factor in any case where overseas claimants seek to bring a case in the United States arising out of an overseas occurrence. Defendants will always invoke the defense and case results are split.[21] The High Court in the United Kingdom has reached the same results.[22]

Measure of Damages under the Warsaw Convention

While the Warsaw Convention specifies the circumstances in which the carrier will be liable, that is, for an "accident"[23] involving either physical injury, wounding or death,[24] the measure of those damages and what is and what is not recoverable for such injuries is "passed through" and to be determined by the court under local law.[25] In *Zicherman* v. *Korean Airlines Co.*, the court found that, based on a plain reading of the Treaty and the post-ratification conduct of the contracting parties, damages and standing to sue are to be determined by domestic law.

Warsaw Limitations on Damages

The original Warsaw Convention, adopted in 1929, specified that a carrier's liability was limited to 125,000 Poincaré, or gold French francs, the then dollar equivalent of approximately US $8,300. This limit could only be exceeded if it could be established that the carrier was guilty of "willful misconduct", as provided in Article 25. Such cases were difficult to win in most circumstances and virtually unheard of outside the United States.

In 1956, the limits were raised by the Hague Convention to twice the original limit, that is, 250,000 Poincaré francs. In 1966, after two high profile accidents, highlighting the very low, unrealistic and out of date limits, the United States filed formal notice of renunciation of the Warsaw Convention. An Intercarrier Agreement was then worked out with the United States Department of Transport, which substituted a flat US $75,000 absolute limit, with no Article 20 defense.

---

21 On the doctrine generally, *see Gulf Oil* v. *Gilbert*, 175 F.2d 705 (4th Cir. 1949).

22 *Milor* v. *British Airways, Plc.*, [1996] Q.B. 702, 706 (Eng. C.A.).

23 Warsaw Convention, Article 17.

24 Warsaw Convention, Article 21.

25 *Zicherman* v. *Korean Airlines Co.*, 516 U.S. 217 (1996).

This applied to any flight to, from or touching the United States. The IATA Accords 1996 provide a two-tier system, with absolute liability from the occurrence of the accident of up to 100,000 SDRs.[26] Plaintiffs may thereafter recover all provable damages under local law, but subject to an Article 20 defense.

Article 20 was in the Convention from its inception. Notwithstanding the provisions of Article 17, making the carrier liable for an accident, that liability can be nullified by Article 20. There is very little case law in the United States on Article 20, since the defense became moot with the adoption of the 1966 Intercarrier Agreement. The airlines were required to waive Article 20, but were protected by a US $75,000 limit. It is generally agreed that an Article 20 defense presents a very high, if not insurmountable, burden for the airlines.

International Travel: When Warsaw Does Not Apply

Because of the definition of "international travel" in Article 1, some trips are not covered by the Convention, even though travel is invoiced from one country to another. To qualify, a trip must start at least in the territory of one "High Contracting Party", that is, a signatory or adherent to the Convention. Because not all nations are signatories or adherents, some interesting results can follow, and care must be taken to examine the itinerary carefully. Article 1 reads:

> "(1) This convention shall apply to all international transportation of persons, baggage, or goods performed by aircraft for hire. It shall apply equally to gratuitous transportation by aircraft performed by an air transportation enterprise.
>
> "(2) For the purpose of this convention the expression 'international transportation' shall mean any transportation in which, according to the contract made by the parties, the place of departure and the place of destination, whether or not there be a break in the transportation or a transshipment, are situated either within the territories of two High Contracting Parties, or within the territory of a single High Contracting Party, if there is an agreed stopping place within a

26 Standard drawing rights are a mix of currencies equivalent to approximately US $135,000.

territory subject to the sovereignty, suzerainty, mandate or authority of another power, even though that power is not a party to this convention. Transportation without such an agreed stopping place between territories subject to the sovereignty, suzerainty, mandate, or authority of the same High Contracting Party shall not be deemed to be international for the purposes of this convention.

"(3) Transportation to be performed by several successive air carriers shall be deemed, for the purposes of this convention, to be one undivided transportation, if it has been regarded by the parties as a single operation, whether it has been agreed upon under the form of a single contract or of a series of contracts, and it shall not lose its international character merely because one contract or series of contracts is to be performed entirely within a territory subject to the sovereignty, suzerainty, mandate, or authority of the same High Contracting Party."

For instance, Taiwan is not a signatory and at least one United States Circuit Court of Appeal has held that it has sovereignty, and is not bound by the signing of the Peoples Republic of China. A round trip itinerary from Taiwan to the United States is, therefore, outside Warsaw, as would be a one-way trip from Taiwan to the United States. However, in the reverse situation, a round trip itinerary from the United States to Taiwan is within the Convention, as the trip originates within the territory of a High Contracting Party, with an agreed stopping place that is not.

In like manner, even though a case may be within Warsaw, it may not be brought in the courts of a non-signatory country. Article 28 confers jurisdiction (four choices) only on courts in High Contracting Parties. For example, in the China Air crash at Hong Kong, Portuguese passengers were on a trip originating and ending in Portugal. Air China was incorporated and domiciled in Taiwan, and even though Taiwan otherwise meets the specifications of Article 29(1) and (2), there was no Warsaw jurisdiction. A case could only be brought in Portugal. The United States Ninth Circuit Court of Appeals has held that even though Taiwan is not a signatory, Air China may still invoke the Treaty and Article 28(1) stating where claims may be brought.

Product Liability Cases in the United States

Early Product Liability Cases

Product liability was generally developed in the courts of the United States by case law, with the early decisions emerging in the early 1960s. Up until that time, a product defect case required that the plaintiff establish negligence, a far from easy task, and perhaps impossible in the case of many products. In fact, prior to the decision in *McPherson* v. *Buick*[27] in 1916, an injured third party could make no claim against a manufacturer based on negligence or otherwise, as there was no privity of contract.

Strict Product Liability

In the 1960s, the courts in the United States began to enunciate a doctrine of strict product liability. The responsibility for the product would no longer turn on questions of negligence, but on the issue of whether or not the product itself was defective. The rationale was that the risk of a defective product should not fall wholly on the injured party, but should be spread among many, through the manufacturer.

In *Barker* v. *Lull Engineering*,[28] a two-prong test was established. The product could be determined to be defective if, upon analysis by the trier of fact, it could fairly be found "not to meet reasonable consumer expectations". Alternatively, if not definable by that test, it would be based on a comparison of the amount of harm the product was likely to do if defective, weighed together with the various factors that went into its utility and usefulness, a risk-benefit type of analysis. The second source of law for a definition of a defective product comes from the Second Restatement of Torts,[29] which defines a defective product as one that is "unreasonably dangerous" when used in the manner which is intended or foreseeable.

General Aviation Revitalization Act 1994

Manufacturers of general aviation aircraft were unsuccessful in limiting their product liability exposure by arguing that compliance with

27 *McPherson* v. *Buick*, 217 N.Y. 382 (1916).
28 *Barker* v. *Lull Engineering*, 20 Cal.3d 413 (1978).
29 Second Restatement of Torts, Section 403A.

Federal Aviation Administration standards preserved a state law cause of action regarding the integrity of the product. However, they struck back and struck gold. The rules with respect to product liability in general aviation were changed dramatically by the congressional enactment of the General Aviation Revitalization Act 1994 (GARA).[30] GARA insulated the manufacturers of aircraft and components by imposing what is called a statute of repose, that is, an absolute fixed time limitation within which to commence litigation, running from the time of first delivery of the product in commercial use. This is in sharp distinction to a statute of limitations, which only arises after the incident has occurred, giving the victim a certain limited time thereafter to file suit. GARA has, in many cases, cut off any cause of action or right to recover damages even before the incident occurs.

The justification for GARA as it went through Congress was that the general aviation industry, once a strong component of the United States export market, had been crippled by product liability lawsuits and overly generous juries. Whatever the merits of that, since there was little hard evidence presented in support, the measure was enacted and billed as "new jobs" legislation. The practical result has been to minimize large portions of the general aviation aircraft industry, and a shifting of the burden of defending and paying onto other entities, such as operators, maintenance and fixed base facilities and, in some cases, air traffic control.

GARA does not apply to larger aircraft engaged in commercial operations. It also allows a new eighteen-year period to commence, when a replacement component is introduced. Efforts by plaintiffs to predicate claims on flight manual updates and revisions as starting new GARA time limits have been met with mixed success.

Governmental Contractor Defense

Irrespective of whether a product liability claim can be made under the Common Law provisions outlined in Barker (reasonable consumer expectation) or the Restatement (unreasonably dangerous), state Common Law can still be displaced and the manufacturer of the product can claim complete immunity based on what has come to be

30 49 U.S.C. 40101.

called the "governmental contractor defense". This defense is not statutory; rather, it comes out of the case law enunciated by the United States Supreme Court in the landmark decision of *Boyle* v. *United Technologies Corp.*[31] The essence of the *Boyle* decision is that if the contractor is following what the government has ordered, in effect, by building the particular type of military hardware to order, then the immunity conferred upon the government, had the government designed and manufactured the hardware itself, is transferred over to the contractor. The underlying government immunity comes essentially from a 1946 United States Supreme Court decision, *Feres* v. *United States*,[32] which exempted from the ambit of the Federal Tort Claims Act claims by servicemen for injury or death while on active duty. The other basis is the discretionary function defense embraced within the Act itself.

The Boyle court laid down a three-prong test that the contractor must show in order to claim governmental immunity. This is a matter of proof, and the contractor must come forward with evidence in support. It must establish that:

(1) The United States provided reasonably "precise specifications";
(2) The equipment conformed to those specifications; and
(3) The supplier warned the United States about the dangers in the use of the equipment that were known to the supplier, but not to the United States.

In Boyle, the Supreme Court explained the function of each prong in the following language:

> "The first two of these conditions assure that the suit is within the area where the policy of the 'discretionary function' would be frustrated — i.e., they assure that the design feature in question was considered by a Government officer, and not merely by the contractor itself. The third condition is necessary because, in its absence, the displacement of state tort law would create some incentive for the manufacturer to withhold knowledge of risk, since conveying that knowledge might disrupt the contract, but withholding it would produce no liability. We adopted this provision lest our effort to protect the discretionary functions perversely

31 *Boyle* v. *United Technologies Corp.*, 487 U.S. 500 (1988).
32 *Feres* v. *United States*, 340 U.S. 135 (1950).

impede them by cutting off information highly relevant to the discretionary decision."

As might be expected, there has been a great deal of debate and discussion back and forth in the lower courts regarding the meaning and application of these words and whether a contractor could meet this burden of proof. One school of thought would read this very narrowly, that is, that the government had to be actually involved in the process, not just rubber-stamping a design, and, further, that the government, rather than the contractor, actually controlled the design. In effect, the contractor's defense would be "the government made me do it".

Another view tends towards the case where, if the contractor can show a paper trail concerning the design and procurement of the product with the government signing off drawings and things of this type on a fairly regular basis, that *ipso facto* creates the necessary approval of reasonably precise specifications. Cases illustrating this defense include *Miller* v. *Diamond Shamrock*[33] and *Gray* v. *Lockheed*.[34]

Special Damage Considerations

Death on the High Seas Act

Generally

Prior to 1920, United States maritime law had held that no cause of action existed for a death claim in international waters.[35] To provide such a remedy, Congress enacted the Death on the High Seas Act (DOHSA).[36] The key language establishing the rights reads as follows:

"(a) Subject to subsection (b) of this section, whenever the death of a person shall be caused by wrongful act, neglect, or

33 *Miller* v. *Diamond Shamrock*, 275 F.3d 414 (5th Cir. 2002), involving Agent Orange damage, which was chemically manufactured for military purposes. The defense in this case was upheld.

34 *Gray* v. *Lockheed*, 125 F.3d 1371 (11th Cir. 1997), involving the design of an aircraft servo valve that malfunctioned. The defense in this case was denied.

35 Harrisburg, 119 U.S. 199 (1886).

36 46 U.S.C. Section 761.

default occurring on the High Seas beyond a marine league from the shore of any State, or the District of Columbia, or the Territories or dependencies of the United States, the personal representative of the decedent may maintain a suit for damages in the district courts of the United States, in admiralty, for the exclusive benefit of the decedent's wife, husband, parent, child, or dependent relative against the vessel, person, or corporation which would have been liable if death had not ensued.

"(b) In the case of a commercial aviation accident, whenever the death of a person shall be caused by wrongful act, neglect, or default occurring on the High Seas twelve nautical miles or closer to the shore of any State, or the District of Columbia, or the Territories or dependencies of the United States, this chapter shall not apply and the rules applicable under Federal, State, and other appropriate law shall apply."

High Seas

Surprisingly, there has been much controversy and litigation over the meaning of this term. Some courts have ignored it entirely and focused only on the doctrine applicable on a United States shore. If an accident occurs more than one marine league from shore (three nautical miles; approximately 3.4 statute miles) and on water, the DOHSA applies. In the TWA 800 litigation in 1998, Judge Robert Sweet of the United States District Court, New York carefully analyzed the exact language of the statute and the term "High Seas" and concluded that the DOHSA trigger requirements were both beyond the three nautical mile measures and on the "High Seas". He then reasoned that, since the crash occurred beyond three nautical miles from the shore, but within the waters over which the United States claimed jurisdiction, such waters were "territorial" and not "High Seas", that is, international waters to which the jurisdiction of no country applies, so the DOHSA did not apply. It would seem, therefore, by the same reasoning, that it would not apply either to an accident occurring in the territorial waters of other sovereign nations, but so far the bulk of the United States cases have not so found. The Supreme Court has not yet spoken on this issue.

Pecuniary Losses

This is the same language that English courts use in applying the original English Wrongful Death Statute, Ford Campbell's Act 1856. That standard is a narrow one, and permits only net economic losses in defending situations. Loss of society is a concept well established in United States domestic law, which permits compensation for intangible, non-economic losses, such as care, comfort, companionship and the loss of other family benefits.

New Death on the High Seas Act

Following the TWA case, Congress amended the DOHSA to provide that, in a case of "commercial aviation", in addition to pecuniary losses, recovery could be had for "care, comfort and companionship".

Liability Location

Careful attention needs to be paid to the enabling statutory language. The wrongful act, default or neglect must occur "on the High Seas", as opposed to the death itself. Thus, arguably, in any product defect case, as in a defective airplane component, the DOHSA should not apply, since the engineering or design flaws occurred on land, not on the water. The case of *Executive Jet* v. *City of Cleveland*[37] also makes clear that all crashes that occur in navigable waters are governed by admiralty law.

Limitations

Damages under the DOHSA are limited to "pecuniary" losses or "care, comfort and companionship" in the new DOHSA, and neither punitive damages nor survival damages are authorized.

Foreign Sovereign Immunities Act

Generally

The Foreign Sovereign Immunities Act (FSIA) is an important part of United States law and is often involved in airline and product cases. A

37 *Executive Jet* v. *City of Cleveland*, 409 U.S. 249 (1972).

foreign sovereign is defined as the foreign government itself, or any organization or company that the government owns in excess of fifty per cent. Thus, many of the world's commercial airlines, being "flag carriers" for their countries, qualify as such. Ownership is measured as at the time of the filing of the suit, not the time of the accident or incident, and cannot be "tiered".[38] For example, in the *Singapore Airlines 06* case in Taiwan, it was held that, since the government of Singapore wholly owned a development company, which in turn owned a majority of the share of the airline, the FSIA did not apply.

Commercial Activity

The FSIA will permit claims to be brought in the United States courts, provided that they are based on commercial activity having an impact in the United States, as opposed to governmental functions, which are absolutely immune.

Trial

No jury trial is permitted in FSIA cases. The case is tried by a United States District Judge. The federal courts have exclusive jurisdiction, and any cases filed in a state court can be removed to the federal court, not just as to the foreign "sovereign", but as to the entire case and all other parties. This rule has many implications where a case may not otherwise be removable, and aviation and product defendants invariably want to get out of the state court and into the federal court.

Note: The author is indebted to Keith E. Patterson for his assistance in the preparation of this chapter.

---

38 *Dole Food Co.* v. *Patrickson*, 1–593 (U.S. 2003).

Index

A

B

C

D

E

F

G

I

L

P

R

S

T

U

V